The Field Archaeology of
the Salisbury Plain Training Area

The Salisbury Plain landscape. Coombes and re-entrants lead into the interior of the Higher Plain from the main river arteries. In the foreground is Water Dean Bottom at Compton where strip lynchets can be traced along the valley sides until they merge with the 'Celtic' fields set around the Romano-British settlements. Roman villages on Compton Down, Upavon Down and, in the distance, Rushall Down all lie to the left of the valley. In the right of the picture lies Casterley Camp facing onto a re-entrant that also leads to Water Dean Bottom. At the bottom a massive round barrow stands alone at the edge of the valley surrounded by levelled 'Celtic' fields. The extent of cultivated Schedule 1 land showing as the rich green of new growth contrasts with the natural coarse grassland of the Higher Plain.

The Field Archaeology of the Salisbury Plain Training Area

by David McOmish, David Field and Graham Brown

with contributions by Mark Corney, Simon Crutchley and Deborah Cunliffe

ENGLISH HERITAGE

Published by English Heritage at the National Monuments Record Centre,
Great Western Village, Kemble Drive, Swindon SN2 2GZ

Copyright © English Heritage 2002
Images (except as otherwise shown) © Crown copyright.NMR
Applications for the reproduction of images should be made to the National
Monuments Record.

First Published 2002

ISBN 1 873592 49 3

Product Code 50098

British Library Cataloguing in Publication Data
A CIP catalogue record for this book is available from the British Library.

Edited and indexed by Veronica Stebbing
Designed by Mark Simmons
Edited and brought to press by David M Jones and Andrew McLaren,
    Publications, English Heritage

Printed by Snoeck-Ducaju & Zoon

Contents

List of Illustrations . . . . *vi*
List of Tables . . . . *vii*
Foreword by Roy Canham . . . . *viii*
Preface . . . . *x*
Acknowledgements . . . . *xiv*
Abbreviations . . . . *xiv*
Summary . . . . *xv*
Résumé . . . . *xvi*
Zusammenfassung . . . . *xvii*

1 Introduction: the Salisbury Plain Training Area (SPTA) 1

The Training Area 2
Modern land use 4
Geology 5
Quaternary geology 6
Quaternary fauna 7
Soils 8
Drainage and water management 9
Survival and distribution of
    archaeological features 11
A history of previous enquiries 13
Orcheston Down: a model sequence 18

2 Earlier Prehistory: the Neolithic and Early Bronze Age (*c* 4500–1500 BC) 21

Long barrows 21
Causewayed enclosures 31
Henges 33
Round barrows 33

3 The Later Prehistoric Periods (*c* 1500 BC–*c* AD 43) 51

Prehistoric field systems 51
Later prehistoric linear earthworks 56
Enclosure and settlement morphology 67
East Chisenbury midden 73
Hillforts 74
Middle to Late Iron Age enclosed settlement . . . 81

4 The Romano-British Period (AD 43–*c* AD 413) 87

The aftermath of the conquest 87
The Romano-British settlement pattern 88
Romano-British cultivation 100
Villa settlement 104
An imperial estate? 106
Communications and market centres 107

5 The post-Roman, Medieval and post-Medieval Periods (*c* AD 413–1897) . . 109

Evidence for post-Roman and
    Anglo-Saxon occupation 109
Estates and territorial boundaries 112
The downland landscape 114
The valley landscape 123

6 The 20th Century 137

The creation of the military estate 137
Military earthworks 138
Re-colonisation of the downs 147

7 Discussion: the Archaeological Landscape of the SPTA 149

The problem of the sarsen stones 151
Agricultural revolution 152
Enclosures 154
A new order... 156
...and decline 157
The archaeology of warfare 159

8 Conclusion 160

'Song of the Dark Ages' by Frances Brett Young . . . 162
Concordance 163
Bibliography 168
Index 174

List of Illustrations

Frontispiece: The Higher Plain. ii

Figure i.1   Plot of archaeological features on the SPTA
              derived from aerial photographic transcriptions
              . . . .*between pages* xviii–1
Figure i.2   Pie chart showing the increase in monuments
              recorded on the SPTA   . . . *between pages* xviii–1

Figure 1.1   Location plan of Salisbury Plain. 1
Figure 1.2   Monument on Chapperton Down. 3
Figure 1.3   Map depicting military use of Salisbury Plain. . . . 4
Figure 1.4   Copehill Down military village (FIBUA). 5
Figure 1.5   Tank track. 6
Figure 1.6   Map showing the geology of the SPTA. 7
Figure 1.7   Palaeolithic biface from Tilshead. 8
Figure 1.8   Map showing relief and drainage of the SPTA. . . . 9
Figure 1.9   Lidbury. 11
Figure 1.10   Map showing 19th-century cultivation on the
              Higher Plain. 13
Figure 1.11   Plan of excavation trenches in Heytesbury North
              Field long barrow. 14
Figure 1.12   Crocker's survey of Casterley Camp, 1812. 15
Figure 1.13   Flinders Petrie plan of Robin Hood's Ball. 15
Figure 1.14   Flinders Petrie plan of Orcheston Down. 16
Figure 1.15   Crawford's air photograph of the Central
              Ranges. 16
Figure 1.16   Extract from OS 6-inch Map showing Crawford's
              plotting of 'Celtic' field systems. 17
Figure 1.17   Church Pits: a model sequence. 19
Figure 1.18   Plan of round barrows, 'Celtic' fields, linear ditch
              and Romano-British settlement on Orcheston
              Down (Church Pits) . . . . . *between pages* 20–21

Figure 2.1   Soil marks of long barrow and ring ditches at
              Figheldean. 22
Figure 2.2   Netheravon Bake long barrow. 23
Figure 2.3   Map showing distribution of Neolithic
              monuments. 24
Figure 2.4   Comparative plans of long barrows. 25
Figure 2.5   Plan of Old Ditch long barrow with linear
              boundaries. 26
Figure 2.6   Plan of Fittleton long barrow with 'Celtic' fields. 26
Figure 2.7   Profiles of long barrows. 27
Figure 2.8   Comparative plans of long barrows. 29
Figure 2.9   Plan of Oxendean long barrow with 'Celtic'
              fields. 30
Figure 2.10   Plan of Kill Barrow with 'Celtic' fields and
              linear boundaries. 30
Figure 2.11   Plan of adjacent long barrows at Milston. 31
Figure 2.12   Plan of White Barrow with linear boundaries. . . . 32
Figure 2.13   Geophysical plot of Sheer Barrow. 33
Figure 2.14   Causewayed enclosure at Robin Hood's Ball. . . . 34
Figure 2.15   Robin Hood's Ball. 35
Figure 2.16   Scratchbury: barrows, enclosure and hillfort. . . . 36
Figure 2.17   Scratchbury. 37
Figure 2.18   Weather Hill. 37
Figure 2.19   Selected round barrows. 38
Figure 2.20   Profiles of round barrows. 39

Figure 2.21   Compton barrow. 40
Figure 2.22   Silk Hill barrow cemetery. 41
Figure 2.23   The archaeological landscape on Snail Down. . . 42
Figure 2.24   Comparative plans of round barrow
              cemeteries. 44–6
Figure 2.25   Plan of Milston Firs long barrow with round
              barrows and linear boundary. 47
Figure 2.26   Snail Down barrow cemetery. 47
Figure 2.27   Snail Down. 48
Figure 2.28   Map showing distribution of round barrows and
              ring-ditches. 49
Figure 2.29   Round barrow in Bourne Bottom at Figheldean. . . 49
Figure 2.30   Round barrow near Sidbury Hill. 49

Figure 3.1   Distribution map of later prehistoric activity on
              the SPTA. 52
Figure 3.2   Plan of enclosure at Lidbury. 53
Figure 3.3   Plan of 'Celtic' fields and linear ditches at Dunch
              Hill (Tidworth Golf Course). 54
Figure 3.4   Comparative plans of coaxial field systems on
              the SPTA. 54
Figure 3.5   Old Nursery Ditch from the air. 56
Figure 3.6   Plot of Sidbury Hill area showing focus of linears. . .58
Figure 3.7   Plan of Casterley Camp. 59
Figure 3.8   Plan of the midden at East Chisenbury. 60
Figure 3.9   Plan of barrows, 'Celtic' fields, linear ditches and
              settlements to the east of the River Avon. . . . 62
Figure 3.10   Double-linear boundary at Sidbury Hill. 63
Figure 3.11   Junction of linear ditches on Slay Down. 63
Figure 3.12   Plan of Romano-British village on Knook Down
              West . . . . *between pages* 64–5
Figure 3.13   'Celtic' fields and linear boundaries on
              Figheldean Down. 65
Figure 3.14   Linear boundary on Chapperton Down. 66
Figure 3.15   Detailed plan of Chapperton Down. 67
Figure 3.16   Platforms on scarp face at Hill Bottom Farm. . . . 67
Figure 3.17   Open and enclosed settlements on Marden
              Down. 68
Figure 3.18   Plans of enclosures at Mancombe Down and
              Chisenbury Trendle. 69
Figure 3.19   Post-holes and hearths at Late Bronze Age
              settlement beneath East Chisenbury midden. . . 70
Figure 3.20   Comparative plans of later prehistoric enclosures
              on the Bulford Ranges. 71
Figure 3.21   Brigmerston U-shaped enclosure. 72
Figure 3.22   Spindle whorls from the midden at East
              Chisenbury. 74
Figure 3.23   Battlesbury. 75
Figure 3.24   Casterley Camp. 76
Figure 3.25   Plan of Sidbury Camp. 77
Figure 3.26   Plan of Battlesbury Camp. 78
Figure 3.27   Knook Down West. 80
Figure 3.28   Casterley Camp annexe. 81
Figure 3.29   Geophysical plan of enclosure on Coombe
              Down. 82
Figure 3.30   Comparative plans of enclosures taken from aerial
              photographic plots. 83
Figure 3.31   Combined aerial and geophysical survey of
              Iron Age and Romano-British features at
              Netheravon. 85

Figure 4.1   Distribution map of Romano-British activity on the SPTA. 87

Figure 4.2   Plan of Romano-British village at Coombe Down. 88

Figure 4.3   Plan of Romano-British village on Upavon Down. 89

Figure 4.4   The Central Ranges: Charlton Down village. . . . 90

Figure 4.5   Plan of enclosure at Church Ditches. 91

Figure 4.6   Plan of earthen dam on Charlton Down. 91

Figure 4.7   Plan of Romano-British village on Charlton Down. 91

Figure 4.8   Implements from Charlton. 93

Figure 4.9   Upavon Down. 94

Figure 4.10   Plan of Romano-British village on Compton Down. 95

Figure 4.11   Plan of Romano-British village on Knook Down East. 97

Figure 4.12   Knook Down East and West. 97

Figure 4.13   Plan of Romano-British village on Chapperton Down . . . . between pages 98–9

Figure 4.14   Plan of Romano-British village at Chisenbury Warren. 100

Figure 4.15   Chisenbury Warren. 100

Figure 4.16   Plan of Romano-British village on Cheverell Down. 102

Figure 4.17   Plan of Romano-British village at Wadman's Coppice. 103

Figure 4.18   Water management at Wadman's Coppice. 104

Figure 4.19   Sheep enclosure at Warden's Down. 105

Figure 4.20   'Celtic' fields on Upavon Down. 106

Figure 4.21   The archaeological landscape of the Central Ranges. 107

Figure 4.22   Seal Boxes from Upavon and Enford, and miniature socketed axes from Casterley Camp. 108

Figure 5.1   Distribution map of Anglo-Saxon activity and material. 110

Figure 5.2   Tithing and parish boundaries along the Avon valley. 110

Figure 5.3   Ridge-and-furrow cultivation on Thornham Down. 111

Figure 5.4   Cultivation remains on Thornham Down. 112

Figure 5.5   Compton strip lynchets. 113

Figure 5.6   Sheep enclosure at Upavon. 114

Figure 5.7   Enclosed site at Imber, used as a warren. 116

Figure 5.8   Sheep enclosures on Orcheston and Figheldean Downs. 117

Figure 5.9   Figheldean sheep enclosure. 118

Figure 5.10   Map showing the distribution of farmsteads and field barns. 119

Figure 5.11   Pond Farm. 119

Figure 5.12   Eastcott Farm. 120

Figure 5.13   Comparative plans of barns and farmsteads. . . . 121

Figure 5.14   Map of Tilshead Lodge. 122

Figure 5.15   Hollow ways on Coombe Down. 122

Figure 5.16   Plan of Longstreet shrunken medieval village. . . 123

Figure 5.17   Plan of East Chisenbury shrunken medieval village. 124

Figure 5.18   Morphology of medieval settlement along the Avon valley. 125

Figure 5.19   Plans of medieval settlement earthworks at Orcheston. 126–7

Figure 5.20   Plan of Knighton deserted medieval village. . . . 128

Figure 5.21   Plan of shrunken medieval village and strip lynchets at Middleton. 129

Figure 5.22   Plan of Compton shrunken medieval village. . . 130

Figure 5.23   Geophysical plot of the chapel at Gore. 130

Figure 5.24   Memorial from Roundway Hospital. 131

Figure 5.25   Plan of West Chisenbury deserted medieval village. 132

Figure 5.26   Tilshead village in 1813. 133

Figure 5.27   Plan of Ludgershall Castle. 134

Figure 5.28   Plan of water meadows at Compton. 135

Figure 5.29   Water meadows at Compton. 136

Figure 5.30   Plan of water meadows at Hindurrington. 136

Figure 6.1   Tented camp at Pond Farm. 137

Figure 6.2   Trenches on Perham Down. 138

Figure 6.3   Distribution map of military earthworks. 139

Figure 6.4   The archaeology of warfare. 140

Figure 6.5   Comparative plans of military trench systems. . . 142

Figure 6.6   Trenches on Knook Down. 143

Figure 6.7   Trenches on Chapperton Down. 144

Figure 6.8   Rifle Range A, Bulford. 145

Figure 6.9   Anti-tank ditch on Knook Down. 147

Figure 6.10   Anti-tank range at Shrewton Folly. 147

Figure 6.11   Splinter-proof shelter. 147

Figure 6.12   Imber. 148

Figure 7.1   Sarsen boulders in the ditch of Figheldean 31 long barrow. 151

Figure 8.1   Land use on the Central Ranges. 161

Tables

Table 1   Extant long barrow dimensions (m). 23

Table 2   Details of internal features within excavated long barrows. 28

Table 3   Frequencies of bell, disc, pond and saucer barrows within cemeteries of more than five barrows. 41

Table 4   Numbers of post-medieval farms on SPTA. . . . 117

Foreword

The archaeological evidence represented in this book is drawn from an area the size of the Isle of Wight and forms the largest Army Field Training Centre in the United Kingdom. It is evident that the high level of preservation of the ancient earthworks in this area is a direct result of its acquisition for military training. This process was largely accomplished by 1900 and brought to completion in the years succeeding World War One.

Paradoxically, the presence of the very organisation that – albeit unintentionally – safeguarded the archaeology, dissuaded the archaeological community at large from seeking access. As recently as the mid-1970s it was widely believed that access to the area was fraught with difficulties and in the main would not be granted. My experience – as County Archaeologist for Wiltshire – and that of others who joined me, was of an unexpected willingness on the part of army personnel to arrange access to ancient features thought to be out of reach and to discuss the problems of their future preservation.

The Nugent Report in 1973 indicated the need for a more effective conservation approach to army training land, and pointed out in particular the value of wildlife and archaeological features on Salisbury Plain. Within a few years of that report, however, an atmosphere of crisis had developed on Salisbury Plain Training Area (SPTA). Two factors contributed to this. The first was the increasing use of the SPTA for armoured training, partly resulting from the expansion of a variety of units. Activities that had been mounted or horse-drawn within living memory, were increasingly being re-equipped for modern warfare, and exercises were evolved that tested their skills over rough, undulating terrain.

The other factor was undoubtedly the development of Conservation Groups, represented on the SPTA by groups in the west, centre and east. The damage reports submitted by the SPTA (East) group in particular indicated a worrying level of attrition of ancient monuments. Not surprisingly, these reports led to some tension between army management and Conservation Group members, and adverse publicity resulted whenever media interest was involved.

By 1980 it was evident to both army management personnel and the archaeologists involved that there was no reliable baseline of archaeological recording on Salisbury Plain and that the lists of sites protected by scheduling as ancient monuments were far from adequate. In 1984–5, therefore, the Wiltshire Archaeology Service was funded by English Heritage to carry out a rapid survey. A database was evolved that indicated some priorities for future protection methods. The same database was used to enhance the scheduling and, as a result, more than 500 monuments on the SPTA were added to the national list of Scheduled Monuments.

This activity in the early 1980s was directed by an SPTA Archaeological Working Party. Its efforts went some way towards solving the problems of the day, but it was evident that further ground survey and aerial photography of Salisbury Plain was needed, particularly if the need for military training continued to increase. The earthwork surveys carried out by the Royal Commission on the Historical Monuments of England (RCHME) fieldwork team during the 1980s began the process of upgrading the quality of archaeological data for the area, and the 1991 Wiltshire County Council aerial survey of the county (in high-quality colour) added to this process. Further air sorties have followed.

The work described in this volume is the end product, therefore, of the processes of concern, debate, and reaction – from the first reports of the Conservation Group workers, about 1970, up to the initiation of the field survey some two decades later. It represents an immense return on investment of both time and money. The gains are both in the academic sphere in which large areas of ancient landscape are seen to survive in totality, and in the management arena where an increasingly valuable training asset is seen to have environmental and historical characteristics of outstanding quality.

Roy Canham
WILTSHIRE COUNTY ARCHAEOLOGIST

Preface

by David McOmish, David Field and Graham Brown

The Survey

Concern about the fate of archaeological sites on the Salisbury Plain military estate was first voiced as early as 1901, when it was suggested that an accurate inventory of 'the tumuli and other objects of antiquarian interest on Salisbury Plain...' be made (Anon 1901a, 4). Some effort was spent achieving this and a few selected earthworks were planned by Percy Farrer (Anon 1915a). Concern for the resource continued, however, and, following the Nugent Report (Anon 1973), which recommended the appointment of Conservation Officers and voluntary Conservation Groups on Ministry of Defence (MoD) landholdings, a meeting was convened at Salisbury in May 1979 between officers of the RCHME, Wiltshire County Council, and the recently appointed MoD Conservation Officer, to consider the problem. A pilot survey sponsored by the Wiltshire Library and Museum Service (Smith 1981) commented on the damage to monuments and suggested that a joint study group be established. A report published by the Wiltshire County Archaeologist, Roy Canham, in 1983, highlighted the archaeological potential of the area. Drawing on earlier work produced by Bob Smith, which had elicited little interest from the Ancient Monuments Board for England, it included a number of sketch transcriptions and called for the RCHME to be involved in a detailed landscape survey of the Training Area (Anon 1983). After the creation of English Heritage (The Historic Buildings and Monuments Commission for England) in 1984, more immediate action was finally taken and it was decided that the Department of the Environment (through English Heritage) would organise an assessment so that the MoD could be advised about site management. A number of vested interests were involved, including the MoD, English Heritage and county archaeological officers, whose varying priorities all needed to be addressed, resolved and integrated into a coherent set of achievable goals. The report was published in 1986 and twelve areas of historic landscape were identified for special protection under Archaeological Site Group (ASG) Management Plans, which were designed to develop a sustainable method of management ensuring that all aspects of land use could evolve together as far as possible (Anon 1986). Following similar projects in Dorset, Hampshire and south Wiltshire, the RCHME fieldwork and analysis began in June 1988 with a pilot survey to assess the archaeological potential of the area.

Methodology

A major challenge lay in developing a survey methodology that would adequately record the archaeology. It was intended that each ASG be covered as thoroughly as possible; all the major earthwork complexes would be recorded by ground survey and the remainder would be included in an aerial transcription at a scale of 1:2 500. Each transcription would then be subject to field verification and amendment. It was soon realised, however, that the ASGs, which concentrated mainly on the well-preserved, but rare, Romano-British villages and their hinterland, failed to acknowledge that the real value of the historic landscape lay in its completeness in comparison with most other archaeological landscapes. Although the main emphasis of fieldwork continued to be directed at the ASGs, hitherto excluded sites and areas were incorporated into the study.

Earthworks, both isolated sites and large complexes, were surveyed using a variety of techniques involving Total Stations EDM equipment and taped off-sets. The majority of the resulting plans were produced using traditional hachures as it was felt that this method best depicted the subtle nature of much of the archaeology. Most sites were surveyed before the general availability of Global Positioning Systems, so the more geographically isolated examples were tied into locally defining features such as fences, tracks, contours and, on a number of occasions, military targets such as tank hulks (which had been separately surveyed onto the National Grid by the military).

This work also highlighted the variable nature of the aerial photographic evidence; ground assessment showed that in some places where no cropmarks or earthworks were depicted on air cover, there was good earthwork survival. Generally, where 19th-century cultivation had destroyed earthworks and where the landscape had been returned to grass, the results from air photography were poor. In response to these factors, and in order to provide an overview of the total archaeological environment, it was decided that, in addition to large-scale survey of the major sites and monuments, ground reconnaissance of negative or poorly represented areas was necessary, and thorough checking of each square kilometre was carried out. By walking in strips separated by 100m, 3,000ha were inspected in this way. In light of the new understanding that the Plain contained an almost continuous landscape of archaeological features of all periods, the project was also included at an early stage within the RCHME's National Mapping Programme (NMP): transcriptions were produced at a scale of 1:10 000 for all archaeological features, including those of military origin, showing as cropmarks, soilmarks and earthworks. The value of this scale, in comparison to that previously chosen (1:2 500), rapidly became apparent in that the work, though less detailed in character, was completed rapidly. All readily available photographs covering the project area were examined, including wartime RAF and USAAF vertical photographs held by the NMR and various prints held by the Cambridge University Collection of Aerial Photographs (CUCAP) and Wiltshire County Council. This survey produced a series of inked overlays on translucent film for the OS 1:10 000 base maps, and a record of the transcribed archaeological features that were input into a RCHME databases, and all of the maps have subsequently been digitised.

Geophysical survey techniques were also employed, the work being carried out by Geophysical Surveys of Bradford, particularly, but not exclusively, on plough-levelled sites. Nine sites were examined in this way. Generally, excellent results were obtained with clear levels of detail, although where earthwork sites were investigated, the detail was less encouraging. On the Central Impact Area it was possible to combine both field survey and fieldwalking, since explosions had disturbed the surface sufficiently to uncover scatters of pottery, worked flint, brick and other stonework.

The Report

This report, therefore, draws on the results of a number of survey techniques: ground, aerial and geophysical. While we realise that analogies from other chalkland environments could be brought in and, indeed, that our results could influence the wider understanding of chalkland archaeology in general, we have focused solely on the physical remains within our predefined study area. The purpose of the report is not to produce an inventory of sites on the Training Area. Instead it provides a commentary on the totality of the archaeology on the Salisbury Plain Training Area, integrating the results of the detailed field survey and enabling landscape contexts or settings to be analysed in great depth. It also provides an overview of the extent and nature of the archaeology, as well as current land-use, and will have a real impact in determining future management strategies.

The results presented here show vividly the quality and completeness of the archaeology (Figure i.1). Importantly, they enable the development of a large area to be understood, not only through the use and adaptation of individual monuments, but also in terms of the changing character of a region, and as such they represent a significant step forward in our knowledge and understanding of the past.

With such excellent survival it is tempting to see the area as a microcosm of the archaeological landscapes that once existed on other parts of the chalk in England. For instance, the post-medieval history and pattern of exploitation on the Marlborough Downs to the north, or the Grovely Ridge to the south, bear comparison to the SPTA. Large expanses of ancient field systems, enclosed settlements and, to a lesser extent, linear boundaries are common to all three of these areas, though the scale and complexity of preservation on the Training Area outstrips the others. This is not to assume some sort of uniformity of human exploitation for all chalkland areas, rather it serves to highlight common aspects of development and to emphasise the value of the now rare archaeological remains. It must be borne in mind that, in national terms, only a small area of chalk downland has been assessed, and, while acknowledging the importance of contiguous areas, the monuments of the study area have remained the main focus.

In terms of sites discovered, the basic statistics are revealing: before the project started approximately 1,500 monuments were known on the Training Area but after completion of the fieldwork this number had risen to nearly 3,000 (Figure i.2). In particular, there has been a substantial increase in the extent of 'Celtic' field systems noted. Large increases have also been observed in numbers of round barrows and prehistoric enclosures, and new lengths of linear earthworks have also been revealed. Two new long barrows were found and a third was noted just outside the Training Area, which, while not a large number, is significant in relation to the twenty-eight sites previously known. The overall increase reflects the intensity of fieldwork and the success of the methodology adopted, but it also says a great deal about the previous state of knowledge and should provide a stimulus for future work. To be able to find new, in many cases upstanding, archaeological sites in southern England is surprising but the reasons for this, in this instance, are very clear. The ground conditions are suitable for earthwork recognition, and land-use, particularly in the 20th century, has meant that plough-damage has been kept to a minimum. Furthermore, previous investigation has not been intensive and has focused on particular areas or types of site, such as barrow cemeteries. The Training Area is, therefore, a fruitful place for archaeological research. The opportunities, however, might be limited to specific areas due to the inherent dangers of the Training Area. It is envisaged that the work of the RCHME will act as a catalyst for future investigation. In particular, it must be hoped that the sort of work undertaken on the Eastern Ranges by Reading University will be extended into the Central and Western areas, since only then can we arrive at a more complete understanding of the archaeological resource of the SPTA and attempt to further develop a coherent narrative of the area's history and glimpse the lives of those who peopled this landscape.

Acknowledgements

This project by the RCHME was conceived by Desmond Bonney and many individuals were involved with aspects of its work. In addition to the authors, members of staff involved in field investigation were Mark Corney, Deborah Cunliffe, Chris Dunn, Carenza Lewis, Alastair Oswald, Hazel Riley, Ian Sainsbury, Nicola Smith and a number of students on placement from Bournemouth, Oxford, Reading and Southampton Universities.

Aerial sorties were carried out by Bob Bewley, Roger Featherstone and Damian Grady; 1:2 500 plots were prepared by Ann Carter, and 1:10 000 plots by Graham Brown, Simon Crutchley, Carolyn Dyer, Kate Gardiner, Katie Roberts and Fiona Small, Geophysical Surveys of Bradford carried out the geophysical work on a number of sites.

Illustrations were prepared and supervised by Deborah Cunliffe. Ground photographs were taken by the principal authors and Ian Leonard, who also provided photographs of artefacts. Julie Lancley added project details to the National Monuments Record, while Felicity Gilmour and Claire Field, librarians at the NMRC, also provided additional help.

Members of staff of the Ministry of Defence, both civilian and military, have been of great assistance. In particular the EH are grateful for the help of Peter Addison, Ian Barnes, Jane Hallet, Lt Col Mike Jelf, Wendy Ives-Nash, John Loch, Major Michael Menage, Major Porto-Wright, Lt Col Geoffrey Rooke, and Paul Toynton. Members of the Conservation Groups, in particular Nell Duffy, also provided additional help.

Roy Canham, the late Alison Borthwick, Duncan Coe and Helena Cave-Penny of Wiltshire County Council provided encouragement and support throughout the project. For discussion in the field or office, our thanks to Professor Richard Bradley, Dr Bruce Eagles, Dr Roy Entwistle, Professor Andrew Fleming, Professor Mike Fulford, Dr Andrew Lawson, Dr Frances Raymond, Dr Andrew Reynolds, and Dr Colin Shell.

Dr Bob Bewley, Mark Bowden, Professor Richard Bradley, Simon Crutchley, Professor Andrew Fleming, Professor David Hinton and Graeme Kirkham commented upon earlier drafts of the text. Thanks are also given to the officers of the Wiltshire Archaeological and Natural History Society, in particular Paul Robinson, for their permission to photograph the artefacts from Charlton Down and Cunnington's sketch of the Heytesbury North Field long barrow. The Society of Antiquaries kindly allowed photographs of Flinders Petrie's survey work at Robin Hood's Ball and Orcheston Down to be used. Photographs were also provided by the Royal School of Artillery, Wiltshire County Council and by Peggy Gye.

Paul Everson, Dr Robin Taylor and Dr David M Jones supervised production of the book.

Abbreviations

AP	Aerial Photograph
ASG	Archaeological Site Group
BGS	British Geological Survey
CUCAP	Cambridge University Collection of Aerial Photographs
DLS	Defence Land Services
DM	Devizes Museum
DMV	Deserted Medieval Village
EDM	Electronic Distance Measuring
ESA	Environmentally Sensitive Area
FIBUA	Fighting In Built-Up Areas
INF/SCH	School of Infantry
MoD	Ministry of Defence
NMP	National Mapping Programme
NMR	National Monument Record
NMRC	National Monument Record Centre
OD	Ordnance Datum
OS	Ordnance Survey
RAF	Royal Air Force
RCHME	Royal Commission on the Historical Monuments of England
SMR	Sites and Monuments Record
SMV	Shrunken Medieval Village
SPTA	Salisbury Plain Training Area
SSSI	Sites of Special Scientific Interest
TVAS	Thames Valley Archaeological Service
USAAF	United States Army Air Force
WA	Wessex Archaeology
WRO	Wiltshire Record Office

Summary

This book is about one portion of an area broadly known as Salisbury Plain: the Salisbury Plain Training Area (SPTA). It is the story of humankind's impact on this environment but it also documents the remarkable remains that still survive in this area. On these Ranges can be found a diverse bio-culture unmatched anywhere else on the chalklands of southern England. On this land are the imprints of past communities, who lived, worked and died here. As successive generations came and went, they left their marks behind, traces of fields, settlements and burial mounds, all still visible on the surface of the Training Area.

The fact that there survives, still, so much, can be put down to one major fact: the area is now owned by the Ministry of Defence and is out of bounds to all but military personnel. The advantages of this, largely even and open terrain were obvious to those looking for new training grounds for cavalry in the late 19th century. Land purchases began in 1897 and so started a process in which all other types of land-use and users were forced out. Today, the estate covers an area of 37,000 hectares, a space roughly the same size as the Isle of Wight. Before the land purchases had begun, this section of the Salisbury Plain had been known, largely, as a desolate windswept place, dangerous and easy to become lost in, and a home to robbers and vagabonds. To cross the downs was seen as an inconvenience on the route from Salisbury to Bath or Marlborough, thence London. The upland terrain now embracing the Training Area stands in marked contrast to the fertile, easily accessed valleys that intersect it and define its southern boundary. When approached from the north and west, the chalk massif of the SPTA stands proud as a very prominent landmark. Towering above the local countryside, it is easy to see why earlier travellers wished to avoid its exposed open downs and, equally, avoid climbing its sharp escarpment edges. For in a lowland landscape of chalk downs and clay vales, these escarpments represented formidable barriers.

The archaeology of the Training Area is, however, often overlooked in archaeological textbooks. Instead, the chalk downland beyond Stonehenge (and elsewhere in Wessex) receives most attention. This is perverse, since in terms of the diversity of monument types, earthwork condition and survival and, therefore, the landscape histories that can be reconstructed, these areas offer only a fraction of that on the SPTA.

There are many reasons why the archaeological remains are so well preserved on the chalk downland. Simply, a combination of good, easily worked and tractable soils allied to intense human activity, shaped and carved the landscape as we see it today; each episode of use built one on top of the other, in such a way that the remains of earlier periods survive clearly or can be seen to influence subsequent developments. This process of accretion stalled, somewhat, from the middle years of this century onwards, with the introduction of new farming techniques, primarily, deep ploughing, which was so pervasive that it obliterated all earlier remains.

The military presence on the SPTA has ensured that this obliteration has not taken place in recent years, so it is no exaggeration to say now that the field remains on the Ranges survive as an island within a sea of arable. A tour of the hinterland of the SPTA clearly emphasises the largely unavoidable damage wrought on earlier landscape features by modern agriculture. This process of levelling and re-inscribing the land has a long history, since the fields and settlements of prehistoric and Roman date that lie across the Plain have themselves, in all likelihood, erased earlier monuments.

Nonetheless, the variety and condition of the extant sites and landscapes enable the construction of a complex narrative of land-use. The earliest monuments are long barrows, the burial mounds for communities who left no other traces of settlement. Other monuments, contemporary with the long barrows, are rare but include the enigmatic causewayed enclosures, sites of ritual, possibly of trade, but certainly of social gatherings. Later, round barrows were built in large numbers on the Plain, concentrated along river valleys and often occurring in clusters or cemeteries. The Training Area holds some of the greatest concentrations of these barrows in the British Isles. Permanent fields and settlements appear to have developed in the Middle Bronze Age, at least 1000 years after the erection of the earliest monuments. This was the first large-scale, long-lasting, colonisation of the Plain but the original extent of these early fields is unknown as a result of the up-take of land and reuse of the fields in the later prehistoric and Romano-British periods. There are only five confirmed hillforts on the SPTA, but there are large numbers of smaller enclosures, presumably farms or their equivalent, though we cannot be sure that some might not have served other, more esoteric, purposes. The discovery of a large Early Iron Age midden mound and associated enclosure at East Chisenbury blurs the distinction between the secular and non-secular, suggesting that ritual was bound up with daily social practices at this time.

By far the most intense period of settlement on the Training Area took place during the 1st – 4th centuries AD, a time of Roman control. There is, however, little evidence of Roman military activity on the Plain. In fact, this was clearly a time of agricultural intensification with close association between flourishing villages, of which we have identified eleven, fields and, certainly by the 3rd and 4th centuries, villas and a market economy. Some of the villages covered large areas; the remains of the village on Charlton Down extend over 25ha and is articulated by a series of tracks servicing well defined, presumably domestic, compounds. The range of artefacts from the sites points to established sedentary agricultural communities.

The fate of the villages on the collapse of the Roman economy in the early 5th century is unknown. From recent excavations at Coombe Down there is evidence of continued activity into the 6th century, but there seems to have been a gradual decline in occupation with the majority of the population becoming established in the villages (which survive today) in the river valleys and at the foot of the chalk escarpment. These villages frequently show evidence of having been occupied in the Romano-British period; this new growth demonstrates either long-term continuity or reuse of ancient settlements. In the post-Roman period the downs continued to be used predominantly as part of a fixed pattern of agricultural exploitation. However, concerns over land tenure and, possibly, ancestral rights are shown by the presence of Anglo-Saxon burials not only in pre-existing burial mounds but also in newly constructed graves.

There are no medieval settlements on the Higher Plain, only sheep enclosures, pasture and the remains of ridge-and-furrow cultivation, which was worked from the settlements in the valleys and more sheltered zones. Nearly all the modern settlements along the Avon valley, for example, display traces of older settlement. The now abandoned earthwork boundaries of properties and associated building platforms are evident, lying side by side within the current village limits. There is much evidence for periodic and intensive use of the downs, always negotiated from the villages in the valleys, while for much of the later medieval period the downs were used as sheep walks and an integrated system of management was evident. This involved the use of a long-established division of the landscape into areas of pasture, arable and meadow interrupted only when the military began its purchasing in the late 19th century. From then on, the use of the downs was equally intense but driven by the requirements of military training; impact zones developed, as did rifle ranges and trench systems. Many of the largest settlements on the Training Area are garrison towns built to serve the influx of military personnel.

This book assesses monuments of all periods and, in adopting this holistic approach to the archaeology on the Training Area, a benchmark for other work has been established. It provides ammunition for further work and analysis, aiding proper management and conservation of the archaeological resource but importantly it presents an understanding and appreciation of the outstanding heritage curated by the MoD on the Salisbury Plain Training Area.

Résumé

Ce livre traite d'une partie de la région généralement connue sous le nom de plaine de Salisbury: la zone de manoeuvres militaires de Salisbury (en anglais SPTA). Il raconte l'histoire de l'impact de l'homme sur cet environnement, mais il répertorie aussi les remarquables vestiges qui survivent encore à cet endroit. On peut trouver sur ces champs de tir une bio-culture variée qui n'a d'égale nulle part ailleurs sur les terres calcaires du sud de l'Angleterre. Ces terres portent les empreintes des communautés passées qui y ont vécu, s'y sont travails et y sont mortes. Générations après générations se sont succédées, sont arrivées, sont reparties, ont laissé leurs marques derrière elles; tracés de champs, occupations, tertres funéraires sont tous encore visibles en surface sur le champ de manoeuvres.

On peut imputer à un seul facteur majeur le fait que tant de vestiges aient subsisté jusqu'à nos jours: la région appartient maintenant au ministère de la défense et l'accès en est interdit à tout individu ne faisant pas partie du personnel militaire. Les avantages de ce terrain, en majeure partie peu accidenté et ouvert, durent paraître évidents à ceux qui cherchaient de nouveaux terrains de manoeuvres pour la cavalerie à la fin du 19ème siècle. Les premiers achats de terres datent de 1897 et ainsi commença un processus qui en élimina tout autre type d'exploitation et tout autre propriétaire. De nos jours, le domaine couvre une superficie de 37 000 hectares, une étendue à peu près équivalente à celle de l'île de Wight. Avant le commencement des achats de terrains, cette section de la plaine de Salisbury avait la réputation d'être surtout une aire déserte, balayée par les vents, dangereuse et où il était facile de se perdre, un repaire de voleurs et de vagabonds. Qu'on soit obligé de traverser les collines en allant de Salisbury à Bath ou à Marlborough, et de là à Londres, était considéré comme un inconvénient. Les terres hautes, parmi lesquelles se trouve maintenant le camp militaire, contrastent violemment avec les vallées fertiles et faciles d'accès qui les entaillent et en forment la frontière sud. Quand on l'approche en venant du nord ou de l'ouest, le massif calcaire du camp militaire se détache clairement et constitue un point de repère très proéminent. Il domine la campagne environnante et il est facile de comprendre pourquoi les voyageurs d'autrefois souhaitaient éviter ses collines exposées et découvertes et, voulaient également éviter d'escalader ses crêtes escarpées. Car dans une région de basses terres consistant en collines crayeuses et en vallées argileuses, ces escarpements représentaient de formidables barrières.

L'archéologie du camp militaire est, toutefois, souvent omise des manuels d'archéologie. A la place, on accorde un maximum d'attention aux collines calcaires situées de l'autre côté de Stonehenge(et ailleurs dans le Wessex). C'est une attitude perverse, car en matière de diversité de types de monuments, de condition et de subsistance des travaux de terrassement, et, par conséquent, de possibilité de reconstruction de l'histoire du paysage, ces régions n'ont à offrir qu'une fraction de ce qui se trouve sur le camp militaire.

Les raisons pour lesquelles les vestiges archéologiques sont si bien conservés sur les collines crayeuses sont nombreuses. Tout simplement, une combinaison de sols de bonne qualité, faciles à travailler et à manier associés à une activité humaine intense ont façonné et sculpté le paysage tel que nous le connaissons aujourd'hui; chaque étape de son utilisation a construit au-dessus de la précédente de telle manière que les vestiges des périodes antérieures ont soit clairement subsisté, soit influencé d'une manière évidente les développements postérieurs. Ce processus d'accumulation ralentit quelque peu à partir du milieu de notre siècle à la suite de l'introduction de nouvelles techniques agricoles, en particulier le labour en profondeur, qui était si pénétrant qu'il a effacé tous les vestiges antérieurs.

La présence militaire sur la zone de manoeuvres a garanti l'arrêt de cette destruction dans les années récentes, donc ce n'est pas une exagération de dire maintenant que les vestiges de champs sur les zones de tir subsistent comme une île dans une mer de terres labourées. Un tour dans l'arrière pays du camp militaire met clairement en évidence les dégâts, en grande partie inévitables, causés par l'agriculture moderne aux divers aspects du paysage antérieur.

Néanmoins, la diversité et la condition des sites et des paysages existants nous permettent de reconstruire l'histoire complexe de l'utilisation des terres. Les monuments les plus anciens consistent en tumulus allongés, tertres funéraires de communautés qui n'ont pas laissé d'autres traces de leur présence. Les autres monuments, contemporains avec les tumulus allongés, sont rares mais comprennent les enigmatiques enceintes à chaussée empierrée, sites à but rituel, voire commercial, mais en tout cas lieux de rencontres sociales. Plus tard, on a construit dans la plaine des tertres arrondis en grand nombre, ils sont concentrés le long des vallées alluviales et se trouvent souvent en groupes ou en cimetières. L'aire de manoeuvres recèle certaines des plus importantes concentrations de ces tumulus dans les îles britanniques. Des champs et des occupations permanents semblent s'être développés plus tard, au moins 1000 ans après la construction des monuments les plus anciens, vers le milieu de l'âge du bronze. Ce qui constitue la première colonisation durable et à grande échelle de la plaine, mais l'étendue originale de ces champs primitifs reste inconnue à la suite de la reprise des terres et de la réutilisation des champs à la fin de la préhistoire et à la période romano-britannique. Il n'existe que cinq camps fortifiés attestés sur le camp militaire, alors qu'il y a un grand nombre d'enceintes de plus petite taille, probablement des fermes ou leur équivalent, bien que nous ne puissions pas être sûrs que certaines n'aient pas servi d'autres desseins plus ésotériques. La découverte d'un important tas d'ordures du début de l'âge du fer et d'une enceinte associée à East Chisenbury vient brouiller la distinction entre séculier et non-séculier, donnant à penser que le rituel était lié aux pratiques sociales quotidiennes de l'époque.

De loin, la période d'occupation la plus intense sur le champ de tir eut lieu entre les 1er et 4ème siècles ap. J.-C., à l'époque où le pays était sous contrôle romain. Il y a, cependant, peu de témoignages d'activité militaire romaine dans la plaine. En fait, c'était de toute évidence une époque où l'agriculture s'intensifiait et où des liens étroits existaient entre des villages florissants, dont onze ont été identifiés, des champs, et certainement à partir des 3ème et 4ème siècles, des villas et une économie de marché. Certains des villages couvraient de vastes étendues; les vestiges du village sur la colline de Charlton Down s'étendent sur plus de 25 ha et s'organisent autour d'une série de sentiers desservant des bâtiments, probablement à usage domestique, bien précis. La gamme d'objets manufacturés provenant des sites atteste de communautés agricoles sédentaires bien établies.

Nous ne connaissons pas le sort réservé aux villages au moment de l'effondrement de l'économie romaine au début du 5ème siècle. A la suite de fouilles récentes à Coombe Down, on possède des preuves ont continué à être actifs au 6ème siècle, mais il semble que le niveau d'occupation ait progressivement décliné, la majorité de la population s'installant dans les villages (qui existent encore de nos jours) dans les vallées alluviales et au pied de l'escarpement calcaire. Ces villages révèlent souvent des témoignages d'occupation à l'époque romano-britannique; ce nouveau développement démontre soit une phase d'occupation prolongée, soit une réutilisation d'anciennes occupations. Au cours de la période post-romaine, les collines continuèrent à être utilisées essentiellement comme partie intégrante d'un système déterminé d'exploitation agricole. Cependant, des préoccupations quant à la tenure des terres et, peut-être aux droits ancestraux sont mises en évidence par la présence d'inhumations anglo-saxonnes non seulement dans des tertres funéraires préexistants, mais également dans des tombes nouvellement construites.

Il n'y a pas d'occupations médiévales dans la partie la plus haute de la plaine, seulement des parcs à moutons, des pâtures et des vestiges de culture en sillons et billons, qui étaient exploités à partir des occupations situées dans les vallées et les zones plus abritées. Presque toutes les occupations modernes le long de la vallée de l'Avon, par exemple, révèlent des traces d'occupations plus anciennes. Les fossés et les talus, maintenant abandonnés, qui délimitaient les propriétés, et les plateformes de construction qui leur sont associées sont évidents, couchés côte à côte à l'intérieur de l'enceinte des villages actuels. Nous possédons beaucoup de témoignages de l'utilisation périodique et intensive des collines, toujours établie à partir des villages dans les vallées, tandis que pendant une grande partie de la fin de l'époque médiévale les collines étaient utilisées pour le pâturage des moutons et que l'existence d'un système de gestion intégré est évidente. Ceci impliquait l'utilisation d'un fractionnement du paysage établi depuis longtemps en zones de pâture, de culture et de prairie, interrompu seulement quand l'armée commença à acheter les terres à la fin du 19ème siècle. A partir de ce moment-là, l'utilisation des collines fut tout aussi intense mais poussée par les exigences des manoeuvres militaires, on développa des zones d'impact, ainsi que des champs de tir et des systèmes de tranchées. Beaucoup des occupations les plus importantes sur la zone de manoeuvres sont des villes de garnison construites pour servir l'afflux de personnel militaire.

Ce livre évalue les monuments de toutes les époques, et en adoptant une approche holistique de l'archéologie dans la zone de manoeuvres, on a créé un ouvrage de référence pour d'autres recherches. Il fournit des munitions pour des travaux et des analyses ultérieurs, il favorise la gestion éclairée et la conservation des ressources archéologiques, mais plus important encore, il offre une appréhension et une appréciation du patrimoine exceptionnel à la charge du ministère de la défense sur le camp de manoeuvres de la plaine de Salisbury.

Traduction: Annie Pritchard

Zusammenfassung

Dieses Buch handelt von einem Teil des Gebietes, welches allgemein als Salisbury Plain (Salisbury Ebene) bekannt ist: Die Salisbury Plain Training Area (SPTA). Es ist die Geschichte vom Impakt des Menschen in diesem Umfeld, aber auch eine Dokumentation der bemerkenswerten Überreste, welche bis zum heutigen Tage dort überleben. Auf diesen Weiten kann man eine vielartige Biokultur finden, die einzigartig auf dem Kalkland im Süden Englands ist. Auf diesem Land sind die Abdrücke von vergangenen Lebensgemeinschaften, welche hier lebten, arbeiten und starben. Als die aufeinander folgenden Generationen kamen und gingen, hinterließen sie ihre Merkmale, Spuren von Feldern, Niederlassungen und Grabhügel sind immer noch auf dem Trainingsgelände sichtbar.

Die Tatsache, daß noch soviel erhalten ist, kann man hauptsichlich dem Umstand zuschreiben, daß das Verteidigungsministerium dieses Land besitzt und es nur vom Militärpersonal betreten werden darf. Das Gebiet mit offenen Terrain war ideal für jeden der nach einem neuen Trainingsgelände für die Kavellerie des späten 19. Jahrhunderts suchte. Erste Landkäufe begannen in 1897, und waren der Anfang eines Prozesses, bei welchem alle anderen Arten der Nutzung dieses Landes und dessen Nutzer heraus gedrängt wurden. Heute umfaßt dieser Besitz 37000 Hektar, ein Gebiet in der Größe der Isle of Wight. Vor den ersten der Landkäufe, war dieser Teil der Salisbury Plain zum größten Teil als ein einsames windurchzogenes Gebiet bekannt, gefährlich und einfach sich darin verlieren, Heimat zu Räubern und Vagabunden. Um das Hügelland auf dem Weg von Salisbury nach Bath oder Marlborough und von dort London zu kreuzen war als Unannehmlichkeit angesehen. Das das Trainingsgelände umgebende Hochland steht in markierendem Kontrast zu den einfach zugänglichen und fruchtbaren Tälern, welche das Gebiet durchziehen und seine südliche Grenzen darstellen. Vom Norden und Westen kommend, steht das Kalkmassiv des SPTA stolz als ein prominentes Landmal. Über die lokale Landschaft ragend, ist es einfach zu verstehen, warum frühere Reisende das offenliegende Hügelland zu umgehen versuchten und die scharfen Steilwände vermieden. Für ein flachliegendes Land von Kalkhügeln und Lehmtälern stellten diese Steilwände ein formidables Hindernis dar.

Die Archeologie des Trainingsgeländes, ist jedoch vielmals übersehen in archeologischen Textbüchern. An Stelle dessen, bekommt das Kalkniederland hinter Stonehenge (und anderseits in Wessex) die meiste Aufmerksamkeit. Das ist unverständlich, da es doch, von Seite der Vielfalt der überlebenden Monumente und Erdwerkskonditionen, nur einen Bruchteil dessen, von dem im SPTA-Gebiet vorhandenen, bietet.

Es gibt viele Gründe warum die archeologischen Überreste so gut im Kalkland erhalten sind. Eine Kombination von guten, einfach zu bearbeitenden Böden, zu der Intensivierung der menschlichen Aktivität beitragend, formte die Landschaft wie wir Sie heute sehen können in so einem Weg, das aufeinander folgende Episoden der Benutzung aufeinander bauten. Dadurch sind Überreste von früheren Perioden erhalten oder machen deren Einfluß auf folgende Entwicklungen deutlich. Dieser Prozeß von Anlagerung verzögerte sich seit der Mitte des 20. Jahrhundert mit der Einführung von neuen Farmmethoden, hauptsächlich Tiefpflügen, welches so tiefgreifend war, das frühere Überreste vernichtet wurden.

Die Gegenwart des Militärs auf der SPTA sicherte das diese Vernichtung hier in den letzten Jahren nicht statt fand, so daß es keine Übertreibung ist zu sagen das die Feldüberreste in diesen Weiten als eine Insel in einem Meer von Farmland überleben. Eine Begehung des SPTA-Hinterlandes macht die größtenteils nicht abwendbaren Schäden an früheren Landschaftsmerkmalen durch moderne Landwirtschaft klar deutlich. Dieser Prozeß der Einebnung und Überarbeitung des Landes hat eine lange Geschichte, da die Felder und Ansiedelungen aus prähistorischen und römischen Zeiten, welche auf der Salisbury Ebene liegen, höchstwahrscheinlich frühere Monumente auslöschten.

Dessen ungeachtet erlaubt die Vielfalt der vorhandenen Standorte und Landschaften eine komplexe Erzählung der Landnutzung. Die frühesten Monumente sind lange Hügelgräber, die Grabstätten für Lebensgemeinschaften welche keine anderen Merkmale einer Ansiedelung hinterließen. Andere Monumente der gleichen Zeit sind selten, beinhalten aber rätselhafte dammartige Einfriedungen, welche Plätze für Rituale, möglicherweise Handel, definitiv aber für soziale Zusammenkünfte waren. Später wurden runde Grabhügel in großer Anzahl auf der Salisbury Ebene gebaut, welche sich in Flußtälern konzentrierten, oftmals in Friedhöfen und Gruppierungen. Das Trainingsgebiet hält einige der größten Konzentrationen dieser Grabhügel in den Britischen Inseln. Permanente Felder und Ansiedelungen ziemen eine Entwicklung späterer Zeiträume zu sein, spätestens 1000 Jahre nach der Errichtung der ersten Monumente, im mittleren Bronzezeitalter. Diese waren die erste groß angelegte, langfristige Kolonisation der Salisbury Ebene, aber die originalen Ausmaße dieser frühen Felder sind unbekannt als ein Ergebnis der späteren Nutzung des Landes in späteren prähistorischen und römisch-britischen Zeiten. Es gibt nur fünf bestätigte Hügelbefestigungen auf dem SPTA, jedoch eine Menge kleinerer Einfriedungen, wahrscheinlich Farmen oder deren gleichen, wo wir doch nicht sicher sein können, daß einige nicht auch mehr esoterische Nutzungen hatten. Der Fund eines frühen Eisenzeitalter-Mittelhügels mit Einfriedung bei East Chisenbury verschleiert die Unterscheidung zwischen sekulär und nicht-sekulär, und regt an, daß die ritualen mit den alltäglichen sozialen Praktiken der Zeit verbunden wurden.

Die bei weitem intensivste Periode von Besiedelung in dem Trainingsgebiet fand wären dem 1. und 4. Jahrhundert A.D., eine Zeit unter römischer Kontrolle. Es gibt jedoch wenige Beweise für römischer militärische Aktivitäten auf der Ebene. Es ist Fakt, daß dieses eine Zeit landwirtschaftlicher Intensivierung mit engen Verbindungen zwischen den florienden Dörfern, von welchen wir elf, Felder und mit Sicherheit im 3.und 4. Jahrhundert Villas und eine Marktökonomie, indentizifiert haben. Einige der Dörfer breiteten sich über große Flächen aus, die Überreste des Dorfes von Charlton Down bedecken 25ha und ist durchzogen von einer Reihe von Pfaden, welche zu gut definierten, vermutlich heimischen Höfen führen. Die Liste der Artefakte von verschiedenen Punkten des Dorfes machen eine seßhafte Gemeinschaft deutlich.

Nicht bekannt ist das Schicksal der Dörfer nach dem Verfall der römischen Ökonomie im frühen 5. Jahrhundert. Von jüngsten Ausgrabungen in Coombe Down gibt es Beweise für kontinuelle Aktivität bis ins 6. Jahrhundert, wobei es angenommen werden kann, daß dann eine stetige Abwanderung statt fand, bei welcher sich die Mehrheit der Bewohner in Dörfer (welche bis in den heutigen Tag bestehen) in Flußtälern und am Fuß der Kalksteilwände ansiedelte. Diese Dörfer zeigen oft Beweise von Besiedlung in der römisch-britischen Periode. Dieser Zuwachs verdeutlicht entweder langzeitige Kontinuität oder Wiederbenutzung von uralten Besiedlungen. In der post-römischen Periode wurde das Hügelland hauptsächlich für landwirtschaftliche Zwecke als Teil eines festen Musters benutzt. Wie auch immer, Sorgen über Landbesitz und das Recht der Vorfahren werden aus dem Vorhandensein von schon bestehenden und neu konstruierten angelsächsischen Grabhügeln sichtbar.

Es gibt keine mittelalterlichen Siedlungen in dem höheren Hügelland, nur Schafeinfriedungen, Weiden und Rippen-und Furchenkultivierungen, welche von den Tälern und mehr geschützten Zonen bearbeitet wurden. Nahezu alle modernen Siedlungen zum Bespiel im Avontal verdecken Spuren von älteren Gemeinden. Die jetzt verlassenen Erdwerksbegrenzungen von Grundstücken und deren Bauplattformen sind sichtbar, Seite an Seite liegend mit den jetzigen Dorfgrenzen. Es gibt viele Beweise für periodische und intensive Nutzung des Hügellandes, immer von den Dörfern in den Tälern umgesetzt, während für die meißte Zeit des späteren Mittelalters das Hügelland für Schaftriebe unter einem integrierten Managementsystem genutzt wurden. Dieses beinhaltete die Nutzung von einer lang etablierten Teilung der Landschaft in Gebiete für Weiden, Ackerbau und Brachland, welche nur dann unterbrochen wurde, als das Militär begann Ende des 19. Jahrhunderts das Land zu kaufen begann. Danach wurde das Land zwar weiterhin intensiv benutzt, diesmal aber von den Bedürfnissen militärischen Trainings vorangetrieben, mit Einschlagzonen, Schießplätzen und Grabensystemen. Die meißten, der größten in Trainingsgelände gelegenen Siedlungen, sind Garrisionsstädte, für den Zustrom des Militärpersonals gebaut.

Dieses Buch schätzt die Bauwerke von allen Perioden ein, und etabliert, durch diesen holistischen Zugang zu der Archeologie des Trainingsgeländes, einen Vergleich für andere Arbeiten. Es gibt Munition für neue weitere Arbeiten und Analysen, hilft ordnungsgemäßen Management und der Erhaltung von archeologischen Ressourcen. Am wichtigsten jedoch erlaubt es ein Verständnis und Anerkennung für das herausragende Erbe, welches vom Verteidigungsministerium auf dem Salisbury Plain Trainingsgelände gepflegt wird.

Übersetzung: Norman Behrend

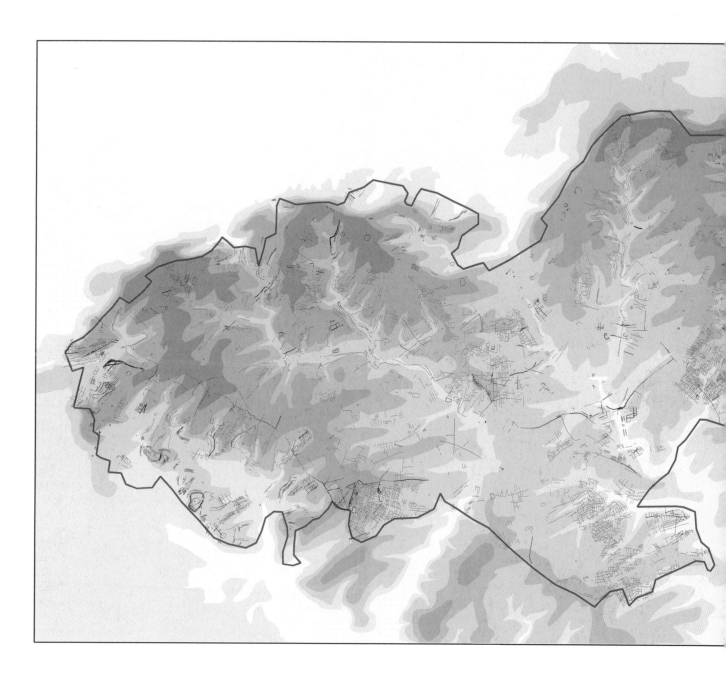

Figure i.1
Plot of archaeological
features on the SPTA
taken from aerial
transcriptions. Field
systems are depicted in
red, while all other
archaeological features
are in blue.

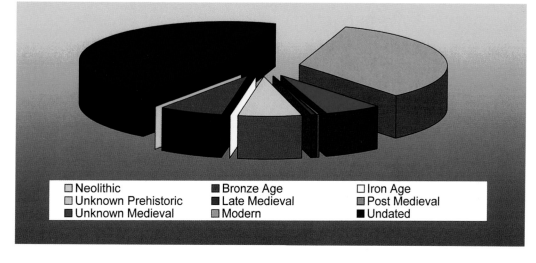

☐ Neolithic	■ Bronze Age	☐ Iron Age
▨ Unknown Prehistoric	■ Late Medieval	▨ Post Medieval
■ Unknown Medieval	▨ Modern	■ Undated

Figure i.2
Pie chart showing the
increase in monuments
recorded on the SPTA.

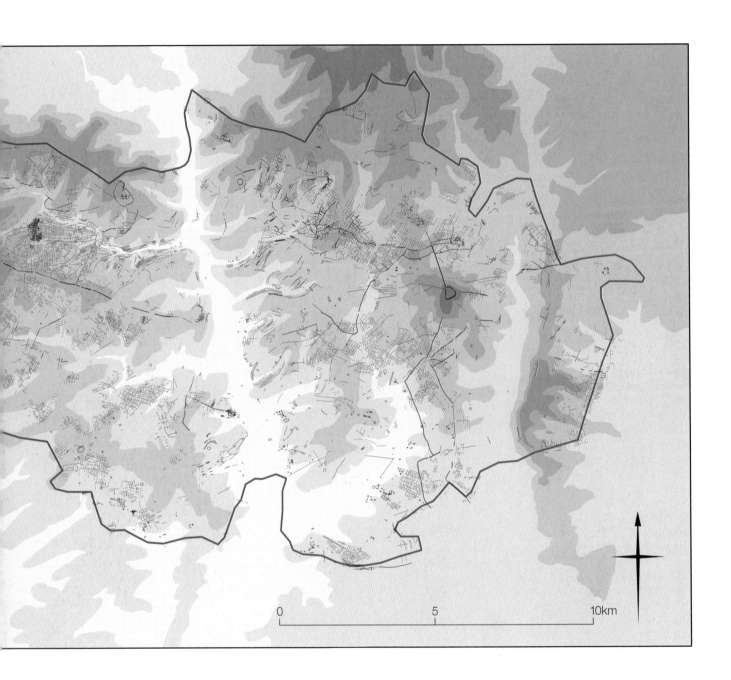

1
Introduction:
the Salisbury Plain Training Area

The Salisbury Plain Training Area (SPTA) is a unique and priceless landscape. This broad swathe of central Wiltshire comprises the largest surviving tract of unimproved chalk grassland in north-west Europe, where the archaeological remains of several millennia of human activity have been extraordinarily well-preserved from the depredations of both plough and bulldozer. The wider area is pre-eminent in the archaeological literature, renowned for monuments such as Stonehenge, and a great deal of our present understanding of prehistoric communities stems from research not only at Stonehenge itself, but at monuments nearby such as Woodhenge and Durrington Walls, and the myriad burial mounds that proliferate. Notions of prehistoric chiefdoms, warrior elites and the Wessex Culture were born here, although to many others, who passed through while on National Service, the nights under canvas in this cold and windswept wasteland have left a less positive memory. By more recent generations the Plain is remembered as a venue for rock festivals and is firmly rooted in the modern mythologies of New Age society as people search for meaning in an increasingly materialistic world.

The Plain itself lies in the heart of Wiltshire in the centre of southern England (Fig 1.1); the city of Salisbury and town of Andover are found to the south and east, surrounded by the rolling chalk hills and picturesque villages of south Wiltshire and west Hampshire. To the north, the fertile, well-watered Vale of Pewsey divides Salisbury Plain from the Marlborough Downs. To the west lies Somerset, where a flatter, lower-lying landscape is dotted with a plethora of hamlets, villages, small market towns and occasional patches of woodland.

Salisbury Plain is very different from these 'domesticated' landscapes. Geologically, it is one of a series of bands of chalk outcrops found across much of southern and eastern England, but here the outcrop is noticeably higher than its surrounding hinterland. The Plain is divided into discrete blocks by the rivers Wylye, Nadder, Till, Avon and Bourne, which have carved out sinuous south- or south-east-flowing valleys, but these are separated from one another by several kilometres of arid chalk downland, the permeable chalk bedrock providing no other easily available source of water. This fact has affected the Plain's usage and historical development. Agricultural policy since the war has encouraged widespread cultivation on the chalk and, as on the Yorkshire Wolds, Sussex Downs, or Cranborne Chase, many of the broad interfluves, particularly away from the military areas, to the south of Stonehenge,

Figure 1.1
Map showing the location of the Salisbury Plain Training Area.

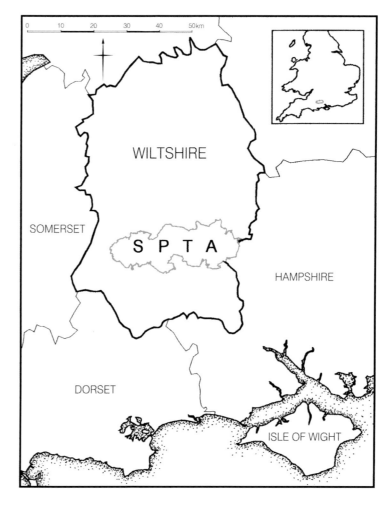

have been intensively ploughed and now form a sea of arable. By contrast, the Training Area survives as a remote and untamed area of unfenced rough pasture overlying steeply rolling hills, mostly lacking tree cover and sparsely settled.

The Training Area

It is not these characteristics alone that make Salisbury Plain unique and archaeologically so important. The most critical factor is the unparalleled condition in which archaeological remains of all periods are preserved across these hills, due to the sheep walks of recent centuries, and to the fact that the northern part of the area has long been under the control of the Ministry of Defence who use it for military training. It is perhaps unexpected, given the destructive nature of warfare, that this particular agency has led to such a relatively high level of preservation, despite damage to some sites by tank tracks or shell craters. Nevertheless, it is important to acknowledge that occupation by the army has saved much of the Plain from the greatest archaeological scourge of the 20th century – modern arable agriculture.

The military estate, known as the Salisbury Plain Training Area, covers nearly 39,000ha, stretching for some 38km east to west and 14km north to south. In places, entire fossilised landscapes survive, containing barrow cemeteries, 'Celtic' fields and linear boundaries and Romano-British settlements, all preserved as upstanding earthworks in a way that cannot be matched anywhere else in lowland Europe. The unexpectedness of this occurrence in southern England, where land is generally so intensively utilised, is evident even to the casual visitor: the rugged grassland of the Training Area appears now as an island within the surrounding countryside where, in all directions, the remains of the ancient land surface have been scoured by intensive modern cultivation and stripped away in advance of construction.

The archaeology is not the only resource to have benefitted from this special treatment. Untouched by the chemical arsenal of modern farming, many rare and vulnerable species of flora and fauna flourish in the SPTA. In recognition of this, more than 20,000ha have been designated as Sites of Special Scientific Interest (SSSI) and Environmentally Sensitive Areas (ESA), reflecting the importance of both the histor-

ical and natural heritage of the area today. The turf on the higher plain is springy and short when grazed, but otherwise the grass grows waist high, and the only noticeable variations in this cover occur on the patches of Clay-with-flints where ranker vegetation predominates. The remainder of the Training Area is covered with a mixture of well-established rough pasture and other formerly arable areas that have reverted to pasture. The main emphasis of modern agriculture here is on cattle and sheep-grazing, with arable restricted to the periphery of the area. Although part of a continuing process, the impact of agricultural improvements by the end of the 19th century was considerable and their effect on monument condition and survival will be considered in a later section.

In historical times few major settlements developed on the Higher Plain. Those that were established there, including Imber, Chitterne, Tilshead and Shrewton, are sheltered in protected valleys or on the slopes above streams and rivers, and were very closely connected with their contemporary communications network. The higher, exposed terrain, that makes up the main body of the Training Area, has not been favoured by either enduring settlement or a comprehensive road network during recent centuries. Although a number of smaller routes and tracks were present in the late 18th century (Andrews and Dury 1773), only a few major roads traversed the area. One of these, the London to Bath road, leads from Chitterne in the south to Coulston on the northern escarpment, and was long known as a haunt for highwaymen. A sarsen stone erected close to the now disused road on Chapperton Down commemorates a robbery and the subsequent death of one of the highwaymen after a chase, which took place there in 1839 (Fig 1.2). Samuel Pepys, travelling nearly two hundred years earlier in June 1668, recorded the difficulties that faced travellers on Salisbury Plain; bad roads and the absence of signposts made it difficult to find the way across open country (Bettey 1986, 195). That the Avon valley has been an important thoroughfare throughout history, is shown by the density of archaeological features along its flanks, and the differences in prehistoric and Romano-British settlement morphology on either side of it mark it out as a transitional or boundary zone. In many ways the Wylye valley is similar. This was, and still is, the major route for those wishing to avoid the Higher Plain. Road and rail routes follow the course of the valley that forms the main link between Salisbury and the major West Country centres of Bath and Bristol. Well-documented archaeological sites lie on the ridge along its southern flank (Corney 1989; English Heritage forthcoming) and these are of a density that clearly suggests that this location, at the edge of one major upland block of chalk and overlooking the river, was of considerable importance. Many of the sites here date to the Late Iron Age – Romano-British period, and it has been suggested that the Wylye valley itself marked a boundary between neighbouring tribes: the Durotriges to the south with the Dobunni to the north, in the area now occupied by the Training Area (Sellwood 1984, 202, fig 13.11). This is difficult to verify in the absence of other corroborative evidence, but finds of Late Iron Age inscribed coins suggest that the valley formed a divide between areas 'controlled' by different tribal confederacies. Further speculation that the Plain was some form of *cordon-sanitaire*, devoid of settlement between two competing zones, has been shown to be rather far-fetched (Van Arsdell 1994, 23–5, map 19); it is simply that prior to the work that has recently taken place on the SPTA, extensive occupation of later prehistoric and Roman date was thought to be largely absent from the area. Instead, it is now apparent that it is the pattern of occupation, not its density, that is different on either side of the pronounced topographical boundary formed by the Wylye valley.

Traditionally, and before the military occupation, Salisbury Plain was more generally known for its large flocks of sheep. Defoe, travelling in 1724, comments on the vastness of these flocks on the downs or 'Carpet Grounds' as he called them (1724–6). However, these observations masked a dependency on mixed farming, a well-established system that saw sheep 'folded' on, and manuring, the arable, thereby ensuring its fertility. Much of the tilled area was confined to the lower slopes above the river valleys, with the river meadow land being reserved for grazing and hay-cropping. This pattern was long established by the Middle Ages; indeed, on the basis of returns in the Domesday Book, the Avon valley was heavily cultivated at this time. Population concentrations were similarly polarised, with the Higher Plain far less populous than other areas.

Secondary products such as cloth were important economic factors in the valleys of Salisbury Plain, particularly in the 14th and 15th centuries when Salisbury became an important centre for the trade. The density of 'Celtic' fields and earlier settlements suggests that, long before the Norman Conquest, the population of the Plain was, similarly, heavily involved in agrarian practices. There is no way of giving anything but the most basic estimates of the population figures for these undocumented, pre-literate, periods and such estimates are further undermined by the inadequate chronological definition of the archaeological sites. It is unclear whether settlements were occupied permanently, or whether the large expanses of settlements and fields were contemporary with one another. What is clear is that the Higher Plain was cultivated during parts of the prehistoric and Roman periods and then largely abandoned, and it was not until the agricultural improvements of the post-medieval period that any concerted attempts were made to re-cultivate the more exposed areas. It has been noted that at this time people moved back onto the downs to work the land from a number of newly built farms, as well as for the established, but rapidly expanding, landed estates. This phase was short-lived and the agricultural depression of the late 19th century, caused by a series of wet, cold summers, poor grain yields, and cheap imports, put an end to it. As the number of workers involved in farming declined and populations moved away from the area, much of the previously arable land was converted back to grass.

Figure 1.2
Monument on Chapperton Down, now protected by wooden posts and barbed wire. The inscription reads 'This monument is erected to record the awful end of Benjamin Colclough, a highway robber who fell dead on this spot in attempting to escape his pursuers after robbing Mr Dean of Imber in the evening of October 21, 1839 and was buried at Chitterne without funeral rights. "The robbery of the wicked shall destroy them Prov.21 v 7". His three companions in Inquiry, Thomas Saunders, George Waters and Richard Harris, were captured and sentenced at the ensuing quarter sessions at Devizes to transportation for the term of fifteen years. "Though hand join in hand the wicked shall not be unpunished Prov.11 v 21".'

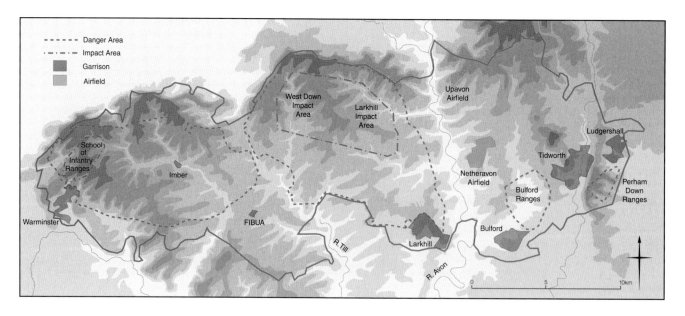

Figure 1.3
Map depicting military
use of Salisbury Plain.

The Agricultural Depression, which resulted in land prices plummeting, was met opportunistically in the final years of the 19th century by a War Office keen to purchase land for its own uses. The largely open landscapes of the Plain proved attractive to the military, and it ceased to be an area in which agricultural needs were uppermost; instead the requirements of military training started to shape the environment and left it much as it is today.

Modern land use

The limits of the military area are clearly defined (Figs 1.1 and 1.3) and the area inside it is now carefully administered under a number of schemes enabling different land usage in different places. Military policy started to influence the landscape very soon after the acquisition of the ranges. Apart from areas along the Avon valley most arable land was returned to grassland. Three categories of land use were identified at the outset. Schedule 1 land was let on agricultural leases and could remain as arable, with compensation being paid for damage done by training. Schedule 2 was arable when purchased but was immediately returned to grassland; Schedule 3 was grassland that remained as such. Schedule 2 land was subsequently subsumed into Schedule 3 and categories 1 and 3 still remain (James 1987, 22–3).

For military use the area is divided into three zones of activity (Fig 1.3):

- The Western Range lies between Warminster in the west and the valley of

the Till, and is used primarily for tactical manoeuvres and firing by both tanks and infantry. The village of Imber, deserted since 1943, lies almost centrally, and, apart from the church and the manor house, is also used for military training. A few kilometres to the southeast of Imber is a purpose-built 'artificial' village (Fig 1.4) of eastern European plan that enables troops to train for Fighting In Built-Up Areas (FIBUA).

- The Central Range stretches from the Till to the Avon in the east and is used mainly as an artillery firing range. The present impact area lies in the north, where the presence of unexploded shells now precludes any other form of land use. To the south of this zone lies a tactical manoeuvre area that is also used by local farmers for temporary grazing and, occasionally, arable cultivation.

- The Eastern Range lies to the east of the River Avon and is used for tactical training. There are also a number of rifle ranges on Bulford Down, two small airfields, at Netheravon and Upavon, and a tank-driver training area to the north of Tidworth.

Recently metalled tracks through and between these areas (Fig 1.5) aim to funnel much tank traffic along specific corridors and help to alleviate the pressure on the natural history and archaeology of the wider grassland.

Some fifty farms lease Schedule 1 land. This is let on a full agricultural tenancy

Figure 1.4
Copehill Down military village (FIBUA). Unlike any of the medieval villages, this nucleated settlement is situated on the Higher Plain. It was constructed by the military to simulate the type of buildings that would be found on the continent, enabling troops to practise combat situations in built-up areas.

and is generally found in areas around the edge of the Training Area, thus providing a buffer between the military and the surrounding villages. On Schedule 3 land, used primarily for training, farmers are licensed to use controlled areas for temporary periods of grazing.

Forestry, where the stands provide cover and camouflage for troops, is also important. Currently 6 per cent of the area of the SPTA is wooded; in addition, large parts of the grass downland, free of cultivation, are now reverting to scrub. In order to increase the level of tree cover, the Defence Land Services (DLS) has undertaken a programme of afforestation. Older plantations, mainly of beech, are, however, a common feature and many of these appear to have been planted during the 18th and 19th centuries. A number were established as a consequence of the growing interest in hunting, while others formed shelter-belts around the new farmsteads on the downs.

The modern settlement and communications pattern is almost completely dominated by MoD developments. The major towns on the SPTA are now essentially garrisons, built and maintained for military personnel. The first establishment was built at Tidworth in 1903, and this was followed shortly afterwards by other developments at Larkhill, Ludgershall, Warminster and Bulford (Bettey 1986, 248). At Bulford a vast complex was constructed during the First World War, and the population, which numbered 341 in 1891 had grown to more than 4,000 by 1931 (op cit, 288). Other camps and RAF bases were built at Figheldean, Rollestone and Upavon, and for much of the resident population the military presence continues to be the principal factor that shapes the local economy.

Geology

The soft rocks forming the landscape not only furnish the Plain with its characteristically subtle topography but also provide the basis for human subsistence in the area, influencing farming patterns as well as providing construction materials for buildings and monuments. Salisbury Plain comprises a mass of elevated chalk more than 200m thick, frequently incised by deep valleys and coombes; it is a landscape of rolling hills and hidden vales. The chalk here formerly comprised a continuous domed unit with the Marlborough Downs to the north, but the summit has been eroded leaving the two isolated chalk outcrops separated by a series of ribbon-like deposits in the Vale of Pewsey. The Salisbury Plain formation extends to the south of Salisbury and into Dorset, while to the east it becomes part of the Hampshire Downs. The area considered in this book, however, is the northernmost part, where the major landscape feature is the dramatic escarpment delimiting the edge of the chalk in the west and north. The available geological cartography was, like much of the pre-survey data on the archaeology of the area, produced during the last century. The present British Geological Survey (BGS) one inch map depicts the entire area as chalk with narrow deposits of Pleistocene drift on the floors of principal river valleys (Fig 1.6). Recently, however, the chalk has been divided into three regional Provinces: the Northern Province, the Transitional zone, and the Southern Province, each of which is in turn subdivided into a series of Members based on the nature of the chalk itself and flint seams within it (Mortimore and Wood 1986, 7). Within the Southern Province, however, the BGS proposes to retain the traditional tripartite terms, Upper, Middle and Lower Chalk (Jukes-Brown 1901, 5) while also applying the new subdivisions (Bristow *et al* 1997). The greater detail will be useful as, among other things, it might help to focus attention on areas of likely prehistoric flint extraction and those suitable for early prehistoric agriculture. No flint is present in the Lower Chalk, and little in the Middle Chalk, although its frequency increases in the higher levels. It is these deposits that provide more easily cultivated land. In contrast the Upper Chalk deposits are of interest in that they contain abundant flint seams, each of a different character (Jukes-Brown 1901, 1–2) and of potential use for both tools and building purposes.

In the military area the Lower Chalk is confined to a strip around the northern escarpment, and small exposures on valley floors to the north-west of Imber and between Urchfont and Tilshead (Jukes-Brown 1905). Similarly, the Middle Chalk is confined to the summit of the escarpment from Coulston Hill to West Lavington (Jukes-Brown 1905), together with the whole length of the Imber Valley and Water

Dean Bottom, west of the Avon valley. Most of the area, however, is Upper Chalk, the greater part being Chalk Rock, although the soft Belemnite Chalk forms Beacon Hill in the south-east. Quarry sections through these deposits, where investigated at, for example, Haxton, Ablington or Milton (Jukes-Brown 1905), display many strata of flint. While these were a primary prehistoric resource, they can also make cultivation difficult where they outcrop at the surface.

The major physical features of the landscape that we observe today were sculpted during the Eocene (38–55 million years ago) and by successive marine transgressions of the Late Pliocene (5–1.6 million years ago) to approximately 200m and 120m above the present sea level (Gifford 1957, 2). These inundated all areas, apart from Sidbury Hill, and left the area of the western and northern escarpment between Bratton and Redhorn, the highest portion of the chalk on the Training Area, standing proud.

Small patches of Clay-with-flints occur on these higher elevations, particularly along the northern escarpments and in a narrow arc around the head of Water Dean Bottom. Another small deposit lies in close proximity to the Reading Beds on Sidbury Hill. Clay-with-flints was formerly more extensive: deposits were recorded during excavations at Casterley Camp (Cunnington and Cunnington 1913, 76) and, more recently, has been noted in excavations at East Chisenbury (Brown *et al* in prep). This is of some importance, given the apparent correlation between these deposits and post-glacial prehistoric activity elsewhere in southern England (Care 1979; Gardiner 1984; Arnold *et al* 1989), for, in the absence of corroborative surface assemblages, the deposit could act as a guide to the likely presence of early human activity.

Quaternary geology

The final shaping of the landscape took place during the Quaternary (1.6 million years to the present day). During this period episodes of glacial and periglacial activity profoundly affected the morphology of the downs. The coombes, which form such a feature of the area, are often short, steep-sided, have blunt ends, and are likely to have formed originally as a result of springs sapping back the head of each coombe (Sparks and Lewis 1958, 26–36). However, the annual cycle of freezing and thawing is thought to have resulted in massive

Figure 1.5
A metalled track provides a focus for tracked vehicles; the aim being to confine vehicle damage to designated areas. Note the white concrete 'dragon's teeth' placed to discourage use of transverse tracks.

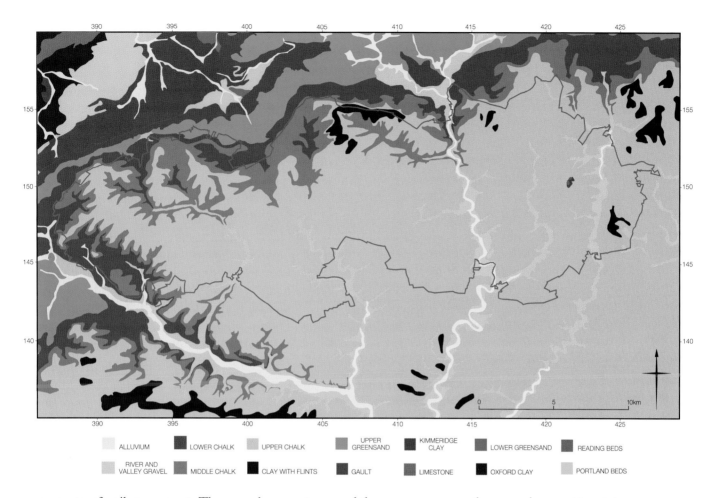

ALLUVIUM	LOWER CHALK	UPPER CHALK	UPPER GREENSAND	KIMMERIDGE CLAY	LOWER GREENSAND	READING BEDS
RIVER AND VALLEY GRAVEL	MIDDLE CHALK	CLAY WITH FLINTS	GAULT	LIMESTONE	OXFORD CLAY	PORTLAND BEDS

amounts of soil movement. The coombes, particularly the dramatic examples in the west of the Training Area, are likely to have been re-moulded as a result: coombe sides facing the sun melted faster than the others and, with the debris being washed down to the river channels, formed valleys of markedly asymmetrical profile. Similar processes also altered the escarpment, and, with recession of up to 1m taking place every century (Fagg 1923), formed the rilling that is so characteristic of the steep chalk-edge slopes. Evidence of cryoturbation, or frost heaving, was found beneath a round barrow at Greenland Farm (Evans 1968, 21), and involutions are frequently noted during excavation of sites in the immediate area, for example, at Stonehenge (Evans 1984, 26; Allen *in* Cleal *et al* 1995, 43). Some of these features can be seen on the summits and slopes, particularly around Boles Barrow and along the valley to the west of Imber, where extensive spreads of soil stripes, remarkably similar in shape to cultivation ridges, have been observed. The effects of later land-use and damage from vehicles have accentuated these natural fea-tures and they now appear on the ground as a series of corrugations or ridges standing to 0.5m in height, though their full extent is best seen from the air. While such soil stripes are recognised elsewhere as soil-marks, extant examples are rare, although they have been recognised at Weeting in East Anglia (Curtis *et al* 1976, 168–71).

Quaternary fauna

Around Salisbury there is some evidence of mammalian and, in particular, hominid activity in the gravel and brickearth terraces at Milford Hill, Fisherton and Bemerton (Blackmore 1804, 243–5; Cunnington 1856,129–42; Evans 1864; 1872, 548–55; Read 1885,117–23; Roe 1969, 5–6; Delair and Shackley 1978; Harding and Bridgland 1998). To the north of Salisbury, however, little is known of the presence of early hominids, but bifaces have been found along the terraces of the upper reaches of the Avon, at Wilsford and Amesbury; the Bourne, at Allington, and Idmiston; and the Wylye at Heytesbury (Grinsell 1952, 436–7). Isolated pointed bifaces have also

Figure 1.6
Map showing the geology of the SPTA, derived and simplified from a map originally drawn by the British Geological Survey.

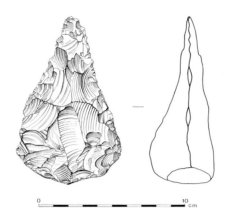

Figure 1.7
Palaeolithic biface from
Tilshead, the earliest
indication of human
activity on the Training
Area.

been recovered from Maddington and Tilshead (Devizes Mus) (Fig 1.7) alongside the Till, and from terrace gravel *c* 20m above the Avon at Figheldean (Roe 1969, 12). While these have a diverse date range, they represent the earliest evidence of hominid activity on the SPTA, and provide an indication that further evidence, perhaps similar to that from the Hampshire or North Downs (Willis 1947; Walls and Cotton 1980; Wymer 1987, 24; Scott-Jackson 1992), is likely to be present. The interfluves or summits capped by Clay-with-flint, in particular where there are limited effects of solifluction and weathering, might harbour important evidence. There is no evidence of *Homo sapiens sapiens*, however, until very much later. Apart from the presence of at least three large post-pits dug early in the post-glacial period at Stonehenge, the flintwork from Casterley Camp, once thought to be of Mesolithic date, on inspection appears to be Neolithic, leaving little evidence of Mesolithic hunter-gatherers on the SPTA.

Soils

Although cultivation is possible on all formations, it has been widely acknowledged that the Lower Chalk is more suited to agriculture, the Middle Chalk is drier and better for pasture, while the thin soil and vast numbers of flints on the surface of the Upper Chalk make it less suitable for cultivation (Reid 1903, 47). Based on such factors as climate, relief, elevation, and soil types, the Land Classification Survey (1947) considered that, apart from valleys such as the Avon, most of the higher chalk comprised medium to poor land. Gifford (1957) usefully divided the features of the chalk uplands into three topographical zones: the Chalk Summit, the Higher Plain

and the Lower Plain, relating each to its potential for settlement and subsistence activities. Like the Land Classification Survey, these divisions are based on a combination of height and the character of soils. Set around the west and northern lip of the Plain is the Chalk Summit above 200m OD. This prominent high-level plateau is today exposed to the elements. Clay-with-flints deposits are common, with small patches of water-retentive Upton, Carstens, and Coombe soils, particularly in the upper reaches of some valleys where there is underlying Middle Chalk (Findlay *et al* 1984). Much surface flint is present, which adversely affects cultivation and, consequently, the area is considered best suited to woodland (Gifford 1957, 5). The Higher Plain, lying between 200m and 120m OD, stretches as far south as Tilshead and comprises an area of broad interfluves with thin and light but well-drained soils (ibid), consisting of a complex mosaic of Icknield and Andover series. Both are light soils, although the Andover series is extremely flinty, making cultivation difficult. The Icknield soils are the most extensive and comprise fine windborne silt, but flints can again cause problems in cultivation and the soil is so thin that lack of rain in the growing season can affect harvests (Findlay *et al* 1984). The ridge tops and interfluves are today exposed to a vigorous and inhospitable microclimate, and, although climatic conditions varied considerably during prehistory, given the increased rainfall after about 900 BC, cereal growth might have been poor in these locations. The Lower Plain, below 120m, extends between Amesbury and Netheravon, south of Shrewton, and the Bulford Ranges below Beacon Hill. The area is drained by the lower courses of seasonal winterbournes as well as the main rivers, and is altogether a more gently undulating and hospitable landscape (Gifford 1957, 6).

Recent investigation in the Wilton area, west of Salisbury, demonstrated that the soil overlying both Upper Chalk and Clay-with-flints contains a loess-derived component (Cope 1976, 166–74), part of a widespread carpet of windblown silt deposited during periglacial conditions (Curtis *et al* 1976, 158). It is generally considered that most of the chalk uplands would have been covered by this deposit (Catt 1978, 14), which varied in thickness but formed a well-drained, mineral-rich mantle that was receptive to early agriculture. However, while the Icknield soils contain a high percentage of this material, weathering since the Devensian has had a marked effect. On many of the steep-sided valleys and re-entrants of the study area, most of the loess particles are likely to have drifted to the valley floors long before Boreal tree cover was established, leaving loess remnants perched on ridge tops, in much the same way as the Clay-with-flints. It is noteworthy, then, that loess was found resting above the Clay-with-flints horizon during excavations at East Chisenbury (Macphail *in* Brown *et al* forthcoming).

Drainage and water management

Salisbury Plain is a relatively dry environment, due mainly to the permeability of the underlying rock formations. There are three major valleys, where the rivers Till, Avon and Bourne divide the SPTA and flow southwards across the chalk (Fig 1.8). The westernmost river, the Till, is now a winter-bourne, but must once have been a more permanent feature. Fluvial deposits suggest that a high-level river of some magnitude formerly ran along the same course. In the east the Bourne rises near Tidworth and flows in a south-westerly direction to meet the River Nadder at Salisbury. The major drainage feature, however, is the Avon. Rising at two points in the Vale of Pewsey, it cuts through the chalk escarpment at Upavon, carving a valley that varies in width from 100m to 600m. Two other watercourses, the Imber-Chitterne Brook and the Nine Mile River, also flow

intermittently southwards across the military training area. The Imber-Chitterne Brook flows south to join the Wylye at Codford St Mary, but it formerly drained smaller streams incised into Coombe Bottom and Longford Bottom to the north of Imber (Barron 1976, 111–12). The Nine Mile River rises on Brigmerston Down on the Eastern Ranges and follows a sinuous course to its junction with the Avon near Bulford, approximately 5km to the south-west.

Both drainage and climate have significantly affected the manner in which the landscape has been utilised, and for this reason modern settlement on the downs is usually confined to spring-lines around the base of the escarpments and within river valleys that either rise in the chalk or run through it. The filtration of rainwater is affected by seams of flint, by fault-lines and by occasional impervious lenses of chalk with high clay content. Thus, water collects at different levels within the chalk, and is increased by autumn rains, so that by mid-winter it begins to rise through 'bourne holes' in dry valleys. Well records this century indicate varying perched water tables of between 91m and 135m above OD (Whitaker and Edmonds 1925). The marly beds at the base of the Lower Chalk are an important source of water and there are strong springs at West Lavington and Erlestoke (Jukes-Brown 1905, 27). Similarly, water is also held in marl seams in the Middle Chalk. Water retention in the Upper Chalk is entirely dependent on the seasons, and, when arid conditions prevail, wells can easily run dry, until recently

Figure 1.8
Map showing the relief and drainage of the SPTA.

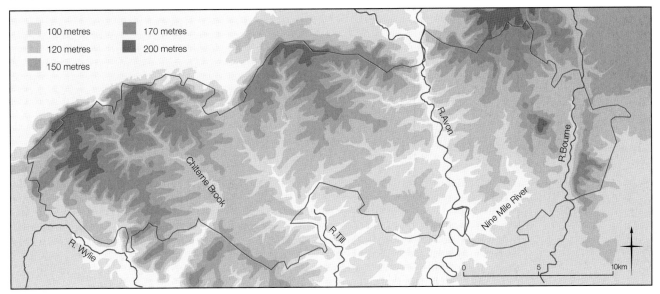

causing problems for villagers and stock. In the early 20th century, for example, Jukes Brown, recorded that the villagers of Chitterne sent carts to Codford daily to obtain water (Jukes-Brown 1905, 53).

Bourne holes occur at points along some valley sides. These are a seasonal source that contain water both before winterbournes begin to flow and after they have dried up. At times when there was a higher water table, particularly during the first half of the first millennium BC (Tinsley 1981, 211; Turner 1981, 256–7), it is likely that some winterbournes carried water throughout the year. Using evidence from Anglo-Saxon charters, Aldsworth (1974, 16) has suggested that the water table in Hampshire has dropped dramatically, perhaps by as much as 36 to 60m during the past millennium, while Andrews and Dury's map of Wiltshire (1773), together with the presence of spreads of gravel, observed both in the field and on the BGS map, suggests that a number of streams started higher up valleys than is indicated on modern maps. At a number of locations, terraces on steep slopes above coombe bottoms appear to have been constructed and in some cases used as trackways, while in others earthen causeways of unknown date have been built to carry trackways across the valley, thus avoiding coombe floors, which in the past are likely to have been wet and often flooded. Today, the authorities extract large quantities of water from the chalk, significantly altering the water table, while the depth of recent wells and boreholes is no longer a guide to levels at earlier periods (see for example, the discussion of well records around the Wilsford Shaft in Ashbee et al 1989, 35–6).

To have access to good water supply is a prerequisite of any permanent settlement on the Chalk and water was probably the single most important factor in determining settlement location and viable forms of subsistence. The knowledge and technology required to excavate wells must have been acquired as early as the Neolithic period, judging by the techniques developed for the frequent digging of shafts for flint nodules; one interpretation of the Bronze Age Wilsford Shaft is that of a well for watering stock (ibid). A large number of abandoned wells of uncertain date exist on valley floors (six wells are shown on the Ordnance Survey 1st Edition 1875 25-inch Map in Water Dean Bottom alone), and it might be that, when winterbournes dried up, these were used for livestock. There is evidence for this from the 19th century, when Lord Normanton's tenants watered stock at wells sunk on the downs (Anon 1902a, 10–11), and a number of often short-lived isolated farmsteads established during the 19th century all obtained water for domestic use from wells. While the physical evidence for springs and wells in earlier periods is elusive, ponds have been recorded at a number of Romano-British settlements. Much landscape engineering appears to have taken place during the Romano-British period in order to secure the massive quantities of water needed for stock, domestic and industrial uses. Cunnington recognised this some 200 years ago:

'...I have often had the question put to me, how the Britons procured water in the Wiltshire Downs? To this question I have answered that in the places inhabited by the Britons, I have generally found in the vallies (immediately connected with them) deep excavations or ponds into which I have conceived the rain water had been directed similar to our present Sheep Ponds; when these filled they had recourse to the neighbouring streams till the period of digging Wells. Immediately beneath this village [Coombe Down] we have a large reservoir that was probably made by the Britons for the above purpose...' (Cunnington MSS Book 8: Devizes Museum).

The construction of ponds might have taken place from at least the onset of the Iron Age. At Lidbury, near Upavon, an enclosure dated by excavation to the Early Iron Age, swerves around a pond-like depression just within the rampart (Fig 1.9) (Cunnington 1917). One of Cunnington's excavation trenches clipped the edge of the depression but encountered no evidence of puddled clay (op cit, 3–14), and the question of the hollow's function was left open. Ponds were noted close to the Romano-British settlements at Knook Down West, Church Pits and Wadman's Coppice, and at Charlton Down a dam and reservoir were built showing the necessity of a good water supply to these communities. A pond lying close to the Romano-British settlement at Coombe Down is mentioned in a Saxon charter of AD 934 (Grundy 1919, 231; Crawford and Keiller

1928, 141). The descriptive place name of Imber (*Imemerie*) also appears in a charter, perhaps indicating a natural waterhole (Crawford 1953, 236). Apart from these examples, however, there is little evidence of water provision after the desertion of the Romano-British villages until the widespread construction of dewponds in the 19th century. Many of these were constructed by the Cruse family, based at Imber, and were of a standard size and distinctive design, being square in plan and usually, although not exclusively, sited on ridge-tops. Davis (1811, 3), reporting on Wiltshire to the Board of Agriculture in the early 19th century, advocated this method of siting dewponds so that dirt and debris did not collect in them.

Survival and distribution of archaeological features

The present distribution of sites is a result of the ongoing processes of attrition, mainly through the increased efficacy of cultivation techniques, which has led to increased rates of destruction. Importantly, differences in the intensity of cultivation have led to uneven survival rates. At a very basic level the landscape can be divided into two broad zones: one of monument survival, the other of monument destruction (Taylor 1971). On the Training Area the zone of monument destruction is very markedly peripheral, and incorporates the Schedule 1 land or area of 'permanent arable' where cultivation continues. There are other small pockets of arable land dotted throughout the area, such as at the source of the Nine Mile River, but these tend to be less well-established due to ongoing military activity, and are utilised for only a few years before being returned to grassland; the monuments here are, therefore, less prone to total destruction. Although archaeological sites are damaged in these zones, they survive as earthworks, but very often only to heights measured in centimetres. The monument survival zone is the grassland of the core Training Area where upstanding earthwork sites can be recorded using intensive field survey techniques and low-level oblique aerial photography.

Figure 1.9
Lidbury. Note how the enclosure boundary curves in order to incorporate an internal depression. The enclosure sits on top of 'Celtic' fields, cut by linear ditches, and overlain by ridge-and-furrow.

11

The very generalised distinction between the zones is not always clear-cut since it is evident that in some parts modification and destruction, sometimes on an enormous scale, began to occur from a very early date; these modifications are themselves features of archaeological interest. In the Impact Area on the Central Range, extensive areas of 'Celtic' field systems have obliterated elements of an earlier landscape. Early sites are less prone to complete surface levelling if they are surrounded by a large bank or ditch that is more difficult to eradicate by ploughing. Single enclosures occur frequently within field systems, and it seems likely that some of these are actually earlier sites, remodelled and reused at a later stage. Church Ditches on Charlton Down is a good example, probably of prehistoric date and subsequently reused in the Roman and, possibly, medieval periods. Similarly, the bank and ditch bounding the Roman settlement on Compton Down are probably reused elements of a prehistoric enclosure.

The distribution pattern of presumed later prehistoric enclosures is very heavily biased towards the areas that remain under arable cultivation on the fringes of the permanent grassland. Most of these enclosures have been ploughed flat and now survive only as cropmarks or soilmarks. We suspect that they were once more widespread, but they are absent wherever later, intense cultivation took place. The distribution pattern for Bronze Age round barrows similarly reflects the effects of cultivation; they are difficult to identify in areas of 'Celtic' fields, or in areas known to have been heavily cultivated during the 19th century that have since returned to pasture; in contrast, they can be seen as cropmarks in modern ploughland. The recognition of the role of subsequent land use, both ancient and modern, in biasing the known distribution of surviving monuments, is not to deny the other main factor in monument survival, that of original scale: the bigger the earthwork, the greater the chance of survival. The same principle applies to the early fields, in many instances now defined by massive lynchets that formed convenient boundaries for more recent episodes of cultivation. This is borne out by the field evidence on the Central Range, where medieval and later ridge-and-furrow fields often reuse earlier boundaries.

The chalk landscape was, from at least the late Anglo-Saxon period, usually divided up according to a set of established principles: the valley floor was used for meadow, the lower slopes for arable and the upper areas for pasture. The arable was by no means fixed and from time to time areas of downland were taken into temporary cultivation and returned to pasture. Cultivation appears to have made substantial inroads on the downland in Wiltshire by the early 18th century when Defoe (1724–6), writing of the upland sheep pastures, noted that '...so much of these downs are plowed up, as has increased the quantity of corn produced in this county, in a prodigious manner, and lessened the quantity of wooll...'. From the late 18th century onwards, Parliamentary Enclosure brought an end to communal, open-field farming and replaced it with a more flexible use of agricultural land. This almost certainly contributed to the ploughing up of much traditional pasture, often destroying any pre-existing earthworks. The extent of each zone of arable varied according to available land, but Cobbett, travelling along the Avon valley in the early 19th century, noted that arable extended back onto the downs for a distance of one or two miles in some places (1830, 297). This, together with extensive cultivation around the isolated farmsteads, had a profound affect on the landscape, and the current appearance of the Training Area owes much to the actions of 19th-century farmers.

The effects of plough damage generally diminish with distance from the main, existing, settlements. This is most noticeable in the parishes on the northern escarpment and along the Avon valley, where the settlements and heavily ploughed land are located in the low-lying vales off the edge of the escarpment or along the valleys. The areas with the greatest chance of earthwork survival, therefore, are those at the greatest distance from villages and farms, at the points where estates or parishes meet. The Romano-British settlements on Chapperton Down and at Cheverell Down, for example, have survived because they lie out on the downs at the junctions of parishes.

Large areas witnessed episodes of medieval and post-medieval ploughing that removed traces of earlier features. In the parishes of Market Lavington, West Lavington and Imber arable cultivation had already seriously damaged pre-existing monuments by the late 18th century. Now, only a fragmented picture of the earlier landscape can be seen, but sufficient detail survives, including truncated lengths of

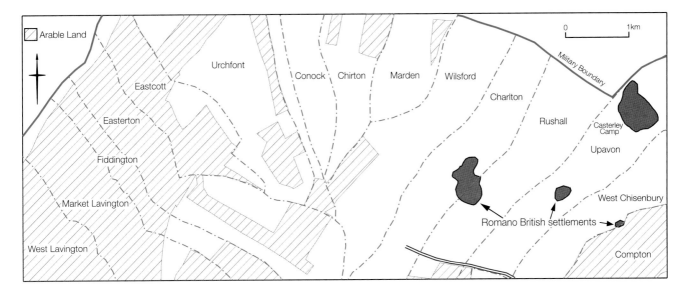

linear earthwork and small patches of 'Celtic' fields, to suggest that the Western Ranges were intensively used in earlier periods. In contrast, in the Centre and East, in the parishes of Charlton, Rushall, Enford, and Upavon, despite some areas being cultivated, others appear to have been unaffected or at least suffered only short-term ploughing (Fig 1.10).

By acquiring large tracts of land in the late 19th and early 20th century that have not been cultivated since, the MoD protected much of the Plain from the worst ravages of modern agriculture. In the 1920s O G S Crawford (1929) stated that military training on Salisbury Plain had destroyed the landscape to such an extent that it did not merit preservation as a National Park. Instead, he favoured the Marlborough Downs. The subsequent reversal of fortunes of these two areas is a sad indictment of the destructive nature of modern farming techniques.

A history of previous enquiries

The chalk downland of Wessex was a stamping ground for many of the greatest names in antiquarian and archaeological investigation. Sir Richard Colt Hoare, working alongside his contemporary, William Cunnington, was the first to consider the archaeology of the Plain on a systematic basis. But it was Cunnington who carried out the earliest documented excavations, principally on burial monuments (Fig 1.11), and his manuscripts provide an insight into late 18th-century life in the area (Cunnington unpublished MSS: Devizes Museum). Colt

Hoare lived at Stourhead, near Mere, just to the south-west of the Plain, and during his travels around Wiltshire he recorded ancient settlements, fields, linear boundaries and burial mounds, many for the first time. His findings, incorporating Cunnington's work, included a brief commentary on the structural details of the excavated sites, as well as the artefacts recovered from them. In addition, Colt Hoare provided an inventory of small-scale plans and excavations occasionally illustrated by areas of relatively detailed survey. In particular, the Knook plan, Casterley Camp (Fig 1.12), Chidbury (Sidbury) Camp, Battlesbury and Scratchbury, drawn for Hoare by his surveyor Philip Crocker, are significant in that they represent the first measured surveys of archaeological sites on Salisbury Plain (Colt Hoare 1810). Colt Hoare's published observations were brief, but provided valuable information, for instance, on the chronology of those Romano-British settlements that he excavated:

'On digging in these excavations we find the coarse British pottery; also fibulae and rings of brass worn as bracelets, flat headed iron nails, hinges of doors, locks and keys and a variety of Roman coins of which the small brass of the Lower Empire are the most numerous, particularly those of the Constantine family...coins of Vespasian, Nerva, Antoninus, Trajan, Gallienus and Gratianus...' (Colt Hoare 1810, 85).

Rudimentary structural details were also noted:

Figure 1.10
Map showing the extent of 19th-century cultivation on the Higher Plain. The shaded area represents the cultivated land in the mid-19th century.

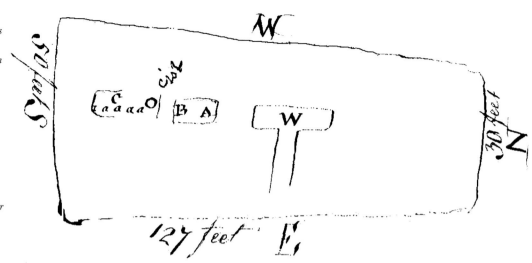

Figure 1.11
Plan of the excavation trenches at Heytesbury North Field long barrow (after Cunnington MSS Book 3: Devizes Museum). Intrigued by the discovery of black earth after an initial excavation in 1800 (W on plan), and lines of similar black earth deposits under Boles Barrow, Knook Barrow, Knook Down, White Barrow, and Old Ditch long barrow, Cunnington cut further trenches into the Heytesbury barrow early in 1804 to try and confirm the nature of the deposit. Trench A–B encountered the deposit at a depth of 2 feet, increasing in height towards the south end. By extending the trench, Cunnington found that it rose to form what was considered to be a circular barrow, the black earth here being 'intermixed with large flints, marl, and a few sarsen stones.' Another trench, C, was cut over the conical mound, and at the base 'we found a large circular cist about 5 feet wide and two and a half feet deep which was cut very neatly in the solid chalk- it contained nothing but the very black earth mixed with Marl, stones, flint, etc. By the side of this cist and farther to the south (marked A on plan) lay a great many skeletons crossing each other in every direction similar to those found in Boles Barrow- from the damaged state of the bones it was impossible to say how many bodies had been interred, but I suppose there were more than ten, perhaps fifteen or twenty... Almost all the bodies were covered with chalk'. Cunnington described the deposit both at Tilshead Lodge and Old Ditch long barrows as black sooty earth and at the latter it occurred as a ridge 9 to 18 inches deep that appeared to extend the length of the barrow.

'...In digging within these villages we have rarely discovered any signs of building with stone or flint, but we have several times found very thin stones laid as floors to rooms. The fire places were small excavations in the ground in which we have frequently found a large flint hearth stone; and in two parts of this village [Knook West] we have discovered hypocausts ... These are regular works of masonry made in the form of a cross and covered with large flat stones cemented by mortar...[we] also found pieces of painted stucco and brick flues; also pit coal...' (ibid).

Flinders Petrie also carried out some of the earliest large-scale surveys at a number of sites. Using coloured crayons to distinguish between bank and ditch, he rapidly planned the hillfort at Knook on 13 September 1877, noting that the British village situated nearby was 'nearly all ploughed up'. The following day he recorded an otherwise unknown sub-rectangular enclosure with associated mounds, 2.5 miles to the east of Netheravon, before surveying part of a field system at Rushall, and a rectilinear sheep enclosure east of Upavon. His plan of Robin Hood's Ball, one of two he made and evidently prepared from a plane-table survey with radiating measurements from a central station, is the earliest recorded for this site. The plan depicts two concentric circuits, one of which is slightly flattened, with no causeways but with four round barrows lying close by (Fig 1.13). Although having no clear idea of the antiquity of the site, he did note the presence of 'chipped

flints scattered about'. He planned an area of Orcheston Down, commenting extensively on the relationships between the barrows, fields and the ditch there (Fig 1.14). Elsewhere he carried out large-scale surveys at the Iron Age enclosure on Mancombe Down, the Everleigh barrow cemetery and Figheldean sheep enclosure, as well as on stretches of 'Celtic' fields and linear ditches (Flinders Petrie portfolio Soc of Antiquaries; BM Add MS 31, 333).

Once the northern part of the Plain had been acquired for military training, archaeological work focused on the area to the south around Salisbury and, particularly, Stonehenge, with only occasional investigations at a few specific sites in the military zone. In 1901 B H Lyell annotated an OS 6-inch map (1897 ed) with the location of barrows and other monuments, although it is not clear whether this was the result of new fieldwork (map held at the Society of Antiquaries, London). During the first two decades of the 20th century, Percy Farrer surveyed a number of sites on Salisbury Plain (Anon 1915a, 5). The Revd E H Goddard (1913) and Maud Cunnington (1914; 1930a) produced early county inventories for long barrows and the Romano-British period generally. The early interest in experimentation with balloons and, eventually, the development of military aviation by the Royal Flying Corps at Larkhill, made it almost inevitable that the SPTA should feature in the earliest aerial reconnaissance (James 1987, 162–3). The earliest recorded survey flight took place in 1924 when O G S Crawford (then Archaeology Officer with the Ordnance Survey), and Alexander Keiller photographed a number of sites on the SPTA, including Coombe Down,

Casterley Camp and the Romano-British village at Charlton Down (Fig 1.15) (Crawford and Keiller 1928). At this time Crawford used his access to RAF photography to begin the compilation of a series of maps entitled 'The Celtic Fields of Salisbury Plain'. These were planned on a scale of 1:25 000 and contained the results of aerial survey as well as those of ground-observation. Only one map, Old Sarum, was published (Crawford 1937), and the map of Amesbury reached proof stage. The rest never progressed beyond the sketch annotations on Ordnance Survey maps that depict the layout of barrows, settlements, linear boundaries and field systems (Fig 1.16), all plotted accurately for the first time.

During the earlier part of the 20th century Maud Cunnington, grand-daughter of William Cunnington, excavated a number of sites in Wiltshire including Casterley Camp (Cunnington and Cunnington 1913) and Lidbury (Cunnington 1917).

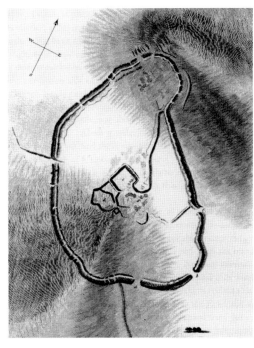

Figure 1.12
Casterley Camp as surveyed by Crocker for Colt Hoare. Crocker shows three entrances only one of which, that to the south, is now considered to be original.

Figure 1.13
The Flinders Petrie plan of Robin Hood's Ball, 1877.

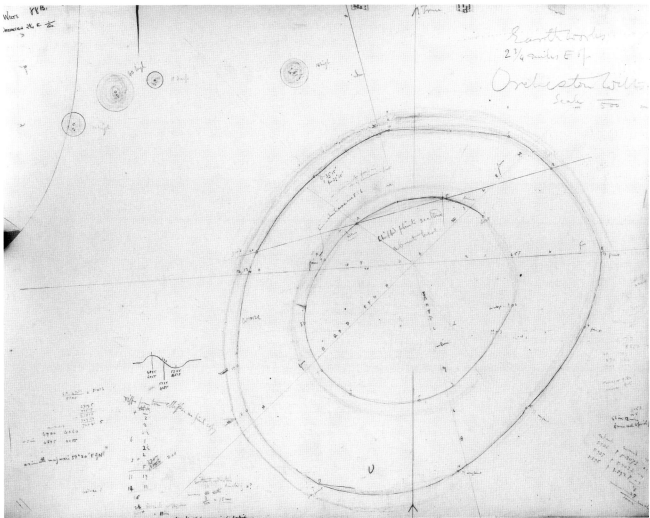

Figure 1.14
Sketch plan and field notes by Flinders Petrie of the relationship between round barrows, 'Celtic' fields and linear ditch on Orcheston Down, 1877 (cf Fig 1.16 (c) and (d)).

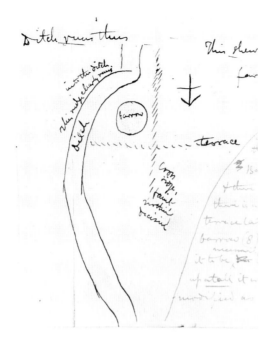

Figure 1.15
Air photograph taken by O G S Crawford, showing the Romano-British village on Charlton and Rushall Downs, 1926.

These represent the first detailed excavations in the area, and paid close attention to stratigraphy and earthwork relationships, frequently highlighting the chronological depth of seemingly simple sites such as enclosures or linear features. Colonel Hawley (1910), a contemporary of Maud Cunnington, also excavated widely, investigating, predominantly but not exclusively, round barrows. The finds from his largely undocumented excavations at the Charlton Down Romano-British village provide a reliable outline chronology for this and other settlements on the Plain (Hawley 1923).

Applebaum's work on the 'Celtic' fields and linear earthworks on Figheldean Down sought to integrate the evidence of cultivated cereal grains found on excavated sites with that of the landscape evidence. He interpreted an area apparently without 'Celtic' fields as a paddock for keeping

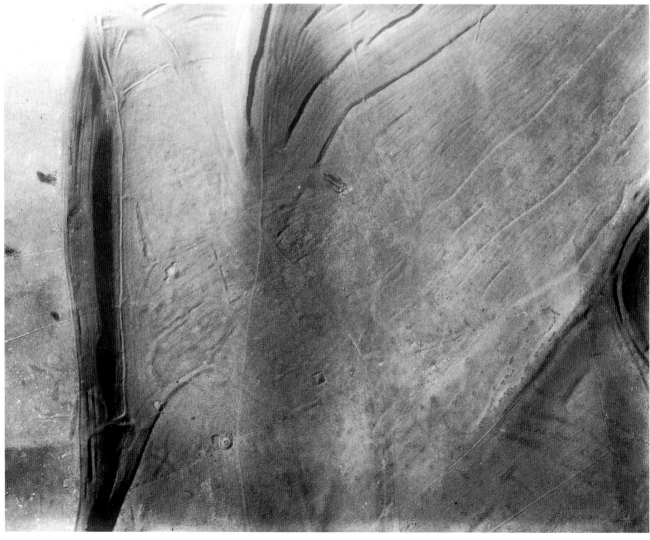

stock that would in turn provide manure for the fields (Applebaum 1954, 110).

Charles and Nicholas Thomas's excavation at the Snail Down barrow cemetery between 1954 and 1957 is one of the most complete in the British Isles of a Bronze Age burial monument group (Thomas forthcoming); but perhaps equally important is Collin Bowen's landscape survey, which attempted to place the site in its local context (Bowen 1978). This influential research carefully analysed the relationship between burial mounds, field systems and the enclosing linear boundaries. His main conclusions, that the barrows were the earliest components, superseded by 'Celtic' fields, then linear boundaries and finally hillforts, and that these boundaries defined large enclosures, presaged many of the results of the Reading University project (Bradley *et al* 1994) two decades later.

The substantial remains of what were presumed to be Roman settlements went largely unnoticed, until the publication by Collin Bowen and Peter Fowler of a paper that sought to characterise the nature of Romano-British settlement in Dorset and Wiltshire (Bowen and Fowler 1966). In this paper, a number of sites were reassessed. Notably, the linear settlement at Chisenbury Warren was surveyed and an aerial transcription of its immediate environs carried out. The re-establishment of these sites as 'villages', rather than haphazard collections of huts and storage pits, was a significant development and defined the nomenclature that is still in use today. This paper recognised for the first time that many of the sites showed evidence of continuity and reuse and that the downland was fully settled for much of the Romano-British period. Additionally, it noted that there was an increase in local communication networks and that almost all settlements were associated with roads and trackways.

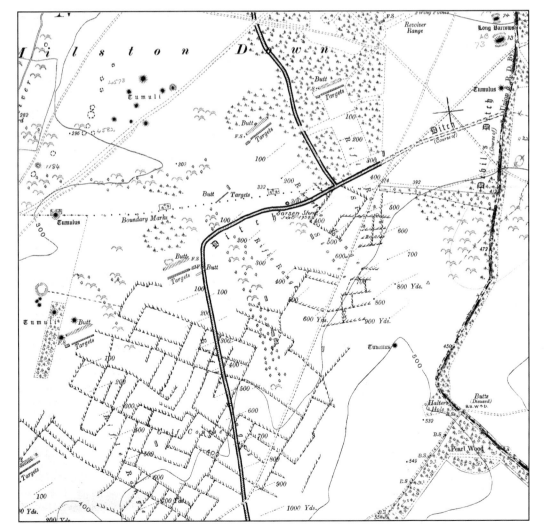

Figure 1.16
Extract from Ordnance Survey 6-inch Map showing part of the Bulford Ranges on the SPTA East, with annotations by O G S Crawford. Notice the symbols for 'Celtic' field banks and lynchets, and how linear boundaries are depicted as cutting through 'Celtic' fields. (not to scale)

Stonehenge and its Environs (RCHME 1979) sought to place Stonehenge in its wider landscape, in particular showing that alongside the well-known ritual monuments there was a plethora of secular activity evolving over a long period of time. The study covered only a small geographical area, including an area on the south-central fringes of the Training Area, but clearly showed that Stonehenge is situated in a landscape that evolved through time to include settlement remains as well as extensive tracts of field systems and linear boundaries. Julian Richards's (1990) *Stonehenge Environs Project* pursued many of the recommendations of the earlier book and focused primarily on providing a context for the early prehistoric periods on the southern edge of the Training Area. A number of sites on the SPTA were excavated, including an area outside the Robin Hood's Ball causewayed enclosure and a hitherto unknown 'short' long barrow, here designated Netheravon Bake 2.

Two Reading University projects examined, first, prehistoric linear boundaries and, secondly, the development of the later prehistoric and Roman landscape within the Eastern Range (Bradley *et al* 1994; Entwistle *et al* in prep). This work consisted of a detailed investigation of the genesis of the landscape in the 1st millennium BC and early 1st millennium AD; a number of analytical observations were made concerning the chronology of these monuments and their relationship with other landscape features, such as 'Celtic' fields, settlements and burial mounds. The results led the authors to identify broad morphological schemes and chronological sequences,

which together show that the earliest construction of the linear boundaries took place some time after *c* 1200 BC. This was followed by repeated alterations to the framework up to the 4th century BC. One of the most important conclusions of the project was that 'Celtic' field lynchets frequently post-date the construction of the linear boundaries, although the present study of a broader area demonstrates that the situation is, in fact, more complex.

The most recent regional assessment is that of Cleal and others, looking at *Stonehenge in its Landscape* (Cleal *et al* 1995). Although they concentrate on providing a comprehensive dating sequence for the monument, they also analysed and discussed valuable environmental data from its hinterland. This enables a fuller discussion of the vegetational and land-use histories of the southern edge of the Training Area, which is used in support of our archaeological field evidence.

In terms of conservation and management of archaeological sites dramatic improvements have taken place in recent years. Roy Canham, Wiltshire County Archaeologist, has been influential in terms of introducing the archaeological viewpoint to the military and underlining the importance of the surviving resource, while the work of the Conservation Groups has also been instrumental in recording and monitoring archaeological features and reporting damage to the military authorities. In recognition of the importance and quality of the archaeological heritage, the MoD has recently appointed an archaeologist with responsibility for the SPTA.

Orcheston Down: a model sequence

It has already been noted that there are specific instances where archaeological monuments of differing ages have influenced subsequent developments. The exceptionally detailed archaeological landscape of Orcheston Down (Figs 1.17 and 1.18) incorporates many key elements of development witnessed less intensively elsewhere, and benefits from having had not only an intensive ground survey at a scale of 1:1000 over the settlement and in the area of the barrows and linear earthwork, but also from an aerial transcription produced at a scale of 1:2500. This survey has generated a detailed

commentary on what might be regarded as the most influential factors in the shaping of the area. In excess of 400ha of land, now under permanent pasture, were assessed. Although the area is used primarily for light vehicle manoeuvres, grazing rights are occasionally granted on a temporary basis.

A broad, flat, gentle south-facing spur, on which the Church Pits Romano-British settlement developed, dominates the local topography. This is flanked to the east and west by wide, now dry, valleys that act as natural routeways to the Higher Plain on the north, and the valley of the Till to the south.

The earliest surviving features recognised here are the four Bronze Age round barrows (Fig 1.17 (a)), located on the southern fringes of the 'Celtic' field system. Arranged in a cluster of three, including a disc variant, with an outlier to the north, the barrows lie on a lower slope that tilts gently to the east and it is from this direction, across the dry valley, that they are best viewed. For groups of people moving through the area via the valley, the barrows would have formed significant landmarks, a usage that might have been deliberately intended by the barrow builders. Sited towards the head of the valley, the barrows might also have marked the position of bourne holes or springs on the valley floor. Although degraded to a certain extent by ancient ploughing, they were not erased by it and it is possible, therefore, that they were intentionally preserved within the field system.

There are, in fact, two coaxial field systems set on different alignments, which abut one another (Fig 1.17 (b)). The field system to the north, which is aligned on a north-east–south-west orientation, extends over an area of 600ha (beyond the limits of the illustration), and can be traced for a considerable distance towards Charlton Down. The southern block, set on a different angle to its neighbour, with lynchets trending north-west–south-east, now covers approximately 200ha, but has been obliterated on the south and to the east and is, similarly, thought to extend some distance to the Lower Plain alongside the River Till. It is impossible to be certain of the overall extent of each system since later ploughing has obscured their peripheries and, indeed, the interface between the two. The systems might not be contemporary and could relate to different episodes of occupation; if so, why one block should avoid rather than reuse the earlier layout, is unclear. It is more likely that they represent the ploughlands of two communities. Within these systems several phases of use are evident, some fields having been enlarged by the removal of subdivisions while others have been reduced in overall size. The field lynchets have built up over the ditch of one round barrow and partly obscured the ditches of others (Fig 1.17 (c)).

At a later stage, a linear boundary ditch (Fig 1.17 (d)) was constructed, which, in the south-east, cuts through, but respects, the orientation of the fields. Farther to the north-west its line is clearly focused on a prominent round barrow and cuts through the lynchet that overlaps the barrow's ditch, beyond which it has been infilled by later ploughing and reuse of the field system. The line of the linear ditch reappears 600m to the north-west (beyond the limits of Fig 1.17) where it is linked with the main east – west linear earthwork, 'Old Ditch West'.

A second linear boundary, which also cuts through 'Celtic' fields, has been reused as the street of the Romano-British settlement that occupies the northern part of the spur on a gentle, south-facing slope. Its course to the south-east, as it curves away from the settlement, is clearly demarcated (Fig 1.17 (e); see Fig 1.18 for clarity). The large hollow (Fig 1.17 (f)), which might have functioned as a central public space in the village, is probably of some antiquity and might even pre-date the linear earthwork. Settlement compounds, which reflect the underlying morphology of the 'Celtic' field system, lie predominantly on the eastern side of the street, although farther south, where the street forks by the hollow, settlement earthworks can be seen on both sides. Given the size of the settlement, reuse of the field system might be

Figure 1.17
Orcheston Down: a model sequence (simplified from Fig 1.18). See pages 18–20 for chronological sequence: (a) round barrow cemetery, (b) junction of coaxial field systems, (c) lynchet lying over barrow ditch, (d) linear ditch respecting barrow, (e) linear ditch, (f) hollow within Romano-British village, (g) Romano-British village (shaded), (h) 19th-century farmstead. Note: small rectangular features represent gun pits.

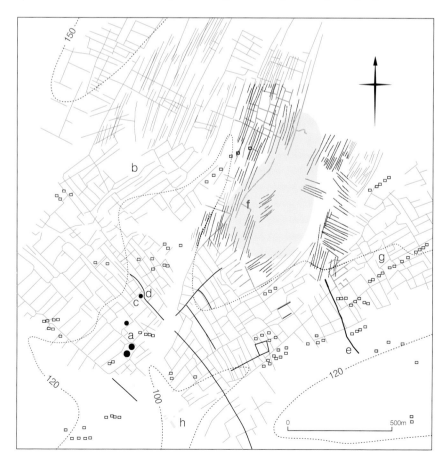

expected to be extensive; it might be that many of the field alterations took place during the lifetime of the settlement. Water for the Romano-British village might, in part, have been provided from a ponded area on the south-eastern fringes of the settlement (Fig 1.17 (g)), where hollowing behind, and heightening of, a pre-existing field bank has created a pond. Overlying much of this northern area is a weave of medieval ridge-and-furrow cultivation. On either side of the valley to the west of the settlement, the ridge-and-furrow extends up the slopes, reusing the 'Celtic' field lynchets. However, on the east, the ridges are slighter, of irregular length and often not parallel suggesting, perhaps, a short-lived ploughing episode. During the 19th century, the northern section of the linear earthwork/Roman street formed part of a droveway across this section of the Training Area (WRO Tithe Map Orcheston St George). The small rectilinear enclosure overlying the 'Celtic' field system to the east of Greenland Farm is a medieval or post-medieval sheep penning and is probably associated with the dew pond immediately to the west. Greenland Farm was itself built in the mid 19th century (Fig 1.17 (h)), reflecting developments elsewhere following the enclosure of the common fields and downs. This farm, together with Keeper's Farm to the west, Prospect Farm and Honeydown Barn to the north (beyond the limits of Fig 1.17), were the only farms established on the downland in the eastern part of the parish of Orcheston St George. At this time much of the land was pasture, although there were closes known as 'bakeland' (former pasture that was broken up and cultivated). Orcheston Down, on which Church Pits is sited, was part of the 890ha Orcheston estate, owned by Miss Mills, that was sold to the military authorities in 1897 (Anon 1902a, 116). Although only 21 per cent was then cultivated it was all soon laid down to grass (op cit, 155). Keeper's Farm, Prospect Farm and Honeydown Barn were dismantled, but

Greenland Farm was retained and became the home of the military range staff.

The area to the north of Greenland Farm hosted a large, tented, temporary military camp during the early years of military ownership, and associated with this a reservoir and a concrete-lined water tank. In order to improve the tactical setting, small copses have been planted, which are used as cover and camouflage in this otherwise 'open' landscape, while to the south of the Romano-British settlement a series of now almost levelled gun pits can be observed.

Through detailed analysis of the field remains at Church Pits we can now establish a clear sequence of landscape development. While acknowledging that the *absolute* chronology of events is unknown, because of the lack of accurately dated sites, the *relative* sequence is clear. The earliest monumental components are the burial mounds of Late Neolithic and Early Bronze Age date. At some later stage, but during the Bronze Age, fields were laid out across the slopes of the downland. The alignment of these fields ignored the topography but largely respected the earlier burial mounds. Linear boundaries sliced through the fields but, similarly, respected the barrows. Beyond the mound later ploughing has destroyed the course of the linear. We assume that much of the earlier field system was re-cultivated and enhanced at this time but it is difficult to identify this since this phase adheres so closely to the pre-established layout. To the north, another linear has been reused as a street within the Romano-British settlement, which, in turn, picks up on the underlying field compounds. The final layers of the landscape reveal medieval and later land-use but still largely within an agrarian economy. The ultimate use, that of the MoD, continues to the present day. It is clear that once a feature exists in the landscape it is often easier to utilise rather than eradicate it, and, in general, this kind of repeated reuse is seen at a wide range of sites across the area.

2
Earlier Prehistory: the Neolithic and Early Bronze Age (*c* 4500–1500 BC)

While Neolithic and Bronze Age monuments on Salisbury Plain have, in general, featured prominently in antiquarian archaeological literature, the military presence has restricted more recent investigation to a small area centred upon Stonehenge and south Wiltshire (RCHME 1979; Richards 1990; Cleal *et al* 1995). The field evidence on the SPTA consists of thirty long barrows, including three recently discovered by air photography (Figs 2.1 and 2.2), one, or possibly two, causewayed enclosures, a small henge and nearly 700 round barrows. In ad-dition, there is a body of data retrieved from 19th-century antiquarian excavations, predominantly of burial mounds, that has long acted as a mine of information for research into the Neolithic and Early Bronze Age and has helped to forge our present day understanding of these periods of prehistory.

Long barrows

The earliest visible monuments in the landscape are the long barrows that form part of the Salisbury Plain group defined by Ashbee, and excluding those around Stonehenge, subdivided by him into two main groups, namely, Salisbury Plain West and Salisbury Plain East (Ashbee 1984, 16–17) (Fig 2.3).

Physical characteristics

Apart from the unusually large Old Ditch Barrow, which measures 115m, the length of mounds varies from 25m to 75m, with a number of examples of approximately 50m and then a gradual decrease as shown in Table 1. At a number of sites, the mound has been partly ploughed, making definitive statements about length impossible. At Tinhead Long Barrow (Fig 2.4 (F)), for example, approximately 20m of the mound has been removed from the east end. Equally problematical is the maximum width of mounds, since erosion has frequently altered profiles. Nevertheless, most widths are within the range 12m to 23m, with a prominent cluster between 18m and 23m. In almost all cases the mounds are slightly trapezoidal in outline, often bulbous or ovoid around the centre, with one end, usually the easternmost, being the widest. In only one example, Old Ditch Barrow (Fig 2.5) is the same width retained throughout the length of the mound.

It is likely that the majority of the long barrows on the SPTA have not been ploughed until recently, and damage is therefore superficial. A few, however, particularly those on the peripheral farmland, are being seriously damaged by ploughing, or sometimes, as at Fittleton (Fig 2.6), by cattle. Nevertheless, it is clear that the centre or easternmost ends of many mounds were built to a greater height, often making them wedge-shaped in profile if not plan (Fig 2.7). In other cases, notably Knook Down (Fig 2.4 (G)), the mounds have a smoothed, dome-like or parabolic profile. Heights range widely between approximately 1m and 3.5m, but two groups are evident. The height of the first of these is about 1m, the second between 2.5m and 3m. Each group has a different visual impact, the second being more substantial than the first regardless of the length of the mound. Some, for example, Knighton Down (Fig 2.8 (F)) and Ell Barrow (Fig 2.4 (A)), are more massive and this must relate to their internal structure. This dichotomy is not the product of ploughing or any other obvious subsequent alteration, but appears to be a result of deliberate construction. The accompanying side ditches usually follow the mound closely, invariably emphasising its shape and height. In some examples, slight ledges within the ditch suggest that recutting might have taken place. Berms, where they exist, are narrow, and in many cases obscured, as a result of soil slumping from the mound.

Figure 2.1

Air photograph of ring ditches and levelled long barrow, upper valley slopes alongside the River Avon. Three new, plough-levelled long barrows were noted alongside the Avon during this project, one near Woodhenge just outside the SPTA boundary, and two others on the eastern flanks of the Avon near Figheldean, which are associated with clusters of later round barrows. One example, 200m to the north-east of Barrow Clump at Ablington (shown here), can only be seen from the air and consists of two short lengths of curving side ditch, which indicates that the mound might have been nearly 40m long. Similarly, the parallel side ditches of the second example, 300m east of Milston, point to a mound 40–50m long.

Siting

While most long barrows are arranged with the higher, wider end to the east, this is not exclusively the case. Arn Hill is oriented towards the north; Amesbury 42 is oriented to the north-east as are a number of examples on Cranborne Chase 20km to the south (Bradley *et al* 1994). Of those aligned roughly eastwards there is marked variation in their precise orientation, from north-east through to south-east (*see* Ashbee 1984, 29). While it has been suggested that this reflects a concern with celestial events, most long barrows, in fact, lie parallel to the contours and it is arguable that orientation was designed to maximise visibility from certain viewpoints (Tilley 1994, 161). Here the long barrow profile (side view) was important. Some long mounds appear to be designed to be viewed from certain positions; many can be seen for great distances when observed from specific locations but with restricted visibility from elsewhere. Long barrows situated around the western escarpment have been constructed on false-crests, such as those at Norton Bavant (Figs

2.4 (C) and 2.8 (G)), Oxendean Down (Fig 2.9), Tinhead (Fig 2.4 (F)) as well as those at Arn Hill and Bratton (Fig 2.8 (B)) (both outside the SPTA boundary), and consequently cannot be seen for more than a few hundred metres into the interior of the Higher Plain. If they were designed to be seen, it would have to be from the valleys and lowlands. The same principles apply to other less dramatically sited examples in the interior. Kill Barrow (Fig 2.10), for example, presents an imposing monument when approached from the valley to its north-east, but from little more than 200m to the west it is hardly visible. In contrast, the pair on Milston Down (Fig 2.11) are situated on the valley floor towards the upper reaches of the Nine Mile River. Rising ground to the north-west, and the imposing Beacon Hill immediately south-east, ensure that visibility is restricted to the valley. This choice of location, with its restricted views, is quite deliberate; if the builders had required a conspicuous site, they might have chosen nearby Beacon Hill, from which the monuments would have been visible over a large part of

Salisbury Plain. There are, however, four long barrows that occupy sites with wide commanding views, being placed close to the highest points in their immediate locales; Knighton, Ell Barrow, Boles Barrow and Knook Barrow. These are among the largest, in terms of height, although neither Boles nor Knook Barrow are on the highest part of the down and each could have been given further prominence if built on the summits nearby. The positioning of two barrows, in parallel, and within 50m of one another, at Milston (Fig 2.11), is unusual and represents one of the closest physical relationships between two long barrows in Britain.

Significant groupings

The long barrows in the west, together with those along the Wylye valley to the south (English Heritage forthcoming), are, with one or two exceptions, regularly spaced, occurring at intervals of approximately 2km. It might, therefore, be feasible to talk in terms of burial monuments acting as markers used to define areas or specific blocks of the landscape. However, at two locations more closely spaced groups of long barrows can be seen. To the west of Tilshead a group of three mounds, Tilshead Lodge (Fig 2.8 (H)), White Barrow (Fig 2.12), and Old Ditch Barrow (Fig 2.5), all situated on high ground, intervisible and within 1km of one another, are each

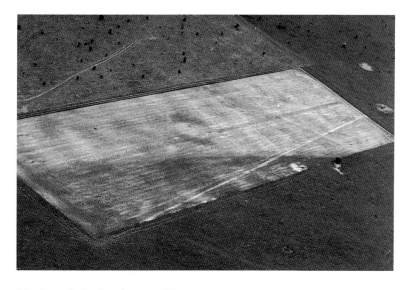

Figure 2.2
Air photograph of
Netheravon Bake 2
long barrow.

Table 1 Extant long barrow dimensions (m).

NMR number	name	length	max width	max height
SU 04 NW 3	White Barrow	75	28	2.5
SU 04 NW 9	Old Ditch	120	23	3.5
SU 04 NW 11	Kill Barrow	39	18	2.0
SU 04 NW 12	Tilshead Lodge	53	13	1.25
SU 04 NE 7	East Down	55	23	3.0
SU 05 SE 22	Ell Barrow	53	27	2.0
SU 14 NW 5	Alton Down	47	15	0.7
SU 14 NW 7	Netheravon Bake 1	33	18	0.5
SU 14 NW 14	Knighton	55	21	3.0
SU 14 NW 41	Netheravon 6	57	22	0.5
SU 14 NE 12	Sheer Barrow	36	25	0.5
SU 14 NE 125	Milston Firs	43	23	2.0
SU 14 SW 23	Durrington Down	45	16	1.0
SU 15 SE 16	Fittleton 5	45	17	1.5
SU 24 NW 33	Milston 31	25	8	1.0
SU 24 NW 34	Milston 40	28	14	1.25
SU 24 NW 93	Milston 39	48	18	2.5
ST 94 NW 16	Middleton Down	55(now 30)	13	3.0
ST 94 NW 17	Oxendean	31.5	13.5	2.0
ST 94 NW 20	Boles Barrow	48	20	3.1
ST 94 NW 28	Norton Bavant	55	18	2.5
ST 94 NE 7	Imber Down 4a	26	23	1.0
ST 94 NE 18	Knook Down 5	25	12	1.0
ST 94 SW 1	Heytesbury North Field	39	21	1.0
ST 94 SE 21	Knook 2	30	18	2.5
ST 95 SW 2	Bratton Camp	69	20	3.0
ST 95 SW 13	Tinhead	77 (now 62)	29 (now 17)	1.0

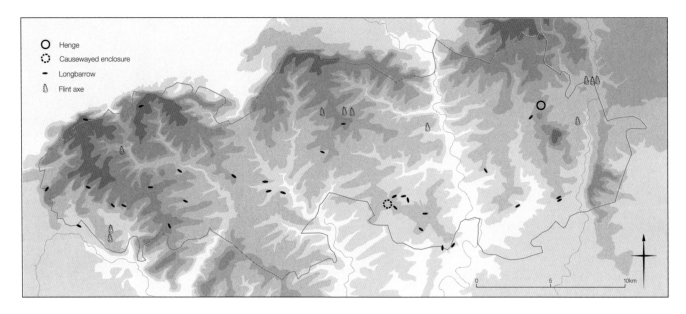

Figure 2.3
Map showing distribution
of Neolithic monuments
on the SPTA.

separated by a re-entrant. Old Ditch Barrow, the largest of the three, and indeed the largest on Salisbury Plain, is centrally placed; all three barrows lie above the valley floor of the River Till, and clearly focus upon it. This river is now a winterbourne, but, taking into account a possible higher water table during the 4th millennium BC, it is probable that the re-entrants separating the barrows contained small streams and that the burial mounds were positioned with respect to the springline. In a similar manner, two long barrows at Norton Bavant are separated from one another by a single re-entrant, and from the mound at Oxendean Down by two more re-entrants.

A second group of barrows lies to the east of the Robin Hood's Ball causewayed enclosure, itself probably contemporary with at least some of them. The most pronounced monument, and the most easterly, is the Knighton Down long barrow (Fig 2.8 (F)), sited on the crest of a prominent ridge. It is intervisible with Ell Barrow (Fig 2.4 (A)) about 6km to the north-west, but also has views across the Avon valley to the east and Stonehenge to the south. There are five more low, long barrows in close proximity; one of these has been mutilated but appears to have a ditch that runs round at least one end, thus inviting comparison with Sheer Barrow (Fig 2.13) and other examples on Cranborne Chase (Barrett *et al* 1991). The most northerly individual in this grouping, Netheravon 6 (Fig 2.4 (E)) lies among 'Celtic' fields, having been slighted by them. Two shorter examples, at Netheravon Bake (Figs 2.8 (D) and 2.2), have been almost

levelled in more recent times and one has recently been excavated (Richards 1990, 265). To the south of this on low ground, and just visible from the outer circuit of the causewayed enclosure on the ridge 500m to the west, lies another low-profile long barrow, Alton Down (Fig 2.8 (E)). A well-defined trench lies along the length of the summit of the mound but there is no record of any formal excavation. Three large sarsens lie in the ditch (*see* Fig 7.1), however, suggesting that there might have been a sarsen chamber within the mound. All of these appear to focus on the head of a re-entrant valley leading north-east to Honeydown Bottom, until recently a winterbourne serving the Avon. Farther to the south, on the western outskirts of the Larkhill Garrison, is a mound of very similar outline. This barrow at Durrington Down (Fig 2.8 (C)), which is now carefully maintained, and which could be classed as an outlier to the above grouping, has been smoothed by cultivation and slightly damaged by the construction of a military railway line. However, its position, above a re-entrant leading to the Avon south of Durrington Walls, indicates that it was part of a group of monuments including those of Amesbury 42, Amesbury 140 (RCHME 1979, 1) and a further example recorded, by the RCHME, as a parchmark, to the south-west of Woodhenge, all just outside the SPTA boundary.

The lack of any long mound in the Codford/Chitterne area might be the product of either differential survival rates or, possibly, real variations in Neolithic land use.

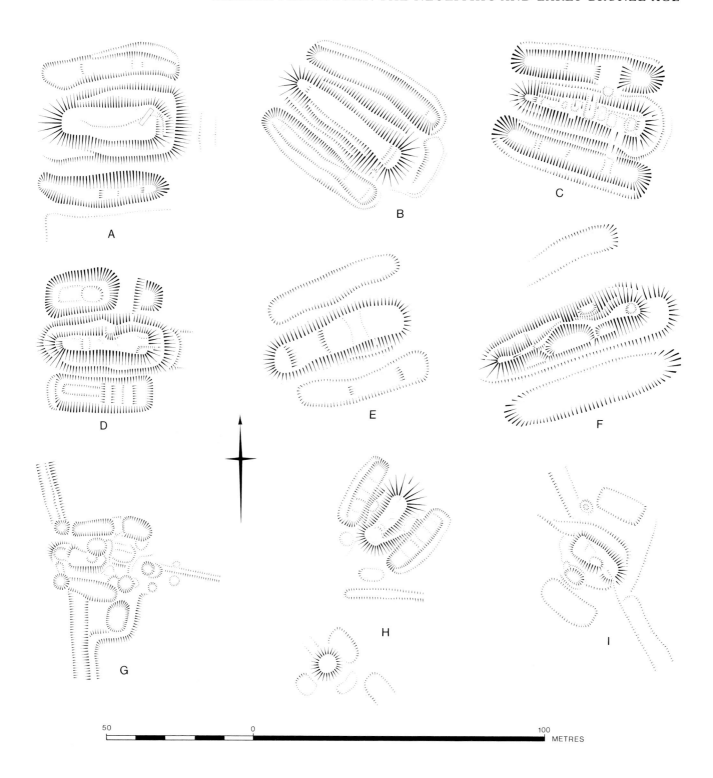

50   0   100
METRES

Figure 2.4

Comparative plans of long barrows. (A) Ell Barrow has been heavily shelled, but retains its form. The rectangular feature at the east end is a target. (B) East Down where the position of an excavation trench can be discerned at the south-east end. (C) Norton Bavant where a series of excavation trenches can be traced on the summit. (D) Boles Barrow. (E) Netheravon 6 surrounded by 'Celtic' fields and partly levelled. (F) Tinhead, partly quarried for chalk, and the east end almost levelled by cultivation. (G) Knook Down lies within an old impact area and has been disfigured by shellfire. The barrow provides a focus for heavily damaged linear earthworks. (H) Knook, a short example with a dramatic parabolic profile and an adjacent round barrow with causewayed ditch. (I) Imber Down is partly levelled and has suffered through its proximity to the village of Imber, where it is a focus for field tracks and more recently for military activity. Notice the possible platform or plinth at the bases of (A), (B), (C), (D) and (H).

Figure 2.5
Twice the length of other long barrows, Old Ditch is also the most massive. Some of the slight undulations on the summit might mark the position of Cunnington's excavations, but others might be the result of tree falls or other recent activities. In terms of scale and topographical positioning, it has much in common with bank barrows. Like other long barrows on the SPTA, the monument became a focus for linear ditches; Old Ditch respects both barrow and ditch, and there is a subsidiary linear adjoining the east end at right angles. During the 19th century Old Ditch was utilised as a park boundary by the owners of Tilshead Lodge, and it is conceivable that the level summit of the long mound is a result of garden landscaping.

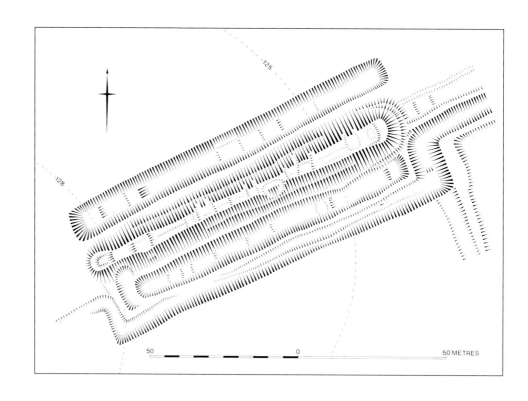

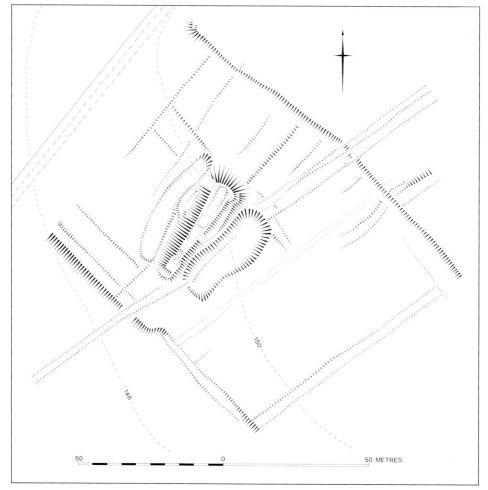

Figure 2.6
Fittleton long barrow, set within a 'Celtic' field system subsequently over-ploughed by ridge-and-furrow cultivation (not depicted). The linear feature slicing through the southern ditch is of military origin. The barrow sits on a plinth and depressions on the summit are likely to represent excavation trenches.

Similarly, while long barrows are sited along the northern scarp summit in the west, they are absent to the east of Tinhead, an area that overlooks the Vale of Pewsey. Construction of monuments on high positions in the landscape inevitably results in a degree of intervisibility, assuming, of course, a suitably open landscape. Unless there are factors that suggest otherwise, intervisibility is therefore likely to be coincidental. The evidence from the SPTA suggests that burial monuments focus upon valleys, river courses and spring-lines, emphasising the importance of the lower-lying land; any visual impact might have been localised, and was often restricted to the immediate valley.

Chronology

Recent excavations at a short long barrow on Netheravon Bake (Richards 1990, 265) (Fig 2.2) indicate a number of phases of activity, although an antler obtained from the primary silt of the accompanying side ditches has provided the only radiocarbon date for a long barrow on the SPTA: 3646–3378 cal BC. This represents the earliest, securely dated human event on the Training Area and falls comfortably within the range for long barrows. Although short long barrows consistently provide evidence to suggest that they might be later than longer examples (for example, Drewett 1986, 31–51; Bradley 1992, 138), reliable dates are considered too few to provide a secure chronology for mound forms (Kinnes 1992, 120).

The antiquarian record

Few records of the 19th-century excavations survive, although the published accounts (Colt Hoare 1810; Thurnam 1871), along with the manuscript notes left by Cunnington and Thurnam, contain interesting details of barrow structure and content and, in the absence of modern excavation, provide valuable information. It is apparent from these early records that mounds merely represent cappings for a series of constructional events, and a number of recurring features can be identified as shown in Table 2.

Mounds or cairns, sometimes circular or ridged in form and situated beneath the long mounds, are frequently mentioned. These cover flint or chalk pavements, sometimes with skeletons, disarticulated

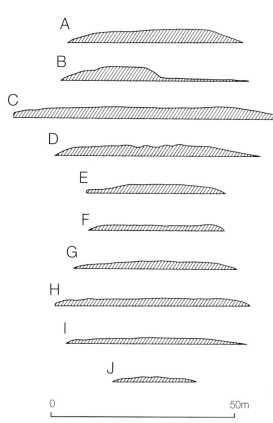

Figure 2.7
Profiles of long barrows.
(A) Boles Barrow, (B) Norton Bavant (Middleton Down), (C) White Barrow, (D) Norton Bavant, (E) Oxendean Down, (F) Durrington Down, (G) Milston Firs (Brigmerston), (H) Tilshead Lodge, (I) Heytesbury North Field, (J) Imber Down.

bones and charred wood placed on them; pits, often referred to as cists, but usually devoid of cultural material, cut into the subsoil; and deposits of black sooty earth often raised into bank-like features. Despite William Cunnington's view that this black sooty earth was decayed blood (Cunnington 1889, 115–17), Colt Hoare had earlier recognised that it might represent decayed turf. This 'turf' was found at the base of a number of barrows; for example, Tilshead Lodge, East Down, and Knook Down. At White Barrow it appeared to cover the floor of the barrow, while at Old Ditch it formed a ridged feature up to 0.45m high that was thought to extend the entire length but that faded towards its edges. In contrast, at Heytesbury North Field, the black earth extended along the centre of the barrow at little more than 0.6m below the surface and increased in height at the southern (prominent) end where it merged with deposits of large flints and sarsen boulders to form a circular mound (Colt Hoare 1810, 72) (Figs 1.10 and 2.8 (A)). This might also have been the case at East Down (Fig 2.4 (B)) where Thurnam recorded human bones in and below the black earth (Cunnington 1914, 403). At Boles Barrow, which has seen more

Table 2 Details of internal features within excavated long barrows.

name (with Grinsell suffix)	sooty earth	pit	pavement	internal mound	excavator
Bratton 1	–	–	–	–	T
Edington 7 (Tinhead)	–	–	–	–	T
Figheldean 31	★	★	–	–	T
Fittleton 5	–	–	–	★	T & WHC
Heytesbury 1 (Bowl's Barrow)	–	★	★	ridged, but later said to be conical	C, T & WHC
Heytesbury (North Field)	★	★	–	circular	C
Knook 2 (Knook Barrow)	–	★	★	ridged	C & T
Knook 5 (Knook Down)	★	★	–	–	C
Netheravon 6	–	–	–	–	T
Norton Bavant 13	no black earth	–	–	★	T
Tilshead 1 (Kill Barrow)	–	–	–	–	T
Tilshead 2 (Old Ditch)	★	★	at both ends	circular	C & T
Tilshead 4 (White Barrow)	★	–	–	–	C
Tilshead 5 (Tilshead Lodge)	★	–	–	–	C & T
Tilshead 7 (East)	★	–	–	–	T
Warminster 1 (Arn Hill)	–	sarsen	★	★	C
Warminster 6 (Oxendean)	–	★	–	–	C & T
Wilsford 3 (Ell Barrow)	–	–	–	–	T

C = William Cunnington, T = John Thurnam, WHC = William and Henry Cunnington; ★ = feature is present

investigation than other mounds, there is uncertainty as to the nature of the large quantity of 'black unctuous earth' that lay beneath the pavement at ground level (and occasionally in the upper layers), and formed a line '...from the small end of the barrow which continued beyond the centre...' (Cunnington MSS Book 3: Devizes Museum). In some cases this turf construction appears to be a primary activity, but there is clearly later use of turf too, and it might be that this distinction was not recognised at Heytesbury North Field. Either way, the presence of quantities of turf suggests that there were considerable areas of grassland around each barrow at the time of construction.

Close to the old land surface, platforms or pavements of carefully arranged flint or chalk nodules appear to have been laid out as at Boles Barrow and Old Ditch. At Boles Barrow, the less well-defined paving was discontinuous towards the west (Cunnington 1889, 114), but at Knook, at 4.5m in length and more than 1.8m in width, it was thought to be more complete.

Single pits occur at the base of a number of barrows, often carefully cut into the natural chalk. None of these contained burials or other deliberately placed objects and most were clean of cultural debris. They varied slightly in shape and size, however, the circular example at Heytesbury North Field, measured 1.5m in diameter and 0.75m in depth (Colt Hoare 1810, 72). At Knook Down a similar pit was nearly 0.9m deep. In contrast, the pit at Old Ditch was oval in plan, 0.9m at its widest, reaching a depth of 0.7m, while that at Knook was semi-circular. The largest, and perhaps most unusual, was at Boles Barrow where the pit was rectangular, 1.8m long by 0.9m wide and 0.7m deep. Most of these pits appear to be placed adjacent to the pavement, and sometimes positioned approximately central to the barrow. The pit at Knook, for example, was located at the west end of the pavement close to the centre of the barrow (op cit, 83), while at Old Ditch it was located next to one of the skeletons that lay on the pavement. At Arn Hill (just outside the SPTA boundary) a monolith of sarsen, 1.5m high and a maximum of 0.9m wide, was located immediately north of the pavement, that is, towards the centre of the barrow. There appears to be a reasonable possibility that the pits beneath other barrows are stone-sockets that once held standing stones, removed prior to construction of the covering cairn and broken up for incorporation in the mound. This might provide an explanation for Cunnington's note that the ridged cairn at Knook incorporated 'large man made stones' (Cunnington MSS Book 3: Devizes Museum). The composition of these internal covering mounds varied greatly but was often of turf or earth. Sometimes cairns of stone, large flints and sarsen were used,

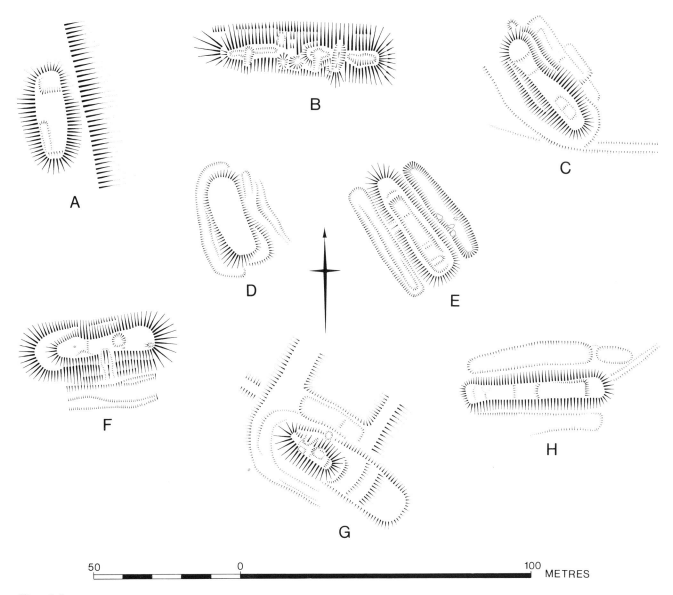

Figure 2.8
Comparative plans of long barrows: (A) Heytesbury North Field, now partly levelled with lynchet encroaching. (B) Bratton, just outside the study area, heavily quarried for chalk, and with excavation trenches still visible. (C) Durrington Down partly disfigured by construction of a narrow gauge military railway around its southern flanks. (D) Netheravon Bake. (E) Alton Down. Note trenching along the crest of the barrow and sarsens lying in the east ditch. (F) Knighton Down, with traces of an excavation trench in the south side. (G) Middleton Down (Norton Bavant) set within a 'Celtic' and later field system, the easternmost end almost levelled. (H) Tilshead Lodge.

Figure 2.9
Oxendean long barrow, set within, though not encroached upon, by 'Celtic' fields, provides a focus for trackways as they ascend the escarpment. Note the trenching at the south-east end of the barrow.

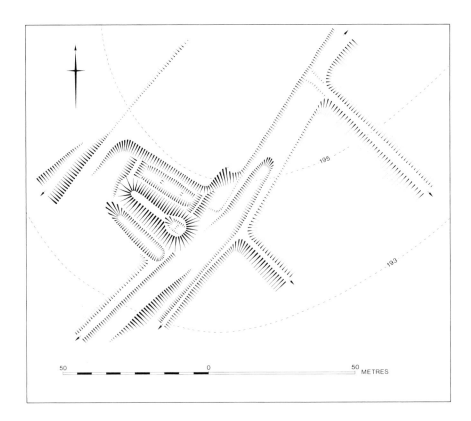

Figure 2.9
Oxendean long barrow, set within, though not encroached upon, by 'Celtic' fields, provides a focus for trackways as they ascend the escarpment. Note the trenching at the south-east end of the barrow.

Figure 2.10
Kill Barrow sits at the head of a shallow re-entrant from where it is highly visible, yet it is invisible from little more than 200m to the west. Its position, close to the parish boundary separating Imber and Tilshead, meant that it acted as a marker for trackways between the two villages, attested by a wide series of traffic ruts. The position of an excavation trench is visible part way along the mound. The barrow, surrounded by 'Celtic' fields that have almost levelled the westernmost ditch, provides a focus for a linear earthwork that cuts through them, but carefully respects the long barrow. Segments of ditch to the south-east of the barrow might mark the abandoned course of other linear earthworks.

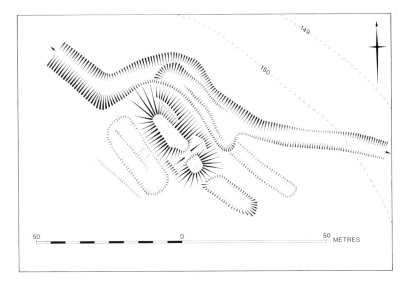

as at Boles Barrow. At Old Ditch the strata of the internal mound could be distinguished as being different from both the black earth and the chalk of the covering long mound. In two cases, Heytesbury North Field and Old Ditch, the mound was circular, while in the former case it was described as conical (Colt Hoare 1810, 72); but at both Boles Barrow and Knook it was evidently ridged, about 1.2m high at Knook and 1.8m at Boles Barrow (op cit, 83). In the latter case it was thought to extend for approximately two thirds of the length of the barrow.

Most of these cairns and earthen mounds covered skeletal material that appears to have been placed on the pavement. At Heytesbury North Field (Figs 1.10 and 2.8 (a)), for example, under the circular earthen core, and to one side of the small circular pit, there were between fifteen and twenty randomly placed skeletons (op cit, 72; Cunnington MSS: Devizes Museum), while at Boles Barrow (Fig 2.4 (d)), to the east of the pit, there were some twenty-five apparently disarticulated skeletons. Three were noted at the west end of the Old Ditch barrow (Fig 2.5). While it is not always clear from these descriptions if skeletons were complete, at least some, such as those from Norton Bavant and those already mentioned from Boles Barrow, appear to have been disarticulated (ibid). Evidence that skulls or long bones had been carefully selected for inclusion in a burial chamber is less obvious. Instead, the descriptions are of skeletons placed in no order '...as upon a skull we found the backbones and ribbs of another skeleton, and upon the neck of another two thigh bones...' at Boles Barrow, or '...a great many skeletons crossing each other in every direction...' at

Heytesbury North Field, and might in fact indicate that the pavement was an excarnation platform. At a number of sites, skeletons do, however, appear to have been articulated, sometimes covering one another or, as at Tilshead Lodge or Old Ditch, tightly contracted (Thurnam MSS: Devizes Museum). In others, they are more carefully placed side by side, like the two at Old Ditch, with a third, the largest, lying transversely at their heads. (Cunnington MSS Book 3: Devizes Museum). At the centre of the Knook Down barrow too, there was an entire skeleton, with three others lying parallel to it 1.2m away. Thurnam, on the other hand, records that, at East Down, eight skeletons were packed tightly together within a cavity 1.2m in diameter and 0.45m deep, a capacity much too small for it to be possible for them to have been complete bodies. These were 'strangely cemented together' in a similar manner to the burnt bones from Kill Barrow, which he felt had been deposited while hot (Thurnam MSS: Devizes Museum). Cunnington recorded the presence of much ash and charred wood on the pavement at Old Ditch together with a number of half-burnt bone fragments. Similar quantities of charred wood were noted at Knook, where all the bones, both human and animal, were more fragmentary, and it was difficult to ascertain the number of individuals present. The presence of ashes, charred wood and burnt bones alongside complete skeletons suggests complex funeral activity (op cit, 90), and some sites, for example, Knook Barrow, Old Ditch Barrow, and Kill Barrow, possibly represent the remains of crematoria. The practice of cremation is best documented in northern Britain (Kinnes 1992, 85), but the evidence for burial here is diverse and recalls findings from a wide range of sites farther afield that include Giant's Hills 1, Lincolnshire, (Philips 1936), Giant's Hill 2, Lincolnshire, (Evans and Simpson 1991), Alfriston, Sussex (Drewett 1975), and Radley, Oxon (Bradley 1992).

Cunnington's trenching at the circular mound, Silver Barrow, Tilshead, demonstrated similarities with the features found below long barrows. The mound, with side ditches, incorporated a 'pavement of rude stones' on which seven interments had been placed. Here, however, the presence of more 'advanced' pottery than in the long barrows was noted (Cunnington MSS:

Devizes Museum). At Westbury, too, where there are several circular depressions rather than a continuous ditch around the base of the round mound, seven or eight skeletons were found intermixed with several large sarsens (Colt Hoare 1810, 54). The nature and date of the mound on Cop Head Hill near Warminster is unclear but, if it is indeed Neolithic, it is likely to belong to a late phase.

Causewayed enclosures

The only certain Neolithic enclosure on the SPTA lies on the south-facing slope of a ridge close to a game covert known as Robin Hood's Ball. It consists of two circuits of bank and an external, causewayed, ditch (Figs 2.14 and 2.15), enclosing a maximum area of 3ha. Neither of the circuits is circular, nor are they concentric; the inner circuit, enclosing about 1ha, and almost sub-square in shape, contrasts with the outer circuit, which is polygonal. In each case there are no interruptions in the bank although at least fifteen causeways occur along the course of the inner ditch, and a minimum of twenty-two along

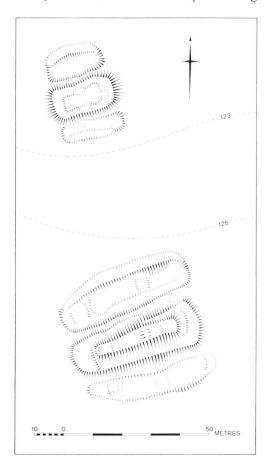

Figure 2.11
Long and 'short' long barrows (Milston SU24NW34 and 93) situated alongside each other at the head of a shallow valley in the lee of Beacon Hill. Note the higher central area on the smaller barrow, and that the longer of the two appears to have been constructed on a plinth.

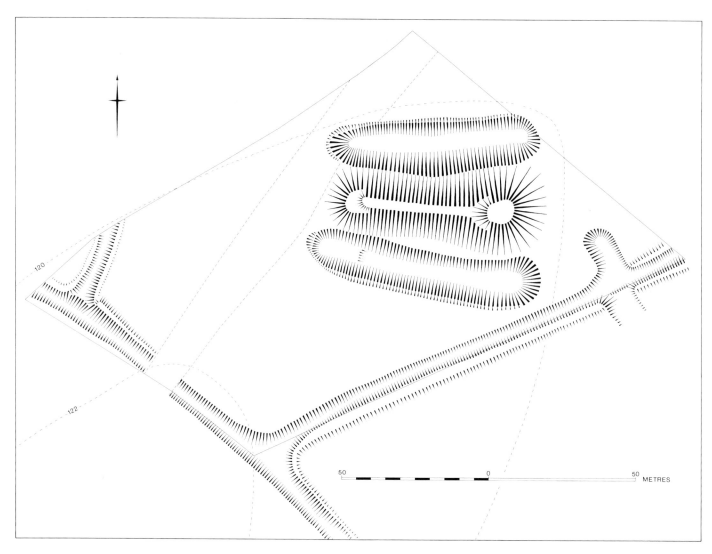

Figure 2.12
White Barrow. The swollen
east end might cover a
chamber, or might be a later
addition. A plinth can be
seen at the distal end, and
the barrow provides a focus
for linear earthworks.

the outer. An elaborate curve and change in the nature of the outer ditch in the west might point to the position of an entrance or, alternatively, indicate that the bank avoids a pre-existing structure.

A group of pits was excavated to the north-east of the outer circuit (Richards 1990, 61) and although it is by no means clear if these were contemporary with the enclosure, animal bone from two of them provided radiocarbon determinations of 3640–3370 Cal BC and 3361–3039 Cal BC. The high percentage of cattle remains recovered from the pits, contrasted with the single grain of emmer wheat (op cit, 65), suggests the presence of cleared grazing land in the vicinity of the monument. Additionally, the bones of red deer perhaps indicate undeveloped countryside that included much local tree cover. Within the area defined by the pit cluster a flint assemblage included more than 200

scrapers together with leaf-shaped arrowheads. Finds of struck flint remain plentiful on the tank track to the north of the enclosure and it seems likely that there was extensive activity in this area.

A second, possible, causewayed enclosure lies within the interior of the hillfort at Scratchbury and consists of a heavily interrupted sub-circular enclosure 3.5ha in area (Figs 2.16 and 2.17). Curwen (1930, 28) first suggested that this enclosure was of Neolithic date but subsequent excavation of the ditch produced only Iron Age finds (Annable 1960, 17). The excavation archive (held in Devizes Museum), however, makes it clear that these do not come from the lowest levels of the ditch. A small oval barrow situated nearby, recalls similar juxtapositions at Hambledon Hill, Dorset (Mercer 1988, 97), perhaps at Whitehawk, East Sussex, and at the Abingdon enclosure (Bradley 1992), and together with the chance find of two ground axes (Devizes Museum), suggests that Curwen's hypothesis needs to be more fully tested.

Henges

Despite the proximity of well-known examples at Durrington Walls, Woodhenge and Stonehenge, only one henge, Weather Hill, is known from the Training Area. This class II henge is slightly oval in plan with a maximum diameter of 72m (Fig 2.18). The circuit consists of a low, spread bank 3m wide, with a shallow internal ditch broken on the north-east and south-west by entrance gaps. Although by no means prominently sited, its position on a broad ridge set back from the River Bourne is more reminiscent of Stonehenge than the usual low, riverine henge positions.

Within a cemetery of more than thirty round barrows on Silk Hill an unusual circular mound, 30m across, is enclosed by a 6m wide bank with a wide and shallow external ditch (Fig 2.19 (e)). There are two opposing entrances through the bank (though not the ditch), thus inviting comparison with henges. The partially levelled Weather Hill henge could easily be mistaken for a disc barrow and it might be that, as Grinsell (1974, 90), Piggott (1973, 354) and others have considered, an evolutionary scheme linking henge monuments to barrows is possible.

Round barrows

Nearly 700 barrows and ring ditches have been recorded, of which more than 550 are found in the east alongside the River Avon and the Nine Mile River. They form part of the massive group noted by Fleming (1971, 141) between Stonehenge and Everleigh, reaching a density of some twenty-five barrows per square mile (RCHME 1970, 427), probably the greatest in Britain.

Across the Plain, barrows survive in a variety of conditions according to the nature of local land use. Cultivation has had the greatest effect, levelling whole cemeteries alongside the Avon and probably elsewhere. In contrast, after eighty years of shelling, Slay Barrow survives as a large, though badly disfigured, mound, while barrows alongside the Nine Mile River, between Bulford and Everleigh, appear to have avoided such damage and remain remarkably intact, presenting some of the finest prehistoric funerary landscapes in Britain.

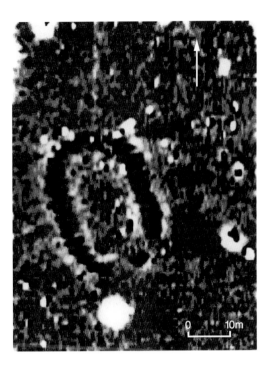

Figure 2.13
Sheer Barrow now survives as an oval mound little more than 0.5m high. A gradiometer plot, however, reveals additional detail. The ditches are continuous around the north-western end, but there are two causeways at the south-east end. A scarp, marking the perimeter of the mound, can be seen with a squared south-east end. (cf Netheravon Bake Fig 2.8 (D)).

Physical characteristics

All the known forms of round barrow are present. Field investigation of a number of cemeteries along the Nine Mile River suggests that the round barrow typology employed by Ashbee (1960) is far too simplistic, however, and that Colt Hoare's observations, more than a century earlier (1810), were far more detailed and relevant. For instance, Colt Hoare described four types of 'druid' (disc) barrow, as well as bell, bowl, cone and broad varieties (op cit, 21–2). Thurnam (1871, 293) acknowledged the presence of these types but incorporated them all under the heading of bowl, bell and disc barrows, and by the 1940s the presence of any other types was completely overlooked (Grinsell 1941, 76). In his gazetteer of Wiltshire barrows, Grinsell (1957) elaborated by identifying fourteen different categories based on characteristics of the plan view, but mainly by the presence of external banks and ditches, describing for example, five categories of bell barrow, two types of pond and two of disc.

Bowl barrows

There is major diversity within the general class of bowl barrows. As with earlier long barrows, at least two different mound heights, of approximately 1m and 2.5m, appear to have been deliberately favoured,

Figure 2.14
Plan of the causewayed
enclosure known as Robin
Hood's Ball. Note the
unusual changes in direction
of the ditches in the
south-west (a), perhaps
the site of an entrance.
Alternatively, they might
avoid a pre-existing feature,
now invisible. A number
of round barrows cluster
around the enclosure.
Note, too, how the parish
boundary (b) runs
diagonally across the site
and that the eastern side
has seen more intense
cultivation than the west
and as a result the
earthworks are less
pronounced.

perhaps hinting at variations in internal construction (Fig 2.20). Observations suggest that Grinsell's widely accepted definition of bowl barrows could be divided into three categories.

Very wide mounds stand to a height of at least 2m, with rounded profiles and are occasionally surrounded by shallow ditches, such as those in the Sling Camp Group. These traditional bowl barrows were, in fact, a distinct type recognised by Colt Hoare, rather than an all-encompassing group.

Lower barrows reach little more than 1m in height, with relatively straight sides, and broad, flat tops, and often lack ditches. These were described by Colt Hoare as broad barrows. Examples occur within the Sling Camp and the Milston 1 Group.

High barrows, often more than 3m in height, of conical form, and with small flat tops, are described by Colt Hoare as cone barrows. Excavation of an example almost 6m high in the Sling Camp Group,

showed it to contain a massive core of compressed wood ash some 2.5m high, which incorporated horizontal and vertical charred posts (Hawley 1910, 618–20), that represented the remains of a massive burnt structure.

Pond barrows

Although a rare type, ten pond barrows have been recorded. When first coining the term, Colt Hoare (1810, 22) described these earthworks with their encircling bank, as resembling 'an excavation made for a pond' and having no mound within the central area, 'which is perfectly level'. Grinsell (1941, 89), however, suggested that the internal area comprised a depression, the soil having been scraped up to form the surrounding bank. RCHME (1970, 422) also described pond barrows as comprising a bank surrounding a depression, sometimes with an entrance gap. Grinsell (1957, 226) recognised a second

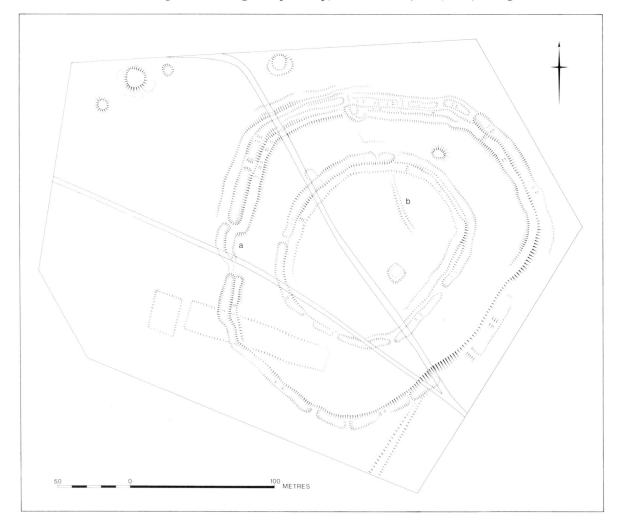

50   0   100
                              METRES

type of pond barrow with a level interior similar to that described by Colt Hoare, and concording with the evidence from recent fieldwork. This is defined, typically, by a circular bank with an external ditch, enclosing a level or sometimes raised platform. Examples on the SPTA show some variation, but the level interior is a common feature. Milston Group 1, which is 31m in diameter overall, is surrounded by a low bank with an external ditch. In the same cemetery another individual, with an overall diameter of 30m, has an external bank with no visible ditch. At Silk Hill, a pond barrow some 20m in diameter, and described by Colt Hoare (1810, 95) '...as if the protuberant part of the sepulchral mound had been cut off and removed...', lies immediately adjacent to a disc barrow (Fig 2.19). The pond barrow on Snail Down, excavated in 1957 (Thomas 1960, 225), was described as 40ft (13m) in diameter with ditches 1ft (0.3m) deep, before excavation. A recent assessment of pond

barrows (Ashbee *et al* 1989, 4–12, 139–43) excluded those with ditches, but incorporated the examples from Silk Hill (Figheldean 39, Milston Down 1 and Milston 45a), all of which have level platforms instead of depressions.

Saucer barrows

Close resemblances in morphology can be detected between pond, disc, and saucer barrows and, as Piggott (1973, 353) suggested, there might also be links with northern enclosed cemeteries. Saucer barrows are a rare type, being generally larger than pond barrows. Surrounded by a ditch with an external bank, the interior comprises a low mound that extends to the edge of the ditch. In the field they are often indistinguishable from pond barrows. Thirteen examples have been recorded; twelve lie to the east of the River Avon, mostly around the Nine Mile River, and River Bourne; in addition, a diminutive example, no more

Figure 2.15
Air photograph of the causewayed enclosure near Robin Hood's Ball showing irregularities in the outer enclosure. The rectangular feature that cuts through the outer ditch (lower left) is a disused rifle butt.

*Figure 2.16
Scratchbury: the
causewayed inner enclosure
was first considered to be
Neolithic by Curwen,
although some of the
interruptions might be a
result of cultivation. Despite
excavation by Grimes
(Annable 1958), the date
of the enclosure has not
been resolved. The oval
barrow (a) provides
circumstantial support for
Neolithic activity here, as
does the presence of chance
finds of Neolithic axes from
the hilltop, while the general
clustering of round barrows
around causewayed
enclosures is frequently
noted (cf Robin Hood's
Ball, Fig 2.14). Air
photographs suggest that
the enclosure ditch might
once have formed a com-
plete, circular, circuit. The
lynchet (b) that obscures it,
is earlier than the hillfort
and excavation suggests
that it was ditched on the
east, possibly as part of an
earlier cross-ridge boundary
or line of a pre-hillfort
enclosure. The sharply
defined linear bank and
ditch (c), which makes a
sharp turn around the
prominent bell barrow, is a
more recent boundary.*

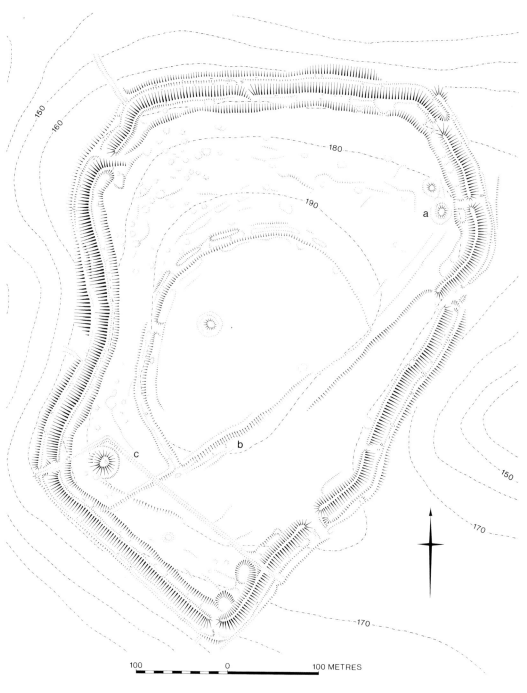

100   0   100 METRES

than 4m in diameter and 0.2m in height survives on the Bulford 'A' Range, at the head of a shallow re-entrant close to the head of the Nine Mile River.

Disc barrows

Disc barrows are the most frequently occurring of the special, or 'fancy', types of barrow, with some thirty-three on the SPTA, mainly on the Eastern Range. They are invariably of large overall diameter, sometimes in excess of 40m, with an encircling ditch and external bank enclosing one or two small, low internal mounds. In some cases, where there has been damage, it is difficult to distinguish between these and saucer barrows, although the latter are usually rather smaller in diameter. A number of types have been identified (Grinsell 1974) according to the nature of the internal mound. Occasional aberrants occur such as at Sling Camp, where a bowl barrow is set eccentrically within an ovoid disc barrow,

Figure 2.17
Air photograph of
Scratchbury hillfort.

Traces of Celtic fields

155

50   0   100
METRES

Figure 2.18 (below)
Weather Hill: a series of
shallow earthworks,
cultivated until recent times
from Everleigh village, and
now partly levelled. The
earliest feature is a class II
henge (a) with entrances
to the west-south-west and
east-north-east, and with
the southern half more
angular than the northern.
Traces of a 'Celtic' field
system on a north-east–
south-west alignment can
be seen, but are obscured
by later earthworks. A
D-shaped enclosure (b),
with the straight side
mirroring the line of an
earlier ditch or hollow
way that might itself be
contemporary with the
'Celtic' fields, lies close to
the henge. Other 'Celtic'
fields on a more northerly
alignment, possibly
contemporary with the
enclosure, are separated
from it by an amorphous
hollow way. The complex
lies at the northern end of
the Sidbury double linear,
which at this point might
be unfinished (c), and
becomes single and
indistinguishable from the
hollow ways and obscured
by earthworks of intense,
and ill-defined, later
activity.

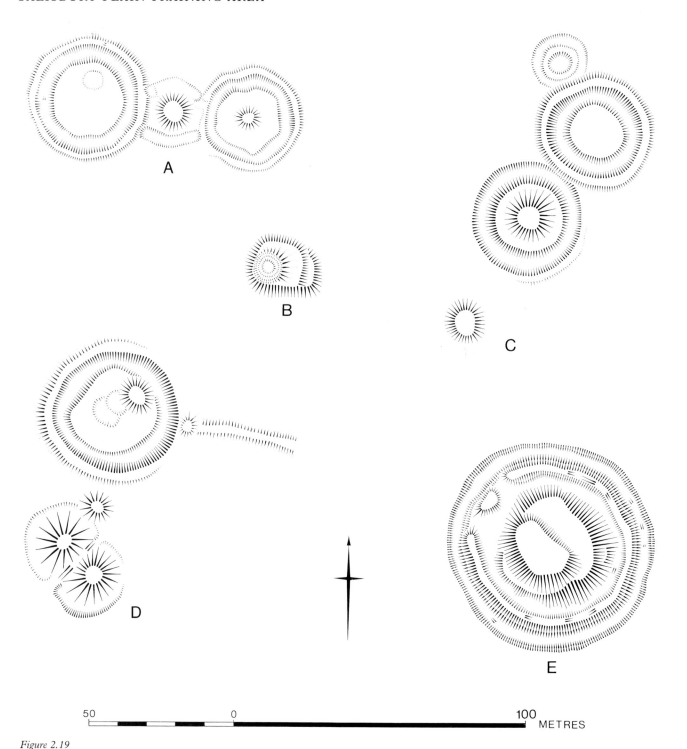

50   0   100
METRES

Figure 2.19

Plans of selected round barrows. (A) Silk Hill, two disc barrows with a smaller bell barrow placed in-between. (B) Diminutive bowl barrow with an external bank, set on the summit of an amorphous mound, possibly of burnt flint, close to the source of the Nine Mile River. (C) Silk Hill bowl barrow. The adjacent bank of the disc barrow straightens to avoid it, but marginally encroaches upon its ditch. The disc also impinges upon the massive bell barrow to its south. A bowl barrow lies a little farther to the south. (D) Bulford Down, an irregular barrow resembling a disc, possibly a cremation enclosure, with depression at the centre and with a small bowl barrow overlapping the inner lip of the ditch. A smaller bowl barrow lies to the east immediately outside the ditch, adjacent to or perhaps on top of, a linear bank of unknown origin. To the south lie two confluent bowl barrows with a third bowl partly overlying the ditch of the northernmost. (E) Silk Hill, a large bell barrow with a two-phase mound and a bank placed around the inner lip of the ditch. Two causeways through the bank, though not the ditch, face north-west. Although the bank lies inside the ditch it is almost henge-like in appearance and, at more than 60m in overall diameter, this is one of the largest round monuments on the SPTA. It is plausible that the site might have been adapted for use as a rabbit warren in the medieval period.

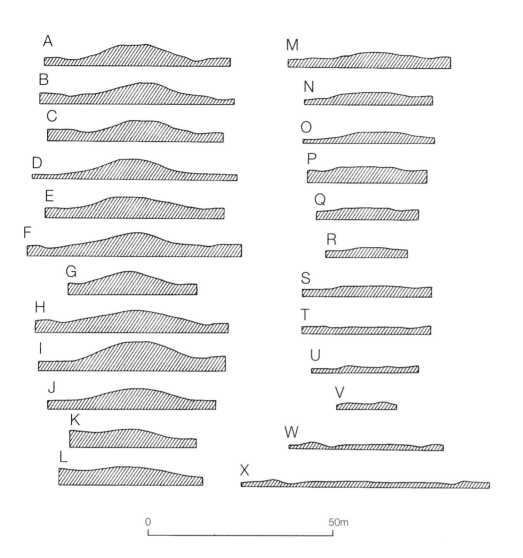

Figure 2.20
Profiles of round barrows:
(A)–(F) bell barrows,
(G)–(I) cone barrows,
(J)–(L) bowl barrows,
(M)–(S) broad barrows,
(T), saucer barrow,
(U)–(V) pond barrows,
(W)–(X) disc barrows.
Silk Hill Group (A), (C),
(D), (V) and (W);
Everleigh (B), (F) and
(X); Milston (E), (N),
(M), (O), (P), (Q) and
(S); Sling Camp (G),
(H), (I), (J), (K), (L),
(R) and (T).

0   50m

or in the Small Arms Range Group, where a mound partly overlies the ditch of an ovoid disc, implying considerable chronological depth to these monuments (Fig 2.19). Whether these ovoid discs are barrows in the true sense, or some form of enclosed cremation cemetery, is not clear.

Bell barrows

Bell barrows, frequently defined by high mounds of curved profile, encircled by a level berm and external ditch, are rare on the SPTA, with only fourteen examples, including a twinned pair. This contrasts markedly with the data from Wiltshire as a whole, where some 125 are recorded in contrast to 100 discs. It might be that some eroded bell barrows have been wrongly classified as bowls, but this, by itself, does not explain the difference.

Chronology

There is clearly a tradition of circular components within burial monuments of Earlier Neolithic date, for example, the mounds identified beneath Old Ditch Barrow and Heytesbury North Field long barrows (Cunnington MSS: Devizes Museum). The round mounds at Silver Barrow and Westbury 7 also covered features almost identical to those found in the long barrows. The large round mound at Compton (Fig 2.21) some 46m in diameter and 6m in height, comparable to some of the Neolithic mounds in Northern Britain, could be considered to be of Neolithic date, simply on account of its massive size. A small number of round mounds situated to the south, Amesbury 71, Mere 13d, and Warminster 10, together with Upton Lovell 2a, are known to be of Neolithic date

10m

10m

0

10m

Figure 2.21
Compton Barrow, the
largest round barrow
on the SPTA, invites
comparisons with
Neolithic round barrows
in Dorset and farther
afield in Yorkshire.

(Kinnes 1979, 10, 21). One of the barrows to the north-west of Robin Hood's Ball has a causewayed ditch (Fig 2.14) and is also likely to be of Late Neolithic or Beaker date.

In general, the field evidence provides no reason to depart from the accepted view that small, low, bowl-shaped mounds were commonly utilised during the Beaker period (2400–1700 Cal BC). Piggott (1973, 340) noted a size difference between the smaller mounds covering burials with what were then considered Early and Middle phase Beakers and larger mounds over burials associated with those of the Late phase, although this needs to be re-evaluated in the light of new dating evidence (Kinnes *et al* 1991). Invariably 'special' types, bells, discs and saucers, are thought to represent 'Wessex' burials (Piggott 1938), and there appears to be a reversion to smaller, low bowl barrows during the currency of Deverel-Rimbury pottery. Whether the cluster of small mounds at Netheravon, or the diminutive bowls and saucer barrows on the Bulford Ranges fall into this latter category, is uncertain.

Within individual cemeteries it is only at Snail Down that some chronological development can be demonstrated (*see* Fig 2.23). As a result of extensive excavations, first by Colt Hoare (1812, 181–186), and more recently by Charles and Nicholas Thomas (Thomas and Thomas 1955; Thomas 1960, 223–7), a sequence of burial activity in round mounds from the Late Neolithic through to the Early Bronze Age can be demonstrated (Thomas forthcoming), and it is likely that, with limited excavation, a similar chronology might be established for Silk Hill and the other cemeteries.

Cemeteries

Apart from the levelled examples sited along the River Avon, some fifteen cemeteries lie alongside or around the head of the Nine Mile River. Many of them contain combinations of 'special' or 'fancy' barrows as shown in Table 3, but only rarely are they found in relationships of special interest. In the northern part of the Silk Hill Group (Fig 2.22), a diminutive bell barrow has been carefully placed in the space between two discs (Fig 2.19), thus binding them physically and, perhaps, symbolically; elsewhere in the same group a disc marginally impinges upon an adjacent bell barrow, as well as slightly overlapping a smaller pond barrow (Fig 2.19).

Other instances of direct relationships are rare. At Sling Camp, a disc and slightly smaller saucer barrow almost touch, as do a second saucer and a broad barrow. Among the Brigmerston Plantation group, a low bowl barrow lies immediately adjacent to a disc, both excavated by Hawley (1910, 621); close by lies an oval mound that surface evidence indicates might have once been two confluent mounds, confirming both Hawley's and Grinsell's views (1957, 183 No 23).

At Snail Down (Fig 2.23), a cemetery with a total of thirty barrows, an ovoid saucer (Collingbourne Ducis 3a) and a pair of conjoined mounds surrounded by a single ditch (Collingbourne Ducis 4), lie in close proximity, as do a bell barrow (Collingbourne Kingston 13) and a disc (Collingbourne Kingston 14); in both cases, however, recent damage has obscured the relationship. Within the Small Arms Range group, a pair of confluent bowl barrows lie close to an ovoid disc (Fig 2.24 (C)), which

has a depression at the centre and an eccentric mound. Between the bowl barrows, in a space some 5m wide, a small mound, of similar dimensions to that within the disc, has been built and this partly overlies the confluent bowl barrow ditch.

Some cemeteries contain the whole range of 'special' barrow types, while others have a more restricted repertoire. Within Milston Down Group 1, for example, only pond and bowl barrows are present, although, on inspection, five of the six 'bowls' are, in fact, low or 'broad' barrows, two of which exhibit a second tier, perhaps implying separate phases of activity.

Arrangement and associations

The arrangement of cemeteries and their association with earlier monuments is complex. Most barrow groups are compact (RCHME 1970, 423) and, although some are scattered, they would fall within the nucleated category described by Fleming

Figure 2.22

Air photograph of part of Silk Hill barrow cemetery showing a bowl barrow with an external bank within the ditch (second from top), a disc barrow with a small 'pond' barrow adjacent (centre), and two disc barrows with a small bell barrow between them (centre left). Note tracks left by vehicles.

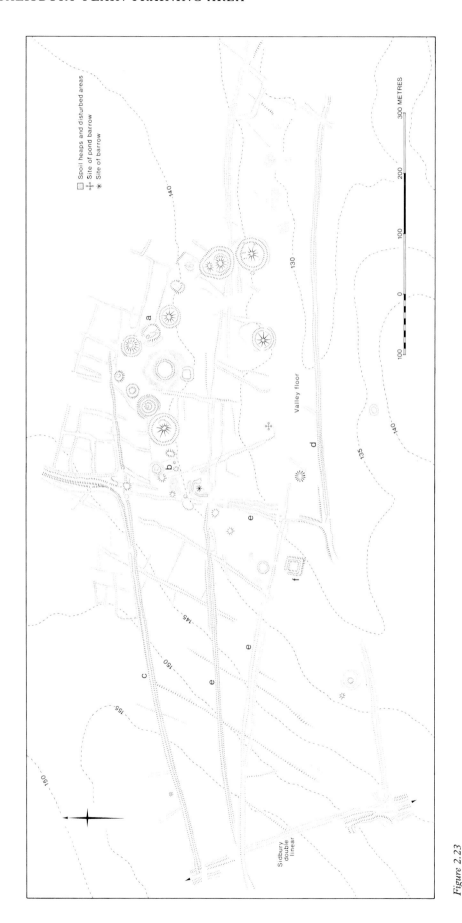

Figure 2.23

The archaeological landscape on Snail Down: the earliest monuments here are the thirty barrows, an oval barrow (a) being among the first to be built. The cemetery is arranged on the slopes of a small, predominantly south-east facing, valley. The whole complex is best viewed from the high ground to the south, particularly Sidbury Hill. All the 'fancy' types of barrow are present and, in one case, a diminutive example has been placed on the berm of a larger bell; in another, a single ditch encircles an adjacent bowl and bell. Many of these were excavated by Colt Hoare who provided names such as Hunter's Barrow (the most north-easterly bell), as a result of the arrowheads and wrist guard found during excavation. Towards the centre of the north-eastern alignment, survey revealed a sub-square enclosure (b), perhaps part of a field system, defined on three sides by banks, but noticeably on a completely different alignment to the later field systems. Three small bowls overlie the southern bank implying that the enclosure is an earlier construction. Excavations during the 1950s by Charles and Nicholas Thomas revealed stake holes here that were attributed to a Beaker date. Linear earthworks, part of the wider complex focusing on Sidbury Hill, cut through 'Celtic' fields. Subsidiary linears branch off from the spinal double linear towards the Bourne valley in the east. One extends along the false-crest of the hill (c), the other just above the valley floor (d), deliberately incorporating the former stream or winterbourne that flowed here. These linears neatly isolate the cemetery from the surrounding area. 'Celtic' fields to the north of the northernmost linear have been slightly realigned as a result of heavy reuse, and the presence of Romano-British potsherds in this area might indicate a date for this later phase of agricultural activity. Deep, modern, tracks (e) run both north to south and east to west across the down, probably to chalk and gravel quarries on Sidbury Hill, and in the Bourne valley, respectively. The square enclosure on the valley floor is a post-Medieval dewpond (f).

(1971, 141–4), the distances between barrows being no more than 100m. Some have linear elements; the Cow Down group of fifteen barrows (Fig 2.24 (c)) and the HQ SPTA group of at least seven (Fig 2.24 (b)) have a prominent linear arrangement on a similar north-east axis to those nearby at Snail Down (Fig 2.24 (b)), although in the former case, barrows are offset from each other, while in the latter, they are farther apart. Within cemeteries there are invariably sub-groups of barrows apparently associated, either simply because of their proximity or, as noted above, because the earthworks actually impinge upon one another. Apart from such relationships, it is rarely possible to deduce the development of a cemetery from field observation alone.

Neither is it clear why only some earlier monuments formed a focus for the development of round barrow cemeteries. A number of round barrows, for instance, lie close to the causewayed enclosure at Robin Hood's Ball (Fig 2.14). One mound encroaches upon the inner ditch, while aerial photographs suggest that a further example once lay across the outer ditch. Equally, round mounds lie adjacent to the Knook Barrow and the Milston Firs long barrow (Fig 2.25). There are, however, numbers of long barrows where there is no such association. The long barrows around Tilshead, for example, are completely devoid of accompanying round barrows, as are the long barrows at Oxendean, Norton Bavant, Bratton, Ell Barrow and Knighton. In fact, most of those sited on scarp edges, or in prominent positions, have not attracted round barrows.

Where co-location does occur, it is usual for just one or two round barrows to be associated with earlier mounds.

The large cemeteries consisting of twenty or more round barrows, have a more complex developmental sequence. The best example is Snail Down, where the most striking feature (Figs 2.23, 2.26 and 2.27) is a linear configuration incorporating eight mounds (Collingbourne Kingston 6–8 and 13–15). Aligned south-west to north-east, and ranging from the valley floor to the false-crest of the ridge above it, they are, with the exception of one bell barrow (Collingbourne Kingston 13) that impinges on the neighbouring disc, regularly spaced. The irregular position of the bell barrow might imply respect for a pre-existing feature immediately to its south-west, and this area also appears to have been the focus for five small bowl barrows, which partly overlie an embanked rectangular feature. Three sides of this are visible on the surface; the fourth, if it existed, has been encroached on by other mounds. Excavations carried out here during the 1950s (Thomas 1960, 224) revealed large numbers of post- and stake-holes associated with Beaker and Grooved Ware pottery, indications of earlier activity. All of this strongly hints that it was an important focal point in the funerary landscape.

Siting

The round barrows are rarely located on the highest and most visible points in the landscape. Slay Barrow, which the later

Table 3 Frequencies of bell, disc, pond and saucer barrows within cemeteries of more than five barrows.

cemetery	bell	disc	pond	saucer	others
Brigmerston Firs 1	–	–	–	–	7
Brigmerston Firs 2	–	–	–	–	6
Bulford Barracks	1	1	–	–	8
Bulford Down	–	1	–	–	8
Cow Down	–	1	1	–	12
Durrington Down 1	–	2	–	1	12
Durrington Down 2	–	–	1	–	8
HQ SPTA	–	–	–	–	8
Milston Down 1	–	–	2	–	7
Milston Down 2	–	–	1	–	11
Seven Barrows	–	–	–	–	11
Silk Hill	2	5	1	–	20
Sling Camp	1	4	–	2	14
Small Arms Range	–	1	–	–	11
Snail Down	6	2	1	2	16

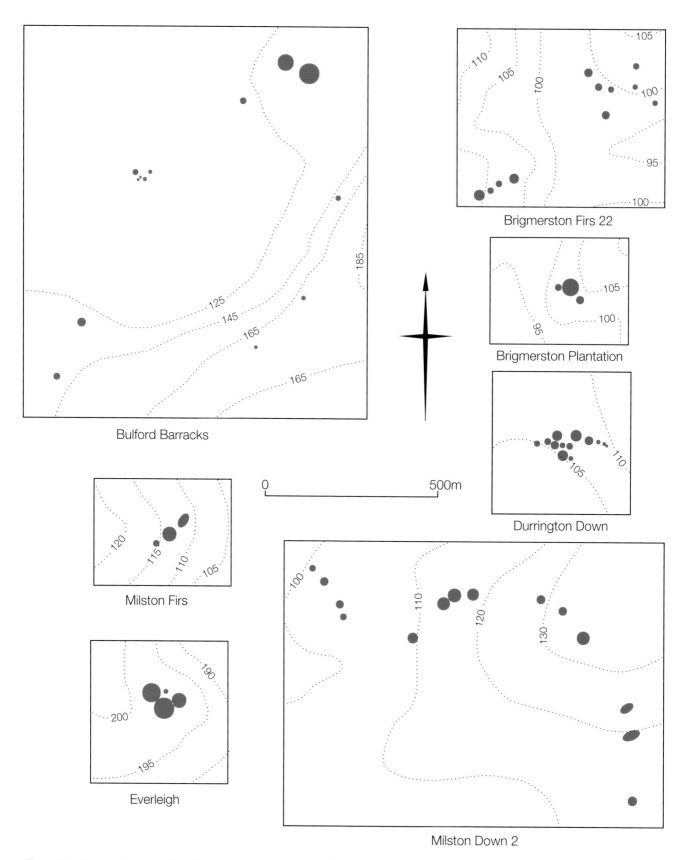

Figure 2.24 Comparative plans of round barrow cemeteries. Part (a) Bulford Barracks, Milston Firs Group, Everleigh Barrows, Brigmerston Firs 22, Brigmerston Plantation, Durrington Down, Milston Down 2. (continued opposite).

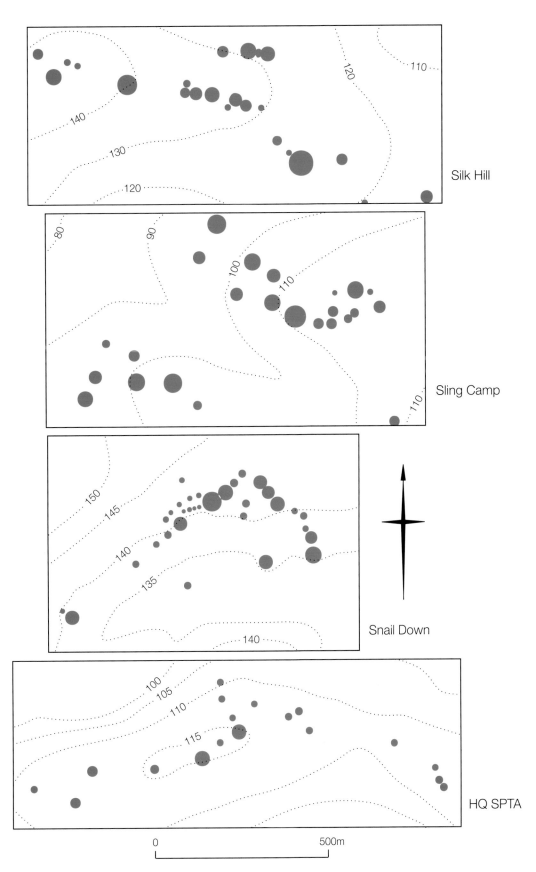

Figure 2.24 (cont'd) Part (b) Silk Hill Group 33, Sling Camp Group 24, Snail Down, HQ SPTA Group. (continued overleaf).

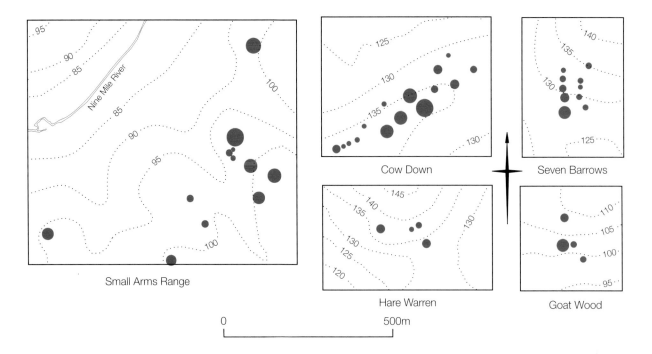

Small Arms Range

Cow Down

Seven Barrows

Hare Warren

Goat Wood

0   500m

Figure 2.24 (cont'd)
Part (c) Small Arms
Range, Cow Down 15,
Seven Barrows Group
12, Hare Warren Group,
Goat Wood Group.

Old Nursery Ditch linear earthwork curves round to avoid, is an isolated example, positioned on the watershed between the Till and Avon valleys. Similarly, there are a few round barrows situated on false-crests close to the escarpment edges. If positioned so as to be seen, as in the case of those at Battlesbury and Scratchbury above Warminster, for example, it would have to be from the valley below. A number of the cemeteries are sited on the slopes and bluffs immediately above or at the head of re-entrants leading down to the Nine Mile River (Fig 2.28). The Silk Hill and Brigmerston Plantation Groups lie to the west, but most groups lie on the east bank of this river and barrow cemeteries along the Avon are similarly distributed. Apart from one small example, which has been placed on top of a larger amorphous mound, possibly of burnt flint (Fig 2.19), no barrows are recorded from the valley floor of the Nine Mile River itself. The Snail Down, Cow Down, and Seven Barrow cemeteries, clearly part of this general distribution pattern, appear to have a similar relationship to the River Bourne. Only rarely are prominent landmarks utilised; instead, the lower slopes were used and some barrows were located on, or close to, the valley floor even though more elevated positions were available. Many barrows were indeed sited on false-crests, although such siting appears almost incidental when individual mounds are considered within their cemetery setting. The

barrows on Snail Down, for example, are situated on the slope of a re-entrant that formerly held water and that provides access to the River Bourne (Fig 2.24 (b)). The cemetery forms a crescent, possibly placed so as to avoid the summit of the ridge, with only one or two barrows sited on the false crest. The rest are arranged at different points down the slope, almost to the valley floor. The re-entrant itself is narrow and these mounds are best viewed from the opposite side of the valley or from the summit of Sidbury Hill 2km to the south. In a similar manner the Durrington Down cemetery (Fig 2.24 (a)), at a little distance from Stonehenge, clusters tightly around the head of a re-entrant, possibly a former spring.

There appears to have been an overriding concern with valley slope locations that provided good drainage and an association with watercourses. The riverine pattern is also emphasised by the distribution of ring ditches and barrows alongside the Avon (Fig 2.28), where, in addition to the HQ SPTA Group, at least nine (mostly plough-levelled) cemeteries lie on the slopes above Durrington, Brigmerston Corner, Ablington, Figheldean, Netheravon, Haxton and Enford along the east bank. Even in other parts of the study area, where round barrows are much less frequent, their position can often be related to former springs or water courses, such as those around the Ladywell spring in the valley to

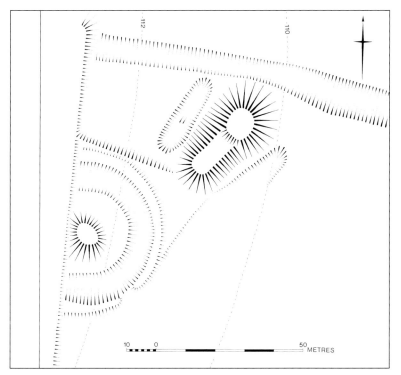

Figure 2.25 (left)
Plan of Milston Firs long barrow. The large easternmost end might indicate the presence of a chamber or an internal structure or might result from a later phase of activity. A now partly levelled disc barrow has been placed close by, while the long barrow subsequently acted as a marker for a linear earthwork that passes close to its north-east end.

Figure 2.26 (below)
Air photograph of the landscape on Snail Down. Wear and tear from vehicular traffic has created a track along the valley floor (top to bottom in centre right), while the barrow cemetery is bounded on the right by a clean linear cut that demarcates an aerial dropping zone. The tank tracks across the summit of barrows can clearly be seen. The false-crested linear ditch lies parallel to it for part of its course, while the lower linear branches off from the vehicle track toward the bottom right. A disc barrow (upper centre) and a saucer barrow (lower right) have been left as excavated during the 1950s. The circles towards the bottom of the picture are the result of manoeuvring tanks.

the west of Imber, the single exception in Bourne Bottom (Fig 2.29), or those within Battlesbury hillfort on the bluff overlooking the Wylye. Colt Hoare, for instance, described and illustrated eleven barrows that formerly stood on the floor of the Ashton Valley to the south of Chitterne just outside the SPTA boundary (Colt-Hoare 1810, 77 and illustrations facing pp 74 and 78) and another in a valley close to a well, south of Imber, none of which survive.

It might also be that barrow cemetery positions were determined by the proximity of a dramatic topographical backdrop such as Beacon Hill and Sidbury Hill, which flank the Bourne and Nine Mile Rivers respectively (Fig 2.30). Beacon Hill dominates the area, and the Sling Camp Group, for example, though separated by a small valley, nevertheless lies below it. Similarly the Cow Down, Snail Down and Seven Barrow Groups are all overshadowed by Sidbury Hill. The cemeteries developed on lower spurs and terraces, often in secluded positions, dominated by these prominent hills.

The antiquarian record

Colt Hoare records the opening of at least ninety-five round barrows on the Training Area. Cunnington investigated some, but most were dug into by Colt Hoare's own workmen, who spent little time recording structural detail, instead digging down directly onto the primary interment usually within a single day (*see* Lukis 1867, 86). Colt Hoare records occasional details concerning the presence of cists that contained grave goods, but the remainder were given scant attention. Only five of those investigated by Colt Hoare on the Training Area are included in Piggott's *Register of Grave Groups of the Wessex Culture* (Piggott 1938, 102–6), although there are greater numbers from those areas to the south of the SPTA boundary. Colt Hoare's field observation skills were, however, finely tuned and he was aware of the relative chronology at complex sites noting, for example, that round barrows underlay the rampart at Battlesbury.

While criticising Colt Hoare for poor excavation technique, Lukis excavated part of the Cow Down round barrow cemetery at Collingbourne Ducis (Lukis 1867) and, although secondary interments were recorded, little structural detail was noted. Subsequently Hawley investigated some seventeen barrows on the Bulford Ranges (Hawley 1910), and, apart from the presence of cists, structural details were recorded at only three of these. Two of the Sling Camp Group outliers contained flint cairns, one of which appears to have

Figure 2.27
Part of the Snail Down barrow cemetery, showing the damage caused by tanks before the Second World War.

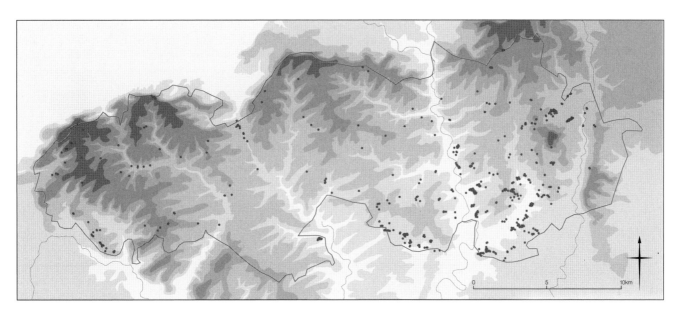

*Figure 2.28 (above)
Map showing distribution
of round barrows including
ring ditches thought to
represent levelled barrows.*

*Figure 2.29
Round barrow protected
by wooden posts on the
Bourne Bottom valley
floor at Figheldean.*

*Figure 2.30
Round barrow on the
lower slopes to the west of
Sidbury Hill.*

slumped into an underlying cist that contained a primary inhumation with an associated axe-hammer. A substantial overlying earth mound contained the remains of seven infants. A cone barrow in the same cemetery comprised a compressed pile of wood-ash, among which were charred upright beams, part, possibly, of a timber mortuary structure. A similar example was described by Colt Hoare on Longstreet Down, where ashes were found to a height of almost 1m (Colt Hoare 1810, 193).

The funerary landscape

Fleming (1971, 152) has drawn attention to the dramatic distribution of barrows between Stonehenge and Everleigh, and Grinsell (1974, 89), too, pointing to the extremely high number of disc barrows situated between Bulford and Milston, considered the likelihood of a ceremonial site existing in the area. Rather than look for a specific monumental construction, however, it would be plausible to see the Nine Mile River valley, itself, as a sacred entity. The general distribution of barrows suggests that rivers themselves, and particularly springs, offered an interface with the spirit world and were considered sacred. Grinsell recognised that barrows were sometimes grouped along watercourses and cited examples, among others, near the Thames, the Kennett between Avebury and Marlborough, the Wiltshire Avon, and the Wylye (Grinsell 1941, 75). New aerial photographic evidence continues to emphasise the riverine distribution and, in this context, the well known concentrations of barrows to the west of Amesbury might be seen as partly reflecting the close proximity of the rivers Avon and Till, rather than, as previously thought, the presence of Stonehenge.

The period of three millennia before *c* 1500 BC has left little trace of activity within the landscape apart from the ritual and burial monuments. Although occasional lithic scatters or chance finds of implements occur, for example a stone axe in an antler sleeve with traces of a wooden handle, which was reported from Imber (OS Record Cards), it is still difficult to identify the presence of significant settlement. Despite intensive fieldwork there is no evidence of fields, farms, houses or domestic enclosures at this date. Clearly a degree of settled activity is necessary to grow and harvest crops, but at this period it might have been no more than cultivation of small garden plots as a supplement to a meat and dairy diet. It is plausible that much activity took place on the valley floors alongside the major rivers and streams. The position of barrows suggests as much. If so, later human and fluvial activity is likely to have ensured that sites are covered in alluvium and colluvium and masked by water meadows and modern settlement.

Increasing intensity of use of the downs during the Early Bronze Age is indicated by the vast numbers of round, as opposed to long, barrows. Many of the former are as massive as the earlier barrows and suggest as much effort in construction, if not visits of greater duration and regularity; it might be that this increased effort reflects a tendency towards settlement in the more favourable landscape positions.

3
The Later Prehistoric Periods
(*c* 1500 BC–AD 43)

During this period Salisbury Plain underwent, possibly, the most pronounced change it has witnessed since the end of the last glaciation 10,000 years ago, for it is at this time that the first physical remains of widespread settlement and agriculture can be identified. The earliest known settlements comprised small enclosures or scatters of unenclosed huts, but through time there was an increased diversity of settlement types and this went hand in hand with an expansion in the areas being farmed. During the 2nd and 1st millennia BC it is apparent that the preferred locations for settlement ranged from river valleys to the summits of hills or prominent ridge-tops. What this means in terms of detailed population figures is unclear, but the proliferation of settlements points to a large and possibly rising population level. The fact that much of the area was enclosed at this time adds weight to this conclusion and the further subdivision of the area by substantial lengths of linear earthwork implies that the control of land was of prime importance.

In marked contrast to the archaeology of the 4th and 3rd millennia BC there is little evidence for burial and ceremonial monuments. This does not necessarily imply that these matters were of no relevance to communities, rather that monuments primarily concerned with this function were no longer built. It is more likely that ritual activities were undertaken at sites that have ostensibly domestic qualities and were more closely integrated with domestic activities. The discovery of a huge midden mound at East Chisenbury, dating to 800–600 BC, might be an example of this.

Prehistoric field systems

The most widespread archaeological remains on the SPTA are ancient fields (Figs 3.1 and 1.17). In plan these are all small and approximately rectangular in shape; indeed, the majority have straight sides.

Individual fields are typically combined with others in an organised fashion (isolated and individual fields could be mistaken for settlement or stock enclosures), creating large conglomerations resembling a chequerboard. These earthworks cover much of the Training Area and, even in areas subsequently levelled by later cultivation, it is still possible to identify slight scarps betraying their former presence.

The antiquity of this form of field enclosure had been recognised by Stukeley (1776, 188–9) and Colt Hoare (1810, 69), but the generic term 'Celtic field' was coined in 1923, apparently independently and coincidentally, by O G S Crawford and E C Curwen (Crawford 1953, 95). Both men were familiar with the clusters of small fields on chalkland slopes, which they had observed during their archaeological careers in Wessex and Sussex respectively. In applying the term 'Celtic', they sought to differentiate these systems from the morphologically distinct elongated fields, strip lynchets and ridge-and-furrow of later periods.

Originally, fences, hedges, ditches or lines of boulders might have marked out the fields, although the field boundaries often survive only as very low banks. However, where these are on slopes, ploughsoil flows downhill to accumulate at the field boundary: such cultivation-created scarps are better known as lynchets. This term, derived from the Saxon '*hlinc*', meaning ridge, can only result from the processes of artificial terracing and large-scale soil movement. The scraping and traffic of animals might create other small linear scarps, but for the creation of the large scarps that form the main elements of the early fields, cultivation is the sole cause. Collin Bowen defined two forms of lynchets (Bowen 1961, 15). Negative lynchets develop through the repeated action of ploughing or digging into a slope, thus creating a pronounced scarp at the upper edge of the worked land. The strength of the negative lynchet is

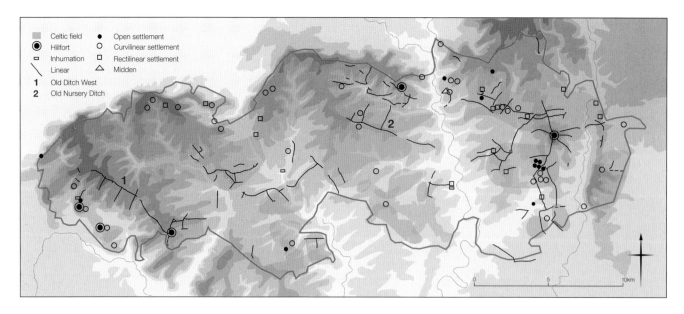

Figure 3.1
Combined plot of
archaeological features on
the SPTA derived from
aerial photographs and
distribution map of later
prehistoric activity.

accentuated by repeated and uni-directional ploughing. The same principles apply to the creation of positive lynchets, resulting from the accumulation of soil along the downhill ploughing edge. Rubbish, stones and other debris cleared from the fields often build up at the ploughing edge and enhance the profiles of the lynchets. However, the strength of these features is more likely to be associated with the steepness of the slope, the length of ploughing, its intensity and the efficacy of the ploughing method, as well as soil movement due to heavy rain. In these circumstances the remaining boundaries lying across the slope, retain something of their original form, appearing as shallow banks. Many of the fields might have been used as livestock paddocks at various times. Repeated usage over many years has meant that in a number of instances the lynchets survive to substantial heights; some of those on the SPTA, such as on Charlton Down, stand to a height of 6m and are among the best preserved ancient fields in Europe. It is unlikely that all of the fields were in use at any one time and, in all likelihood, there existed a mixed agricultural regime in which extensive tracts of 'Celtic' fields were reserved as fallow or pasture.

Distribution

Given the wide distribution of extant ancient fields, it is clear that the absence of field remains in some areas has to be explained. There are a number of factors at work here, and one of the most significant

is the effect of agricultural practices in post-Roman times. This is particularly noticeable in the western part of the survey area, which is cloaked in ridge-and-furrow cultivation formerly worked by the Imber villagers. Other areas that are devoid of 'Celtic' fields, such as river valleys, might never have been ploughed or, as is more likely, the evidence might have been destroyed by modern development, the creation of water meadows and intensive farming practices. It is, of course, entirely feasible that areas without 'Celtic' fields were never ploughed with enough intensity to leave behind traces of lynchets. Alternatively, they could have been areas of established and, presumably, managed woodland, while other gaps in the distribution of fields might reflect different forms of landholding or tenure.

Dating

Refined dating of field systems is notoriously difficult. Cultivation was certainly underway by the Early Bronze Age on the Marlborough Downs (Gingell 1984, 153), and similar evidence was noted in the environs of Stonehenge (Richards 1990, 274). The Deverel-Rimbury enclosure at South Lodge in Cranborne Chase (Barrett *et al* 1991, 150) sits on top of a 'Celtic' field system. For relative dating we have to rely on associations with better dated forms of earthwork, such as enclosures and linear ditches, but given the effects of subsequent activities it is now difficult to identify areas that did not see development in the

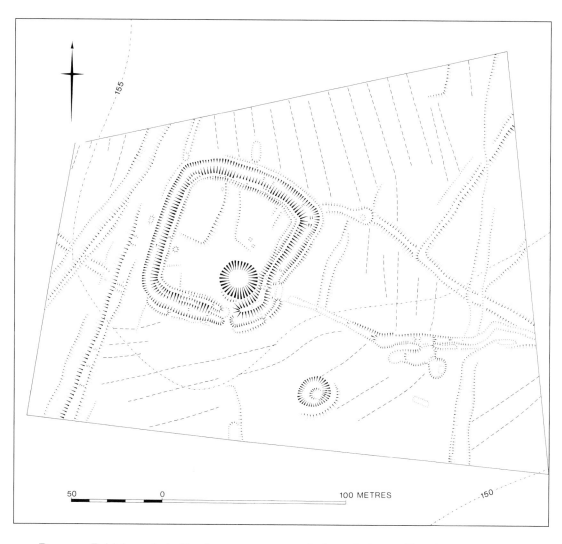

Figure 3.2
*Plan of Lidbury: the
enclosure overlies 'Celtic'
fields and incorporates a
large depression near the
entrance. It seems likely
that it held water, but
excavations found no
evidence that it was a pond
(Cunnington 1917). The
rampart had at least two
phases, and was possibly
preceded by an open
settlement. The first enclosure
was associated with
furrowed bowls of Early
Iron Age date (8th–6th
centuries BC), after which
the depression was dug and
the rampart rebuilt to
incorporate it. The second
phase was associated with
pottery currently dated to
the 5th–4th centuries BC.
The enclosure ditch
truncated a linear
earthwork, while much
of the surrounding area
is obscured by ridge-and-
furrow cultivation.*

Romano-British period. On the rare occasions when it is possible to observe undisturbed prehistoric fields, or at least a system established at this date, it can be seen that the field banks are very flattened. For example, the field banks near Lidbury (Figs 3.2 and 1.8), which are part of a system that underlies the enclosure there, stand to a height of less than 0.3m. On Snail Down, the shallow banks of a prehistoric field system can be seen interspersed within the barrow cemetery (Fig 2.23). They have been truncated in at least two places by east–west aligned linear ditches and have seen redevelopment and enhancement, at a later stage, in the area to the north of the northernmost linear boundary. The excavator, Thomas, believes that this early phase of field system is of Middle Bronze Age date (Thomas forthcoming).

Other less secure dates are glimpsed in those instances where fields have been slighted by linear ditches of the late 2nd and 1st millennia BC, such as on the Bulford Ranges or at Tidworth (Figs 1.15 and 3.3). Where such associations occur, in no instances can the *initial* phase of field construction be shown to post-date the linear earthwork. The layout of the 'Celtic' fields is, therefore, best placed in the Middle Bronze Age period, contemporary with Deverel-Rimbury pottery, roughly between 1500 and 1000 BC.

Morphology

Individual fields are grouped together into a field system and occasionally cover very large areas. Two main types of 'Celtic' field system are apparent: regular and irregular. The regular systems, termed 'cohesive' by Bradley and Richards (1978), and now referred to as 'coaxial' (Fleming 1987) consist of a field layout that appears to form a grid pattern. The degree of regularity in terms of size and shape is

Figure 3.3
Plan showing relationship of linear boundaries on Dunch Hill and Tidworth Golf Course to the 'Celtic' field system. Note that the field boundaries are slighted by the linear earthwork. Dense vegetation alongside the linear earthwork prevented survey here.

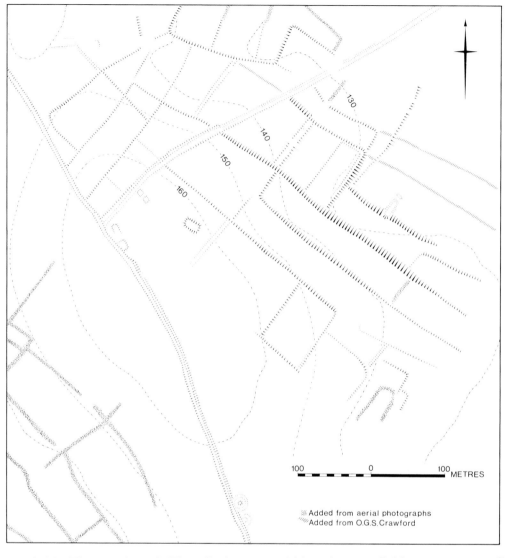

100   0   100 METRES

⌗ Added from aerial photographs
⫽ Added from O.G.S.Crawford

Figure 3.4 (opposite)
Comparative coaxial fields showing the commonality of axial layout, the uniformity of field size and overall extent (estimates of gross acreage/hectarage): Maddington Down 1,300 acres (526ha); Rushall Down 1,500 acres (607ha); Netheravon Down 500 acres (202ha); Milston Down 247 acres (100ha); Figheldean Down 3,700 acres (1497ha); Longstreet Down 2,400 acres (971ha).

remarkable (Figs 1 and 1.17). They display a common symmetry of layout with the predominant axis being north-east–south-west (repeatedly 26–30 degrees east of north) (Fig 3.4), although occasionally there are areas where cultivation, or the topography, emphasises the axis at right angles to this. This axial geometry is adhered to regardless of the underlying topography, and the systems appear to have been laid out either in one large undertaking or in a series of episodes following rapidly one after the other. On average, the blocks of coaxial fields cover between 1 and 15 sq km with the main spinal elements, in some instances, running for a length of 4–5km. These separate groupings might relate to the work of an individual group or farmstead or might have been the responsibility of a collective of smaller farms.

Although most fields appear, superficially, to be rectilinear, on closer inspection there is a wide degree of variability in shape and size. This is exemplified on Orcheston Down (Fig 1.18) where two main forms of field can be identified. The most prevalent are square examples with some as small as $25m^2$ in area but few exceeding $50m^2$. These fields sit at the heart of the coaxial systems here and so are integral to the earliest phase of activity. In contrast, those fields on the periphery, while adhering to the overall symmetry of the system, are of a markedly different shape, being elongated. They also enclose smaller, narrow, plots covering areas up to $30m^2$. There are indications, particularly on the fringes of the southern coaxial block, that these narrow fields result from ploughing across the subdivisions of earlier examples.

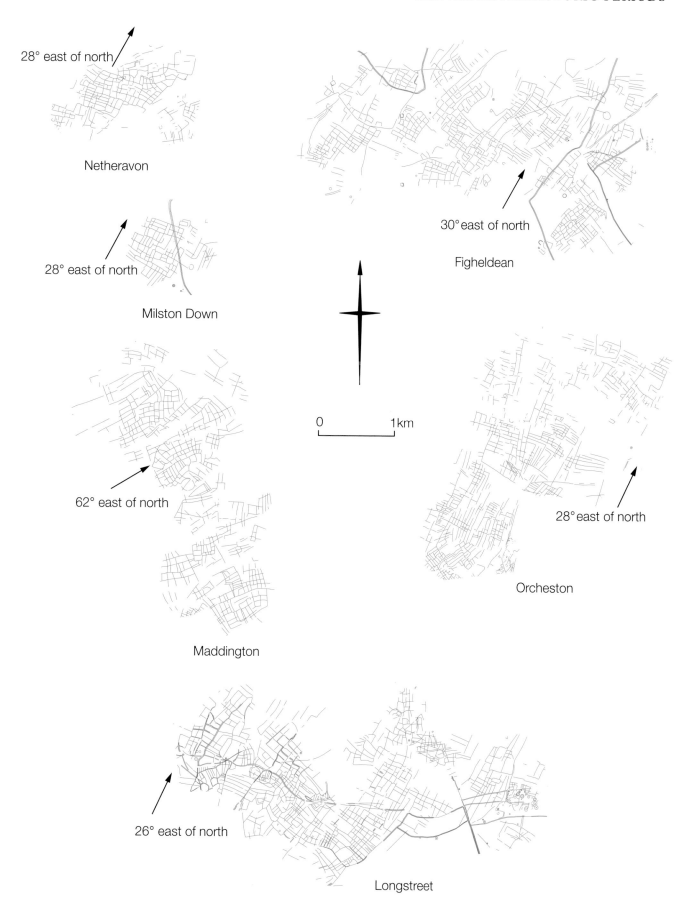

28° east of north

Netheravon

28° east of north

Milston Down

30° east of north

Figheldean

62° east of north

Maddington

28° east of north

Orcheston

0   1km

26° east of north

Longstreet

The fields underlying the Early Iron Age enclosure at Lidbury, best seen within its interior, each enclosed an area 25m by 35m. Those outside the enclosure are larger, up to twice this size, indicating that enlargement took place at a stage within the prehistoric period since these fields are slighted by a linear earthwork of early 1st millennium BC date. Similarly, on the Central Impact Zone, the 'Celtic' fields, particularly those on Upavon and Thornham Downs, show clear evidence of having been enlarged. Here, individual fields on the south-facing slopes are markedly elongated, with some attaining a length of 200m in comparison with a width of 50m. Within these fields, slighter cross-divisions can be seen, often partially and deliberately obliterated in order to create the long fields. This pattern of field modification, either enlarging or contracting, is repeated at several locales and was, presumably, governed by the intended use of the field. There might, for instance, have been strict rules governing field size during their construction, which might, in turn, have been related to the amount of land that could be easily dug, ploughed, maintained or harvested in a given time (perhaps of one day). Nevertheless, the state of preservation of individual fields is often good enough to enable the identification of field entrances and access ramps leading from one field to its neighbour; there are also elements of routeways through the fields, surviving either as terraced tracks or embanked paths.

'Celtic' fields in the wider landscape

Other traces of 'Celtic' field systems can be seen spread across much of the area not included within the coaxial layout. These fields appear much less organised, seemingly occurring in clusters that display a wide variety of shape and size. Field size is very similar to that noted earlier, with individual fields rarely more than 0.5ha in area. Often, later damage has removed much of the field evidence for these less regular systems, known as 'aggregate' fields, so that an already haphazard pattern has been further disrupted. The most telling observation, however, is that in almost all instances where association can be observed, aggregate fields post-date coaxial layouts. This can be clearly seen along the southern fringe of the Training Area to the south-east

of Knook Castle where there are a number of coaxial systems, each separated from its nearest neighbour by an average distance of 1km. The interstices are filled with clusters of fields, apparently randomly conjoined, and these systems might also cover very large areas. Quantifying their extent is difficult, partly because many areas have suffered later damage and alteration, but mainly because it is now impossible to identify the outer edges of these groups (Fig 3.4). The lynchets that make up these systems are frequently slighter than their coaxial counterparts, which might point to a less intensive and shorter history of use or, alternatively, to a less prominent construction technique. Settlement within aggregate systems is equally difficult to identify, although unusually shaped fields, such as those with curved lynchets or others that define small trapezoidal or triangular areas, might point to the presence of former settlements set within the fields. Aggregate field systems represent a completely different way of organising the landscape and seem to imply that the social regime epitomised by the coaxial fields had collapsed or was less relevant to the contemporary community.

Later prehistoric linear earthworks

Linear earthworks, variously called ranch boundaries, linear ditches and linear boundaries (Bowen 1978), can be found in other areas of the British Isles, such as the Yorkshire Wolds, the Berkshire Downs and the Chilterns but nowhere as well-preserved as on the Training Area. Here at least 70km of linear earthwork can be traced on the ground or from aerial survey. The defining feature is the ditch, usually V-shaped in profile, and varying in maximum width from 2m to 8m. In the vast majority of cases the ditches are flanked on both sides by low banks, which, in some instances, later ploughing has eroded. These linear earthworks extend for considerable distances: the shortest are rarely less than 500m, but the longer ones extend for distances in excess of 15km, as in the case of Old Ditch West. The original pattern has clearly been altered by subsequent events such as ploughing and infilling, but enough survives for it to be clear that a number of linear elements are interconnected and appear to form discrete divisions in the landscape. Occasionally these elements form large

Figure 3.5 (opposite) Air photograph of the Central Impact Area (the black spots are shell craters) showing the linear boundary Old Nursery Ditch, extending along the false crest of the interfluve between the Avon and Till. A tank track has developed alongside for part of its length. 'Celtic' fields, overlain by ridge-and-furrow, can be seen to the left of the linear ditch.

enclosures, such as that on Dunch Hill, which covers an area of nearly 3ha. On the SPTA this network of linears, labelled the 'Wessex Linear Ditch System' by Collin Bowen (ibid), is seen to be composed of two main parts, spinal and subsidiary linears.

Spinal linear earthworks, such as Old Ditch West or Old Nursery Ditch, are the most substantial and best preserved, forming the main components of the linear system (Fig 3.1). They are placed in very prominent positions, often following contours along a false-crest, or positioned along watersheds (Fig 3.5) or flanking escarpment edges (and thus the river valleys), and form the main backbone from which the smaller subsidiary linears emanate. They are generally aligned roughly east–west and run for several kilometres; their massive scale enhances their survival. Occasionally, these linears focus on particular locations: good examples are at Sidbury Hill, where six linears meet at a junction destroyed by the construction of the hillfort (Fig 3.6), Casterley Camp (Fig 3.7), which is the focus for at least three linear earthworks, and the East Chisenbury Midden (Fig 3.8), where six linear ditches and a pit alignment converge (Raymond *in* Brown *et al* forthcoming).

In contrast, subsidiary linears run for much shorter distances, are lesser earthworks, and occupy very different topographical locations. Subsidiary linears, in most instances, spring from the spinal elements and can be seen to extend along the main axis of spurs or ridges, thus defining small parcels of land centred on valleys.

Three main forms of linear earthwork were noted:

- Simple lengths of ditch. Some instances are accompanied by a single bank, and in others the bank material has been removed or ploughed away.

- Parallel embanked linear ditches with a medial bank.
- Multiple ditched and banked linears.

Many linear earthworks are on a scale that suggests they were refurbished at frequent intervals, and this might have gone hand in hand with changes in the way they were used by contemporary society. Their simplicity of form masks complexity of construction and maintenance. Excavations show that ditches were kept open and cleared on a regular basis, and that the banks were substantial constructions, often comprising a small turf stack at the core upon which successive layers of chalk and soil were then heaped (Bradley *et al* 1994). Their significance to prehistoric communities must have been immense, more so given the labour requirements for their building and maintenance.

Figure 3.6
Aerial transcription of round barrows, 'Celtic' fields and linear boundaries at Sidbury Hill. Linear boundaries can be seen approaching the hill from six directions. All linear boundaries post-date the 'Celtic fields', and this relationship is seen most clearly in the area to the north of the hillfort.

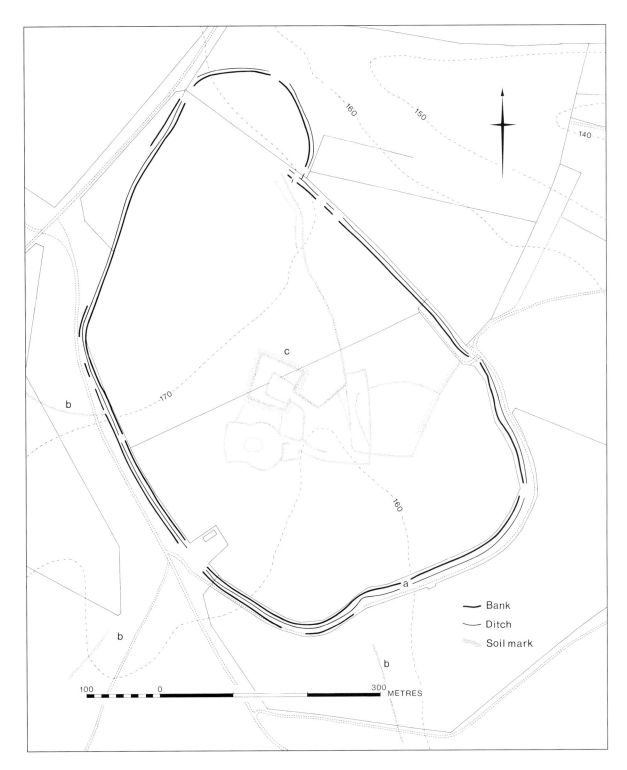

Figure 3.7
Plan of Casterley Camp. This is the largest hillfort on Salisbury Plain. The rampart, however, is slight, in places no more than 1m high, and the long straight lengths are, in fact, reminiscent of many linear ditches. The incorporation of the head of a coombe within the circuit of the enclosure is also unusual. An entrance placed adjacent to this encourages the view that the siting was deliberate and that the coombe was used as a formal approach to the site (a). As at Sidbury Hill and the East Chisenbury midden, linear ditches focus on the site (b), again implying an important status for Casterley during the Late Bronze Age. Soil marks of a Late Iron Age and Roman viereckschanze (ritual enclosure) at the head of the coombe, and possibly the site of a spring, give further emphasis to its special significance (c). Finds of miniature socketed axes (Robinson 1995) nearby suggest that the site served a religious purpose, possibly as a clearing in woodland.

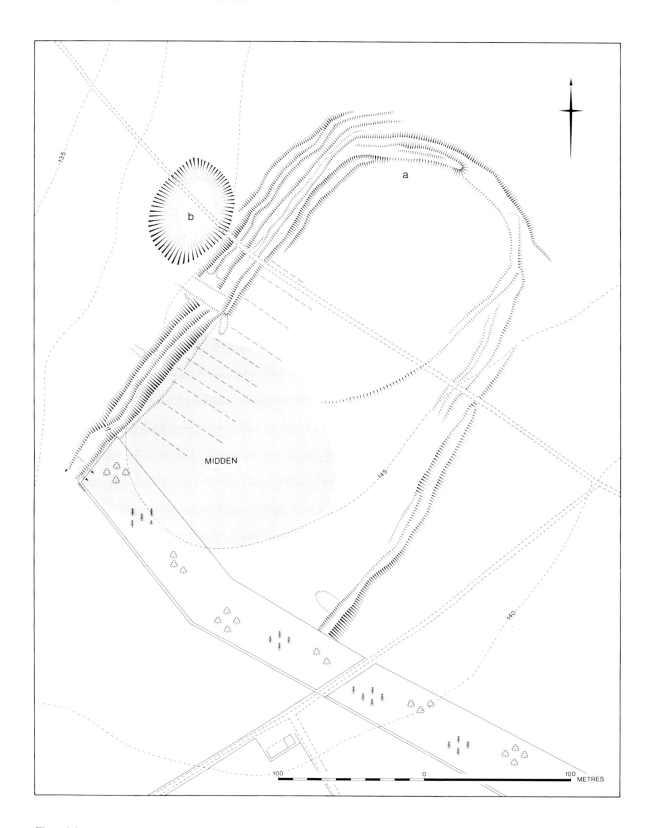

Figure 3.8
Plan of the midden at East Chisenbury. This massive mound situated on a prominent spur partly overlies an embanked enclosure (a) and dates to the Early Iron Age (between 800 and 600 BC). Now at best 2.5m high, the mound was formerly considerably higher (compaction and the effects of cultivation having taken their toll) and would have been visible from the Marlborough Downs several kilometres to the north. Much of the chalk interleaved within the mound might have come from the large quarry (b).

Dating

The dating of linear earthworks is tenuous. Only those on the Eastern Range have a reliable chronology (ibid). The earliest phase of construction dates to between 1200 and 1000 BC. This dating is based on a number of spinal linear earthworks that cut through settlement areas associated with Plain Ware pottery of post Deverel-Rimbury date (op cit, 126). At a later stage, principally between 800 and 600 BC, many linear earthworks appear to have been reworked while others were newly constructed. Reworking continued thereafter throughout much of the 1st millennium BC. At their earliest, linear earthworks post-date the construction of the coaxial field systems. Subsequent refurbishments, however, are likely to be contemporary with later episodes of cultivation, and this complex chronology is apparent in the intricacy of the field remains. Away from the Eastern Range, dating is relative and can only be postulated where there are identifiable relationships with other monuments, usually barrows, settlements and fields.

Distribution

On the Western and Central Ranges, the linear earthworks divide the landscape up in an orderly fashion; the spinal and subsidiary elements are clearly identifiable. The most pronounced of these spinal linears are aligned ESE–WNW, in places reflecting the main axis of the watershed, while others, lying parallel to the main south- or north-facing escarpment edges, mirror the natural longitudinal axis of the chalk ridges on the Plain. They are frequently multiple, perhaps reflecting their importance over a considerable period of time. It is likely that their massive original scale enabled them to withstand later damage and also served as a template for later use. Some of these spinal linears extend over substantial distances: Old Ditch West runs for at least 16km and Old Nursery Ditch extends for more than 11km (Fig 3.1). Although they appear to ignore the underlying topography, they have been carefully placed in the landscape. Old Ditch West runs along the upper edge of the main southern escarpment, cutting across narrow spur necks just above the breaks of slope leading into re-entrants, and delimiting the Higher Plain from the valley below. Similarly, Old Nursery Ditch runs along the central spine of the ridge that separates Thornham and Slay Down but has, again, been placed so as to be seen best from areas to the north.

On the Western Range, Old Ditch West acts as a spinal linear since a number of slighter linear earthworks extend from it on the north and south. Intermittent strands of linear earthwork, some as long as 1km, can be seen to the north, but their course has been obliterated by cultivation; to the south their layout and extent is much fuller. Here it can be seen that the subsidiary linears respect the topography, having been laid out along spur projections or on other stretches of flat ground, usually at, or nearly at, right angles to the River Wylye. At its eastern limit Old Ditch West terminates against another linear earthwork aligned at right angles, which runs for several kilometres to the south-east before feeding into the linear system to the west of Stonehenge (RCHME 1979). The subsidiary linears to the north of Old Nursery Ditch appear to have been laid out with little regard for local topography. Often they follow the contours but also cut across dry valleys. They are invariably interconnected with other sections of linear earthwork.

To the east of the Avon there is a sharp rise in the number of linear earthworks, paralleling the greater density of round barrows here. This more intense subdivision of the landscape might be related to the need to demarcate an area that was heavily settled and farmed by the 1st millennium BC or perhaps less intensively worked in the Romano-British and later periods. There are no surviving linear earthworks aligned perpendicularly to the course of the Avon, although we suspect that in some cases their courses might be preserved within the line of later tithing boundaries. Instead, the main concentrations of earthworks are found on the western slopes of the Bourne valley, or on the relatively flat plateau farther to the east; many have been laid out with reference to pre-existing landscape markers, which range from natural features, such as Sidbury Hill, to the man-made, such as round barrows and earlier settlement.

Farther to the east, however, a number of these boundaries are set perpendicularly to the River Bourne. To the south of Sidbury Hill, the linears extend towards Tidworth and the Bulford Ranges where they form large rectangular enclosures, including the previously mentioned example on Dunch Hill (Fig 3.9).

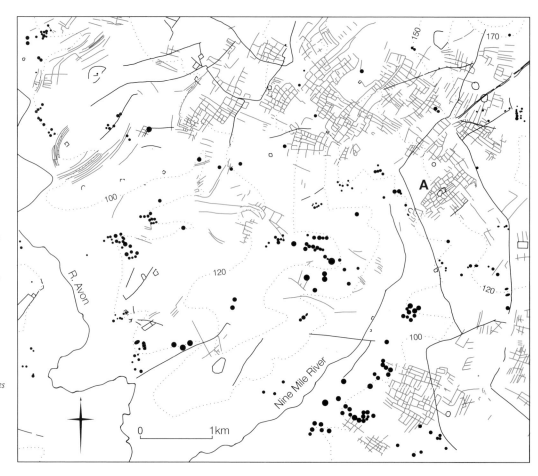

To the north of Sidbury Hill lies a double-ditched linear earthwork with a medial bank. The eastern length is less substantial and less evenly dug, while excavation suggests that the western ditch, dug perhaps as early as 800 BC, is earlier and originally continued beyond the terminal of its eastern counterpart (Bradley *et al* 1994, 134). The line of the ditch might have continued and linked up with another that extends to the south-west from the hilltop. The Sidbury double-linear continues to the north-west for a distance of nearly 2km and clearly performs a spinal function since a number of other subsidiary linear banks and ditches run off perpendicularly from either side of it (Figs 3.6 and 3.10).

Associations

During fieldwork it was repeatedly noted that the intersection of linear ditches overlay significant hollows, the shape and extent of which varied considerably. The hollow to the south-west of Snail Down, for example, is triangular in outline with a very shallow profile no more than 0.5m deep. Its surface, which is

unworn, is level and five linear earthworks emanate from it. An example along Old Nursery Ditch on Slay Down is oval in shape; it has a depth of 1.5m, and is more hollowed; again, a linear feature leads out from it at right angles (Fig 3.11). Their date and original function are uncertain, although they are likely to be another form of monumental landscape marker that possibly influenced, and was subsequently incorporated in, the layout of the linear system. The hollows share common topographical locations in that they are sited on false-crests and are usually visible over large distances. At least four were included in the line of Old Nursery Ditch as it traversed Slay Down. All are located with good vistas to the north and would have been clearly visible from this area. It is plausible that they represented early territorial markers, or alternatively, meeting places, perhaps communally recognised as significant, thus explaining not only their prominence, but also their later inclusion in the linear earthwork system.

In all surviving instances, the linear earthworks can be seen to cut through fields, thus post-dating them. On Dunch

Figure 3.10
The unusual double-linear boundary to the north of Sidbury Hill, now protected by wooden posts shown in the middle part of the photograph.

Hill (Fig 3.3), for example, a linear boundary sliced through a number of pre-existing fields, whose overall coaxial nature is brought out clearly by the aerial survey (Fig 1.1). However, the strength of the lynchets that flank the linear ditch clearly indicates that reuse of some of the 'Celtic' fields took place at a later date, post-dating the construction of the linear earthwork. On Snail Down and Tidworth Down, linear earthworks also clearly truncate earlier fields. Similarly in the vicinity of Knook Down

West, Old Ditch West makes a marked right-angled turn to the north (Fig 3.12); this is probably due to its link with a pre-existing linear earthwork, which is aligned on a north–south axis and bounds a block of fields to the east. The fields on Figheldean Down (Fig 3.13) were long thought to respect the linear earthworks (Applebaum 1954, 107). In fact, both field-work and the aerial survey plots make it clear that the fields continue, confirming Crawford's assertion that later cultivation

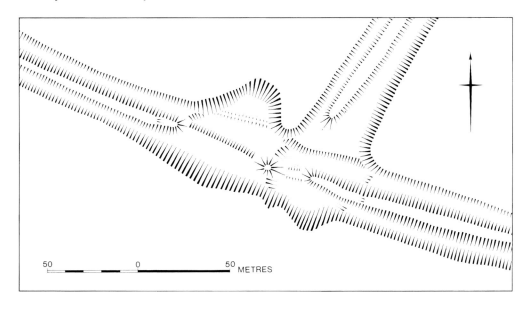

50 0 50 METRES

Figure 3.11
Junction of the spinal 'Old Nursery Ditch' with a subsidiary from the north. There has been much wear and tear along the course of the spinal linear, but it is nevertheless clear that both linear elements drop down into a previously hollowed area.

had destroyed the remains of earlier fields on one side of the linear (Crawford 1924). We must emphasise that there are no observable instances where linear earthworks were slighted by the early phase of 'Celtic' field use, although, arguably, only the most prominent earthworks have survived; other minor or less substantial lengths of bank and ditch might lie buried within fields. The abrupt north-western termination of the Orcheston Down linear earthwork, for instance (Figs 1.15 and 1.17), might be due to over-ploughing in the prehistoric or Roman periods.

All the main spinal linear earthworks run close to, or alongside, pre-existing burial monuments. In the west, Old Ditch West originates on Boreham Down, 300m to the north of the Oxendean long barrow. Farther to the east it runs close to Boles Barrow, Knook Barrow, and the two barrows on Tilshead Down. Likewise, the main linear earthwork on Chapperton Down, which runs for a distance of 6km, first becomes apparent, at its western end, close to the round barrows on Rough Down and, along its course, winds around Kill Barrow (Figs 2.9 and 3.14), making a series of unexplained right angled turns, presumably to avoid a feature of former importance (Fig 3.15). On the Central Ranges, Old Nursery Ditch originates very close to Ell Barrow and runs to the south-east, curving around Slay Barrow *en route*.

The purpose of linear earthworks

Linear earthworks might have performed a number of functions ranging from arable or pastoral concerns to social and territorial matters, while many might have been composite constructions incorporating diverse elements. This is only to be expected of a class of monument that had a very long currency. The sheer scale of construction of the linears and their distribution suggests that the primary function was a form of socially determined land division. The relationship between Old Ditch West and its subsidiary linears, predominantly those to the south, points to a sophisticated method of land organisation. The smaller linears are set at right angles to the main spinal ditch and define strip-like territories up to 500m wide. These focus on the Wylye valley to the south, and enclose a range of habitats, so that each strip includes valley floor, river terraces and downland. This can also be seen on Thornham Down where a series of

subsidiary linears branch off from Old Nursery Ditch and head towards the valley and Charlton Down. Some of the strips along the southern edge of the Training Area run for several kilometres down to the river and it is plausible that each represents the landholding or farm of a family group. Elsewhere, the surviving picture is too fragmented to make comparable assertions, although there is a hint of similar land-use on the western slopes of the Bourne valley. Farther to the south along the River Bourne, strip territories have been identified by Collin Bowen (1978).

The scale of construction and positioning of the main spinal linears suggest that they might also have performed more communally oriented roles. The careful positioning of Old Ditch West along the upper edge of the southern flank of the chalk plateau, resembles that of 'contour reaves' noted on Dartmoor (Fleming 1988). The major spinal linears mark boundaries in the landscape between areas of differing use, and often, perhaps, tenure. Old Ditch West might have served to differentiate between land to the south, owned and worked by individual groups, and land to the north, which was a shared resource, possibly common land. Unfortunately, due to later ploughing, it is not possible to determine if a similar form of land division existed farther north of Old Ditch West, though fragments of linear earthworks in this area suggest that it did and that a multi-period and more complex pattern of land division was in operation. During their time of use we assumed that fields slighted by the linear system would have been abandoned or perhaps used as part of communal grazing areas, before being re-cultivated at some stage in the later prehistoric and Roman periods.

The construction and maintenance of the linear system must have demanded a considerable investment in terms of labour and it seems likely that the earthworks were designed to make important statements about land ownership. Many linears, located in striking topographical positions, are carefully placed so as to maximise their visual impact. Old Nursery Ditch is best seen from the north and must have formed a prominent reference point for contemporary communities living and working on Thornham Down. Likewise, Old Ditch West appears to have been deliberately sited so as to be highly visible from the south. The most prominent, however, is the double-linear that approaches Sidbury Hill

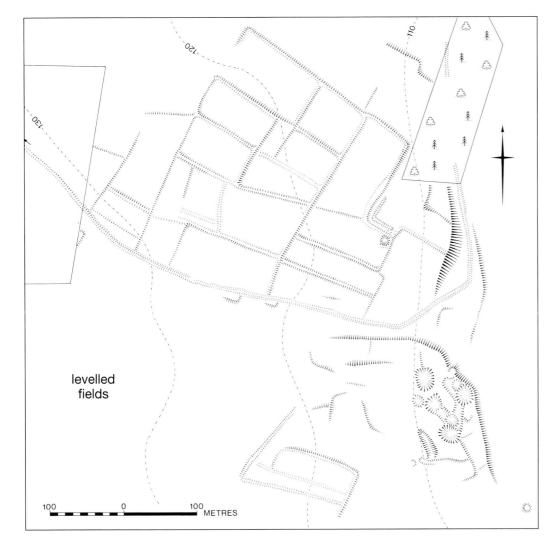

levelled
fields

100   0   100
METRES

Figure 3.13
Plan of 'Celtic' fields and
linear boundaries on
Figheldean Down.
The linear earthwork,
once thought to bound
the 'Celtic' fields, can
now be seen to slice
through them. Their
current arrangement has
been influenced by recent
agricultural activity, which
has levelled the earthworks to
the south of the linear ditch.

from the north-west. Re-cut as early as the 8th century BC on the line of an earlier ditch, it apparently originates just below the crest of the slope to the west of the Snail Down barrow group. The double-linear pre-dates the construction of the hillfort here but, standing on the summit of the hill and following the line of its features, the viewer is struck by the visual effect it creates. In a sense the two ditches and the medial bank channel the sightline to and from Sidbury, and it is tempting to speculate that this is deliberate and was engineered so as to provide an accentuated focus for activities on the hilltop.

The frequent association of linear earthworks with earlier monuments, such as burial mounds and settlements (*see*, for example, Figs 2.5, 2.10, 2.11 and 2.25), suggests deliberate attempts to integrate linears within the pre-existing monumental landscape. The builders of the linear earthworks were, possibly, seeking legitimacy for their own demarcation of the landscape by associating it with the earlier signs of occupation.

In a secondary context, perhaps the most basic use of linear features was as trackways or roads, particularly after the ditches had silted up or were backfilled; a number were used at a later date as streets or tracks within Romano-British settlements on the SPTA. Although no original breaks or gaps, indicative of gateways and access points could be identified along the courses of the linears, it is clear that many, particularly the spinal elements such as Old Ditch West or Old Nursery Ditch, were sufficiently wide to have taken small vehicles such as carts. They might have been used as drove roads for livestock and, in a busy agricultural landscape incorporating tracks as well as fields and settlements, the position and subsequent usage of these highways must have been heavily controlled.

Figure 3.14
Linear earthwork crossing
Chapperton Down. The
linear purposefully avoids
Kill Barrow long barrow
(top) and then makes a
number of elaborate curves
to avoid pre-existing
features (centre) before
continuing, making slight
sinuous curves as it cuts
through the underlying
'Celtic' field banks.
Note the shallow ridge-and-
furrow that overlies much
of the 'Celtic' field system.

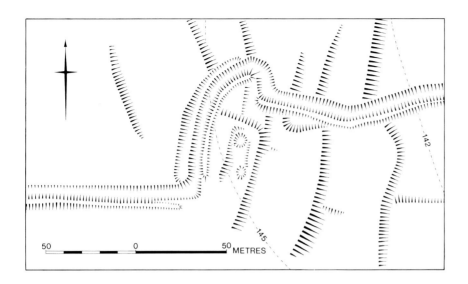

Figure 3.15
The linear boundary cuts
through 'Celtic' fields on
Chapperton Down, but
makes a number of
angle changes to avoid,
presumably, important
pre-existing features.
The depressions could
represent hut sites.

Enclosure and settlement morphology

The use of the word 'settlement' is here taken to incorporate a wide range of activities not necessarily confined to the traditional understanding of sedentary domestic occupation, since it is clear that sites might have performed a wide range of functions. Three main forms are present, namely, unenclosed settlements, hillforts and small enclosures.

Unenclosed settlements

These are the least easily identifiable and rarest forms of prehistoric settlement, and are infrequently noted as earthworks.

They are usually composed of small clusters of terraced platforms, the stances of former structures, often on hillsides. These settlements only survive in specific locations, usually those that have avoided subsequent cultivation, such as the edges of fields, or on steep slopes that have remained unploughed (Fig 3.16). One example can be seen on the slope to the west of Marden Down enclosure (Fig 3.17), where six small crescentic scarps mark the position of a former unenclosed settlement. A similar instance occurs on a steep south-facing scarp near to New Zealand Farm. Where ploughing has effectively removed all surface traces, open settlements might be identified by clusters of pits, post-holes and other dark spots visible

Figure 3.16
Traces of settlement: hut stances revealed as narrow ledges precariously situated on the steep escarpment edge near Hill Bottom Farm.

67

Figure 3.17
Open (a) and (b) enclosed
settlement on Marden Down.

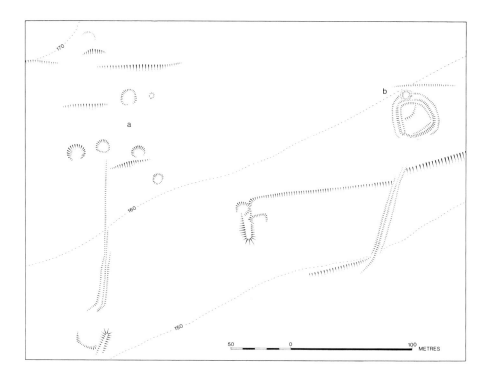

as crop, soil or parch marks. In other instances they might be identified in ploughed fields as concentrations of dark soil associated with surface finds of pottery, bone and flint, as on the cultivated area on Brigmerston Down.

Many open settlements have, doubtless, been masked by the construction of later sites, and it is likely that others have been buried within fields or under other features. The sinuous S-shaped lynchet 100m to the north of Knook Castle, for example, is likely to have formed around a former settlement (Fig 3.12). Excavation shows that a number of later prehistoric enclosures have had earlier 'open' phases. At Lidbury, for example, excavation of the enclosure by Cunnington (1917) uncovered the residual remains of an earlier unenclosed settlement that was occupied in the 8th century BC. On the northern approaches to Battlesbury hillfort and possibly truncated by its ramparts, construction work revealed an extensive spread of pits, post-holes and shallow lengths of ditch that belonged to an open settlement occupied between 700 and 500 BC, therefore pre-dating the hillfort (Chadwick and Thompson 1956). Unenclosed settlements could stretch over large areas. The settlement outside the double-ditched enclosure at Chisenbury Trendle (Fig 3.18) can, in suitable conditions, be seen as a spread of parch-marked pits and post-holes covering an area in excess of 3ha.

The settlement that underlies the Early Iron Age midden at East Chisenbury (Fig 3.8), consists of a dense scatter of truncated post-holes and hearths (Fig 3.19) (McOmish 1996). This settlement, as yet undated, is likely to belong in the post-Deverel-Rimbury period, between 1200 and 800 BC. A similar settlement existed on Strawberry Hill on the edge of the northern escarpment overlooking the Vale of Pewsey. A vast quantity of pottery of Late Bronze Age–Early Iron Age date was found here, along with pits, post-holes and short stretches of ditch, during excavations along the course of a water trench (Anon 1988a, 180–1). Artefacts of this date have also been found on the ploughed slopes of Brigmerston Down, often lying close to known enclosures.

The linear earthworks leading onto Dunch Hill cut through unenclosed settlements dated to between 1200 and 1000 BC (Bradley *et al* 1994, 127), although it is unclear whether a substantial length of time separated the abandonment of the settlements and the construction of the linear earthworks. Excavation of an artefact scatter on Dunch Hill shows that it derived from a now buried, unenclosed settlement consisting of round and oval houses, which was occupied in the second half of the second millennium BC (Anon 1997a, 158). These examples of unenclosed settlements suggest that this form of habitation might

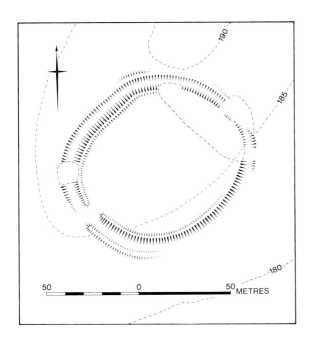

Figure 3.18
Plans of enclosures at Mancombe Down and Chisenbury Trendle. (left) Mancombe Down enclosure comprises a bank with external ditch enclosing some 0.4ha. Slight traces of a counterscarp bank survive on the north-east and south-west, but this might have been created by more recent ploughing around the area of the enclosure. The entrance is on the south-west. (below) Chisenbury Trendle was levelled during World War II, as its banks posed a threat to landing aircraft; a tarmac runway now bisects the site. Sufficient survives to establish that the southern part of the enclosure is more angular than the northern and that the enclosure, like others, lies over 'Celtic' fields. East- and west-facing entrances can be seen. The presence of a number of pits to the north-east (beyond the survey area, and not shown) were revealed by parch marks and might mark the position of an earlier open settlement.

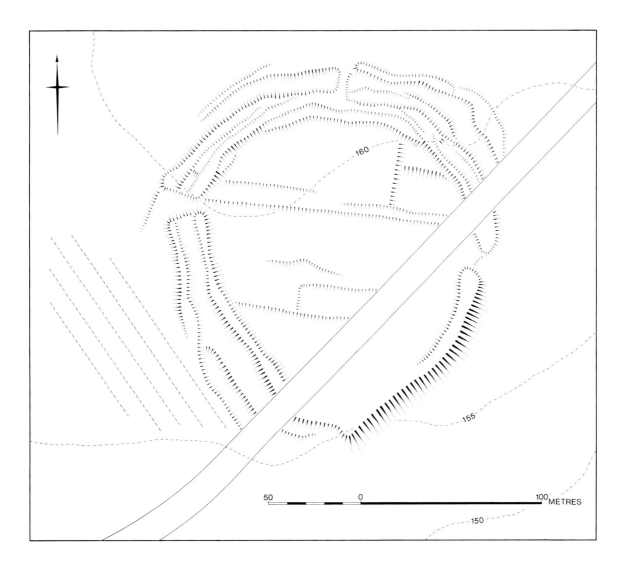

Figure 3.19
Post-holes and hearths
beneath the massive
midden mound at East
Chisenbury.

have been a great deal more common than was once thought. Indeed, it is plausible that for much of later prehistory the open form was the dominant settlement 'type'; however, it is rarely noticed and is under-represented due to its lack of monumentality.

Small enclosures

These are the most frequently observed form of enclosure. The first to be built date largely to the early 1st millennium BC, but often continued in use after the Roman Conquest. A number of prehistoric enclosures have now been excavated on the Training Area (Lidbury, Mancombe Down, Pewsey Hill, Widdington Farm, Coombe Down), enabling us to assign dates to similar, though uninvestigated, sites with some confidence.

Both curvilinear and rectilinear enclosures are found, although, within these broad categories, morphology varies considerably. The defining feature is a bank with an external ditch, most commonly part of a univallate circuit. Each enclosure is furnished with one simple entrance gap, normally facing south east; in the case of rectilinear enclosures, corners are never angular but slightly curved. The size is fairly standard with the majority, particularly rectilinear individuals, falling in the 0.2 to 0.5ha range. The largest examples, usually curvilinear, rarely extend beyond 2ha in area. Often these enclosures occur in clusters, as on Coombe Down and Brigmerston Down. Only the larger curvilinear examples

are sited on prominent hilltops. Otherwise, all other topographical locations are used, with shallow hillside slopes a favoured location for smaller, rectilinear, enclosures. It is plausible that the size of the enclosure is a good indicator of date since it appears that on the basis of excavated examples at Widdington Farm, and in the area to the north of Coombe Down, curvilinear enclosures larger than 1ha in area date from *c* 600 BC through to, and beyond, the Roman Conquest. Typical of these is the example at Chisenbury Trendle (Cunnington 1932) (Fig 3.18). Excavations, conducted when part of the enclosure circuit was levelled, found Early Iron Age scratched-cordoned bowls. As noted above, the site, which covers 2ha in area, sits on top of fields and, on the basis of parchmark evidence, overlies an unclosed settlement. As far as can be gauged from the meagre dating evidence at present available, larger curvilinear enclosures became more common through time.

It is likely that settlement systems consisted of both open and enclosed sites. The drive to enclose previously open settlements, might relate to the need for defence, but the external stimuli that might have provoked this are difficult to identify. None is placed in a defensive location and the boundaries might simply have been to keep animals out, or, indeed, in. They could also have had a symbolic value, however, and it is worth bearing in mind that many of the settlements are enclosed within banks or ditches on a scale far grander than is obviously necessary for the small areas enclosed.

The densest concentration of rectilinear enclosures is on Brigmerston Down where there are at least five small examples within an area of 6 sq km (Fig 3.20). They lie immediately to the east of the Nine Mile River, clustering around its springline, and located in close proximity to round barrows and possibly contemporary linear earthworks. The majority overlie lynchets from earlier fields, and fieldwalking in their vicinity indicates that they form only part of much more extensive scatters of Middle to Later Bronze Age activity (Bradley *et al* 1994, 126). It is not possible to say if this relates to the remains of large-scale settlement, or settlement shift over a considerable period of time. Indeed, it is entirely plausible that the enclosures demarcate areas that are not specifically related to typical settlements. The lack of well-developed,

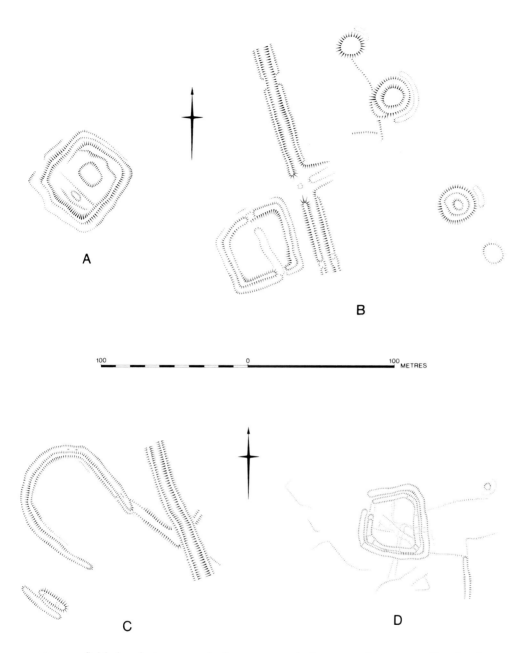

A

B

100 ———————— 0 ———————— 100 METRES

C

D

Figure 3.20
Comparative plans of later
prehistoric enclosures on the
Bulford Ranges. (A) Dunch
Hill superimposed upon a
'Celtic' field system (not
illustrated). Dense scatters
of struck flint and Deverel
Rimbury pottery found
outside the enclosure indicate
that it is positioned on top
of, or close to, an earlier site
set within contemporary
fields. (B) The juxtaposition
of the enclosure on Milston
Down and the linear
boundary is striking. The
breaks through the linear
and in the northern bank of
the enclosure appear to be
recent. Note stepped
arrangement indicating
phased activity on two of the
adjacent round barrows.
(C) Brigmerston U-shaped
enclosure lies over 'Celtic'
fields, of which only part is
depicted. Again the proximity
of a linear ditch is striking.
To the south-west of the
enclosure lies a short length
of bank with a slightly longer
ditch to the south – once
thought to be a long barrow
with a 'Celtic' field lynchet
obscuring one side; if so, it is
a small example, and is best
interpreted as, potentially, a
settlement set within the
fields. (D) Ablington Furze,
with its entrance in the
north-west corner, overlies
traces of 'Celtic' fields. A
round barrow lies less than
50m away.

contemporary field lynchets around them suggests that they were not the farmsteads of arable farmers. Instead, the main association with linear boundaries, seen clearly on Brigmerston Down, points to stock-based concerns and it is plausible that these sites housed shepherds tending flocks of sheep and smaller numbers of cattle. As well as providing residential space, secondary activities related to sheep husbandry, such as cheese-making and textile production, could also have been undertaken within the enclosures.

The enclosures are all placed on gently sloping, south-facing ground, which maximises the available sunlight and provides a good vista over the surrounding landscape. The northernmost enclosure of the group, Dunch Hill (Fig 3.20 (A)), overlies a field system and there is an extensive scatter of Middle to Late Bronze Age pottery immediately to the east, suggesting that activity was long-lived, possibly pre-dating the enclosure and spread over a large area (Bradley *et al* 1994, 55; 127). A more complex relationship between settlement and fields can be seen approximately 300m to the south. Here, there is another curvilinear enclosure, Brigmerston East (Fig 3.9 (A)) open on its east side but now flattened by ploughing. Only the ditch can be seen on aerial photographs, enclosing an area of 0.2ha.

Figure 3.21
Air photograph of an
unusual U-shaped enclosure
on Brigmerston Down
that lies close to a linear
earthwork (from bottom
left to upper right, a narrow
gap in the trees marking
part of its course). On the
opposite side of the enclosure
lies a simple, long mound
that shares the same axis as
the underlying 'Celtic' field
system, and which might be
the remnants of an enclosure
similar to that recorded at
Thorny Down, Wiltshire
(Stone 1937).

Contiguous with the eastern side, is another ditched enclosure, again levelled, of a similar size, though rectilinear in outline. In effect, these enclosed elements open out into one another, and both slice through the lynchets of an underlying field system, but lynchet build-up around the periphery of the enclosure clearly demonstrates that ploughing recommenced at a date sometime after the construction of the enclosure boundary.

The variation in morphology is well illustrated by the largest, and perhaps most unusual, enclosure on Brigmerston Down. This consists of a curvilinear or 'U-shaped' bank with external ditch open to the south 'enclosing' 0.4ha (Figs 3.20 (C) and 3.21). The defining bank is very low and spread and has been heavily damaged by burrowing rabbits; nonetheless, it remains clearly distinguishable from the slight traces of embanked fields that underlie it. One very low field bank has been truncated by the course of the

enclosure, and other ephemeral linear features were observed to the north and east. Either the enclosure was constructed in a landscape of abandoned fields or it made the local fields redundant. A linear boundary, which also cuts through the 'Celtic' fields, runs approximately 20m to the east. The Deverel-Rimbury pottery, found in rabbit scrapes on the bank of the enclosure during survey, might be residual from an earlier phase of settlement and provide a rough *terminus post quem* for the enclosure.

The much more rectilinear example, which lies to the south of this, Milston Down (Fig 3.20 (B)) similarly, comprises a broad and spread bank with an external ditch. No substantial traces of underlying field system can be seen in the immediate area of the enclosure, although shallow scarps, which might derive from ploughing, have impinged upon the eastern fringes of the four round barrows, the closest of which lies 30m to the east. Again, the enclosure is situated close to the linear boundary. Another 300m to the east a more extensive group of barrows has been recorded, some of which were opened in the early 20th century by Hawley, who observed that many had secondary cremations in urns of Early to Middle Bronze Age date (1910, 621).

Other enclosures of the early 1st millennium BC are scarce on the SPTA. Lidbury is a particularly complex example (Fig 1.9). The enclosure, lying on top of an unenclosed settlement, was itself remodelled on at least one occasion about the middle of the 1st millennium BC, and was possibly reused as a cattle or sheep pen in the medieval or post-medieval period (Fig 3.2). The enclosure boundary swerves to avoid what might have been a pre-existing pond, and within the interior there are traces of the earlier fields. At Ablington Furze (Fig 3.20 (D)), a rectilinear enclosure 0.5ha in area is similarly defined by a bank and external ditch that cut through earlier lynchets; the low mound that lies to the east might be a small round barrow or, alternatively, a pronounced corner of the almost levelled field system. A circular enclosure on Mancombe Down covers an area of 0.4ha (Fig 3.18). It overlies a field system and excavation showed that it might have originated as early as the 8th century BC (Fowler et al 1965). An enclosure partly underlies the Early Iron Age midden at East Chisenbury but might have been contemporary with it, at least in its earliest stages (Fig 3.8). It is, therefore, securely dated to the period before 800 BC. Covering 4ha in area and curvilinear in outline, it has a massive, spread, bank and external ditch. Colt Hoare remarked on the strength of the enclosure boundary, which has subsequently been much worn down by cultivation (1810, 192).

The majority of the identified enclosures are clustered in an arc along the southern and eastern flanks of the Training Area (Fig 3.1), mirroring the concentrations of round barrows. This distribution, like those of earlier monuments, probably reflects bias in survival, a result of the differing agricultural practices across the Plain, as well as the intensity of field investigation.

East Chisenbury midden

The huge midden mound at East Chisenbury, dating to between 800 and 600 BC, is one of the most important discoveries of the RCHME project (Brown *et al* 1994; McOmish 1996). Similar in scale to that found at Potterne (Lawson 1994), the mound survives to a height of 3m with a maximum diameter of 200m, and spreads over an area of at least 2.5ha, sitting on the west-facing edge of a spur that overlooks, and protrudes into, the Avon valley. It has been truncated along its northern side by a later 'Celtic' field system and ridge-and-furrow ploughing has scarred the entire area (Fig 3.8). To the east of the mound, and apparently partly overlain by it, the arcing bank and external ditch of an enclosure can be seen. To the north of the enclosure, and some 40m to the north-east of the midden, there is a substantial circular hollow, 20m in diameter and 3m deep, its profile smoothed by the plough. This hollow is also overlain by ridge-and-furrow, though avoided by the 'Celtic' field lynchets and is of prehistoric date but uncertain function.

A small evaluation trench towards the perimeter of the mound revealed dark layers of ashed sheep dung (Macphail in Brown *et al* forthcoming), while lighter layers comprised tips of bone-rich coprolitic material. Of the great quantities of butchered bone from the site, most is sheep; initial assessment suggests that this includes a large proportion of neo-natal lambs (Serjeantson *in* Brown *et al* forthcoming), and an assessment of the mandibles from the excavation concluded that sheep dairying took place on the site or in its immediate vicinity. The large number of spindle whorls from the small evaluation trench also suggests that there was an extremely high dependence on sheep (Fig 3.22). On the basis of furrowed bowls occurring throughout the profile, and with a Sompting-style socketed axe at the base of the deposit, the mound is likely to have accumulated in less than 100 years. The amount of sheep dung and carcasses represented on the site is enormous. The implications, therefore, are of an intensity of sheep farming rivalling, perhaps, even that of the post-medieval period.

Elsewhere, it has been pointed out that prehistoric fields on the Marlborough Downs were manured up to the time they were abandoned (Gingell 1984, 153). Almost certainly this practice was also carried out on the SPTA. However, it would appear that during the 7th century BC, rubbish here was not put out on the fields as manure, but was stored and allowed to build up into a huge mound. The high percentage of butchered bone and personal

Figure 3.22
The faunal assemblage
at East Chisenbury is
dominated by sheep.
They were economically
important, not only for
their meat and milk but
also for secondary products
such as wool, as demon-
strated by the recovery of a
number of spindle whorls.

ornaments from a small sample of the mound suggests that this is more than farmyard rubbish, as does the flat-based fine tableware and the presence of human skull fragments. This interpretation is further enhanced by the discovery of a series of linear boundaries, including a pit alignment, focusing on the site (Raymond *in* Brown *et al* forthcoming). Allowing for compaction and the effects of cultivation, the mound might once have been considerably higher and, indeed, must have been monumental. The position of the mound on a prominent spur above the River Avon, with views across Salisbury Plain and to the Marlborough Downs, is a significant focal point and it is possible that the highly visible midden mound was used in a symbolic manner. On the one hand it might represent the result of competitive or ritual feasting, or of communal festivals (the sacrifice of sheep in large numbers is still practised at festivals by some societies and religions), but, equally, it might be that the mound was itself an expression of status, reflecting social standing.

Hillforts

The most prominent enclosures are the hillforts, of which there are five definite examples: Battlesbury Camp (Fig 3.23), Scratchbury Camp (Fig 2.17), Knook Castle (Figs 3.7 and 3.27), Sidbury Camp (Fig 3.25) and Casterley Camp (Fig 3.24). A sixth, Bratton Castle, lies just outside the study area on its north-western periphery, and a seventh, Yarnbury, a few hundred metres to the south, not far from Maddington Down. The bivallate southern

enclosure at Ludgershall, which is curvilinear in outline, might also have been a hillfort before remodelling in the Middle Ages.

Hillforts are traditionally distinguishable from other contemporary sites on the basis of their:

- topographical position, normally on prominent hilltops or other similarly distinctive locations
- large internal area, usually greater than 2ha
- strong encircling boundary and occasional multivallation, supposedly related to defensive requirements

A detailed analysis, however, shows that a wide range of locales on the SPTA was exploited by the hillforts. Some developed on sites that had been previously used for settlement, while others were placed in areas demarcated at an earlier date by enclosures or burial mounds. It is also likely that some sites developed on prominent, well-known, and frequently used landmarks, previously unmarked by monumental structures.

It is clear that only the builders of Sidbury Camp made use of an easily defensible location (Fig 3.25). The domed summit of the hill forms an important landscape feature and one, given the density of linear features focusing on it, that was already heavily marked out before the construction of the Iron Age enclosure. After damage to the enclosure, excavations across the inner bank found Middle Iron Age pottery (Megaw 1967); finds of Early Iron Age pottery suggest that there might have been a preceding settlement of this date on the hilltop (Bradley *et al* 1994, 134). The subtriangular hillfort is univallate except on the south-east where an additional bank has been added. There is only one original entrance. This is in the north-west angle and consists of a simple gap in which the northern rampart terminal has bifurcated to provide both an inturn and a slight projecting hornwork. The entrance is enclosed within a later, rectilinear, annexe of 1ha.

The hillforts of Battlesbury and Scratchbury lie in close proximity to one another at the southern ends of chalk spurs that project from the southern edge of the Training Area, both in dominant positions. They are strategically located at the point where the valley of the River Wylye widens to the west, providing access to the lowerlying areas of clay and the Reading Beds (*see* Sherratt 1996). Farther to the east the valley narrows considerably and is deeply cut, affording one of the most important thoroughfares through the chalk downland, avoiding its higher plains. This location, at a major topographical junction, had been significant for millennia before the construction of the Iron Age hillforts. The area is the focus of Ashbee's Salisbury Plain West Group of long barrows and there is a marked concentration of Late Neolithic and Early Bronze Age barrows on the valley floor here (English Heritage forthcoming). The most common assumption about the relationship between the two hillforts is that one site supersedes the other. This was encapsulated in a report by a local archaeologist, Major-General Sir John Willoughby (personal communication). He stated that Scratchbury was abandoned after construction, since its builders found out that it was indefensible due to the ramparts being placed too far downslope. A move to Battlesbury was, therefore, initiated and here the defences were strengthened and made to correspond much more closely to the terrain. The bare facts are correct. Scratchbury (Fig 2.16) is indeed built in a

less defence-minded location than its neighbour. The univallate defences enclose an area of 17ha but lie so far down the slope that it is possible to view much of the interior from outside the enclosure. The most substantial section of the boundary is the part that, effectively, lies across the spur-approach, facing east. It is straight and broken by two entrances, one at the north, the other to the south. The hillfort is, unusually, furnished with a third original entrance, located close to the north-western corner of the enclosure. Within the interior traces of a number of phases of activity can be seen. The earliest established remains are those of the Neolithic and Early Bronze Age cemetery noted in Chapter 2, but the date of the inner enclosure is unknown and might, in fact, be Neolithic. Aerial photographs show that the enclosure continued in an arc farther to the east, and in all likelihood formed a circle now partly ploughed out by medieval or post-medieval cultivation. As it survives, the enclosure is truncated by a linear scarp, itself overlain by the hillfort rampart close to the north-eastern entrance. The function of this scarp is unknown, but it shares a similar alignment with many of the

Figure 3.23
Air photograph of
Battlesbury hillfort.

Figure 3.24
Air photograph of Casterley
Camp. Note that the soil
marks at the centre of the
enclosure, the site of a
possible viereckschanze
(later prehistoric/Romano-
British ritual enclosure),
encompass the head of a
coombe.

'Celtic' fields in the area and might be related to arable cultivation. The linear feature, on excavation, was shown to have a ditch on its eastern flank and so might have been a cross-ridge boundary preceding the hillfort. The incorporation of these earlier features suggests that the builders of the hillfort did not act in ignorance of their surroundings, and that the positioning of the ramparts and ditches was a deliberate choice, designed to permit an open view of the interior from lower-lying ground to the south-west. The

presence of at least seventy hut platforms within the interior also suggests that, rather than an early abandonment, there was a period of occupation on the site; this number is likely to have been much larger but for the effects of later ploughing.

Battlesbury (Fig 3.26) lies 1km to the north-east of Scratchbury from which it is separated by Middle Hill. This only partly interrupts the line of sight between the two, and the juxtaposition of both hillforts with Middle Hill seems deliberate. Battlesbury is effectively a contour fort consisting of two lines of bank and ditch enclosing 9.7ha. Like its neighbour, the defences, in part, serve to cut it off from the rest of the chalk spur on which it sits, particularly on the north-

western angle of the defences. It has two entrances, one to the west, the other facing east, and these are much more complex than those now visible at Scratchbury. The eastern example consists of a flanked entranceway

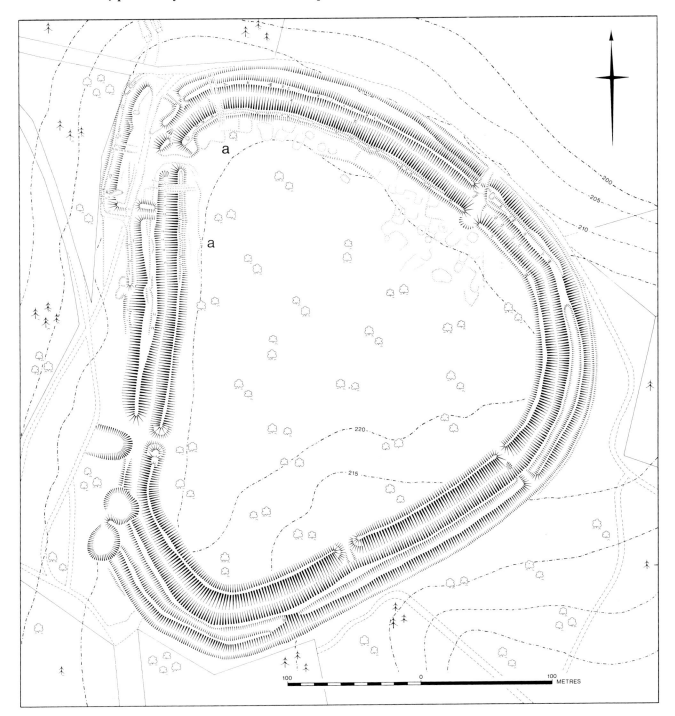

Figure 3.25
Plan of Sidbury hillfort, which occupies one of the most conspicuous eminences on the Training Area. Small-scale excavations (Megaw 1967) indicate a Neolithic presence, and the linear boundaries that focus on the hill perhaps imply an important function here during the Late Bronze Age. The interior was covered with thick vegetation at the time of survey, but a well-defined quarry scoop within the rampart was noted (a). Other, slighter features once thought to be hut stances, might be geological or result from gravel diggings. The central area of the hillfort has been removed by extensive post-medieval gravel quarrying.

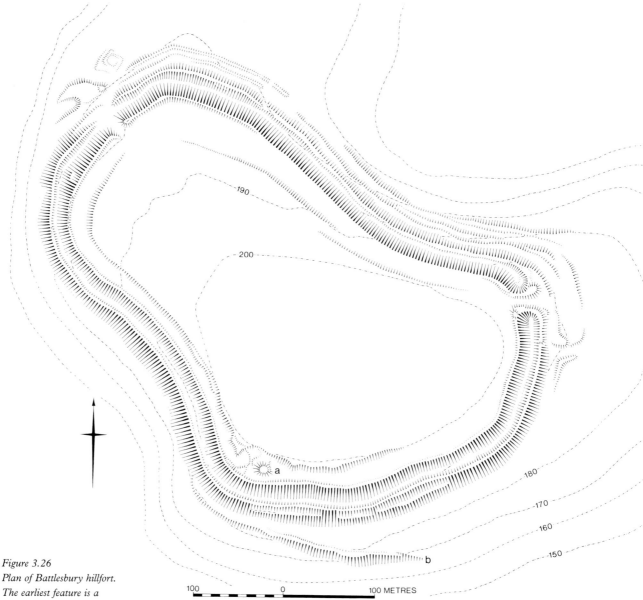

190

200

180

170

160

150

a

b

100   0   100 METRES

Figure 3.26
Plan of Battlesbury hillfort.
The earliest feature is a
small barrow cemetery on
the bluff overlooking the
headwaters of the River
Wylye to the south. One
barrow stands proud (a),
a second is partly exposed
lying beneath the hillfort
rampart, while a third is
almost covered by soil
creep from post-medieval
cultivation of the interior.
Within the plough-levelled
interior, aerial photographs
show the remains of 'Celtic'
fields, an element of which
emerges from underneath
the outer rampart close to
the south-western apex (b).

40m in length, with an external hornwork or façade. At the western entrance an inturned gap is flanked externally by a sub-triangular platform upon which there is a small circular mound, built, possibly, to restrict views into the interior. In this area, a number of human skeletons were found in the earlier part of 20th century, leading to speculation about the existence of an Iron Age cemetery (Whimster 1981).

The Battlesbury site was already heavily settled by the time its ramparts were constructed and slight traces of 'Celtic' fields pre-dating the ramparts can be seen within the interior. On the southern ellipse of the defences, a substantial scarp protrudes from underneath the counterscarp

bank and might relate to this earlier phase of field system or, perhaps, an earlier enclosure. All of the evidence points to this area as having been intensively used in the later prehistoric period. The hillfort defences date to the Middle to Late Iron Age on the basis of artefacts recovered from a mound overlain by the tail of the inner rampart; one of these, a glass bead, has been given a date of post-300 BC (Guido 1980). This accords well with other finds from pits within the interior, which, again, suggest that the hillfort was occupied from a late stage in the pre-Roman Iron Age and continued to be used throughout the following two or three centuries (Cunnington 1924, 368–73).

Paired hillforts are noted in other parts of the country, for example, at Hod Hill and Hambledon Hill in Dorset. It is impossible to be sure of their function, but in all likelihood they encompassed a wide range of activities including settlement, agricultural storage and defence (both real and symbolic). The construction and maintenance of the defences must have been undertaken by large numbers of the local population, and the sites might also have formed arenas for communal functions such as trade and exchange. They were, perhaps, also places where people gathered for ceremonial purposes, recalling the role of earlier causewayed enclosures. In this scenario, the hillforts might represent the communal centres of two groups, and the elaborate and labour intensive boundaries might embody an element of symbolic display as well as reflecting a highly competitive relationship between the two.

Knook Castle and Casterley Camp, although classified as hillforts, bear little resemblance to the three sites already described. They are both plateau forts, built on relatively level ground, lacking the advantages to be gained from any natural topography. At 1.7ha in area, Knook Castle (Figs 3.7 and 3.27) is the smallest hillfort on the Training Area and is only distinguishable from other later prehistoric enclosures by the strength of its surrounding defences, made up of a substantial rampart, fronted by a deep and wide ditch broken in the south-east by a simple entrance gap. The boundary has been damaged in a number of places, primarily by later ploughing within the interior and by cattle erosion, but it is most pronounced when viewed from the south; however, the site offers no obvious military advantage. In plan the enclosure is, again, unusual: it is rectilinear in outline and slightly concave along its long sides, with an angular protuberance in the north-western corner. Its peculiar shape owes a lot to the influence of pre-existing features; the ramparts overlie an earlier field system, with the curious kinks coinciding with those points where the bank and ditch cut through elements of the fields. Internal ploughing has removed all traces of detail contemporary with the hillfort defences.

The largest enclosure noted, Casterley Camp, encloses 27.5ha within a single line of bank and external ditch (Fig 3.7). This boundary lies on a level plateau on the north-eastern fringes of the Plain overlooking the Avon Valley. It is in a particularly poor position for defence, exacerbated by the fact that the boundary sweeps down into a shallow coombe on the south; this is the location of the sole original entrance to the enclosure (Fig 3.24). The circuit in places seems to be incomplete, consisting of short straight lengths of shallow bank and ditch separated by gaps no more than 1m wide. Only on the eastern flank, set well back from the edge of a steep escarpment, do the ramparts reach a substantial height with a correspondingly wide and deep ditch. Here, their course is noticeably straight for a length of 200m and it is suspected that this section has been rebuilt at some later stage (*see* p 84). To the north-east, a semi-circular annexe protrudes to include the upper end of a wide coombe (Fig 3.28). This has given rise to the suggestion that the annexe is the only surviving element of an earlier circular enclosure superseded by the hillfort. No trace of the return of the enclosure can be seen within the hillfort interior, either on the ground or from aerial photographs, and none was forthcoming during excavations here (Feachem 1971). It is perhaps more plausible to view the annexe and the adjoining eastern flank as an alteration to an initial construction plan.

Casterley Camp sits at the junction of a number of linear boundaries. At least three approach from the west, and another runs to the south from the entrance. Within the interior, other linear ditches are associated with an enclosure complex, one of which might be a *Viereckschanze* (ritual enclosure) (Corney 1989). Cunnington suggested that the hillfort, linear ditches and earliest phase of the internal enclosures were probably coeval, based on the general presence of Middle to Late Iron Age 'bead-rim' pottery (Cunnington and Cunnington 1913), but this might have been residual from the putative phase of rampart reconstruction on the western flank. Late Bronze Age metalwork, including a palstave and bronze stud, have been found in the immediate vicinity of the hillfort (Grinsell 1957, 115). Other activity is attested by a number of Early Iron Age pits within the interior (ibid).

The site of Broadbury Banks, on the northern escarpment edge, has previously been classified as an unfinished hillfort on the basis of its apparently incomplete defences. Approximately 5ha are enclosed within an oval circuit that is open to the

Figure 3.27
Air photograph of earthworks on Knook Down West (south at the top). Knook Castle hillfort lies at the top and the Romano-British settlement at bottom right. Despite being extensively masked by ridge-and-furrow, the earthworks of the 'Celtic' fields are clear enough to indicate that they have influenced development of the landscape. The S-shaped lynchet (upper centre) is particularly important, as it is likely to have developed around a pre-existing feature possibly a settlement.

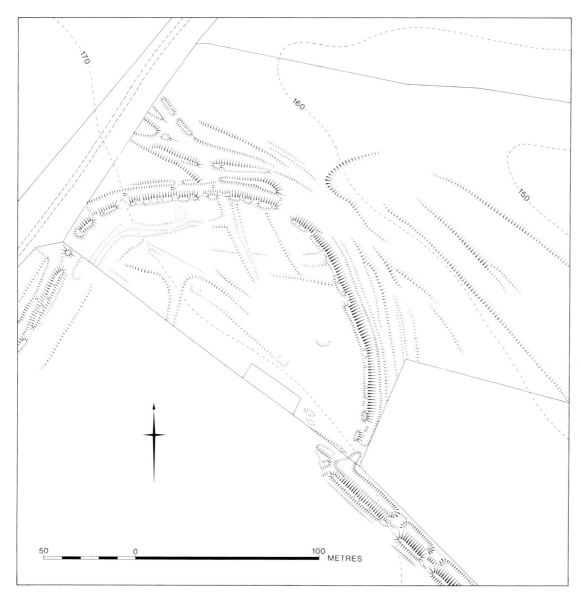

Figure 3.28
Detailed plan of
the annexe at
Casterley Camp.

south and sits on a steep north-facing slope. Colt Hoare excavated here but found no traces of occupation (1810, 4). Field reconnaissance would suggest, on the basis of the very wide, worn and shallow ditch and the slight accompanying bank, that this is not an enclosure but a rather fortuitously curvilinear stretch of medieval or post-medieval hollow way leading from the downs to the Vale of Pewsey.

Middle to Late Iron Age enclosed settlement

Recent work east of the River Avon has produced evidence for widespread settlement and agricultural activity in the closing centuries of the 1st millennium BC (Entwistle personal communication).

The enclosing ditch at Chisenbury Field Barn revealed a complex sequence, producing material of Middle Iron Age to Romano-British date, much of it sealed by deep ploughsoil (Entwistle *et al* 1993, 7). Two other sites, Warren Hill and Everleigh, have provided firm Middle Iron Age dates (Entwistle personal communication). Both are circular, or sub-circular, in outline and 85 to 125m in diameter. At Coombe Down geophysical survey has revealed a partly bivallate enclosure beneath the Romano-British settlement (*see* below p 82). Excavation of the inner ditch produced a saucepan pot from the primary silts and pre-Flavian samian from the secondary silting (Entwistle personal communication), suggesting that the enclosure was occupied throughout the Iron Age. The geophysical plot shows clear evidence of zoning within the enclosure (Fig 3.29), including a linear strip devoid of features, probably a street leading from the north-eastern entrance. On the north-west side the enclosure is univallate and features a curious 'stepped' alignment, which suggests it was respecting a pre-existing field-system.

Although limited in number and of variable form and area, these small bivallate enclosures represent a morphologically distinct type and can be compared to similar examples, of proven Late Iron Age date, found east of the River Avon and extending into western Hampshire. The best known examples are at Boscombe Down West, Wiltshire (Richardson 1951) and Suddern Farm, Hampshire (Cunliffe 1991). Both are dated to the Late Iron Age and viewed by Cunliffe (ibid) as being a distinctive 'Atrebatic' form of settlement.

To the west of the Avon, and in a prominent position overlooking the valley, an enclosure at Widdington Farm (Fig 3.30) resembles Chisenbury Trendle in both extent and morphology. Excavation has established its Iron Age date, although it post-dated The Trendle by perhaps a century (Ent-wistle personal communication). A curvilinear enclosure on Pewsey Hill, similarly, began its life in the middle centuries of the 1st millennium BC (Entwistle

personal communication). Other undated, though potentially Iron Age, sites were found on Stoke Hill, Copehill Down and Battlesbury (Fig 3.30). Stoke Hill has a curvilinear annexe attached on its northern side. Another enclosure at Maddington Down has similar dimensions to The Trendle. In this case, however, a 'Celtic' field system overlies it, and the line of the enclosure can now only be seen as a series of disjointed lynchets.

Another group of sites to the west of the Avon display markedly different morphologies and, judging from the associated finds, are of a different status and function to the sites described above. At Netheravon, immediately west of the river cliff of the Avon, air photography, supplemented by extensive geophysical survey, surface collection and limited excavation, has revealed an enclosed, nucleated settlement of the Late Iron Age and Romano-British periods (Fig 3.31). The enclosure encompasses an area of approximately 8ha and is univallate, except on the east, overlooking the Avon, where an earthwork terrace to the east of the modern road might indicate a second ditch. The site is defined on its eastern side by a 150m length of ditch, parallel to the river. To the north and south the ditch turns through approximately 90 degrees, while the western side, by contrast, follows an irregular course, almost

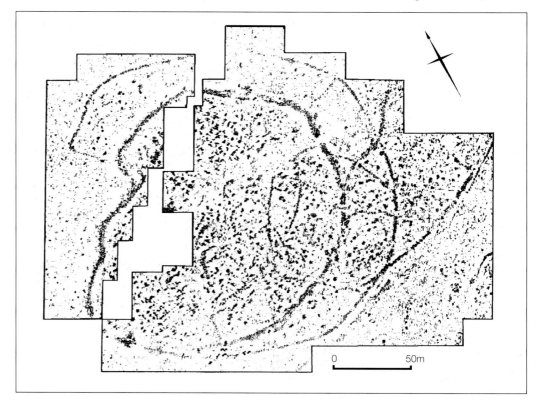

Figure 3.29
Geophysical plan of the enclosure and Romano-British settlement on Coombe Down. The outline of the double-ditched, Iron Age enclosure underlying the Romano-British settlement, can be clearly seen. Much of the additional detail noted relates to house sites and working areas within the settlement.

0   50m

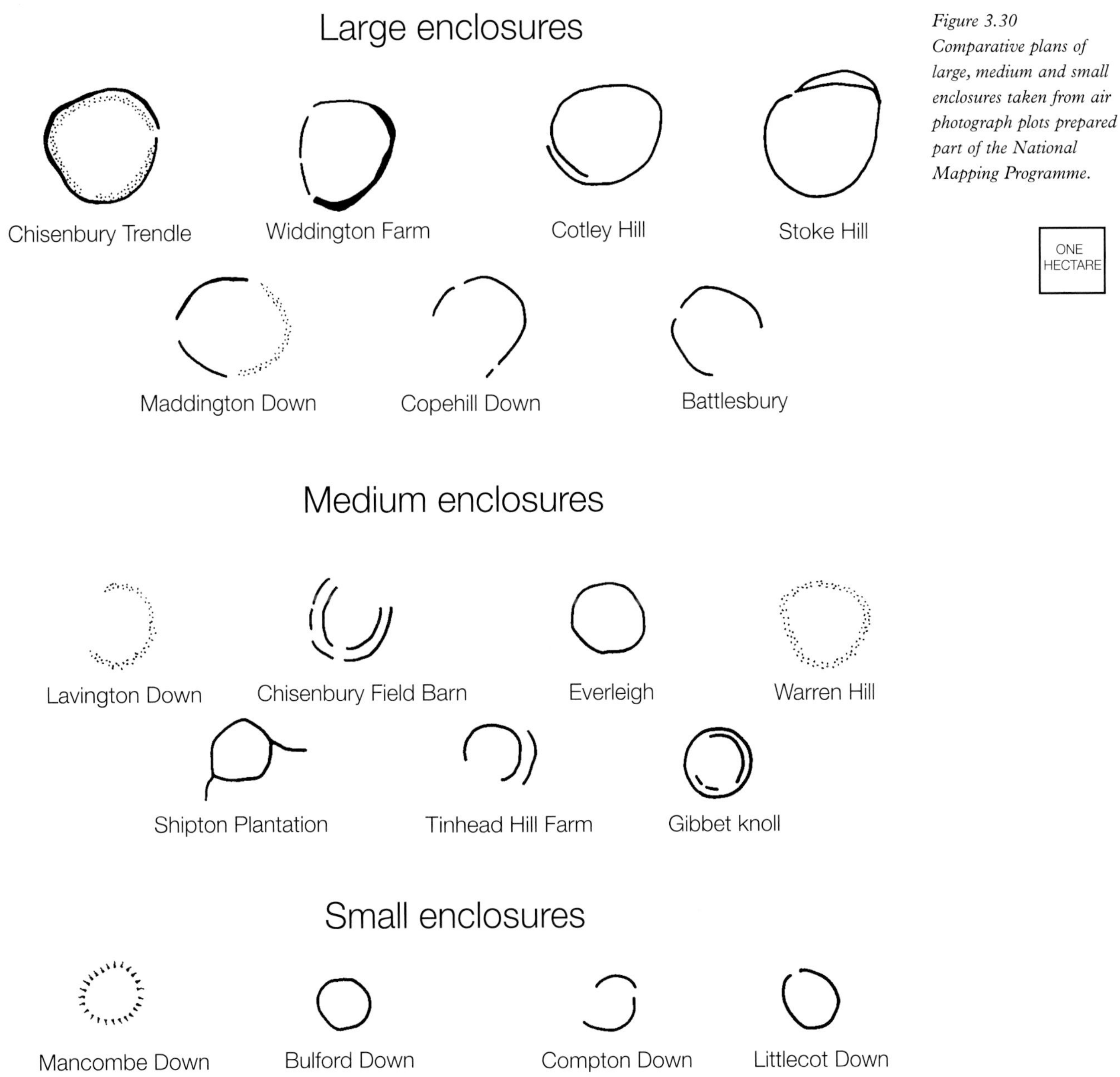

Large enclosures

Chisenbury Trendle   Widdington Farm   Cotley Hill   Stoke Hill

Maddington Down   Copehill Down   Battlesbury

Figure 3.30
Comparative plans of
large, medium and small
enclosures taken from air
photograph plots prepared as
part of the National
Mapping Programme.

ONE
HECTARE

Medium enclosures

Lavington Down   Chisenbury Field Barn   Everleigh   Warren Hill

Shipton Plantation   Tinhead Hill Farm   Gibbet knoll

Small enclosures

Mancombe Down   Bulford Down   Compton Down   Littlecot Down

certainly the result of abutting a pre-existing field system, similar to that noted at Coombe Down (*see above* p 82). There are two entrances: one in the west with inward curving terminals, and one on the south side approximately 50m from the south-east angle. Another possible entrance, on the north, might be hinted at by a pair of curving ditches, located by geophysical survey, and possibly representing a track heading for a point on the northern circuit 50m from the north-west corner. Geophysical survey and air photography indicate a very dense pattern of internal features including, in the south-east corner, a number of circular structures. In the north-east corner, which is the highest point within the main circuit, the geophysical survey recorded a small polygonal enclosure, 0.5ha in area, of unknown date or function but conceivably a shrine or temple. Excavation, in advance of service trench works in 1991, located the ditch of the enclosure close to the north-east and south-east corners of the circuit (Graham and Newman 1993, McKinley 1999). Although restrictions prevented full excavation, the depth of the ditch was estimated to be in excess of 3.5m and contained pottery of Middle to Late Iron Age date. Surface finds from the enclosure include a Durotrigian coin, a Late Iron Age type of strap union, a terret, a La Tene I *fibula* and a number of Late Iron Age *fibulae* (S Burgess personal communication. Records in Salisbury Museum).

This evidence strongly suggests that the Netheravon enclosure is a 'valley fort' of Late Iron Age date, comparable with sites in the middle and upper Thames Valley, such as Dyke Hills, Dorchester-on-Thames and Cassington Mill, Oxfordshire.

Approximately 2.5km to the north of the Netheravon enclosure, at Fifield Folly, cropmark evidence, coupled with surface finds of Late Iron Age *fibulae* (S Burgess personal communication), might indicate another site with a Late Iron Age origin. Located on an east-facing spur, 500m from the Avon, the site is clearly looking to the valley rather than the interior of the Plain. The air photographic evidence suggests a settlement extending over 4ha, associated with ditches and pits but apparently unenclosed. A large proportion of these features might be of Romano-British date, as much material of this period has also been found here.

Casterley Camp has already been discussed in relation to a possible Late Bronze Age or Early Iron Age origin and association with a discrete group of linear ditches. Within the main circuit, placed at the head of a shallow south-facing coombe, a group of earthwork enclosures was observed by Colt Hoare (1810, plan facing p177) (Fig 1.12). This complex, severely degraded by ploughing during the 19th century, was investigated between 1909 and 1912 by Cunnington (Cunnington and Cunnington 1913), and found to be of Late Iron Age and Romano-British date. The remains comprise a pair of conjoined enclosures, one curvilinear, the other rectilinear. These face south-east and open out into another irregular-shaped enclosure, linked by a linear ditch to the north-east rampart of the hillfort (Fig 3.7). The air photographic evidence coupled with the results of the Cunningtons' excavation make it clear that this complex has a long and complicated history. Despite this it is possible to reconstruct the earliest phase with some certainty. The southernmost (curvilinear) enclosure was of 'banjo' type: the original curving back of the enclosure is clearly shown on Colt Hoare's plan (1810, plan facing p177) and CUCAP air photographs; the rectilinear north-west extension of the enclosure is a subsequent addition. The adjacent rectilinear enclosure also represents at least two phases, both possibly

within the Late Iron Age. A great point of interest at Casterley Camp is the large quantity of non-local Late Iron Age pottery recovered from the enclosure complex. These ceramic imports are found in association with early Savernake products, an industry that is now known to have a pre-conquest origin (Corney 1997b; Timby forthcoming). In addition to the ceramic assemblage, some of the metalwork also suggests a higher status or special function with the iron and copper-alloy *fibulae* inviting comparison with the votive deposits from the putative Late Iron Age shrine on Cold Kitchen Hill. It is also possible that the eastern defences of the hillfort were refurbished at this date. Although the Cunningtons stated that they could not distinguish stratigraphic evidence for such an event, they recorded the discovery of butt-beaker sherds in the primary ditch fill on this side (Cunnington and Cunnington 1913, 102). From this overall finds assemblage it is clear that during the closing decades of the Late Iron Age, Casterley Camp was linked with other long-distance exchange networks, including regional *oppida*, that had access to imported Roman luxury goods. It has been argued elsewhere (Corney 1989) that the association between 'banjo' type enclosures, rectilinear enclosures (possibly *Viereckschanzen*), pre-Roman conquest imports and other substantial earthworks might indicate Late Iron Age high status and politico-religious centres on the Wessex chalk. It is in this context that the internal enclosure complex at Casterley Camp is best viewed.

The Late Iron Age on the SPTA was a dynamic period, in which, if the increasing complexity and density of the settlement record is anything to go by, there was a large population increase. There is also evidence for the emergence of coin-using groups and long-distance trade, through *oppida* and coastal *emporia*, with the Roman Empire expanding under Augustus and his immediate successors. It has already been demonstrated that along the Avon valley and eastwards from it, there is a pattern of distinctive Iron Age enclosure types. The area also has a distinctive pattern of indigenous ceramics and lies at the southern limit of 'Irregular Dobunnic' silver coinage (Robinson 1977; Van Arsdell 1994). Indeed, the distribution of this coinage suggests that it was probably centred upon a major Late Iron Age complex in the Marlborough region (Corney 1997b).

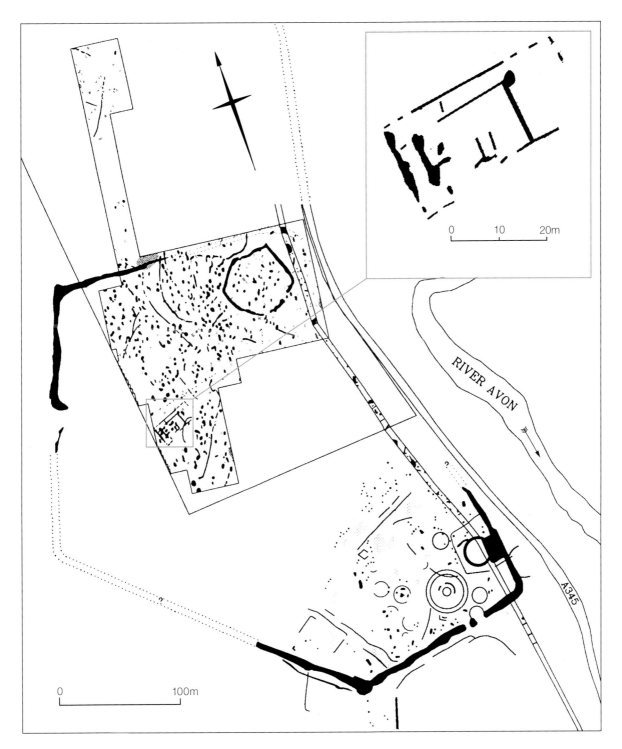

Figure 3.31
Composite plot from geophysical survey and air photographs of features at Netheravon. Four, possibly five, of the ring ditches in the south-east corner are likely to be round barrows forming a small cemetery on a terrace overlooking the River Avon. Other ring ditches appear to be roundhouses based on their association with pits and linear features. The dominant feature is that of a large polygonal enclosure of Late Iron Age and Romano-British date, with an entrance to the south, lying at the mouth of a shallow re-entrant valley. The survey further revealed the robbed-out remains of a corridor villa and a wide range of pits, post-holes and other anomalies. The inset shows, in detail, the villa.

One possibility, based on the evidence from Netheravon and Casterley Camp, is that a major trade route existed from Hengistbury Head, via the Avon valley and the Vale of Pewsey, to the main centre near Marlborough.

Farther west there is a marked absence of settlement and artefactual evidence until the Warminster region and the fringes of the Wylye valley. Late Iron Age coin distribution patterns here strongly suggest a junction between two highly distinctive zones. South of the Wylye the coin and ceramic assemblages are 'Durotrigian' and associated with large settlements of the type encountered at Stockton Earthworks, Hanging Langford Camp, Ebsbury and Hamshill Ditches (English Heritage forthcoming). In the Warminster area and the western end of the Vale of Pewsey the dominant coin distribution is 'Dobunnic' (Van Arsdell 1994), extending as far south as the shrine above the source of the Wylye at Cold Kitchen Hill (English Heritage forthcoming). Van Arsdell (1994, 23–5, map 19) goes so far as to suggest that the western half of Salisbury Plain was a 'no man's land' between neighbouring tribal confederations. This is perhaps an extreme view; the general lack of clearly identifiable Late Iron Age settlement on the western side of the Plain might testify more directly to the damaging effects of later agricultural regimes.

4
The Romano-British Period
(AD 43–c AD 413)

The Roman conquest of AD 43 and the annexation of much of southern Britain into the Roman Empire seems to have led to fundamental changes in the archaeological record. Apart from the incursion of troops as part of the military operation, there are no other records of accompanying large-scale folk movements, but the changes wrought on the inhabitants of the countryside were profound. In many areas a new road system was established, often using the military routes, and an organised town and market network developed. Much of what took place during the period of Roman rule probably stemmed from an indigenous source, stimulated by the imposition of Imperial tax and a market economy dealing with the widespread supply and consumption of a range of new commodities, and underpinned by a coin-using economy.

The aftermath of the conquest

While there are no Claudian military sites and no records of campaigns in the region, forts might be postulated at Cunetio (Mildenhall) (Corney 1997b) and Westbury. Stray finds of 1st-century military equipment are recorded from Casterley Camp, Rushall

Down and 'on the Downs' at Edington (Griffiths 1982), and might represent losses by patrolling cavalry units during the early years of consolidation. The major observable development during the period from AD 43 through to the final collapse of the Roman administration sometime in the 5th century is one of agricultural intensification and then decline. Pre-existing fields were redeveloped and expanded, and in some areas new layouts were established on a scale not witnessed previously. Massive lynchets and terraces developed and, for the first time on the Training Area, these were associated with the extensive remains of settlement. Eleven Romano-British settlements survive as earthworks, and other levelled examples are known (Fig 4.1). In many instances, it is likely that these sprang from smaller, Late Iron Age precursors.

At the time of the conquest Salisbury Plain was already heavily farmed, with large areas of fields and small clusters of open and enclosed settlements. The nature of the suspected precursors to the Romano-British settlements is undefined. Occasional unusual features, however, such as the curved lynchet trackway at Coombe Down (Fig 4.2) or a similar feature at the heart of the

Figure 4.1
Distribution map of
Romano-British sites:
(1) Knook Down West,
(2) Knook Down East,
(3) Chapperton Down,
(4) Cheverell Down,
(5) Wadman's Coppice,
(6) Orcheston Down,
(7) Charlton Down,
(8) Upavon Down,
(9) Compton Down,
(10) Coombe Down,
(11) Chisenbury Warren.

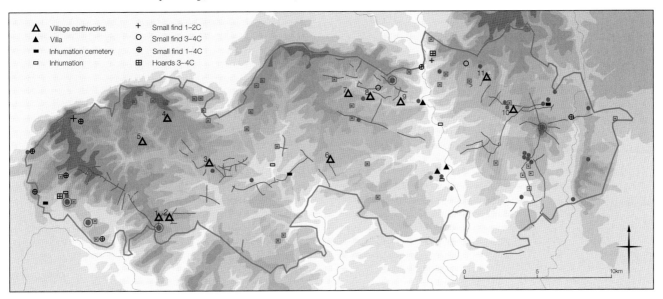

Figure 4.2
Plan of Romano-British
village at Coombe Down.
A series of sub-rectangular
building compounds and
associated trackways
lies on the summit and
slopes of the chalk spur;
the layout has been
influenced by earlier
structures (cf Fig 3.30).
A large dam across a
re-entrant (a) provides
a large cistern that might
be the Seathing Pond of
the Saxon Charters.

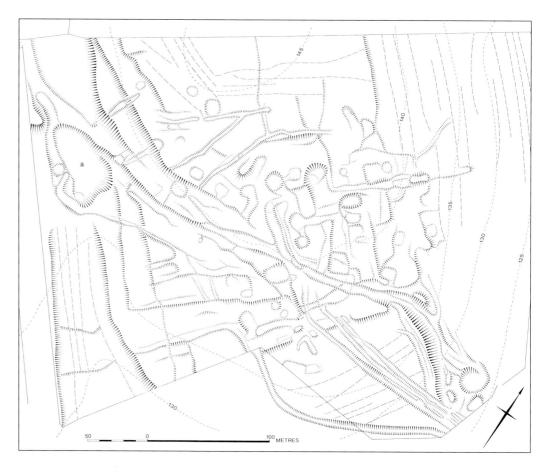

Charlton Down settlement, point to the reuse of earlier components, possibly enclosures. This interpretation was confirmed by excavation at the former site and is suspected at the latter site. A semi-circular length of hollow way, which loops down over the escarpment edge to the north of the partly destroyed Upavon Down settlement, also looks suggestively like an earlier enclosure (Fig 4.3). But perhaps the most convincing earthwork evidence can be seen at Compton Down where the Romano-British settlement is bounded on the west by a bank and external ditch, broken by a single entrance that strongly resemble the defences of a prehistoric enclosure. It is likely that many of the enclosures, built in the centuries preceding the conquest, either continued to be occupied or were re-occupied at this time. The sprawling, open, nucleated settlements were, however, an innovation. Their rise must surely relate to the agricultural intensification witnessed during the Roman era when they would presumably have housed those who worked the fields. In no instance has it been possible to identify higher status elements, such as larger and better-defined houses or building compounds, so status might have been displayed by other means; more probably the 'land owners' lived 'off-site'.

The Romano-British settlement pattern

It is the quality, preservation and variety of the large, unenclosed, settlement remains that rank them among the most important monuments in the region. The quality of the surviving earthworks makes it possible to undertake a detailed morphological analysis, although a refined chronological sequence is hampered by the lack of modern excavation. The exception is the area to the east of the River Avon, where excavation has provided a limited framework for the development of the settlements at Chisenbury Warren, Coombe Down and Beach's Barn (Entwistle personal communication).

Settlements survive as earthworks at Knook Down West, Knook Down East, Cheverell Down, Chapperton Down, Orcheston Down, Charlton Down, Upavon Down, Compton Down, Chisenbury Warren, Coombe Down and Wadman's

Coppice (Fig 4.1). The original number of settlements is likely to have been much greater than this since many less substantial sites have been destroyed or remain hidden. Levelled examples are thought to exist at Tilshead, Snail Down and Rainbow Bottom, Enford, among others. Immediately beyond the boundary of the study area settlements are known on Winterbourne Stoke Down, and at Codford (Colt Hoare 1810), Maddington Down (McKinley and Heaton 1996), Durrington Walls (Wainwright *et al* 1971) and Butterfield Down (Rawlings and Fitzpatrick 1996). Two basic settlement forms can be discerned: compact and linear.

Compact villages

Compact villages mainly occur to the west of the River Avon and are most graphically illustrated by the settlement on Charlton Down (Figs 4.1 and 4.4). Here, the earthworks

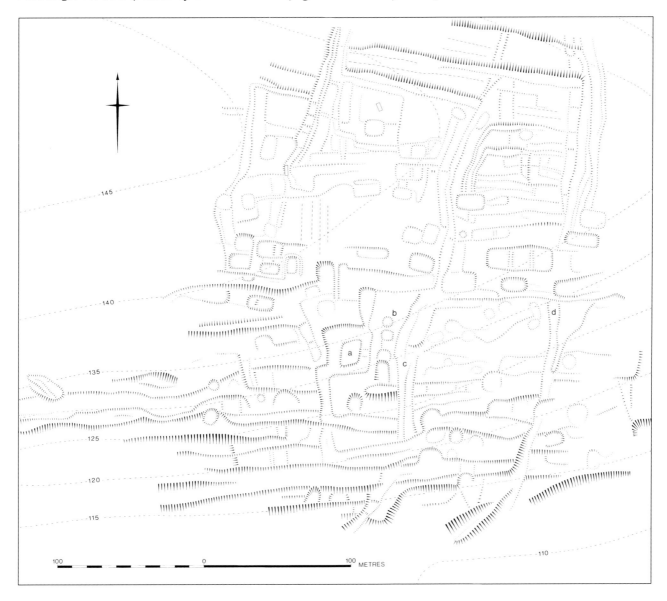

Figure 4.3

Plan of the Romano-British village on Upavon Down. Terraced into a pre-existing 'Celtic' field system, the settlement stretches for some 300m along a south-facing hillside above a narrow, steep-sided coombe. At least thirty hut scoops can be identified, often in small units consisting frequently of a main sub-rectangular depression, sometimes a circular subsidiary hollow, and a rectangular plot of land, perhaps a garden. At the centre of the settlement lies a small, sub-square enclosure with a hollow way leading from it to the valley floor (a). Immediately east of this is a series of regular depressions or 'reservoirs' (b) leading downhill to culminate in a large dam-like bank, all of which lie alongside another north–south hollow way (c). A third hollow way, 100m farther east, also runs to the valley floor (d).

Figure 4.4
Air photograph of the Central Impact Area, showing a major Romano-British settlement on Charlton Down (right foreground) that has spread out across the 'Celtic' field system, with its streets leading transversely across the hillside and into the valley. A massive dam lies across the valley floor adjacent to the settlement (centre bottom), while nearby is the rectangular enclosure 'Church Ditches'. In the distance (top left) is the settlement on Upavon Down. Here it is possible to walk along Romano-British streets in one settlement, through its fields and on, into the next settlement. The small white spots are tank hulks, painted and used as artillery targets.

cover a roughly rectangular area of approximately 25ha and are set at the western end of a broad, flat-topped chalk spur defined to the north and south by deeply incised valleys. The earthworks are set within an extensive pre-existing field system, and, given the finds of Iron Age pottery from the site, it is plausible that the settlement originated at an earlier, pre-Roman stage. A number of 'streets', which might in some cases be reused linear ditches or field tracks, give access to the fields. Within the village, shorter trackways lead to the house sites set within embanked, terraced or ditched compounds, usually, though not exclusively, rectilinear in outline and possibly originally enclosed by fencing or hedging. These, in turn, feature multiple rectangular platforms, terraces and depressions, representing the sites of former buildings and yards. Up to 200 potential building sites have been identified. Surface finds and observation suggest that some of the buildings were quite substantial, featuring stone footings (mainly flint, but including some Greensand), and ceramic and Pennant sandstone tiled roofs. Approximately 150m

south of the settlement, and linked to it by the continuation of one of the village streets, a small square enclosure, known as Church Ditches (Fig 4.5) could, on the basis of its morphology and comparison with sites such as Cold Kitchen Hill (Nan Kivell 1925; 1926), represent a small enclosed shrine originating in the Late Iron Age (Grinsell 1957, 99). The head of the coombe, separating the settlement from Church Ditches, is cut off by a substantial earthen dam (60m wide at its base (Fig 4.6)) that is integrated with a track running south from the settlement and therefore most probably of Roman date. The bank even now impedes drainage; the associated reservoir would have covered an area of at least 1ha and might have held up to 10,000 cubic meters of water. This feature, along with a similar but smaller example at Orcheston Down, is one of a number identified on the Training Area, and provides a rare insight into Romano-British water management on the Wessex chalk (Field 1999).

The Charlton Down village (Fig 4.7) was investigated by Hawley between 1897 and 1899 and described by him as 'Rushall Down'

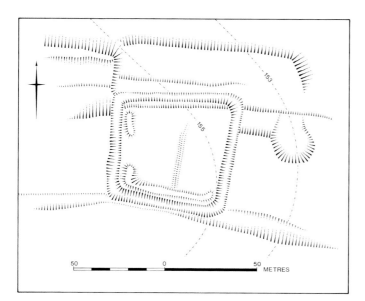

Figure 4.5
Plan of enclosure at Church Ditches. The interior is featureless apart from a small trench of recent military origin. No entrance is visible, but Crocker's survey produced for Colt Hoare, shows a wide inturned entrance on the east side (1810, 112, 175). Although the interruption in the internal bank is still evident, any corresponding causeway across the ditch has been obliterated by modern damage. The enclosure is set within a well-developed field system and appears to have been superimposed upon it. Some 20m to the east is a large hut scoop also cut into the field. Middle Iron Age ceramics have been recovered from the primary silts of the enclosure ditch (Grinsell 1957, 269 No.191).

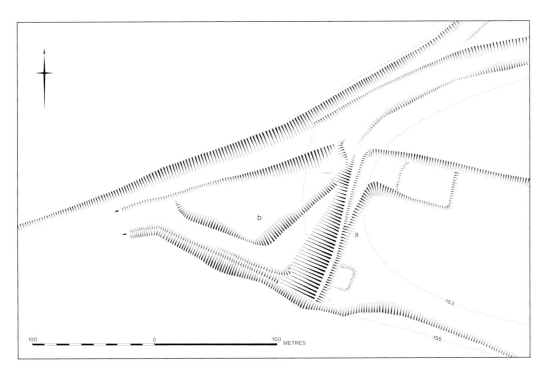

Figure 4.6
Plan of the dam on Charlton Down. This lies at the head of a valley, now dry, about 150m from the south-western extent of the Charlton Down settlement. The head of the valley has been cut off by the construction of a large bank (a), against which water has clearly ponded. The reservoir (b) is sub-triangular in area, covering roughly 1ha and it has been estimated that it would have held 10,000 cu m of water.

Figure 4.7 (following page)
Plan of the extensive Romano-British village on Charlton Down. This, the largest Romano-British settlement on the SPTA, covers some 26ha and comprises more than 200 hut sites situated on the summit and slopes of a downland spur, bounded by deeply incised valleys on its north and south sides. It is surrounded by contemporary field systems forming a continuous archaeological landscape extending beyond Upavon Down, a neighbouring village, 1km to the east. To the south-west a massive dam has been constructed across the valley (Fig 4.6), and farther to the south lies the Church Ditches enclosure (Fig 4.5). The form of the village is dictated by a pre-existing field system and settlement clearly spread out into fields as development took place. On the western fringe, at an interface with the fields, a large depression (a), at the junction of four hollow ways, possibly represents a 'village green' or, alternatively, a pond. The central area of the village, which lies on the summit of the down, has been damaged by shelling as well as a short episode of ploughing in the 19th century, but it is clear that structures here are of a markedly different nature to others on site, and consist of a number of close set rectangular village compounds (b), set on a common alignment with a major trackway (c). The hollow way that leads south from the 'village green' (d), towards a dam/reservoir on the valley floor, might have been connected with the supply of water to the settlement or the replenishment of the reservoir. In its final phase the settlement was served by two north–south trackways, both providing access to the valley floors, as well as feeding a number of lesser tracks that led out into the fields. One of these (c) led to the enclosure at Church Ditches (Fig 4.5). Two post-medieval dewponds (e) cut the Romano-British earthworks.

celtic fields

celtic fields

celtic fields

100   0   100 METRES

(though it spreads across several parishes). The excavations have never been fully published but finds include a bronze plaque of Minerva (Devizes Mus), numerous small finds including coins from Gallienus (AD 253–68) to the House of Theodosius (AD 378–411), a small stone altar, a variety of building materials and 1st–4th century pottery, though the majority dates to the 3rd–4th century (op cit, 100). Much evidence of agriculture, such as sickles and quernstones, as well as carpentry tools, saws and dividers, and household objects, was recovered (British Museum; Devizes Museum). In addition, pottery, stone, brick and tile, as well as a worn *as* or *dupondius* of Domitian (AD 81–96), were noted as surface finds during the RCHME survey (Fig 4.8).

The lack of modern, controlled excavation makes a detailed analysis of the site difficult. It is unknown whether the area represents the maximum extent of occupation at any given time, or is the result of gradual settlement shift. It is clear from the survey that there is a great deal of morphological variation within the settlement, with building plots and settlement compounds becoming larger and more widely spaced on the periphery. Even so, these plots are less well defined than those at the core of the settlement, and are seen as being used

Figure 4.8

Top left (a) Evidence of agriculture. Scythe and quernstone from the Romano-British settlement on Charlton Down (Devizes Mus 558f). Quernstone (0.28m diam) inscribed with numeral XXIII indicating, perhaps, that it was the property of an estate (Robinson 1997, 143).

Bottom left (b) Evidence for private property. A door-latch lifter (top) and a key from a tubular padlock (bottom; 0.17m long) together with an iron razor from the Romano-British settlement on Charlton Down (Devizes Mus 554, 555b, and 558).

Top right (c) Specialist tools. Top to bottom: blacksmith's tongs, spokeshave, handsaw, carpenter's dividers (max length 0.15m), from the Romano-British settlement on Charlton Down (Devizes Museum 542, 558 a, b and d).

Bottom right (d) Close-up of handsaw (total length 0.17m).

Figure 4.9
Air photograph of
Romano-British settlement
on Upavon Down showing
trackways cutting
transversely across the
hillside.

for a shorter period of time. It might be that these peripheral building plots represent overspill onto 'greenfield' sites, areas previously under cultivation. In particular, the central area of the village stands out. Here, the surviving features are shallower, having been degraded by episodes of ploughing, as well as several decades of shelling, and consist of a number of close-set rectangular units each approximately 50m by 40m in size. Within these presumably domestic compounds there are rectilinear house platforms, and this small but densely occupied space, covering 2ha, is likely to be the early core of the village. Immediately to the west of this a large hollow, 55m wide and 1.5m deep, sits at the junction of a number of tracks and might be the site of a former 'village green' or pond, which, conceivably, reuses an earlier hollow. Surface distribution of pottery suggests that the village was at its most extensive during the 2nd to 4th centuries.

Approximately 1km to the east of Charlton Down, is another, smaller, occupation area. This is probably contemporary with its larger neighbour since it appears to be

connected to it by a double-lynchet trackway, itself integrated within the field system that covers the area between the two settlements. This second village, Upavon Down (Figs 4.3 and 4.9), sits on a south-facing hillside above a narrow steep-sided coombe and sprawls over 13ha, but might once have been more extensive since military damage is particularly evident along its northern edge. The village is, again, composed of a number of building compounds that are set along narrow paths or lanes and take their form from underlying fields. These tracks feed out into the surrounding field system and provide immediate access to the now dry valleys to the north and south. Within the settled area there are at least thirty building platforms, and close to the centre lies a sub-square enclosure, 30m by 30m in extent, with a hollow way leading south from it. This enclosure has an unusual morphology, and it might be that it is the site of a shrine, temple or some other public building. Flanking its eastern side are a series of well-defined hollows, probably ponds, leading downhill and culminating in a large dam-like bank. Upavon Down was also investigated by Hawley, who does not appear to have noted the full extent of the village on the southern flank of the hillside (Hawley 1923, 230). He described it as being embanked, with an internal cattle enclosure, presumably referring to the prominent paddocks and field boundaries along the summit of the ridge.

The village on Compton Down (Fig 4.10) lies approximately 700m south-east of that on Upavon Down, and is located in a prominent position at the apex of a narrow east-facing chalk spur at the head of a coombe that leads to the River Avon. The site, which occupies an area of 4ha, has been heavily damaged by shellfire and military trenches but clearly overlies an earlier field system. Unusually for a Romano-British village on the SPTA, it is enclosed by a slight bank and external ditch, possibly of Iron Age date, on the west and for a short distance on the north. A narrow causewayed entrance breaks the line of the bank and ditch and within the interior there are a number of levelled areas and subdivided fields into which more than a dozen sub-rectangular hut platforms have been terraced. No hollowed streets or tracks can be seen in association with the site and it seems most likely that the settlement represents a small

family holding or homestead, contrasting with larger contemporary sites in the immediate vicinity.

The other major villages of compact form are Knook Down West (Figs 3.12 and 3.27) and Knook Down East (Figs 4.11 and 4.12). The former appears to have reused an earlier linear earthwork as a north–south main 'street', which ultimately gives access to the Wylye valley some 3km to the south-west. The core of the village is 400m to the north of Knook Castle hillfort and is grouped around a hollowed area, possibly a pond, at the junction of three 'streets'. This part of the village covers an area of approximately 6ha, the westernmost part having been damaged by ploughing. In form the village, like Charlton Down, consists of a series of rectilinear compounds, the largest of which are up to 60m^2 in area, and some of which overlie elements of the adjacent field system. Rectilinear and circular recessed platforms, presumably the sites of former domestic and related structures, can be seen within the compounds. To the south, a linear extension of the village consists of two large compounds attached to the east side of the main north–south street. These each cover an area of approximately 1ha,

Figure 4.10
Plan of the Romano-British village on Compton Down. Located at the east end of an east–west oriented spur at the confluence of two branches of Water Dean Bottom, it lies over a 'Celtic' field system, elements of which have been modified and utilised as strip lynchets, some showing traces of ridge-and-furrow cultivation. Settlement remains consist of more than a dozen rectangular hut depressions terraced into both sides of the hill, possibly representing two phases of activity. The spur was cut off by a low bank (a), now spread 14m wide in the south, but is narrower and better defined as it curves around the northern flank of the hill. This strongly resembles other later prehistoric fortifications, such as promontory forts. From a central entrance a further bank (b) extends along the summit into the interior. Associated settlement is obscured by later activity, but seems to have incorporated narrow terraces or subdivided fields (c). Cutting through some of these features is a series of large hollows or scoops (d to g). A group of three huts (h), possibly the main and subsidiary buildings of one unit, lie close together on a terrace on the southern hill flank. Farther south, small plots (j), if not other house sites, could also be gardens. No hollowed street is present, either as a settlement focus, or leading out to the fields or to the valley bottom. The remains are likely to be those of a small community, perhaps even a single farmstead, reusing or continuing to use the site of an earlier enclosed settlement, contrasting with other Romano-British settlements in the area.

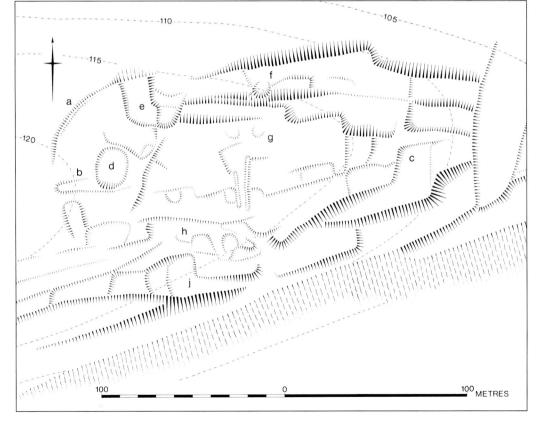

100   0   100 METRES

160

150

b

a

140

130

a

c

d

and are defined by banks with external ditches. Within each enclosure there are extensive remains of square and rectangular buildings, a number of which appear to have been robbed out.

Remarkably, only 600m to the east of Knook Down West, and connected to it by a length of hollow way, another Romano-British settlement of compact form survives on Knook Down East. Extending over a distance of 300m and covering an area of 3.5ha on a gentle, south-facing slope, the village is served by a single sunken track, and by a reused linear boundary aligned north–south. Aerial photographs suggest that, at an earlier stage, the village consist-ed of one large enclosure, which was subsequently subdivided by the track. The best preserved elements of the settlement now lie on its eastern flank, where a number of embanked compounds, enclosing rectilin-ear building platforms and yards, can be seen. Other slighter features, much degrad-ed by ploughing, survive on the western side and were recorded by Colt Hoare in the early 19th century (1810, 84–5). A detached part of the village can be seen 50m to the north, again flanking the hollow way and composed of shallow rectilinear hollows. To the east and south of the settle-ment a well-preserved field system retains a number of unusual features, including probable access ways and surface indica-tions of a single rectangular structure, pos-sibly a barn (Fig 4.11 (b)). At the base of the slope, to the south of the settlement, a number of tracks converge on a pond. Although it has undoubtedly been main-tained until recent times, there is little doubt that this pond was contemporary with the Romano-British village. North-west of the village is a large area (approxi-mately 9ha) devoid of cultivation remains and bounded on its north side by a linear ditch. It is tempting to view this as dedicat-ed woodland associated with the village.

Figure 4.11 (opposite) Plan of the archaeological landscape on Knook Down East. Like Knook Down West the Romano-British village focuses on a north–south street, again a reused linear boundary (a). The linear cuts through the 'Celtic' field system, which, unmodified by later cultivation, is better preserved than at Knook Down West, to the extent that a low-banked structure, perhaps the remains of a field barn (b), was recorded in the corner of one field. The best-preserved building com-pounds lie to the east of the street and front onto it. To the west, the buildings appear much more haphazardly positioned, but this is due to later damage. In the south the street forms a T-junction with a track providing access to a pond (c) on one side and the coombe leading towards Knook Down West on the other (d).

Figure 4.12 Air photograph (looking west) showing the relationship of the Romano-British settlements at Knook Down West (background) and Knook Down East (foreground). Traces of levelled 'Celtic' fields, as well as the original 'street' between the two villages (centre right), can be observed on this photograph, also the position of the former Quebec Farm (hidden by trees upper right).

The Knook Down village complex is of special importance because it has suffered very little damage from military training or agriculture. In addition, the proximity of the settlements to the Iron Age hillfort, and the reuse of the linear ditch system in the immediate vicinity, could suggest a continuous sequence of land use from the pre-Roman conquest period, but the majority of Colt Hoare's discoveries and the more recent stray finds (Grinsell 1957, 116), are of Romano-British date, however, and, as with most of these villages on the Training Area, 2nd–4th-century material dominates the record.

Linear villages

Other villages are all of general linear form. Chapperton Down (Fig 4.13 (foldout between pages 98 and 99)) has developed alongside a linear hollow way, which is likely to be a reused prehistoric linear boundary since it links to the known boundary systems at either end. The hollow way is aligned on a north-west–south-east axis and runs for a distance in excess of 1km. It is truncated at its northern end by a pond, and the remains of settlement compounds can be seen on either side of it, though predominantly on the slope to the north. Each unit or compound appears to conform to a standard dimension, usually defined by an embanked rectilinear enclosure 25m by 15m in area. Within these compounds are small clusters of sub-rectangular recessed platforms, probably representing former domestic structures. Bearing this in mind, the excessive length of this settlement suggests that in its final form it derived from a number of coalesced settlement units. These are surrounded by a 'Celtic' field system and superimposed upon it, ignoring its orientation. This is unusual, and it might be that Chapperton Down was not an agriculturally based settlement but rather one that was associated with a major routeway, in effect a roadside settlement or staging post on the route from Bath (Aquae Sulis) to Salisbury (Sorviodunum).

Orcheston Down (Fig 1.18) has a north–south hollow way that runs for a distance of 350m. This street leads into a large hollowed area, which might have functioned as some form of central public space, and then bifurcates immediately to the south. The eastern arm, which can be seen on aerial photographs extending farther to the east, is clearly a reused linear earthwork, as is the main village street.

On either side of it are remains of small sub-rectilinear settlement compounds, the majority of which fall into the size range of 35 sq m to 60 sq m in area. Post-medieval ploughing has erased all but the coarsest detail; nonetheless, rectilinear and circular hollows are visible within these compounds. On the eastern fringes of the settled area a large pond, which is likely to be of Roman date and reuses elements of an earlier field system, again demonstrates the importance attached to water management by the inhabitants of these villages. Quantities of 1st–4th century pottery were found in the area during field survey, suggesting that the site might have been occupied throughout the Roman period.

Chisenbury Warren lies at the eastern end of the coombe known as Rainbow Bottom, 4km east of the River Avon. The site again occupies a south-facing slope and covers an area of approximately 5ha (Figs 4.14 and 4.15). The earthworks are best preserved over the westernmost 300m of the village and show a number of clearly defined and regularly spaced properties, 30m to 45m wide and up to 70m in length, fronting onto a street that survives as a substantial terrace way. Within each property rectilinear hollows are apparent, including a number of more substantial examples at the rear. This suggests a differentiation between these larger buildings and the smaller ancillary structures closer to the road. Excavation revealed a Late Iron Age origin for the settlement and identified evidence for occupation shift through to the late Roman period (Entwistle et al 1994, 10–17). The earliest features represent Late Iron Age spade-dug cultivation, succeeded by settlement of 1st–2nd-century date. The later Roman village was concentrated towards the south-west, where the earthwork remains are best preserved. Structural remains included stone buildings set into terraces in the hillside. Evidence for cultivation and the continued accumulation of deep plough soils in lynchets adjacent to the site was dated to the 3rd and 4th centuries (op cit, 17). One trench also produced evidence for iron smelting, probably of later Roman date (ibid).

Two kilometres south-east of Chisenbury Warren, occupation at the Late Iron Age site on Coombe Down (see p 82 above) has been shown by excavation to have continued into the Romano-British period (Entwistle et al 1993, 10–17; 1994, 17–24). By comparison with the other villages on the Training Area, Coombe Down is, with an area of

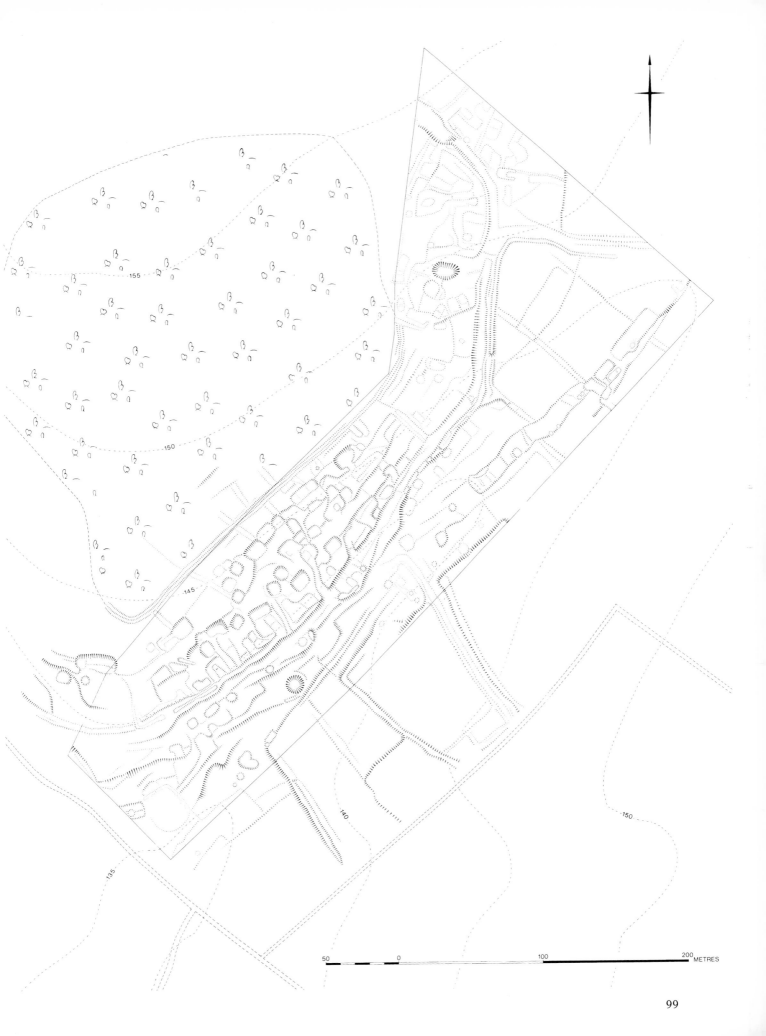

155

150

145

140

150

135

50   0   100   200 METRES

Figure 4.14
(previous page)
Plan of Romano-British
village at Chisenbury
Warren. Although having
the appearance of a
single-row settlement, a
morphology better
recognised in medieval
villages, the site history
is much more complex.
Settlement did, indeed,
focus on the linear street,
but the property divisions
represent the result of
occupation shift over a
considerable period of time.
Excavation suggests a
Late Iron Age origin for
this settlement, with
occupation continuing
intermittently through to
the late Roman period.

Figure 4.15 (opposite)
Air photograph of the
Roman-British settlement
at Chisenbury Warren
(looking north-west).
The 'street' lying parallel
to the valley floor is clearly
visible, as are house
platforms to the right of it.
'Celtic' fields are extant on
the opposite side of the
valley and extend to the
valley floor. Later quarrying
has extracted a narrow
strip of gravel that lay
along the valley floor. The
later warren lay among
the trees (centre right).

approximately 2ha, comparatively small. It is of linear form and sits at the south-western end of a chalk spur, with the settlement area lying to the north of a track or street (Fig 4.2). The settled area has been heavily ploughed in modern times and much of the detail, therefore, is missing; nonetheless, a number of sub-rectangular building platforms and lengths of low walling can be identified, which share an alignment with the underlying field system. The re-entrant to the west of the site appears to have been dammed, creating a large pond, possibly contemporary with the village. Indeed, this might be the spring pond *'Igean seath'* or 'Combesdeane Well' mentioned in AD 934 and AD 1591, respectively, although Crawford identified these features with 'Sadler's Pit', which he placed immediately to the south-east of the village (Crawford and Keiller 1928, 140). In the early Roman period the site appears to have been a small arable farming community. Cultivation continued in the late Roman period and, on the evidence of the quantified ceramic fine wares, the status of the village appears to have been higher than that of the neighbouring centres at Chisenbury Warren and Beach's Barn (Entwistle *et al* 1994, 23). There might have been a reduction in farming activity in the 5th century, but in the late 5th or 6th century a sunken-floored building was constructed adjacent to a field boundary (Entwistle *et al* 1993, 14).

The linear village on Cheverell Down (Fig 4.16) lies at the head of a south-facing re-entrant. Ploughing has heavily damaged the village but several sub-rectangular building platforms can be seen, some of which are placed within compounds, themselves reflecting the outline of an underlying 'Celtic' field system. Here too, a flight of dams across the re-entrant provided a secure water supply.

At Wadman's Coppice (Fig 4.17) a number of platforms associated with Roman pottery, were noted on the west side of the sheep enclosure. According to Cunnington, the village might have been more extensive, perhaps more than 300m in length, and almost certainly incorporating an adjacent enclosure (Cunnington MSS Devizes Museum). The settlement was placed close to the head of a re-entrant that contained a flight of dams, which, even today, hold water (Fig 4.18). A cemetery of Romano-British date, comprising fifteen skeletons, some contained within wooden coffins, was found nearby during military trenching in 1916 (Engleheart 1915–17, 500–1).

Late Roman fine wares and part of a *tegula* have been recorded from the probable sheep enclosure on Warden's Down (Grinsell 1957, 46) but no earthworks commensurate with settlement have been noted by the present survey (Fig 4.19). Similar finds have come from a number of sites, including an enclosure to the west of Slay Barrow, on the Central Ranges and from close to Tilshead.

Romano-British cultivation

Much of the evidence for the extent of Romano-British cultivation rests on the association of field systems with known villages. Other extensive areas of well-developed fields, not directly associated with known villages, survive, suggesting that new sites await discovery or that the villages worked very large areas. The field patterns around Knook and Church Pits have already been described and, although they originate in the pre-Roman period, there seems little doubt that there was consolidation and expansion as the Romano-British villages spread over existing fields.

On the Central Ranges, and to the east of the River Avon, molluscan evidence points to a marked intensification of arable farming in the Roman period. This is especially clear around Sidbury Hill and Weather Hill (Bradley *et al* 1994, 108, 111 and 120), while at Chisenbury Warren similar evidence was recovered for an intensification of arable production during the late Roman period (Entwistle *et al* 1994, 9–10). Perhaps the most intensive agricultural activity took place around the settlements of Charlton, Upavon and Compton (Figs 4.4, 4.9 and 4.18). Fields here have been so intensively worked that lynchets standing to a height of 6m have been created (Fig 4.20). Breaks of slope and ledges on the scarp face point to different phases of activity and in some cases it is possible to distinguish up to three phases. The aerial survey plot shows the skeletal outline of the fields, but ground observations indicate that, in almost every case, shallow subdivisions are present, as well as shallow ramps for access to the fields and entrances between contiguous paddocks. These fields on the Central Impact area, which were integral to the villages, remoulded an earlier agricultural landscape to such an extent that no gaps can now be discerned. It is noteworthy, however, that those fields closest to the villages are less well preserved.

This might mean that they were less intensively cultivated or that they were put to a different use. In places the orientation of the fields coincides with that of the contours and here the earthworks develop a 'strip-like' appearance, with well-developed terraces extending for a distance of 750m but with no cross-divisions. On further investigation the fields around the Charlton Down settlement (Fig 4.21) can be broken up into at least five main blocks, each coinciding with a piece of downland itself

Figure 4.16
Plan of Romano-British village on Cheverell Down. Situated at the head of a south-facing coombe, the settlement earthworks stretch for 300m along the west side of a street (a) and consist of more than thirty-five hut stances and hollows, some subrectangular, others circular, terraced into the hillside and set within a preexisting landscape of 'Celtic' fields. In some cases compounds consist of a large scoop with a smaller subsidiary building together with an attached open area, perhaps a garden. A major bank (b), one of a series across the valley bottom, might have been used to pond water.

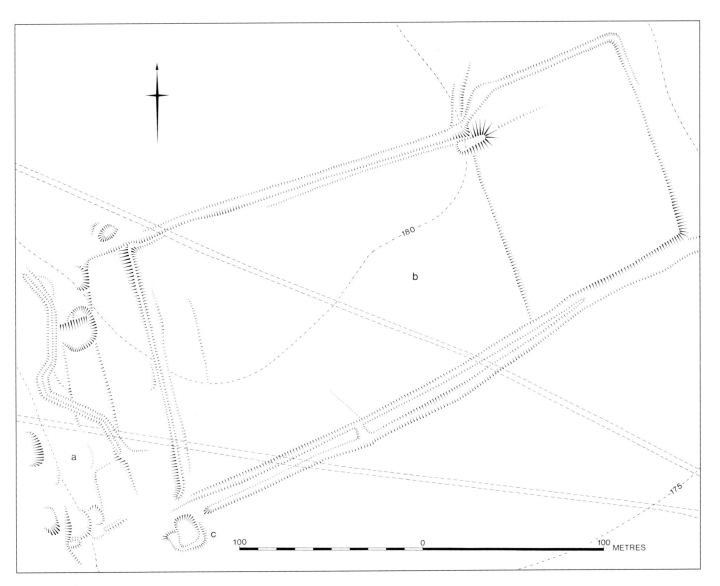

defined by natural valleys and other pronounced breaks of slope. Each constituent block covers approximately 100 ha and the whole area is bounded to the south by Old Nursery Ditch, a prehistoric linear boundary. To the south of this the 'Celtic' fields have been less intensively worked and it is tempting to see the linear boundary (which is dramatically 'skylined' from the north) as having been used at this time as a southern boundary to the cultivated lands being worked from the Romano-British villages to the north. There is no evidence that these fields extended across the village earthworks. Instead, as can be seen on Charlton Down and other sites, settlement spread from an earlier core onto former arable, 'greenfield' sites. Prominent pre-existing lynchets might have been levelled in anticipation of development that

never materialised; alternatively, these buffer zones might have been used as pasture for milking cattle or sheep or as storage areas for tools, agricultural machinery and harvested crops. In addition, sheep and cattle could easily have been housed and fed here. Thus the separation between domestic, pastoral and arable might have operated much like the 'infield-outfield' agricultural systems known from the medieval period. The crops grown during this time would have included wheat and barley, but more exotic crops such as vines should be suspected, especially in those areas with an eastern or southern aspect.

Water supply could have proved a problem with such large villages and extensive cultivation. The provision of many villages with dams, cisterns and ponds might even have been part of an attempt to

Figure 4.17

Plan of Romano-British village at Wadman's Coppice. Situated on the east slopes of a small south-facing coombe, the site consists of half a dozen hut stances placed within the remnants of an earlier 'Celtic' field system (a). A more recent military trench cuts through the settlement. To the east of the settlement, and extending across the summit of the hill is a sub-rectangular, ditched sheep enclosure with an internal subdivision of later date (b). A post-medieval pond, adjoining the west end of the hollow way, lies to the south of the enclosure (c).

furnish the fields with an irrigation system, as much as providing water for domestic and stock use.

In addition to the above evidence, notice should also be taken of the number of 'grain driers' or malting kilns that have been recorded, ranging from Knook Down and Codford on the west to Sidbury in the east, including the so-called 'hypocausts' recorded by Cunnington and Colt Hoare.

Three substantial examples have been excavated in recent years: at Durrington (Wainwright *et al* 1971), Butterfield Down (Rawlings and Fitzpatrick 1996) and Beach's Barn (Entwistle *et al* 1993, 5). All are of later Roman date, probably 4th century, and point, possibly, to the introduction of new agricultural products and an intensification of cereal production as a result of late Roman provincial policy (Corney 1997b).

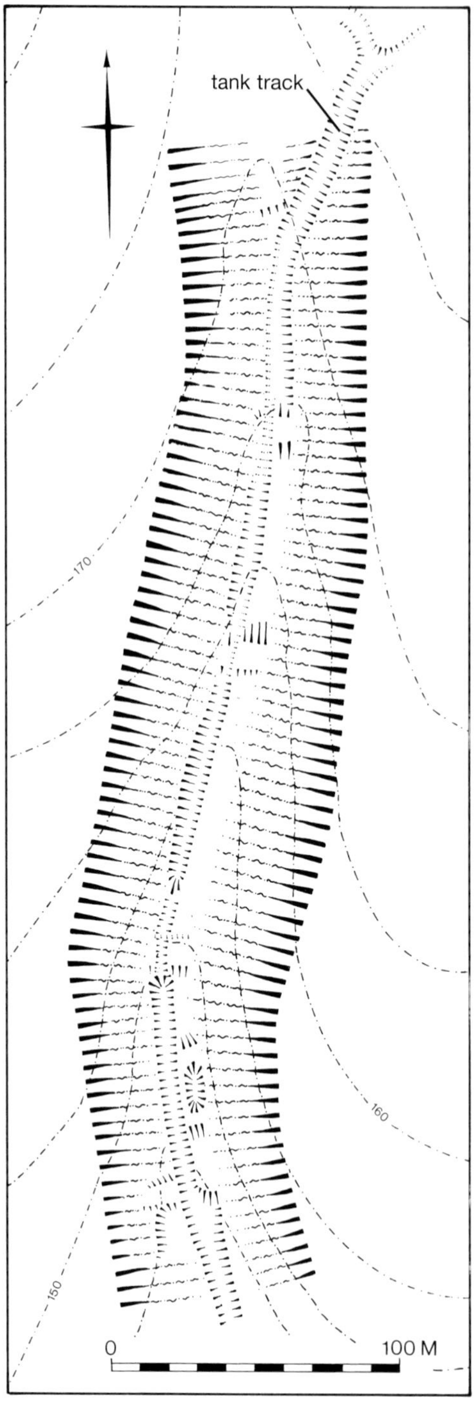

Villa settlement

Prior to the SPTA survey, the known Romano-British settlement pattern appeared anomalous, when compared to other areas of the Wessex chalk, in terms of the apparent lack of villas. The evidence for villas on or near Salisbury Plain was indeed limited. A major villa complex was known at Pit Mead, in the Wylye valley near Warminster (Colt Hoare 1821, 108), while at Netheravon, in the Avon valley, part of a substantial building was investigated by Hawley (Grinsell 1957, 91). Another large villa complex is known to exist under Manningford Bruce church in the Vale of Pewsey (Johnson and Walters 1988). These three sites alone suggested that a more extensive pattern of villas might exist around the fringes of the Plain. Careful examination of the Wiltshire SMR, coupled with information from local farmers, has resulted in the identification of two more villa sites on the SPTA; a number of others are suspected.

Some 500m to the south of the building recorded by Hawley at Netheravon, large quantities of Romano-British material, including building stone, tile, more than 100 coins (from the 1st to early 5th centuries), brooches, lead weights, two steelyards and a hoard of pewter vessels have been recorded (Stuart Burgess personal communication). Geophysical survey (Fig 3.31) located a large Roman villa of winged corridor form set just below the crest of a hill on a south-facing slope within the western defences of the Late Iron Age enclosure at Netheravon. The villa measures approximately 36m east–west and 20m north–south at the wings. A weak linear trend to the north of the villa building might indicate a boundary wall. Excavation, in advance of a service pipeline, 150m east of the villa, recorded extensive traces of Romano-British settlement, presumably associated with the villa

Figure 4.18
Water management at Wadman's Coppice. Lying south-west of the Romano-British settlement (Fig 4.17), several large banks cut across the coombe floor and, even now, pond water.

tank track

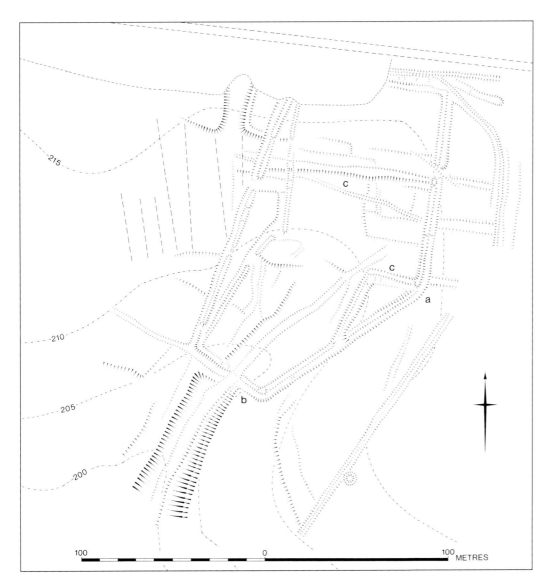

Figure 4.19
Sheep enclosure at Warden's Down. This enclosure lies at the head of a re-entrant above one of the steep-sided coombes that leads south towards the village of Imber. The polygonal enclosure covers an area of 1.5ha, and consists of a bank of relatively sharp profile with a corresponding external ditch (a). An entrance gap exists in the bank on the south side leading into the re-entrant (b). Other small subdivisions and additions suggest that the enclosure has been remodelled on a number of occasions (c). The enclosure overlies slight traces of a 'Celtic' field system, but ridge-and-furrow cultivation has largely destroyed these earlier fields.

(Graham and Newman 1993). The bulk of the material associated with the settlement was of 3rd- and 4th-century date, although earlier material was also present. It is quite possible that the villa at this site represents a continuation of the Late Iron Age enclosed settlement described above (*see* p 85).

Five kilometres north of Netheravon, at Compton, where Water Dean Bottom joins the River Avon, pipeline laying in 1966 exposed quantities of Roman building debris, plaster, pottery and other materials (Anon 1967, 126). Geophysical survey failed to locate any structural remains but, during the drought of 1995, air photography recorded a series of parchmarks on a south-facing slope immediately to the north of Compton Farm Cottages. Although somewhat indistinct, the marks appear to show part of a double-ditched enclosure of at least 1ha with traces of internal stone structures. On the opposite side of the valley re-entrant, another two buildings have been located by fieldwalking (S Burgess personal communication; Entwistle *et al* 1994, 4). Finds from this site include Pennant sandstone roof tiles, a flue tile, *fibulae* and four 4th-century coins. The cumulative evidence strongly suggests that Compton was also the site of a villa with extensive associated structures. The location of the site, at the confluence of Water Dean Bottom and the River Avon, places it in an ideal position to exploit the extensive field systems around the villages on Charlton and Compton Downs. A little to the south, and on the east side of the Avon, at Littlecott, another building associated with Pennant sandstone roof tiles and

Figure 4.20
Ground photograph of
'Celtic' fields on Upavon
Down enhanced by
cultivation in the Romano-
British period. The dark
spots are old tank targets,
enabling the massive scale
of some of the lynchets to
be gauged.

pottery of Late Iron Age to late Roman date has been recorded in the ploughsoil (Entwistle *et al* 1994, 3), while to the north high status finds might indicate similar activity in the Upavon area (Fig 4.22). In addition to the sites investigated above, there are other potential villas lying outside the SPTA along the springline at the foot of the chalk escarpment in the Vale of Pewsey. Two, those at Charlton and Edington, have been confirmed by geophysics and field-walking. Others, such as West Lavington (Grinsell 1957, 120) and Erlestoke (op cit, 70), are suspected due to the considerable quantities of Roman building materials, including roofing tile, wall plaster and window glass, that have been found locally. In the Avon valley, the west wall of Amesbury parish church contains large amounts of reused Roman tile, suggesting the presence of a substantial Roman building in the vicinity, and a probable villa site has also been located in the Till valley south of Winterbourne Stoke (English Heritage forthcoming).

An imperial estate?

It has long been suggested that Salisbury Plain and other areas such as the Fens of East Anglia were part of an imperial estate; that is, territories taken under the direct control of the military government after the Roman conquest. This view was first proposed by Collingwood (Collingwood and Myres 1937) and it has been repeated by subsequent writers on Roman Britain.

Frere, for instance, pointed out that the area (extending as far south as Cranborne Chase) has an absence of villas and, furthermore, no towns, yet was heavily settled in pre-Roman times. This led to speculation that the whole area had been converted into an imperial estate as a punishment for the resistance shown at the conquest (Frere 1987, 266). Esmonde Cleary (1989, 106) adds the suggestion that soil exhaustion in late prehistory also contributed to the lack of villa settlement. Recognition of Roman imperial estates is derived solely from the discovery of inscriptions referring to them (Crawford 1976, 36) and, as no such finds exist for Salisbury Plain, identification here is speculative. The contrast in settlement patterns between imperial estates and those in private hands is not sufficiently detailed to enable recognition of an imperial estate on the basis of archaeology alone (Hingley 1989, 128).

At present, therefore, it is impossible to be categorical about the nature of land ownership on Salisbury Plain during the Roman period. It is entirely plausible that the area might have been held as an imperial estate in the early years of conquest and afterwards reverted to private tenure and here it is worth noting that, from what little evidence exists, there seems to be a hiatus in settlement and cultivation sometime in the 2nd century, with the majority of the villages and villas reaching their zenith in the 3rd and 4th centuries. Furthermore, the status of the agricultural workers might have varied a great deal within and between private and imperial estates.

Much of the work might have been done by tied workers, possibly even slaves, but the rich range of artefacts recovered by Hawley from the settlements on Charlton and Upavon Downs is not commensurate with what might be expected from a slave colony. In all likelihood there existed a close working relationship between the villages and villas, with the latter located in the river valleys, functioning as estate centres processing and transporting out the goods produced by the downland settlements. The find of a Roman quernstone with the number *XXIII* incised on its upper surface on Charlton Down suggests that it was part of an inventory of equipment held on an estate, in this instance perhaps based on the villa in the valley at Charlton or at Compton (Robinson 1997, 141–3). This would seem to suggest that by the later Roman period Salisbury Plain was not part of an imperial estate. Its status during the first two centuries after the conquest is at present unclear and an answer must await more fieldwork.

Communications and market centres

Evidence for a formal road network serving Salisbury Plain is non-existent. The route of the road from Sorviodunum to Cunetio (Margary 1955, 44) is largely conjectural, but it ought to cross the Eastern Range on, or close to, the line of the 'Old Marlborough Road' to the north-east of Salisbury. If this was the case, it would have served the settlements at Beach's Barn, Coombe Down and Chisenbury Warren, all of which lie within 3km of the route postulated. The villa settlements in the Avon valley would also have required a route to serve them and, though evidence is lacking, a Roman (or earlier) origin for the present roads should be considered. Similarly, the line of the Till valley forms a natural route between the Central and Western Ranges, linking the villages of Shrewton, Tilshead and West Lavington. A track linking Tilshead to Imber, probably part of a

Figure 4.21
Aerial transcription of archaeological landscape on the Central Ranges. The fields to the south of Old Nursery Ditch (a) are simpler and less well developed than those to the north where proximity to the villages ensured a more intensive use. Indeed, the linear boundary might have served as a property or land-use division during the Roman period. Other, subsidiary, linears (b) have become fossilised in the Roman landscape as double lynchet trackways or prominent field boundaries, and access lanes (c) lead to the higher ridge rather than the valley floors. Blank areas are simply those areas that do not respond to aerial survey, but where field investigation has shown there are further features.

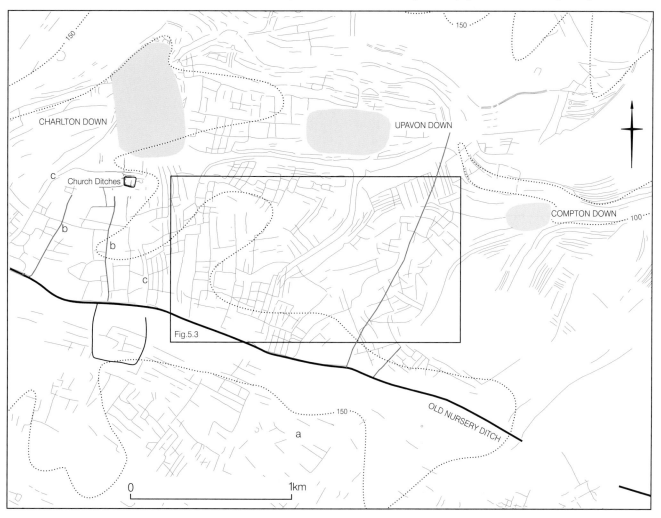

Figure 4.22
(a) Seal boxes decorated with a bee (diameter 24mm) and a sheep (diameter 20mm), from Upavon and Enford respectively (Devizes Mus:1984.46.11 and 1993.532).
(b) Miniature socketed axes, probable votive offerings, from near Casterley Camp (maximum length: left 21mm, centre 21mm, right 17mm), (Devizes Museum: 1994.130.1; 1994.130.2; 1984.46.5 (Robinson 1995)).

much larger network between Salisbury and Bath, and incorporating the settlement on Chapperton Down, might also have existed. The verification of these as early routes must again await more work.

Local networks of tracks serving settlements and their surrounding landscape are known from ground and aerial survey. As Gifford (1957, 7) suggests, the major routeways would have avoided crossing steeply undulating coombes, travelling instead along valley floors or the ridges of interfluves. This can be seen at Charlton, where at least three trackways follow the courses of earlier linear boundaries south from the Romano-British village to a ridge that, in historical times held a by-way. This would then have linked into a long-dis-

tance route through Netheravon towards Winchester in the east and the Vale of Pewsey in the north.

Beyond the Plain there are three sites that might have functioned as nucleated market centres, Sorviodunum (Salisbury), the probable 'small town' at Westbury Ironworks, largely destroyed in the 19th century (Grinsell 1957, 76–7), and Cunetio (Mildenhall) (Corney 1997b). The latter site might have been the most important in the region, and studies of Savernake Ware distribution, for which it was the market centre, have demonstrated that Salisbury Plain is within the marketing area served by the town (Hodder 1976). Indeed, quantities of such pottery have been found in villages on Charlton and Upavon Down.

5

The post-Roman, Medieval and post-Medieval Periods (*c* AD 413–1897)

The impact of political, environmental and economic change at the end of the 4th and into the 5th centuries AD on the settlement and land-use of Salisbury Plain, while unclear in detail, is with a broader view quite striking. The chalk uplands were emptied of settlements, long established cultivation patterns were abandoned and by the Domesday Survey settlements seem to have developed predominantly along the valleys and in the margins of the Training Area. The stages and mechanism of this transition are not fully understood, but might reflect the disruption and social upheaval that have been recognised elsewhere in southern England during this period (cf Cunliffe 1973; Fowler 1975, 123; Branigan 1976, 97). On Salisbury Plain, the more favourable valley positions, almost certainly already occupied, continued to be a focus for settlement. In contrast, the settlements on the Higher Plain gradually contracted, possibly due to a collapse of traditional markets and changing environmental circumstances making it ever more difficult to cultivate the marginal ground (Dark and Dark 1997, 19).

Evidence for post-Roman and Anglo-Saxon occupation

Along the length of the Avon Valley, from south of Salisbury to Pewsey, there is evidence of early Anglo-Saxon activity and cultural influence in the form of cemeteries and chance finds. A cluster of 5th-century sites have been recognised around Old Sarum but the majority are of 6th- and 7th-century date (Eagles 2001, 209). At Compton, north of Amesbury, four sherds of organic-tempered pottery, a sherd of late Anglo-Saxon date and one of 12th- or 13th-century date, were found in a service trench with Romano-British pottery dating to between the 1st and 4th centuries (Anon 1967, 126), and although organic–tempered ware has a wide date range from the 5th to 9th centuries, its possible association with Romano-British pottery suggests use, in this instance, at the earlier date. Farther north three button brooches are known from Upavon; two of them dated to the 5th century were found on the lower slopes of the downs at Widdington south-west of the present village, while the third is from the village itself (Anon 1985, 257). Recently, a copper alloy brooch in the form of a bird was recovered from Brigmerston Farm, Milston (Anon 1991, 148), while other material of early Anglo-Saxon date has been discovered on the lower slopes in Bulford, and Figheldean (Fig 5.1) (Grinsell 1957).

A similar pattern of evidence exists along the Bourne valley. At Collingbourne Ducis, a 5th- to 7th-century settlement comprising eight sunken-featured buildings was excavated (Pine 1998); it lay approximately 150m from a previously recorded 5th-century cemetery where some thirty-three inhumations had been uncovered (Gingell 1978). Other finds of 5th-century material have come from Collingbourne Kingston nearby (Eagles 1994, 15). Some twelve km west of the Avon, at Grove Farm in Market Lavington, a settlement lies adjacent to a late 5th–7th-century cemetery (Williams and Newman 1998).

Later Anglo-Saxon artefacts are also present at Knighton Farm, Enford, Durrington and East Chisenbury (Anon 1981, 206; Anon 1985, 257; Anon 1988b, 185; Anon 1990, 229; Anon 1991, 148). Unfortunately, the precise location of a chance find of a copper alloy disc brooch from Durrington went unrecorded, but it too derives from the bluffs above the river, either close to or within the present settlements.

On the Higher Plain, in the area of the Romano-British settlement on Coombe Down, a sunken-featured building was built in a hollow bounded by a negative lynchet and trackways. Occupation debris from the vicinity of the building included both Romano-British material, sherds of organic-tempered ware and early Saxon stamped pottery (Entwistle *et al* 1993, 12; Anon 1994, 154). It might be reasonable to conjecture that a number of the Romano-British settlements and fields could have continued in use but with a gradual abandonment and shift in settlement to the valleys.

In a number of cases excavations of barrows by 19th-century antiquarians have revealed intrusive burials of early Saxon date, a practice that was widespread elsewhere in England (Williams 1997).

In seven cases, these inhumations were in long barrows, although examples in round barrows also occur. The choice of these sites for burial re-affirmed their sacredness, as well as the significance of ancestors. They once again became focal places in the landscape, reserved for the dead with perhaps other unmarked burials in the vicinity,

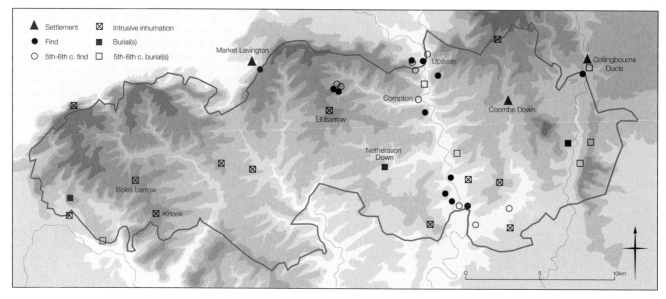

Figure 5.1
Distribution map of Anglo-Saxon activity and material.

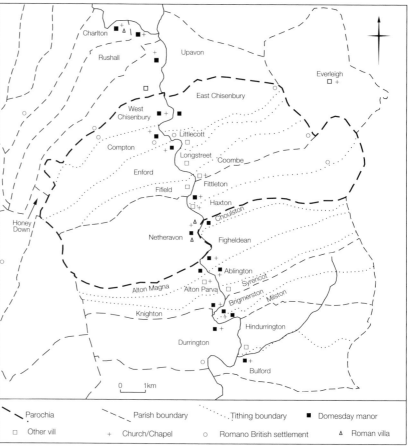

Figure 5.2
Tithing and parish boundaries along the Avon valley. The land covering the northern part of Bulford parish represents the tithe-free land, which included Hindurrington. Although some of the settlements were not specifically mentioned until the 12th or 13th centuries, some were possibly in existence much earlier. Everleigh, for example, was mentioned in an early 8th-century charter. Similarly, the Domesday entries for Enford probably include the holdings of Fifield, Longstreet and Littlecott.

and thus came to play a special role in defining local land-use by marking tenurial or territorial arrangements. Some were specifically named in 10th-century charters. Boles (or Bowl's) Barrow, for example, first mentioned in 968 (Gover *et al* 1939, 168), lies in an elevated position close to a later parish boundary that also served as a Hundred boundary. The Knook long barrow contained four headless, intrusive interments, which were found 'a little-way under the turf near the centre of the barrow' (Cunnington MSS Book 3, 33–4). This site, which again lies close to a Hundred boundary, has been interpreted as an 'execution' cemetery (Grinsell 1957, 80). Three Saxon intrusive burials occur in round barrows (Grinsell 1957), two lie on either side of the Nine Mile River, while the third lies farther north on the slopes overlooking Figheldean and the Avon. Although the numbers are few, the location of such burials in barrows, close to the river, helps to indicate a riverine pattern of Saxon settlement.

Apart from the intrusive inhumations, other Saxon burials have been identified from levelled cemeteries at Elston and Shrewton, and on Perham Down, near Tidworth. Here a cemetery dating to the late 6th or early 7th century contained four extended skeletons each accompanied by iron shield bosses and spearheads (Wilson and Hurst 1969, 241; Robinson 1987, 132; Nenk *et al* 1993, 287). At West Chisenbury, Enford, a shallow grave containing a skeleton with a socketed iron spearhead was excavated and, apparently, other burials lay nearby (Cunnington 1930b; Meaney 1964, 267).

A cemetery comprising seven small round barrows, situated on a south-facing slope just above the valley floor on Netheravon Down, compares favourably in form to other Saxon examples in Wiltshire and southern England. None is larger than 8m in diameter and 0.5m in height, although the possibility that they could be of Middle Bronze Age date should not be ignored (Struth and Eagles 1999).

Place- and river-names of Latin and British origin are thought to indicate the survival of a British population in the area. Urchfont is one of three settlements in Wiltshire that incorporates the Latin *funta* element, meaning spring or fountain (Gelling 1978, 83–6). The settlement lies at the foot of the northern escarpment near Wickham Green, itself a Latin name incorporating the element *wicham* meaning a Romano-British habitation (op cit, 70–74). Chitterne contains the British *ceto* element meaning wood, while Conock (Ekwall 1960, 121) Chute Forest and the River Avon, are both also names of British origin.

Figure 5.3

Aerial transcription of cultivation on Thornham Down. Some of the ridge-and-furrow is clearly contained within the 'Celtic' field lynchets (a), in other cases it ignores the earlier fields (b). Although one tithing boundary follows a prominent lynchet (c), a second (d) cuts across the landscape ignoring the underlying 'Celtic' fields, suggesting that the area was pasture when the boundaries where set out.

Estates and territorial boundaries

Bonney has argued that the incidence of Saxon burials discovered on territorial boundaries might indicate that the latter were established by at least the 7th century (Bonney 1976). A number of these boundaries also lie close to, or beside, Romano-British villages, indicating that there might still have been some recognisable feature in the landscape when each boundary was established. This is not to argue that the Romano-British villages were still occupied, but rather that there was a link with these places, even if it was merely use as seasonal pasture. At the very least, the deserted settlements would have been used as markers to orientate those working in the area and consequently likely to develop a special place in folklore and memory. The eastern extremities of Enford parish are marked by the deserted Romano-British villages at Chisenbury Warren and Coombe Down, while at Compton the tithing boundary with West Chisenbury cuts across the spur immediately to the east of the deserted Romano-British village there. A similar situation can be observed at Chapperton Down, Cheverell Down, Church Pits and Knook Down where each lies no more than 100m from a later boundary. Gelling has noted that where names with the Latin *wicham* element are neither later parishes nor Domesday estates, they lie on a parish boundary (Gelling 1978, 73), and Wickham Green, on the boundary between Urchfont and Easterton, is one such local example (ibid).

Most medieval parish boundaries on the SPTA form the characteristic pattern so prevalent on the chalk downland of Wessex (*see*, for example, Taylor 1994, 214; Lewis *et al* 1997, 107), whereby they extend in a rectangular, or 'finger-like' fashion from the valleys onto the Higher Plain (Fig 5.2). Within many parishes there were a number

Figure 5.4
Air photograph of 'Celtic' fields on Thornham Down overlain by ridge-and-furrow.

of estates, or tithings, that appear to have functioned as separate economic units throughout the medieval period. The tithing divisions ensured that each settlement had a balanced share of the available resources, with their meadows close to the river, arable fields extending from the settlement onto the downs, together with pasture and rough grazing. Through a combination of cartographic analysis and fieldwork, it is possible to trace these tithing boundaries for a considerable distance onto the Higher Plain. Spaced out along the Avon valley, they each measure between 4 and 7km in length. Close to the settlements they were probably established by the late Anglo-Saxon period, but their farthest limits might not have been defined until very much later, possibly in the 13th or 14th centuries when the Higher Plain was again being intensively exploited. In 1267, for example, an Augustinian priory was granted land at Honeydown (London 1979, 322) at the extremity of Upavon, Rushall and Enford parishes, a holding that can possibly be identified with the wedge-shaped piece of land abutting the respective parish boundaries and today known as Honeydown Ridge (Fig 5.2).

Almost any extant topographical or natural feature was used to define these later boundaries: in the 16th-century perambulations of the Duchy of Lancaster's estates, prehistoric linear earthworks and barrows were specifically mentioned (Anon 1860, 186–200). Some boundaries respect the edges of prominent 'Celtic' fields; the southern boundary between the parishes of Bratton and Edington, for example, is dog-legged where it follows the lynchets. There were instances, however, where prominent prehistoric earthworks were avoided – for example the boundary between Charlton and Rushall – indicating that the earthworks themselves were regarded as of little consequence.

Although Hundreds are not specifically mentioned in documents until the mid-10th century, they might have evolved from earlier institutions (Cam, 1944, 84; Yorke 1995, 125). In contrast to local tithing boundaries, their areas are defined by the watersheds of the rivers Avon, Till, Wylye, and along with the Vale of Pewsey, each valley being central to a Hundred. This emphasises the importance of valleys as the preferred zones for settlement and communication.

Figure 5.5
Strip lynchets still in use alongside Water Dean Bottom at Compton, with a large round barrow on the bluff, for example.

The downland landscape

Following the example of the Anglo-Saxon settlement pattern established for the Wylye valley (Hooke 1988, 135), the chalklands of Wiltshire might have presented relatively open countryside by the 11th century, with cultivation confined to the lower valley slopes but with extensive areas of pasture on the Higher Plain. Much of the area, certainly Netheravon, Warminster, Tilshead and Rushall, was in the king's hands or belonged to one of the great monastic houses that held land at Coulston, Bulford, Edington, Imber and Enford (Thorn and Thorn 1979).

Cultivation

Traces of ridge-and-furrow overlying 'Celtic' fields is a widespread feature of the Higher Plain, particularly on Thornham, Charlton and Knook Downs. On the spur connecting two Romano-British villages on Upavon and Charlton Down, ridge-and-furrow occupies both the southern slope and summit, and extends for up to 650m along contours. On Thornham Down it covers an area of more than 150ha as far south as the linear earthwork, Old Nursery Ditch, which might have defined the limit of this cultivated zone (Fig 5.3). Each ridge varies from 5m to 10m in width, and the furlongs are generally aligned on, and in many cases contained by, the 'Celtic' field lynchets. However, there are cases where ridge-and-furrow ignores these earlier fields and slices through the lynchets at an oblique angle. Although some of the shallow cross-divisions have been destroyed, in most cases the underlying 'Celtic' fields have not been levelled by this later phase of ploughing, which might indicate a relatively short period of cultivation and, possibly, a mere temporary extension onto the more marginal land. Most ridge-and-furrow appears to conform to parish boundaries but near the linear ditch on Thornham Down it crosses the boundary from Charlton into Rushall, indicating that the boundary had either not been defined or lay elsewhere when these fields were being cultivated (Fig 5.4). Ridge-and-furrow overlying 'Celtic' fields is present both inside and outside Knook Castle (Fig 3.27). Here the furlongs that lie parallel to the linear earthwork are in excess of 300m in length, and partly overlie the earthworks of the Romano-British village.

Elsewhere in Wessex, ridge-and-furrow cultivation on the downs has been dated to the 13th or early 14th century (Taylor 1997, 17; Fowler 1975), and a similar date can be suggested for the furlongs here. At Enford, for example, documents specifically mention furlongs above *Wolterdene* (Water Dean),

Figure 5.6
Sheep enclosure at Upavon. This enclosure, covering some 4.5ha, lies at the head of a small re-entrant on the Higher Plain to the east of Upavon and was described as a 'sheepe penning' on an 18th-century map (WRO 135/42/45). On its southern side, facing the re-entrant, there is a small entrance (a). In the north-west, set against the underlying 'Celtic' field lynchets, are two parallel linear banks that probably represent the remains of a sheepcote (b).

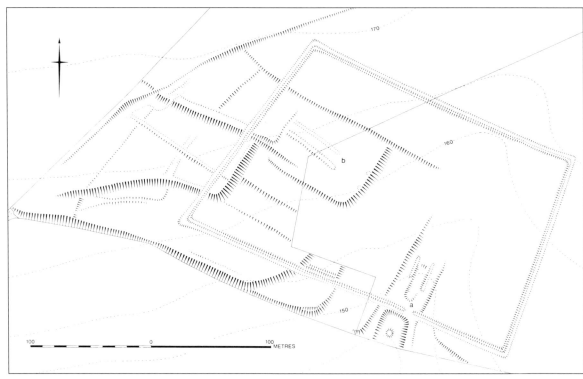

Waddene, and *Westersdene* (Wexland Dean) in the 13th century (Harrison 1995, 12), and in 1340 the demesne at Erlestoke included 125ha (300 acres) on the hill *'when sown'* (Stokes 1914, 139). It is also possible that some cultivation occurred on the Higher Plain much later. During the 16th and 17th centuries there was an extension of arable cultivation and temporary intakes for 'catch crops' on both lower slopes and Higher Plain (Bennett 1887, 35; Kerridge 1951, 115). At Collingbourne Ducis, for example, aside from the common field and its three enclosed fields, the manor farm included an outfield (Crittall 1980b, 111) that might represent a new field out on the Higher Plain. Extension of the village arable also continued here into the 18th century when much of Snail Down was cultivated (ibid).

Strip lynchets, long narrow terraces on the sides of hills, are much in evidence around the fringes of the chalk. Examples occur above the Greensand at Bratton, Tinhead and Rushall, while along the Wylye valley they are present on the eastern, lower slopes of Battlesbury hillfort and on Middle Hill farther to the east. Along the Avon valley, too, they can be observed at East Chisenbury, Upavon and Compton. Occasionally they can also be traced farther into the Higher Plain, some considerable distance from any settlement. On Bishopstrow Down strip lynchets are set on a south-facing slope some 2.5km from the settlement and close to the extremity of the tithing. Another curious example on Strawberry Hill in Great Cheverell, comprises a series of short lynchets on a south-facing slope, coupled with the absence of interconnecting ramps or accessways, and this, together with the place name, might indicate a horticultural function.

The strip lynchets at Compton are among the best preserved and most extensive; here they survive up to 2.5m high with treads 25m in width and up to 290m in length (Fig 5.5). Very shallow scarps between terraces indicate the former existence of other lynchets that have since been levelled. They are tiered along the contours on the slopes of the narrow valley, with ramps providing access to the terraces above. Farther west, towards the interior of the Higher Plain, a small platform that might have been the site of a building lies on the uppermost of a series of much narrower lynchets. These do not extend beyond the tithing boundary, but they do appear to utilise former 'Celtic' fields by ploughing over cross divisions, and a graduated sequence can be traced along the valley sides onto the Higher Plain, where the strip lynchets become less prominent and the earlier 'Celtic' fields are left standing proud. The process can also be traced at Middleton on Middle Hill, near Warminster.

Strip lynchets are generally regarded as dating to the medieval period and, like the episode of ridge-and-furrow on the Higher Plain, might have developed or, in some cases, been constructed in response to an increasing population coupled with a shortage of suitable arable land. However, it is equally conceivable that those at Compton originated at a much earlier date as the physical nature of the thin tithing, sandwiched along a narrow valley, might have encouraged the use of terraces to maximise the area available for cultivation.

Sheep enclosures

Large flocks of sheep, kept primarily for their wool and meat, were a common sight on the downs throughout the medieval and post-medieval periods. They also provided a valuable source of manure for the arable fields, which became increasingly important as larger areas were brought into cultivation. During the winter months flocks were housed in permanent sheep enclosures (Hare 1994, 161). Typically these are rectangular or trapezoidal in outline and comprise a small bank that might originally have been surmounted by a hedge or hurdling with an external ditch, although examples with internal ditches are occasionally found. Some might also have contained a structure to house both sheep and shepherds. Excavated examples on the Marlborough Downs have been dated to the 12th–13th centuries (Cunnington 1910a, 590–98; Fowler *et al* 1965, 62–6). Documents indicate that in at least one case, at Enford, much of the enclosure and internal building were constructed of stone (Hare 1994, 161). Some, such as a curious square example, known in the late 18th century as the 'Shepherd's Garden', on Rushall Down, are quite small, in this case less than 0.25ha (Andrews and Dury 1773). Adjacent to a major drove route between Netheravon and Market Lavington, it might have been used as a

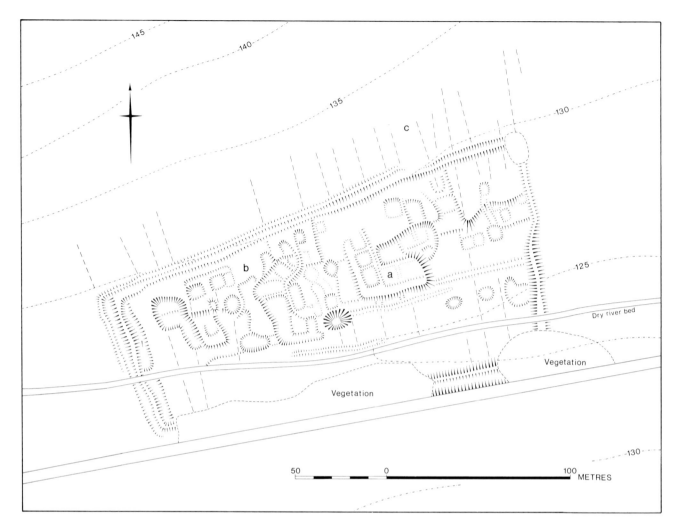

Figure 5.7

An enclosed site at Imber incorporating a sequence of varied building platforms; the largest covers 35 sq m (a). To the west is a brick-lined well. Potsherds noted on site indicate activity from the Romano-British to post-medieval period. Cartographic evidence shows that the site was also used as a warren. The trapezoidal enclosure incorporates an area of c 3ha and is typical of many other sheep enclosures. On the river terrace, there is a series of sub-rectangular enclosures, possibly building platforms (b). Periglacial soil stripes, resembling ridge-and-furrow cultivation, underlie the site (c).

temporary dwelling. Occasionally, more than one sheep enclosure occurs in a tithing and these might have catered for different flocks: two enclosures on Wilsford Down lie beside one another, each measuring 200 by 140m. They were described as 'Water Den Lamb House' in the late 18th century (ibid). These again are sited close to a drove route on an east-facing slope, and each has a much smaller internal enclosure set in a corner that was either used for segregating sheep or as accommodation for a shepherd. These enclosures were invariably sited on the edge of the open fields, on the lower slopes of the Higher Plain. Upavon (Fig 5.6) is a good example; where, the large rectilinear enclosure straddles the head of a re-entrant, indicating how the slopes of the valley were used to funnel the sheep into the enclosure.

Other larger sheep enclosures, polygonal in plan, exist on the Higher Plain. A good example lies adjacent to the Romano-British village at Wadman's Coppice in the

parish of Imber (Fig 4.17). Another on Warden's Down in the parish of Bratton, covers an area of 1.5ha and lies at the head of a re-entrant valley, which again provides a funnel into the enclosure entrance (Fig 4.19).

Prehistoric enclosures also appear to have been reused for this purpose. The sharp profile at Lidbury, an enclosure similar in size and form to those on Figheldean Down (Figs 5.8 and 5.9) and Shepherd's Garden, suggests reconstruction in the medieval or post-medieval period. Similar activity is likely to have taken place at Knook Castle, and, by the 19th century, at other hillforts, such as Battlesbury and Casterley.

Whether any of these sheep enclosures later developed into farmsteads as at Overton Down on the Marlborough Downs (Fowler and Blackwell 1998, 79), cannot be determined from the surface evidence alone. The large southern enclosure at the Knook Down West Romano-British village, close to the hillfort, might be one example, since it has a much sharper profile than the rest of the earth-works there (Figs 3.12; 3.27); the enclosure on Warden's Down, is another example.

Sheep washing was, of course, only practicable close to a source of water. Cartographic evidence indicates that there was a sheep wash at Compton, in Water Dean Bottom, and it might be that the enclosures at Imber, which lie astride the Imber Brook, provide earthwork evidence of such activity. Here, the western enclosure, known in the late 18th century as the 'Cony', contains evidence of small scoops and embankments flanking the canalised brook, showing that there was an attempt to pond the water and create a suitable locale for washing (Fig 5.7). Farther east the same stream cuts through another probable sheep enclosure. While it is unclear if they are contemporary, each is situated in order to utilise water from the stream.

Downland settlement in the 18th and 19th centuries

Prior to the Parliamentary Enclosures of the late 18th and early 19th centuries only seven farmsteads and five field barns lay on the Higher Plain, most located near the north-west escarpment, with a smaller number situated on either side of the Avon some 2.5 km from their respective villages (Fig 5.10) (Andrews and Dury 1773). While it is unclear when these farmsteads were first established, at least one, Widdington Farm in the parish of Upavon, is mentioned in documents as early as 1331 (Gover *et al* 1939, 324).

Table 4   Numbers of post-medieval farms on the SPTA.

year	farmsteads	field barns	cottages
1773	7	5	–
1845	13	20	–
Late 19th century	24	38	6
1904	18	34	–

The 19th century witnessed a period of re-colonisation of the Higher Plain as landowners brought more land into cultivation, and cartographic evidence reveals that, by the end of the century, the number of farms had increased dramatically (Figs 5.11 and 5.12; Table 4). The fortunes of many, however, were short-lived, due principally to the Agricultural Depression in the third quarter of the 19th century, which culminated in land being sold-off to the military. Some farms continued to be used until the land was required for more intensive military training; a few, however, were adapted by the military, for use as range control buildings, or as training features. Ultimately the majority were either destroyed or dismantled.

Until the beginning of the 19th century there were few downland farms. Following the Parliamentary Enclosures the numbers increased dramatically, and after the Tithe Commutation Act in the mid-19th century the number of farmsteads doubled. The earthworks of many of these farmsteads and

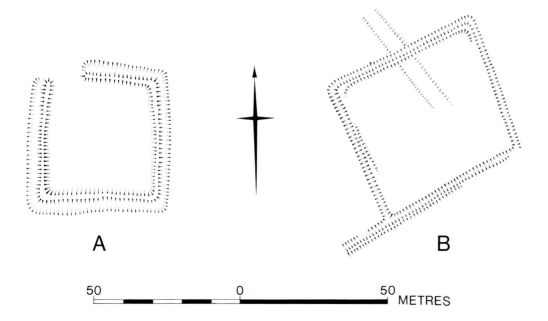

A

50   0   50 METRES

B

Figure 5.8
Sheep enclosures on Orcheston and Figheldean Downs. (A) The enclosure on Figheldean Down lies on the lower slope of a broad re-entrant and is positioned on the southern edge of a prominent 'Celtic' field lynchet. A pond, which is probably contemporary with the enclosure, overlies a linear ditch to the east (not shown). (B) The Orcheston Down enclosure is positioned on gently sloping ground close to the foot of Orcheston Down. In area, 0.5ha, it is similar in size to Figheldean and is defined by a ditch with an internal bank on the southern side, but no entrance. Like others it overlies a 'Celtic' field system (not shown).

117

Figure 5.9
Air photograph (looking north-east) of 'Celtic' fields on Figheldean Down. Reuse has partially obscured an earlier linear earthwork that curves from bottom right to run across the centre of the photograph. At the head of a re-entrant a medieval sheep enclosure lies over, and obliquely to, the fields.

field barns survive as very shallow rectilinear platforms and enclosures covering an area of up to 0.25ha (Fig 5.13). On Summer Down, for example, in the parish of Market Lavington, the remains of two farmsteads are set only 300m apart. The westernmost, probably the earlier of the two, lies on the valley floor and consists of a series of rectangular compounds, while the other, comprising at least two buildings, is terraced into a north-facing hillside. The brick and tile rubble in the area, together with a square pond nearby, would suggest a 19th-century construction date.

Each farmstead generally comprised one or more barns, a shelter shed, and a cartshed arranged in a rectangular fashion around a yard, and often surrounded by a shelter-belt of trees. The houses were frequently contained within this layout, or sometimes set to one side, and were substantial buildings, constructed mainly of brick with either slate or thatch roofs. Materials for each building had to be brought in, often from a considerable distance, and some buildings incorporated

reused materials. A foundation stone at a farmstead on Eastcott Down (Fig 5.12) is a moulding, possibly from a redundant building in the village. Water for each farmstead and its stock was provided from a well and either a rectangular or circular dewpond.

Field barns, while incorporating features appropriate to farmsteads, differed; they were essentially an outfield store and muck-yard or a shelter for cattle situated on the Higher Plain at some distance from the 'home' or 'parent' farm. There is some variation in size and form, ranging from a single building, with perhaps a small fenced enclosure on one of its longer sides, for example, Old Bake Barn on Rushall Down, to more developed units that were sometimes inhabited and, morphologically, cannot be distinguished from a farmstead. Of the twenty field barns mapped on the Central Range at the end of the 19th century, only five were uninhabited single buildings, while the remainder were of the more developed type. There was no topographical preference

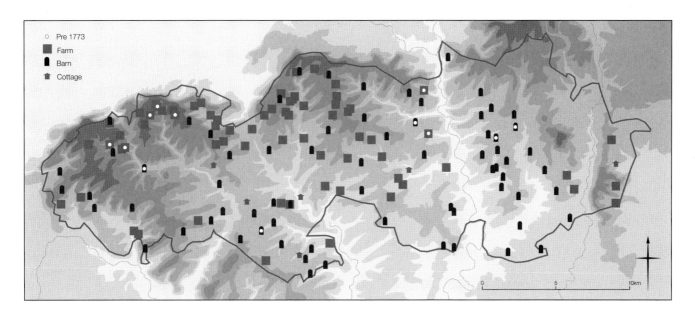

in the siting of either farmsteads or field barns; what is apparent, though, is that they were set conveniently within their holdings.

The size of farm holdings varied considerably. Slay Down Farm and Pond Farm, in the parish of Upavon, were only 52ha and 85ha respectively, whereas Candown Farm in the neighbouring parish reached 235ha. Compton Farm, centred in the Avon valley, comprised more than 364ha and, as well as the farm, incorporated two inhabited field barns situated on the Higher Plain. Much of the land itself was enclosed by wire fencing, and although this was removed in the early 20th century, isolated posts remain, indicating the extent of some of the former field boundaries.

Exploitation of marginal areas

The results of an increased interest in hunting during the 18th and 19th centuries (Williamson 1997, 111) can be observed at a number of places where small coverts were planted to encourage game. Although hunting leaves little archaeological evidence, its effect on the landscape is striking here. The most extensive and visually dramatic covert lies in the parish of Marden,

Figure 5.10
Map showing the distribution of farmsteads and field barns. Note how the field barns are located predominantly to the east of the Avon. These were the downland barns of the home farms in the valley, although many developed into more substantial complexes. Isolated cottages were also built on the downs to house farm labourers who would otherwise have had to journey some distance to their fields. In the west, the large open area denotes Imber where there were no downland farmsteads or field barns.

Figure 5.11
Pond Farm, a photograph taken about 1910, showing the isolated farmstead.

where two narrow beech plantations extend for nearly 2km onto the Higher Plain. One of these lies astride the parish boundary, while the other cuts across the centre of the parish thus emphasising the marginal nature of such areas at this time. Another good example is at Netheravon where a hunting box was built sometime after 1734, probably on the site of a former manor house. The building, which subsequently became known as Netheravon House (Stevenson 1980, 167), along with three coverts planted at the extremity of the parish, provided an ideal field sports environment for which the estate became renowned (Cobbett 1830, 61).

Further evidence of such exploitation is present at Tilshead where the levelled remains of Tilshead Lodge, an early 18th-century hunting or sporting lodge, are situated. The lodge and its enclosed grounds straddle a shallow valley, and once covered an area of some 55ha, with the lodge itself located near the north-eastern corner. The grounds are defined by a polygonal enclosure now distinguished by a line of beech trees; the southern side utilises a prehistoric linear boundary and long barrow as part of its course (Fig 5.14). Within the southern part of the enclosure a series of platforms that cut into the slope result from later use as a temporary military camp. To the south of the lodge, traces of associated formal

gardens, defined by slight rectilinear enclosures, lie among dense undergrowth. Eighteenth-century field names suggest that equine pursuits were important in the vicinity: Tilshead Race lay to the south, with Horse Down to the north. Horse racing and hunting were also important pursuits at both Everleigh and Tidworth from at least the 17th century (Crittall 1980a, 139; Stevenson 1995c, 157), although no field evidence remains.

The poor, but well-drained, downland pastures of Salisbury Plain were ideal for rearing rabbits and from the 13th century these proved to be an important source of revenue (Bond 1994, 145; Hare 1994, 164). Large warrens were normally located on the Higher Plain on less productive soils close to the extremity of parishes, while smaller examples were situated closer to settlement where space allowed. At Fittleton, for example, a small warren was present on the northern edge of the village from at least the late 19th century (OS 1st edition map). Similarly at Imber, former settlement earthworks about 500m to the west of the village were reused for farming rabbits (Fig 5.7). To the north-east the earthwork bank of a warren enclosure survives on the northern edge of the Romano-British village at Chisenbury Warren in the parish of Everleigh (Fig 4.14). Here, the irregularly shaped ditched enclosure, known as

Figure 5.12
The earthworks of a farmstead in Eastcott. The trees are the remains of shelterbelts and orchards. The building platform (left of centre) is marked by a substantial, lone bush, while the large depression close to the trees is a pond. The vehicle hulks to the rear are military targets.

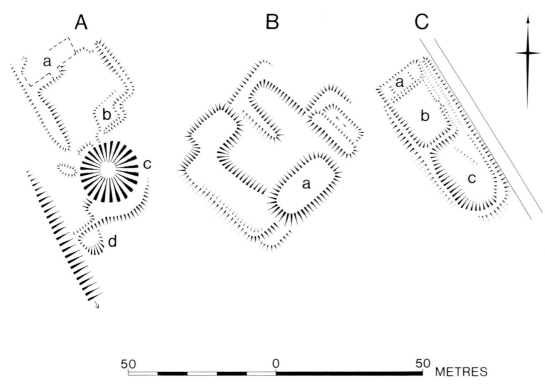

50   0   50 METRES

Figure 5.13
Comparative plans of barns and farmstead earthworks. (A) Eastcott. The farmstead is set against a lynchet, which also forms the parish boundary. The farmhouse (a), built on foundations of brick and sarsen stones, is positioned at the north end of an embanked enclosure. To the south is another probable building platform (b). The most prominent feature is the pond (c), which measures 2.5m deep with a bank on the south side. Another building platform (d) is evident beside the lynchet. (B) Compton Bake was one of two downland field barns belonging to Compton Farm. As the name implies it was established in the 19th century on previously uncultivated land. The site lies at the head of a wide valley more than 2km from the farm and consists of a central yard with building platforms set around it; these platforms represent the residence (a), with barns, a cart-shed and stabling on the other three sides. (C) Old Barn, Market Lavington. This field barn is one of five farmsteads set along the Market Lavington to Tilshead track. It comprises a building platform (a) beside a rectilinear embanked enclosure (b). A narrow entrance in the north-east side opens onto a path leading to a large pond in the south (c).

Jenner's Firs, covering an area of approximately 6ha, might be the warren documented at Everleigh in the late 13th century, and which, by 1346, was said to be contained within a small close (Stokes 1914, 171). Place-names identify the location of a number of other warrens in the area: Warren Down (which covered a large part of the southern extremity of the parish of Market Lavington), Warren Farm in Tidworth, Warren Hill on Perham Down and Warren Plantation in Shrewton. The site at Shrewton covered an area of 120ha during the late 19th century (Anon 1902a, 41).

Pillow mounds of post-medieval date (Williamson and Loveday 1988, 298) are rare and principally survive on the northern escarpment. In Luccombe Bottom, near Bratton, four mounds are dispersed along the north-west facing slope, while immediately north, on Piquet Hill, a further group of three mounds, initially thought to be ditched bowl barrows are, in fact, pillow mounds. A further example, excavated by Cunnington in the early 19th century when he mistook it for a burial mound (Colt Hoare 1812, 82), lies adjacent to Conegar Hill, in the parish of Heytesbury at the head of a wide coombe on the Higher Plain. This isolated long mound, measuring 22m by 8m and ditched on only three sides, is the only example of a long pillow mound

on the Training Area and it might be that rabbit farming on the Higher Plain was so successful that such artificial runs were considered largely unnecessary.

By the beginning of the 20th century, far from being an asset to the local economy, rabbits, or more particularly their burrows, were considered a major problem, particularly for horses on the new military estate (Anon 1902a, 19). As a result, in 1897, 14,000 rabbits were killed and warreners employed to fill in the holes (op cit, 32).

Communications

The present north–south communication pattern on Salisbury Plain is primarily the result of the creation and upgrading of roads during the past two hundred years. During the 20th century a number of military roads have been built and many older routes closed. Despite these changes, elements of the medieval and earlier communication pattern can still be detected.

Long-distance droveways linking principal market centres in the county and farther afield, are thought to be of considerable antiquity. Many are routed, coincidentally, alongside or within a few hundred metres of a parish or tithing boundary. Most avoid settlements and, wherever possible,

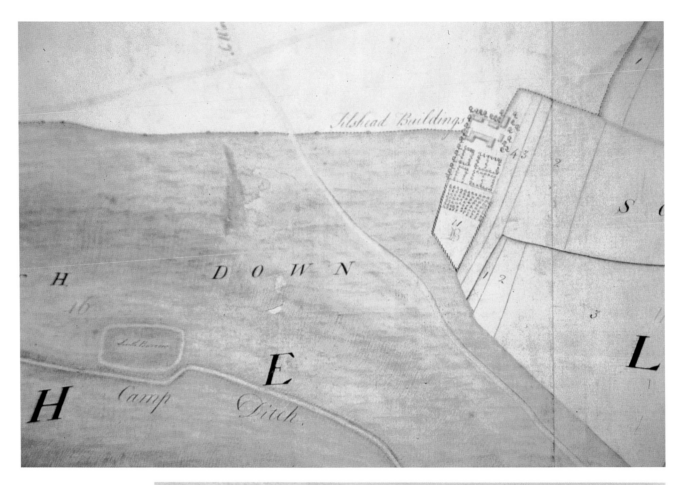

Figure 5.14
Tilshead Lodge: plan of
house and gardens shown
on an estate map of 1760
(WRO 1252/1). Note also
how the linear earthwork,
which is utilised as a park
boundary, avoids Old
Ditch long barrow, here
described as 'South Barrow'.

Figure 5.15
Medieval and later hollow
ways on Coombe Down,
incised into the hillside.

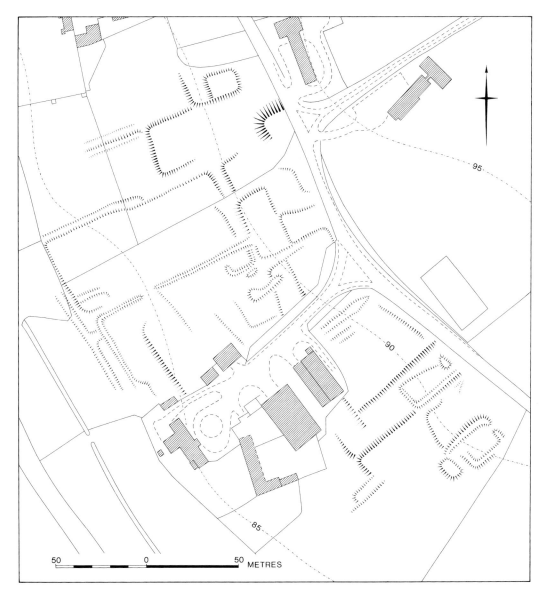

Figure 5.16
Plan of shrunken medieval village at Longstreet. Earthworks here comprise seven regular property boundaries extending from the lane towards the water meadow. The building platforms lie at the eastern, higher end. Although the date of abandonment is unknown, at least two buildings were in existence in the late 19th century.

the steep coombes instead favour the high ground. The road from Sarum to Bath, for example, a poorly defined track marked in places by milestones, passed close to its Roman predecessor on Chapperton Down and only descended to the low ground where it was found difficult to circumnavigate a coombe. Traffic ruts, lying parallel to each other, created a broad swathe of corrugations up to 100m wide. Other than these high level droves, river valleys provided the main arterial routes from at least the Saxon period onwards (Cossons 1959, 254). Local tracks linked settlements and provided access to the arable fields and downs. At West Chisenbury two tracks led from the medieval settlement onto the Higher Plain, and another example linked the settlement to neighbouring villages along the Avon val-

ley. In the parish of Upavon, a track leading from the village towards Tilshead can be traced as a deeply incised hollow way across Compton Down where it cuts through a 'Celtic' field system. Similarly, well developed hollow ways cross Snail Down *en route* to gravel quarries and snake across the Romano-British village of Coombe Down and on to the Avon valley (Fig 5.15).

The valley landscape

Settlements

The Domesday Survey provides the earliest documentary evidence for many settlements, although it is clear that those mentioned might not lie in the same location as later settlement with the same name.

Figure 5.17
East Chisenbury village,
with West Chisenbury on
the opposite river bank.
Surrounding Chisenbury
Priory, which, during the
medieval period was a cell of
the alien priory at Ogbourne
St George, is a large sub-
circular enclosure formed by
a bank and ditch in the
west, the road itself. A hollow
way, together with the
earthworks of at least four
building platforms (a), is set
into the gentle, west-facing
slope east of the manor
house, forming the southern
extent of the village. The
back of the platforms, and
the remainder of the east
side of the settlement to the
north, is marked by a
prominent 'Celtic' field
lynchet (b). Water for a
garden within the emparked
area was drawn from a leat
(c), and flowed south along
the back of the properties,
through the park, and back
to the river (adapted from
Ordnance Survey 1st edn
map, 1887).

However, place-names such as Chisenbury, which means 'dwellers on the gravel' (Gover *et al* 1939, 328); the *ford* element in the place names Bulford and Enford; and the river element in Netheravon and Upavon; together with the presence of at least three Domesday churches in valley locations, provide the strongest indication that, by the 11th century, settlement was present along the valleys of both the Till and Avon.

The earthworks of shrunken and surviving settlements show that the pattern was one of either compact, regular nucleated hamlets and villages, and smaller irregular hamlets. The regular examples generally lie parallel to the river, with either a single or double row of tofts set between a street and back lane or other boundary feature. At Longstreet (Fig 5.16), for example, tofts are defined by earthworks on either side of a farmstead at the southern end of the village. Each toft measures 30–35m in width and extends from the street for up to 150m to the edge of the water meadows. At the higher end of each toft, near the street, are rectilinear building platforms. This regularity of toft width suggests a degree of deliberate planning, perhaps reorganisation from an earlier settlement pattern, or a planned expansion from an earlier core, although it is by no means clear whether such an arrangement was imposed or resulted from a consensus among tenants.

The restrictions of the topography, and a desire not to encroach upon the more fertile land on the lower slopes when faced with population growth, was a major factor behind reorganisation here. In contrast at Enford, there was little reason to reorganise in this way as the settlement occupied a wide river terrace.

East and West Chisenbury lie on opposite banks of the River Avon and the communication pattern suggests that they might have developed around the site of an ancient river crossing. This pairing of settlements on either side of a river is a repeated feature of the medieval settlement pattern, not only along the Avon, but along other chalk downland streams in Wessex. East Chisenbury displays the characteristics of a regular double-row village with tofts arranged on either side of the street (Fig 5.17); it is noticeable how, although of similar width, the tofts on one side are almost half the length of those on the other.

At Bulford there appear to have been at least two phases of development. The earliest probably incorporated a group of properties arranged along the north side of the Nine Mile River, close to the confluence with the Avon. This included the church, the oldest part of which possibly dates to *c* 1100 (RCHME 1987, 117), and the present manor house. Later expansion is evident on the opposite bank of the Nine Mile River, where properties extended alongside a street (Fig 5.18). Similarly, the compact layout of Haxton (Fig 5.18), on the opposite bank to Netheravon, might have a similar history. The early focus, with tofts set around a central green, lay close to the river. To the east of this nucleus a group of regularly placed properties arranged on one side of a street was probably a later development.

The village of Orcheston today appears as a polyfocal settlement, but actually combines Orcheston St Mary and Orcheston St George (Fig 5.19), two markedly different settlements bounded at the northern and southern limits by their respective churches. Orcheston St George is the most southerly; north of its church lies the present manor house, with a regular compact line of properties ranged principally along the east side of the road. Orcheston St Mary lies farther to the north, where the early focus of settlement probably lay around the confluence of the Till with a prominent tributary; later expansion occurred along a north–south routeway that passed by the west of the church.

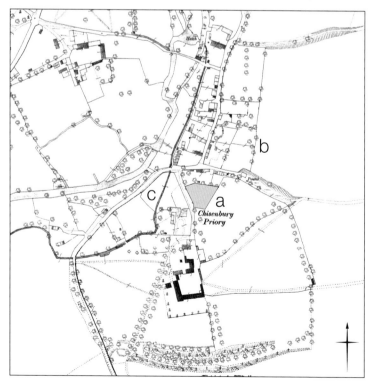

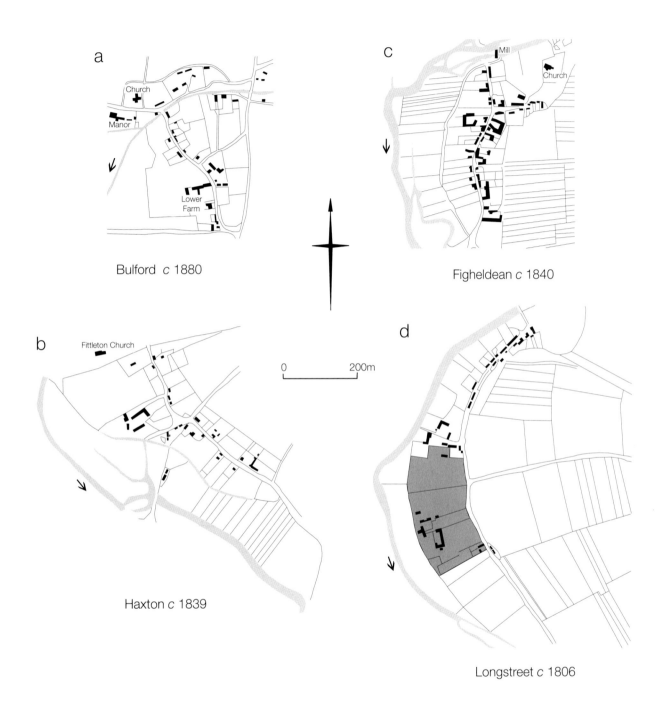

a

Bulford *c* 1880

c

Figheldean *c* 1840

b

Haxton *c* 1839

0   200m

d

Longstreet *c* 1806

Figure 5.18
Examples of medieval settlement along the Avon valley. (a) Bulford (c 1880). The earlier core at Bulford might have been along the Nine Mile River, with later expansion along the street to the south. (b) Haxton (c 1839). The eastern end of the settlement appears to be regularly laid out between two lanes, with a separate element sited near the river crossing to Netheravon. The area with regularly spaced boundaries on the southern side of the lane is a water meadow. (c) Figheldean (c 1840). Here the church, manor and mill form a complex to the north, with the remainder of the settlement arranged on both sides of a street parallel to the river. (d) Longstreet (c 1806). The shaded area represents the surveyed area in Figure 5.16.

Finally, the area between the two settlement nuclei became infilled.

Smaller irregular hamlets are also frequent. That at Knighton Farm, on the Avon north of Durrington, is set on rising ground and comprises a number of irregular building platforms placed within 'Celtic' fields that provided convenient boundaries for

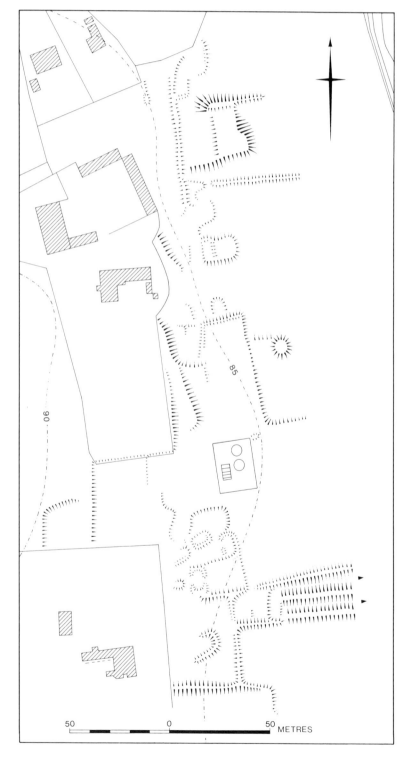

compounds (Fig 5.20). The reuse of a pre-existing feature such as a field lynchet, either to form the back of the tofts or as a building platform, can be seen at other settlements such as Coombe, Middleton (Fig 5.21) and Compton (Fig 5.22), and recalls associations noted in the Romano-British villages.

Few traces of the deserted settlement at Gore remain. Situated on the east side of a slope in the upper reaches of the River Till, this small hamlet, first documented in the Domesday Book, once formed a detached tithing of Market Lavington. Much of the hamlet probably underlies the present 19th-century farmstead, although there are slight earthworks to the south of this. Geophysical survey here located the site of the chapel (Figs 5.23 and 5.24), but field-walking produced no clear evidence of medieval occupation immediately adjacent. Earthworks of similar size and form interpreted as chapels survive at Knighton, West Chisenbury and Coombe.

Small farmsteads at Choulston and Syrencot, where there are no associated earthworks, were always smaller than their neighbours and in each case the documented medieval settlement probably underlies the present farmstead. The earthwork remains of the small irregular hamlet of Hindurrington, however, a site abandoned by the 16th or early 17th century (Stevenson 1995b, 67), lie on a terrace about 1km north of Bulford, on the east bank of the River Avon. The site covers an area of approximately 1ha and consists of a series of rectilinear building platforms, with a deep hollow way leading down the river bluff to a possible mill site and the river itself.

In some cases manorial complexes can be identified within existing settlements, although much of the evidence comes from later estate maps and obscures the probability that the location of the manor house moved with time. The earthworks at Knighton Farm demonstrate that the *curia*, including a chapel and manorial fishponds, were separated from the remainder of the settlement by a hollow way. At West Chisenbury (Fig 5.25) a single row settlement, positioned along the northern side of a street, is separated from the manorial complex that included the site of a chapel-of-ease (Brown 1996). Enclosure and Tithe maps both reveal that at Figheldean the manor, mill and church are all isolated from the rest of the settlement (Fig 5.18). Similarly, at Netheravon the church and

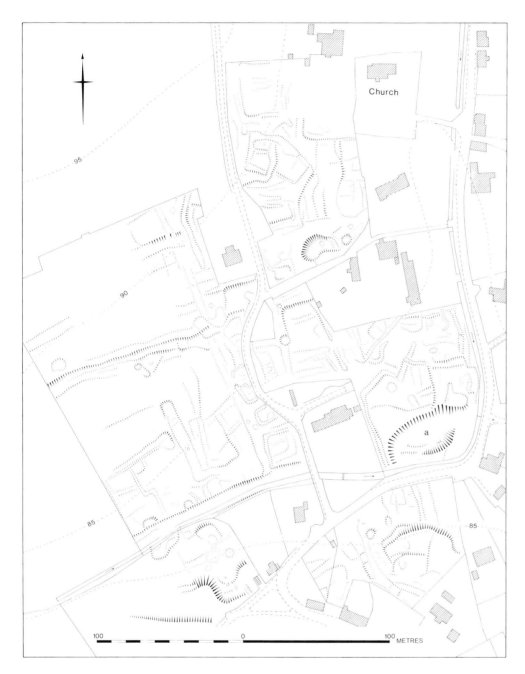

Church

100   0   100 METRES

Figure 5.19 (opposite & this page) Plans of shrunken medieval villages at Orcheston. (A – opposite) Orcheston St George. The remains of several properties survive arranged in a single row facing onto an embanked street to their west. Several rectangular structures are visible within the properties with the well-defined circular mound of a dovecot in the centre of the site. (B – this page) Orcheston St Mary. The settlement lies at the junction of the River Till and one of its tributaries with a large ponded area (a) marking their confluence. Settlement earthworks extend north from here to St Mary's church. South-west of the church a series of properties is aligned along a north–south route and perhaps represent later expansion. Sherds of 12th- to 14th-century pottery were noted in this area. Many of the settlement earthworks appear to respect the alignment of the underlying 'Celtic' fields – note the prominent field corner in the south.

later manor house stand detached from the remainder of the village. This suggests that, as a result of expansion, settlement shifted and that the earlier focus, no longer apparent, lay much closer to the church.

Although there is no evidence of large-scale emparking, some of the lesser gentry created small pleasure grounds that, in places, involved the removal of earlier settlements. At East Chisenbury, building platforms lying close to the manor house (Fig 5.17) represent the southern end of the village that was removed during the 17th century. Substantial improvements were made to the grounds, including the creation of a water garden. The pleasure ground is contained within a sub-circular enclosure, necessitating the diversion of the north–south road along the Avon valley. The house, with its impressive 18th-century front (Pevsner 1975, 240), was approached along an embanked formal tree-lined avenue. On the south side of the enclosure a deep cutting known as 'Gladiator's Walk' was probably used as a shaded, picturesque walk.

A small pleasure ground was also created to the north of the manor house at Imber sometime in the 18th century, probably forcing the abandonment of houses along the south side of the park. The now derelict manor house, with gardens to the north and adjacent farm buildings, was then enclosed by an ornamental setting of trees, a number of which survive.

Towns

As the name indicates, Tilshead is situated on the upper reaches of the River Till, and analysis of the present morphology reveals that it comprised a regular village with toft boundaries laid out on either side of a street along which the river formerly flowed. Some tofts in the north are defined by a prominent bank and ditch, while others are marked only by a hedge-line. Properties here, at approximately 34m in width, are similar in size to those in other regular settlements in the region. Within some of the tofts are building platforms, principally on

the river terrace, above the present street level and on a similar line to the church. Along the southern side of the settlement fewer toft boundaries are evident and they appear wider than in the northern part. The back lane, unlike that to the north, is marked by a hollow way for part of its course. The church of St Thomas lies at the eastern end of the village, with other settlement earthworks to the south-east. The field evidence is supported by a 19th-century map (Fig 5.26) that depicts a relatively open area to the south of the church, with a broader street, perhaps the area of a former 'green'. It seems probable that the settlement was originally situated on a river terrace, at the same elevation as the church, with a wide central green that had been encroached upon by the early 18th century.

Despite the earliest fabric only dating to *c* 1100, the church is similar in plan to the late Saxon church at Breamore in

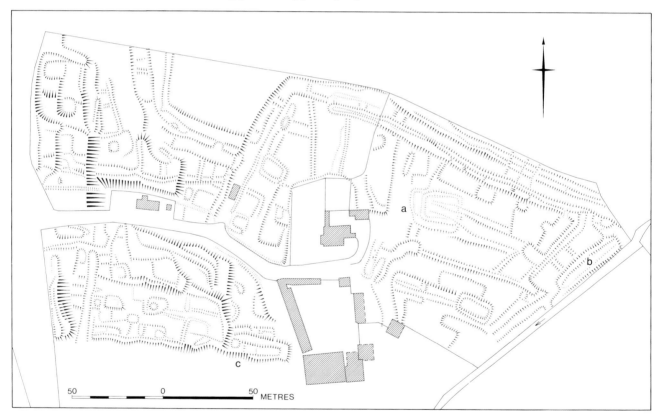

Figure 5.20

Plan of deserted medieval village at Knighton. Settlement earthworks covering an area of about 3ha are set around a farmhouse, bounded in the west and north by a hollow way with a leat in the south-east. A number of probable building platforms are positioned along the inner side of the hollow way and share a similar orientation, while to the east of the farmhouse a sub-rectangular platform (a), might be the location of the manorial chapel documented in the mid-13th century. A rectangular fish pond (b), which is divided into three compartments, lies farther east along the edge of the leat. The southern side of the settlement is defined by a prominent lynchet (c), which also forms the parish/tithing boundary. This lynchet formed part of a 'Celtic' field system, parts of which have been slighted by building platforms. The earthworks appear to represent a small cluster of farmsteads, together with their outbuildings, set within small compounds.

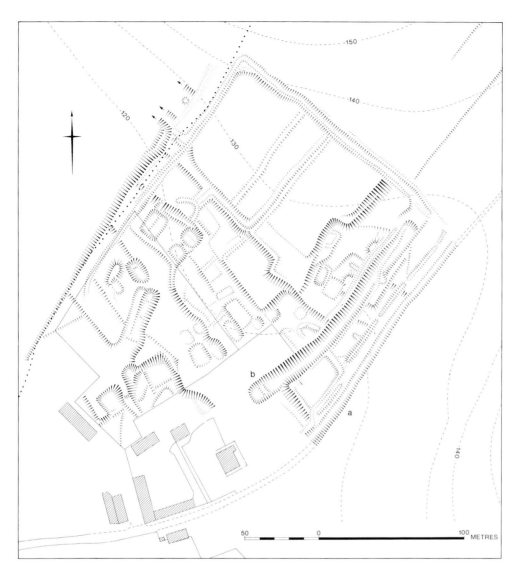

Figure 5.21
Plan of shrunken medieval village and strip lynchets at Middleton. The remains of the settlement at Middleton lie beside the parish boundary on the south side of Middle Hill. The settlement, represented by a series of sub-rectangular building platforms cut into a former 'Celtic' field lynchet, is bounded in the north and west by a boundary bank and, in the east, by a hollow way (a) that leads onto the downs. Between the hollow way and a deep cutting (b) is a 19th-century garden set on a level platform that includes a number of subdivisions. The function of the deep cutting remains unclear; however, it is unlikely to be a hollow way since it does not extend beyond the boundary bank.

Hampshire (RCHME 1987, 11–12) and it might be that an earlier building existed at Tilshead. It is also notable that the church appears to lie within a curvilinear enclosure. By the late 11th century Tilshead was one of ten boroughs in Wiltshire (Thorn and Thorn 1979, 1, 7), and the size of its holding makes it likely that it was then the focus of a large estate centred on the Till valley (Freeman 1995, 117). However, the 1334 tax assessment shows that it had lost its borough status and failed to prosper as a town during the medieval period.

In contrast, Ludgershall was not created until the later 12th century. It might have succeeded a traditional place of congress, perhaps a reused hillfort, the precursor to the medieval castle (*see* below); but its formal creation as a planned layout of rows of burgage plots defining a market area was clearly linked with the 12th-century development of the castle (Everson *et al in* Ellis 2000). It is sited at the head of a dry valley where the medieval settlement pattern is otherwise one of farms and hamlets located at intervals along the valley floor. Certainly, by 1194 Ludgershall had been granted borough status, and a fair and market were held here from the 13th century (Stevenson 1995a, 128). The earliest surviving fabric of the church of St James also dates to the 12th century (Pevsner 1975, 314) and, despite its present rather detached position away from the core of the town, it can be shown to be integral to the planned 12th-century layout.

Morphological analysis (Everson *et al* 2000) reveals a complex pattern of development and suggests that the town extended southwards from the castle. The first phase, dating to *c* 1190, is the

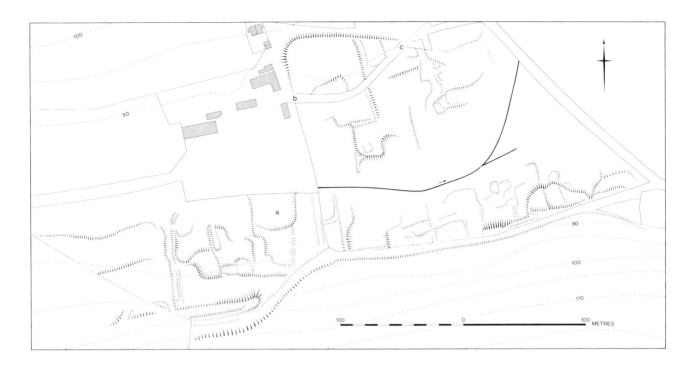

*Figure 5.22 (above)
Plan of shrunken medieval
village at Compton. The
settlement is situated at the
bottom of a steep-sided
coombe on the west bank
of the River Avon. The
earthworks form two
distinct elements separated
by a stream that flows
intermittently from Water
Dean Bottom to the River
Avon. To the north of the
stream there are a number
of house platforms and
paddocks set out in an
irregular fashion.
A depression (a) by the
stream was probably a
pond; (b) and (c) mark the
line of a service trench
where quantities of Romano-
British material, including
pottery and pieces of lead,
were found. It was also
along this line that four
sherds of grass-tempered
ware and a sherd of late
Anglo-Saxon pottery were
also found. To the south of
the stream other building
platforms back onto a lane
at the foot of the escarpment.*

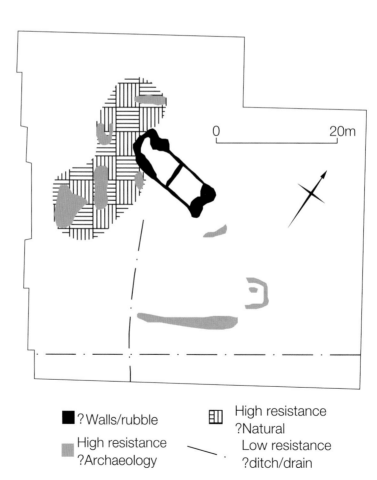

? Walls/rubble

High resistance
?Archaeology

High resistance
?Natural

Low resistance
?ditch/drain

*Figure 5.23 (left)
Geophysical plot of the
chapel at Gore. The site
lies in an arable field to
the west of the present
farmhouse and shows the
rectilinear walling of the
chapel, with further
indications of probable
buried features to the
west. The linear feature
of high resistance to the
south of the chapel might
be part of a boundary
wall.*

Ludgershall Castle

The only castle within the study area is at Ludgershall. It lies on the northern edge of the medieval borough and on the south-eastern fringe of the Forest of Chute. The well-preserved earthworks (Fig 5.27 (a) and (b)) include the fragmentary remains of medieval buildings, principally a solar tower of 12th-century construction, stone-built royal lodgings adjacent to it, and a Great Hall, all within the castle's northern enclosure. The survey shows that the curvilinear northern enclosure was inserted or superimposed onto an earlier southern enclosure, the postulated hillfort, also of double-bank and ditched form. This latter element became an outer court to the northern enclosure, which itself was remodelled in the late 12th century. In its place two very large elongated mounds were constructed. Elsewhere, the inner rampart was realigned into rectilinear rather than curvilinear alignments, suggestive of an ornamental use.

The northern enclosure covers an area of approximately 1.7ha, with a central platform 75–80m in width, with successive Great Halls standing precisely at the centre. Along the north-eastern section of the outer bank (corresponding to the sector occupied by the royal residential apartments), there is a wide, level platform or terraced walk overlooking the park with access to the first floor of the buildings. A ramp lies at the west end of the terrace, which leads to a gap in the outer bank and provides a way into the park. These elements of regularity and detail of form, the relationships between buildings and the wider emparked landscape, suggest a designed, ornamental and symbolic intent of a sort now widely recognised in great medieval residences, for example at Bodiam Castle in Kent (Taylor *et al* 1990), although without water as a dominant feature.

There is, however, an unresolved issue about the chronology of the site. The survey evidence alone might suggest that the high status residence and attendant landscape was the castle's sole and original function, along with the stone buildings of the latter half of the 12th century. However, a combination of excavated and documentary evidence demonstrates an earlier 12th-century phase of military use of a ringwork. The designed and ornamental aspects would therefore represent a radical alteration, though still *c* AD 1200.

Figure 5.24
Memorial from Roundway Hospital to the antiquary, Dr John Thurnam, now in Devizes Museum, reusing a stone with 12th-century decoration that he himself reportedly recovered from the site of the chapel at St Joan à Gore. This might have originated as a grave-marker similar to those excavated in situ as head and foot stones at Old Sarum Cathedral (St John Hope 1914, fig 5), but it has been recut for a secondary use.

establishment of burgage tenements on the east and south sides of the town, with the church a defining feature on the west. Sometime between 1200 and 1340, an ecclesiastical block developed around the church forming a built-up front on the west side of a very long market square. The next stage occurred in 1348 with the creation of an enclosure, the eastern side of which survives as an earthwork hitherto thought of as town defences; the western side is divided by a series of lanes overlying the north end of the market square and half the eastern side. This intrusion represents an extension to the castle and its attendant landscape. The market area and access to the town were redefined, in part, by the establishment of rows of 'rents'. The surviving market cross, itself stylistically of mid-14th-century date and carrying an iconography of resurrection, was probably originally erected centrally in the redefined market square. Only in the 16th century, after a change of ownership, was the present arrangement, based on a broad north–south street, imposed and the former open market infilled by encroachment.

Figure 5.25
Plan of deserted medieval village at West Chisenbury. The earthworks of a small hamlet are situated partly on the river terrace with the remainder on the floodplain. In the east are traces of a floated water meadow (a). Another water meadow lies to the north, but its main drain utilises a former track (b). In the south is a modern farmstead (c) with ditched closes or paddocks. A modern road cuts across the earthworks, but the former route lay 200m west on the lower slopes of the downs. Situated to the north are platforms of a single-row settlement with other properties lying on the river terrace. An Anglo-Saxon inhumation was found during house construction at (d).

The medieval buildings, with the exception of the solar tower, were systematically dismantled and levelled in the 16th century. Slight earthworks on the platform of the northern enclosure appear to be the remains of a formal garden extending across the levelled buildings, but incorporating the tower. It might have functioned as a banqueting house and stand, with additional emblematic significance for the Catholic Bridges family, owners in the later 16th century. Their residence, described as a 'lodge', might have adapted the medieval gatehouse and have stood in the centre of the south side of the northern enclosure.

Water meadows

Among the most distinctive and pervasive features of the chalkland river valleys, are the floated water meadows. These were constructed on both sides of the River Avon, and it is clear from the surviving earthworks that as much suitable land as possible was utilised in this way. In plan they comprise a series of parallel earthen ridges of varying length with corresponding furrows. Each ridge, known as a 'carrier' or 'carriage', has a narrow water channel cut centrally along its length, although as a result of heavy silting these are not always visible. On wide carriers there might be two such channels. Lying parallel to the carriers are furrows, or 'drains', that empty into a larger main drain that ultimately leads to the river. Other features, sluices, hatches and aqueducts, were all designed to control and direct the flow of water. Two main types of water meadow were identified. In one, the main drain and carrier lay at right angles to the side carriers and drains, while in the second they formed a herring-bone plan. Combinations of the two also occur as at Compton and Hindurrington (Figs 5.28. 5.29 and 5.30), and as there

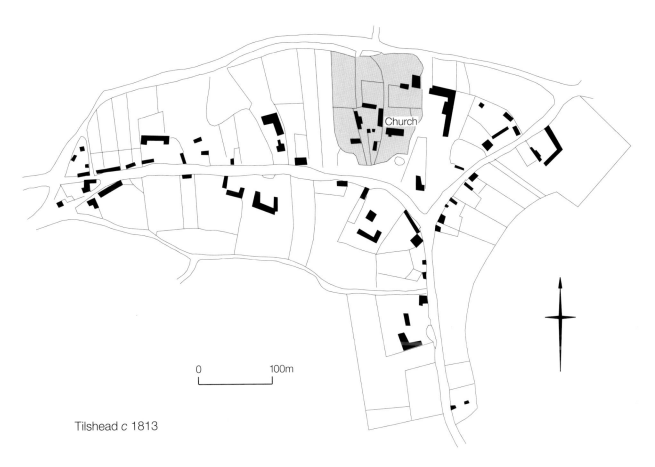

Tilshead c 1813

appears to be no chronological difference between these layouts, they were probably adopted for topographical reasons. Prior to the floating of meadows much of the land was already meadow, although, in at least one instance, a former hollow way appears to have been incorporated into the system (Brown 1996, 81).

Floated water meadows were crucial to the agricultural prosperity of the region. Prior to their introduction the number of sheep kept on an estate was determined by the availability of fodder crops during the winter. Since sheep were crucial for the manuring of arable fields, the area under cultivation was directly related to the number of sheep that could be kept. The floating of the meadows effectively provided an earlier growth of grass with the result that more sheep could be fed through the

winter, and, in consequence, more land could be manured and cultivated. Water meadows first appear to have been in operation along the Wylye valley from about 1635; however, it was not until the period 1650–1750 that they began to make a widespread impact in Wiltshire (Kerridge 1953, 111). Some of the earliest records of meadows to be converted were those at Milston and Hindurrington (Duke 1914, 161),which were constructed in 1660, although the meadows on the larger estates were probably floated somewhat earlier. Water meadows continued in operation until at least the Agricultural Depression of the late 19th century, and in some cases they persisted in use until the early 20th century, by which time there was a marked reduction of arable land following military acquisition.

Figure 5.26
The village plan of Tilshead in 1813 (re-drawn from WRO: Tilshead EA). The regular property boundaries extend either side of the street forming a curved block to the west of the church. There is also a regular layout of boundaries on the eastern side of the village. Note the curvilinear boundary (shaded area) to the south of the church, perhaps the remnant of an earlier enclosure.

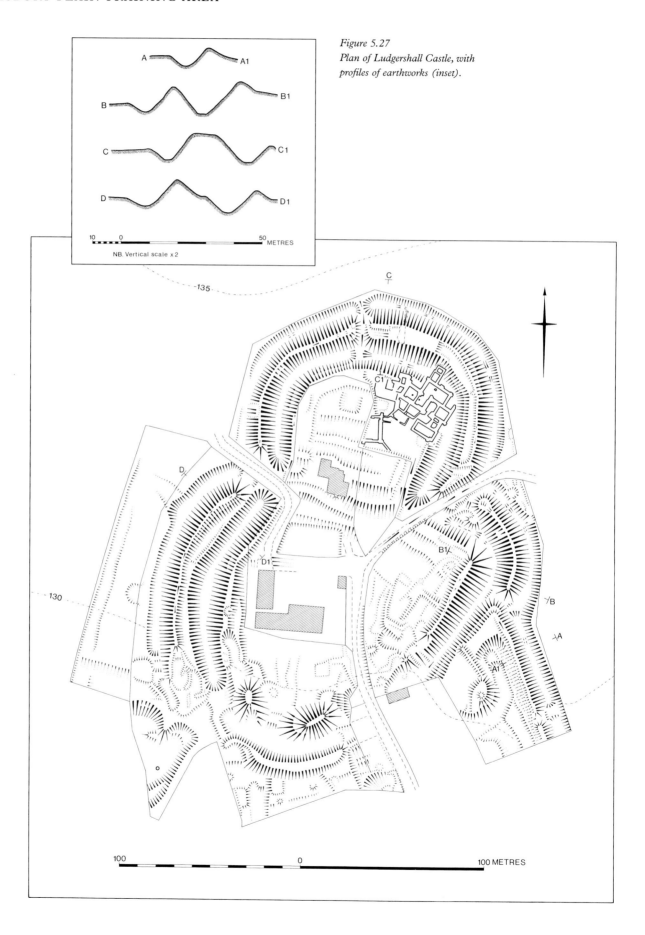

Figure 5.27
Plan of Ludgershall Castle, with profiles of earthworks (inset).

NB. Vertical scale x2

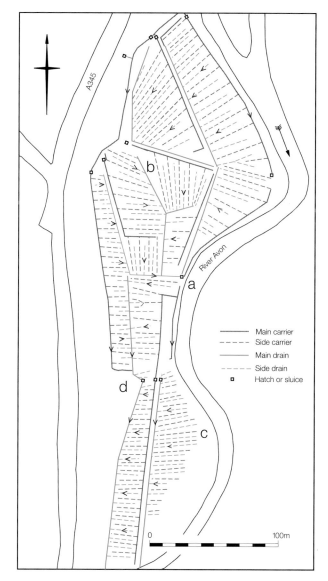

Figure 5.28
Plan of water meadows at Compton. There are two distinct meadows: the northern meadow, which extends as far as the main drain to the river, and a southern meadow, which is supplied by water from a brick aqueduct (a). From the earthwork survey a probable sequence of construction of the water meadow can be made. Having prepared the land, the main drains and main carriers were constructed; these were probably dug in a single operation. Sluices and hatches would then have been constructed and finally, the side carriers and drains were dug. Making best use of the land was crucially important, since water meadows were so highly valued; this can best be seen in the curious Y-shaped drain at (b) with the attendant 'fan' arrangement of the side carriers and drains above it.

Water for the northern meadow was provided from the river through a large iron hatch and was initially directed along the main carriers on either side of the meadow. The channel for the eastern main carrier is no longer visible, although its position would have been along the higher ground close to the riverbank. The main carrier supplied water to a series of side carriers, each about 0.2m high. In the west, the main carrier channel survives as a ditch up to 2m wide and 0.3m deep. Along the western course, control of the flow of water to three subsidiary main carriers was achieved by brick sluices and culverts to other parts of the meadow. Water from the northern meadow ultimately drained back into the river at (a). The southern meadow was supplied with water via the aqueduct (all that survives is part of the brickwork). Two main carriers are evident here, although the course of the eastern example (c) is no longer visible.

135

Figure 5.29
Air photograph of water
meadows along the River
Avon at Compton.

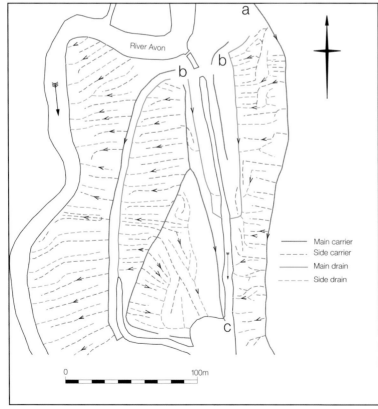

Figure 5.30
Plan of water meadows at Hindurrington. The water meadow here covers an area of 5.7ha and extends continuously to both the north and south of the surveyed area. The greater part of the meadow is encompassed by a wide bend in the River Avon. The main carrier (a), took a course parallel to the river in the north. This carrier, which has been eroded in places to the north, supplied water to three other main carriers (b), which in turn, fed the side carriers in a similar manner to the Compton meadows. Significantly, all the main carriers are lower than the side carriers, and sluices would have been used to raise the level sufficiently for water to flow along the side carriers. It is also likely that a former watercourse was utilised in the meadow; the main drain (c), might have been a former stream associated with the deserted medieval settlement on the river terrace to the east. The water meadow at Hindurrington is markedly different to that at Compton (Fig 5.28), the carriers and drains being far more sinuous; in addition, the side drains in the west empty directly into the river and not into a main drain as elsewhere. Small mounds of earth indicate the location of sluices at Hindurrington, although no brickwork is evident. The well-preserved earthwork remains also include the channels for the side carriers as well as those for the main carriers.

6
The 20th Century

The creation of the military estate

Prior to the establishment of permanent training areas, large-scale military manoeuvres were conducted on privately owned land. This was considered highly unsatisfactory by the military authorities as the agricultural calendar placed inevitable restrictions on training; furthermore, protracted negotiations were sometimes necessary concerning such matters as the establishment of temporary camps and the supply of water for large numbers of troops.

To counter these difficulties, in January 1897 the Under Secretary of State for War proposed the acquisition of a large area of land on Salisbury Plain for the purpose of military manoeuvres. Initially, 40,000 acres (16,000 hectares) were to be purchased (Salisbury & Winchester Journal, 30 Jan 1897), the primary purpose being to enable troops, particularly cavalry, to manoeuvre unhindered over large tracts of land. The undulating downland of the Plain appeared ideally suited for this purpose. In addition, infantry training was to take

place, necessitating the establishment of permanent rifle ranges. In 1898, a further proposal was submitted for an artillery range, designed to take the pressure off the range at Okehampton on Dartmoor (Anon 1902b, 63), to be created on the west side of the River Avon. These decisions had considerable advantages for the army; as gunnery practice, for example, no longer needed to be divorced from tactics and soldiers could be trained in a more realistic setting (Headlam 1937, 30). This provided an 'unrivalled field for tactical instruction' (Anon 1901b, 15). Although, initially, no permanent barracks were envisaged, this decision was soon reversed when the full potential of the Plain was recognised, and in 1899 barracks were established at Tidworth, Bulford, and, later, Ludgershall, Larkhill and Warminster.

Land purchases began in August 1897, with acquisitions to the north of Amesbury on both sides of the Avon, and farther to the east at Tidworth. Most of the estates covered between 200 and 400ha, although three large purchases accounted for some 43 per cent of the total area.

"POND FARM CAMP". SALISBURY PLAIN. 1909.

Figure 6.1
A tented camp adjacent to Pond Farm in 1909. Unlike some temporary camps that became permanent many, like Pond Farm camp, survived only briefly, in this case until c 1911 when the area was absorbed into the artillery danger area.

Figure 6.2
Military trenches at
Perham Down overlying
'Celtic' fields.

The majority were secured by negotiation, but some had to be compulsorily purchased. Within five years more than 16,000ha were in military ownership. More than half the total had been either arable or pasture, but within a short period of time 83 per cent had been turned over to grassland (Anon 1902a, 156), thus emphasising the shift from an agricultural regime to one dominated by military training. Further purchases, primarily in the east, were made during the first half of the 20th century, when 6,200ha were acquired (James 1987, 237) and then in the decade before the Second World War a further 10,000ha was purchased (ibid).

Cavalry training began in 1897, initially only between May and October, with the soldiers being accommodated in temporary tented camps on the Higher Plain (Fig 6.1). In all, eighteen such camps were established by 1906 (James 1987, 242), although this number fluctuated during succeeding decades. These camps, by their very nature, have left little trace of their existence, although earthworks interpreted as field

kitchens cut into 'Celtic' fields have been identified at Tidworth golf course, while at other temporary camps such as West Down South camp, large concrete ponds or reservoirs remain. Farming was allowed to continue on the downs as long as it did not impinge upon military training (Salisbury & Winchester Journal 13 Feb 1897), but fencing, which had been extensively used, had to be taken down and this clearly imposed restrictions on farming practices. On one estate of 1,100ha, some 16km of fencing was removed (Anon 1902a, 62). This arrangement was only temporary, and, when land was finally required for continuous training, the farmsteads were either dismantled or converted for military use and by 1902 the area occupied by the Larkhill artillery danger area had been completely depopulated (Anon 1902b, 2) (Fig 1.2).

Military earthworks

Though the impact of the military on the entire area has been substantial, the most distinctive military remains survive on the chalk plateau. Used extensively for training since the turn of the century, the intensity of use increased dramatically prior to, and during, the two World Wars, and at other periods of conflict. It is sobering to reflect that British Forces have been continuously engaged in some form of conflict since the Second World War and this has resulted in uninterrupted activity on the SPTA. In order to cater for this intense use, a whole new garrison infrastructure, with barracks, schools, churches and hospitals, together with new roads and a railway, were established. An impression of the transformation can be obtained from the words of an officer, who, writing in 1916, observed that: '...at times one could easily imagine oneself at the front, with the constant gun practice going on, and the exploding of mines, trench mortars and grenades to say nothing of the incessant rifle fire. Trenching and mining of all kinds are practised extensively here. If you have never seen a large hutted camp, you must imagine a huge town built entirely of wooden huts of various shapes and sizes according to their requirements, but as the streets in our case are not named, it is very difficult to find one's way about.' (Guy 1981, 1–2).

The impact of this activity over such a short period of time has been profound. Not since the Romano-British period has the effect on the landscape been so dramatic and, even now, land-use is continually changing as new tactics and weaponry demand fresh approaches and an upgraded infrastructure. It is difficult to present a comprehensive assessment of the military earthworks since, by their very nature, many were only temporary, while others were reused for a variety of purposes. Nonethe-less, there are extensive remains of features such as rifle-ranges, gun emplacements and large tracts of trench systems, all of which played a crucial part in military operations on the Plain during the 20th century.

Trench systems

Trenches were a major feature of land warfare during the 19th and the first half of the 20th century and although infantry trench systems have been identified elsewhere in the country, at such places as Penally in Wales (Thomas 1997, 5), Cannock Chase in Staffordshire (Welch 1997), and Otterburn in Northumberland (Charlton and Day 1977, 137), only on Salisbury Plain do they survive on such a large scale (Fig 6.2). Practice trenches were being dug by at least 1902 when 'three 4 foot deep S-shaped Boer trenches, filled with standing dummies, were fired at both by guns and howitzers with fair effect' (Anon 1902b, 23). Since then, large numbers of trench systems have been constructed, and indeed, apart from the 'Celtic' fields and linear ditches, military trenches are the most extensive earthwork monuments on the Training Area. These have been mapped as part of the aerial photographic transcription of the area (Figs 6.3 and 6.4), ranging from the small slit trenches close to the aircraft hangers at Netheravon to fully developed systems, such as those near Shrewton Folly and Perham Down, that extend over a considerable area (Fig 6.5). The trenches are remarkable both

Figure 6.3
Distribution map of military earthworks and garrisons. The largest area of trenches lies to the south of Imber, on Knook Down, where a variety of different trenches are evident. Other large areas of trenches include a complex west of Shrewton Folly, and another on Perham Down and the southern fringes between Bulford and Tidworth. There are two anti-tank ranges on the Training Area, although the one at Shrewton is no longer used.

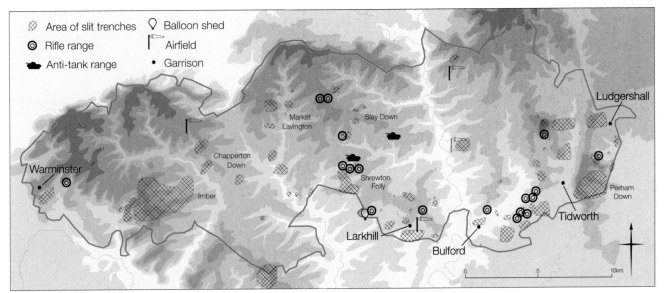

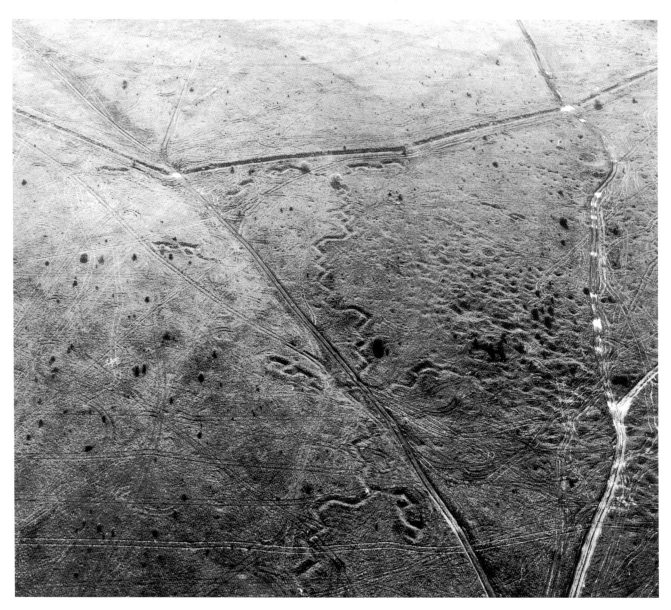

Figure 6.4
The archaeology of
warfare. An extensive
system of zigzag World
War I trenches on Knook
Down have been heavily
shelled leaving an area
of craters (lower right).
The straight lengths of an
anti-tank ditch (from top
left to right) are probably
later in date.

in their magnitude and scale of survival, and in a number of places, such as on Compton Down and New Copse Down, obstacles such as wire entanglements secured by screw pickets are still in place.

In their developed form trench systems were composed of three distinct elements: a front line, support trenches, and a reserve, all of which were connected by a further series of communication trenches (Anon 1997b, 19). The front line consists of a trench from which firing took place, with a command, or supervision trench, immediately to the rear; a parados or a bank was sometimes constructed behind the trench (Solano 1915, 71) in order to give protection to the troops from enfilade fire and to minimise the effect of shells bursting on a

trench. In plan the firing trench consisted of T- or L-shaped fire bays, within a crenellated or zigzag linear arrangement (Anon 1918, 5; Anon 1997b, 25). Behind the front line, and separated from it by at least 50m, were the support trenches. As the name implies, these were designed to provide support to the troops in the front line in the event of an attack or withdrawal. Finally, the reserve line was between 400 and 600m from the support trenches (Anon 1997b, 20) and consisted either of trenches or dugouts similar in design to the forward examples. This line was essentially the battalion reserve, its purpose being local counter-attack. Trenches and dugouts were connected by a series of communication trenches that afforded a covered approach.

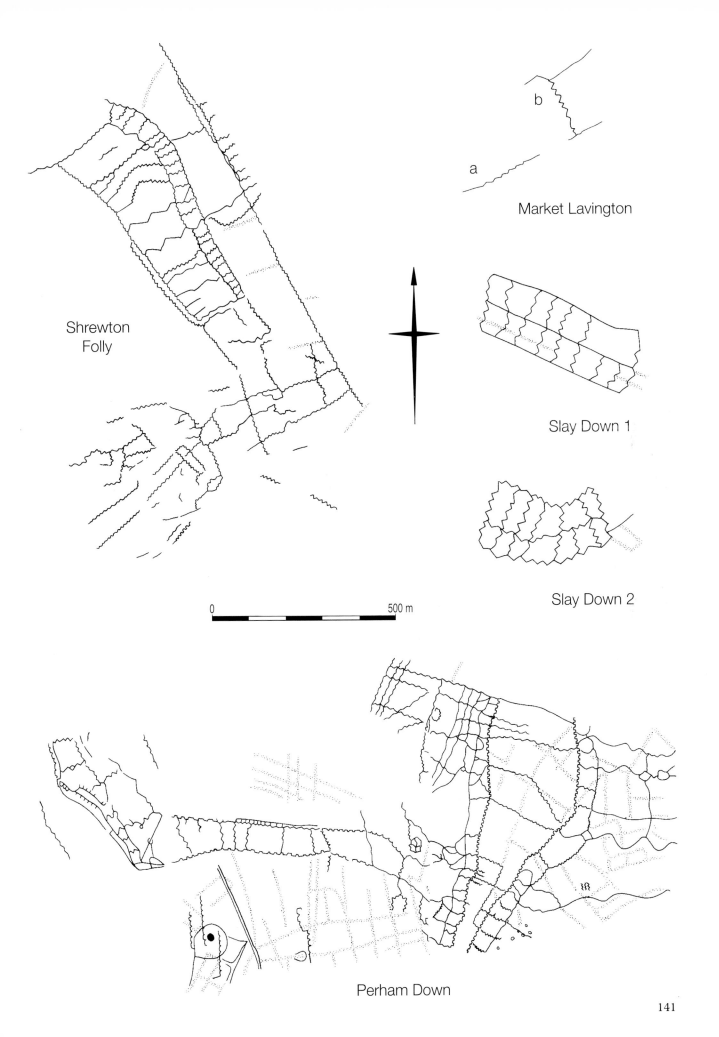

Shrewton
Folly

Market Lavington

b

a

Slay Down 1

Slay Down 2

0   500 m

Perham Down

141

Each communication trench would curve to provide protection, apart from the last 40m section, which was straight in order to give a good line of fire (op cit, 31). In addition to these main features, shelters and smaller specialised trenches, such as bombing trenches, advanced posts, and machine gun posts, were also constructed. A bombing trench was normally dug at an angle off a communication trench, but within grenade range of the front line, and was used to harass the enemy in the event of the front line falling into enemy hands (op cit, 20). The advanced posts were constructed up to 30m in front of the front line, the purpose being to keep the enemy's snipers and observers at a distance (Anon 1915b, 43). Other small trenches leading off the front line were used as exit and entry points for patrols.

Among the oldest trenches are those located in the artillery impact zone; these might well have been used for 'live firing' practice since the orientation of the front line was directed towards the 'danger area'. On Slay Down, two systems each comprise a front line and two support trenches connected by communication trenches (Fig 6.5).

The trench systems at the southern end of the parishes of Market Lavington and West Lavington vary from single sinuous lines to more complex examples. Two of these are of particular note since they illustrate the probable sequence of construction following an initial 'contact' with the enemy, as advocated in various military manuals (for example, Solano 1915, 39; Anon 1997b, 23). These trenches lie on a spur of Warren Down, above a deeply incised re-entrant (Fig 6.5 (a) and (b)). The first stage can be seen in the western trench (a) where individual 'scrapes' have been dug; these are further developed into small trenches that are then linked together to form a continuous, sinuous, front line. The second example, 100m to the north-east (b), illustrates how soldiers practised an approach to a front line. Here the front line was dug on the top of the slope in the south, and a zigzag communication trench, linked to two other linear trenches, was dug from the valley to the north so that soldiers could approach the front line undetected.

The most spectacular example of an early trench system lies near the Perham Down rifle ranges (Figs 6.2 and 6.5). Covering about 100ha, at least three separate trench systems of which the eastern is the most comprehensive, comprise the usual array of front lines, support and communication trenches, and illustrate the ebb and flow of warfare where successive firing lines were constructed as the battle progressed.

The largest area of trenches is situated on Knook Down, 2km to the south of Imber village (Figs 6.4 and 6.6). This complex is multi-period in date being used up to, and during, the Second World War. The most conspicuous element, and one of the latest, is a deep and broad linear trench, probably part of an experimental anti-tank ditch, dug in 1943 (Public Record Office; War Office 199/54). To the east of it, and overlying a long barrow and 'Celtic' field system, are further trenches that, in plan, form a rectangle 900m by 500m, with a small honeycomb of subsidiary trenches in the south-east corner. More large trench complexes are present in the north and to the west of the anti-tank ditch. This system, together with another on Chapperton Down, appears to have been deliberately shelled, possibly to demonstrate the effect of artillery bombardment on, or above, the trenches.

The example on Chapperton Down (Fig 6.7) lies on the west side of a re-entrant and is a good illustration of how the military not only utilised landform when siting trenches but also utilised pre-existing earthworks such as 'Celtic' fields. Three trenches, each measuring between 100–150m in length, are situated on rising ground with the firing trench on the brow. One hundred metres in front of the firing trench is an isolated crenellated trench. The firing line is approached along a communication trench extending 750m from the valley bottom in the south and significantly the trench uses the 1.5m height of a lynchet to provide additional cover from the west.

Rifle ranges

Musketry was a crucial art for infantrymen, requiring constant practice. Live firing practice was, and is still, carried out on rifle-ranges, the first being established in 1870 before the land was purchased (James 1987, 144). This 900 yard (823 metres), later 1000 yard (914 metres), range was situated on the south side of Mancombe Down near Warminster, where the targets were positioned on the side of the hill beyond, so that the slope formed a natural 'backstop'. The range continued in use until about 1937 when barracks were built on the site (op cit, 145).

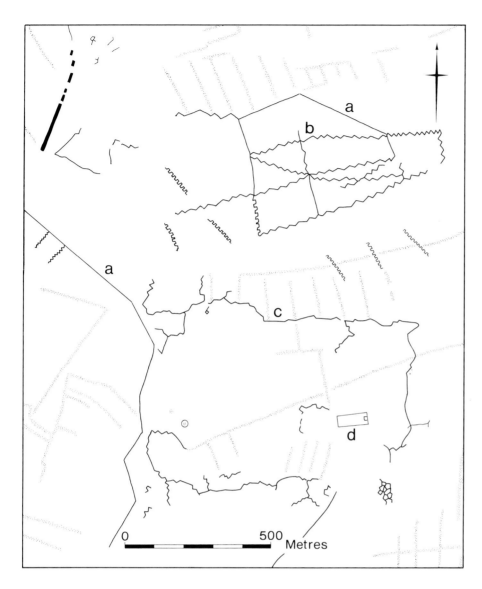

Figure 6.6
Military trenches on Knook Down. This complex plan illustrates the diversity of military trenches of different periods, set over a fragmentary 'Celtic' field system. The linear anti-tank ditches (a), which measure 7m in width and 2.5m in depth, were designed to form a physical barrier against enemy tanks and would have been used in conjunction with other obstacles such as tree trunks and concrete blocks. To the east are First World War trenches (b), with additional crenellated trenches to the south and west. A much larger system lies to the south (c), which is morphologically distinct from the others and might reflect a change in military tactics. Set neatly within the trench system is a sheep enclosure (d).

Each range comprised two distinct elements: a target butt and a number of firing points at fixed distances from it. The target butt or backstop, comprises a linear earthen bank, up to 160m long and approximately 3m high, separated by a wide berm from a parallel ditch, in which the targets were placed. Shots would hit the butt to the rear of the target. In some cases a hollow to the rear of the butt was used as an administrative point and cover for troops during firing. Facing the butt, and parallel to it, were the firing points; the most distant consisted of a continuous trench with earth placed to form a slight bank to the rear, while intervening firing points might be marked by lines of stones set at regular intervals from the butt and providing varying degrees of difficulty in marksmanship.

Within two years of acquiring the land the army had constructed rifle ranges at seven locations; the main concentration was at Bulford where five ranges covered an area of 1.2 sq km and varied in length from 800 to 1000 yards (731 to 914 metres) (Fig 6.8). A further range was constructed on Rushall Down, with the firing point positioned on one ridge and the butt on the next, some 800 yards away. Two other ranges had been constructed on Wilsford Down by 1900, one of 800 yards and another of 1000 yards; in each case the butts were situated to the east of the firing points. Although the constituent parts of these two ranges were the same, the butt and firing point at the northerly range was three times as large as the southerly one. This might denote variety in function, either use of

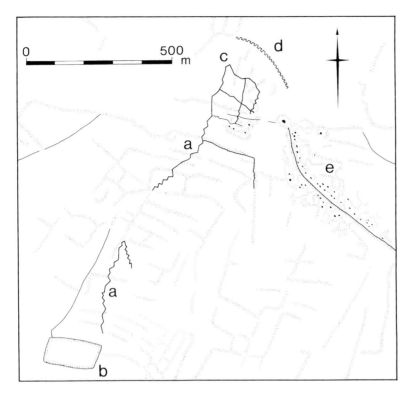

Figure 6.7
Military trenches on Chapperton Down. The communication trench (a) extends from the Berrill Valley in the south, near a sheep enclosure (b), to the three trenches on the brow of the hill (c). Another communication trench to the east of (a) overlies a 'Celtic' field lynchet. The relationship between the trenches and the crenellated trench (d) to the north, is unclear since there are no further earthworks here. To the east lies a Romano-British settlement (e).

larger targets, use by novice marksmen or use of different weaponry. Wilsford Down Farm North, situated between the two ranges, might still have been inhabited at this time, although it was soon abandoned. Other farms were certainly affected by the construction of rifle ranges. At Newfoundland Farm, for example, firing was directed towards the farm, which meant that occupation would '... presumably become untenable ...' (Anon 1902a, 60). The ranges on Wilsford Down and Rushall Down were probably used for only a relatively short period of time, since the area in which they lay was subsequently incorporated into an artillery range danger zone (Anon 1901b, 16). They remain the earliest surviving unimproved rifle ranges on Salisbury Plain.

Throughout the succeeding decades other rifle ranges were constructed and some existing ones expanded, while others were abandoned as training needs changed. Among the latter are a complex of four butts constructed some time between 1901 and 1924 at Robin Hood's Ball, one of which cut through part of the causewayed enclosure. This range was abandoned probably because of the constraints it would have placed on manoeuvres in the area beyond the butts.

Anti-tank warfare

The development of the tank during the First World War revolutionised land warfare for much of the 20th century (Fig 6.9). In order to counter the threat of tanks on artillery positions new tactics were developed that would enable gunners to fire at moving targets approaching at differing angles and speeds. These tactics required slick, concise procedures and constant practice if the gun detachments were to be proficient. In order to provide realistic practice an 'anti-tank' range was constructed in 1916 on the southern edge of Shrewton Folly and the earthwork still survives (Cross 1971, 184) (Fig 6.10). This range overlay a 'Celtic' field system and comprised two parts, a firing line where the artillery guns were deployed, and a target. This was a canvas or hessian screen shaped like a tank, which was mounted on a trolley and towed along a railway line at varying speeds. The gun detachments were required to 'aim-off' their guns, taking into account factors such as the speed of the tank and angle of approach. The range, which covers an area of approximately 65ha, incorporates part of an earlier rifle range butt, behind which a rail terminal and administrative point was constructed.

Field gun emplacements and splinter-proof shelters

Field gun emplacements, or gun pits, are most prevalent on Orcheston Down and to the south of Imber. Since the earth is usually reinstated after each pit is no longer required, such positions can invariably only be identified archaeologically as soil or crop marks. They generally cluster in groups of three, four, or six arranged either in a straight line or staggered, although randomly placed examples also occur; they were typically placed below a hill crest so that the flash or smoke from the gun would be less apparent. Other structures close by might represent the command posts from which the guns were controlled and which facilitated communication with an 'observer' some distance away. A gun pit on Alton Down is typical, defined by a sub-circular earthwork about 10m in diameter and 1m deep with sides revetted by corrugated iron to prevent the walls collapsing. There were also additional trenches or bunkers around the perimeter for storage of ammunition and equipment. Farther north, on the Larkhill impact area, temporary 'scrapes' were possibly used as gunpits by smaller, anti-tank guns,

Figure 6.8
Rifle range A, Bulford,
with part of C range (top
left). Among the Sling
Camp barrow group are
the earthworks of a much
smaller, now disused, pistol
range. The cone barrow
excavated by Hawley,
which was found to have a
core of ashes and charred
beams, lies at the corner
of a cultivated patch of
downland (right of centre).

since here the 'scrapes' are much shallower than the usual gun pit, thus enabling the gun to fire at a much lower trajectory.

The first splinter-proof shelters were constructed before 1901 on the southern side of the Larkhill Impact Area (OS 25-inch map, 47/14, 1901) and comprise rectangular concrete structures set within a deep depression, partly buried by a mound of earth approximately 10m wide and 1.5m high. Internally these shelters are revetted with corrugated iron. Their specific purpose is unclear but they are unlikely to have been observation posts since visibility to the north, into the danger area, was extremely limited. The siting of some of these shelters on the flanks of rifle-ranges, however, would suggest that they might have been used as picket posts, defining the limits of the range and preventing trespass.

The military railways

A number of railways were constructed on the military estate, connecting the major garrisons to the main civilian lines in order to move both troops and supplies. A branch line between Ludgershall and Tidworth was completed in 1901 and four years later another was built to link Amesbury and Bulford. The line from Larkhill to Amesbury, built in 1909, became the longest of those constructed (James 1987). There is little surviving evidence of these railways on the SPTA. However, the Larkhill branch line, which extended as far as the animal hospital at Fargo, survives as a curving earthen embankment north of the present road between Larkhill and Shrewton, where it skirts around a long barrow on Durrington Down.

Airfields

The SPTA played an important role in the development of air warfare, with eight airfields constructed between 1910 and 1986 (op cit, 168), two of which, at Upavon and Netheravon, are still in use today. While there was an earlier balloon school at Rollestone, the earliest airfield was constructed in 1910 at Larkhill. This incorporated eight hangars and a runway covering approximately one kilometre. A number of the former hangars remain standing and represent the oldest aeronautical buildings still in existence in the country (op cit, 163).

The airfield to the west of the present military camp at New Zealand Farm was in use during World War II. A perimeter ditch extended southwards from the main track in the north and enclosed an area of approximately 176ha. Within this boundary are a number of splinter-proof shelters. No clearly defined runway has been identified, although aerial photographs depict a number of hangars and at least one hut in the vicinity. During the 1950s the airfield expanded with the marking out of clearly defined runways orientated roughly north-east–south-west.

Impact areas

Perhaps the most dramatic change in the landscape in the 20th century is on the 'impact areas'; zones where artillery and aircraft munitions detonate. Although there were formerly others, two are currently still in use, the Larkhill and Westdown Impact areas, which together cover a continuous area of approximately 47 sq km. These are characterised by undulating downland, selected to present challenging scenarios to the 'observer' who acted as the 'eyes' of the guns, and with occasional targets such as obsolete tanks, vehicles or other features dotting the landscape. Around the edges of the impact area, particularly on the south, there are a number of observation posts in the form of long, narrow bunkers with an observation slit

to the front (Fig 6.11). Early examples of both bunkers and towers, remain extant and lie hidden within the impact area.

The archaeological evidence of a disturbed land surface and associated structures shows that some zones have been intensively targeted in the past, particularly Warren Down, in the parish of Market Lavington, and part of Rushall Down. In these places, the ground surface is heavily pocked by shell holes with the result that, in some cases, any underlying archaeological remains are difficult to distinguish.

Re-colonisation of the downs

A recurring theme has been the periodic colonisation of the downs followed by contraction to the more favourable valleys. The military are continuing this process with their own forms of settlement. The most notable is the 'ghost' village situated on the Higher Plain on Copehill Down (Fig 1.4). This uninhabited nucleated village is composed of types of building encountered on the continent and thus provides realistic training scenarios for warfare in a built-up environment. The village of Imber has been adapted in a similar way, although remnants of the former village remain (Fig 6.12). Elsewhere former farmsteads have been converted for military purposes, providing cover in an otherwise open landscape.

Figure 6.9 (opposite, top) Anti-tank ditch on Knook Down to the south-east of Imber.

Figure 6.10 (opposite, bottom) Earthworks of an anti-tank range at Shrewton Folly, incorporating traces of a dismantled railway.

Figure 6.11 Splinter-proof shelter of concrete used for observing the accuracy of shellfire.

Figure 6.12
Imber nestles at the junction of two valleys with that of the Imber Brook at the centre of the Western Range. The church survives (centre left), protected in its compound, as does the derelict manor house (centre top). A few other original brick buildings remain, but these have been supplemented by a collection of breeze block constructions built for military purposes. Medieval earthworks lie around the church and to the west of the manor house. The village of Imber was depopulated during the Second World War and has been used for military training ever since. During the post-medieval period there were four farmsteads arranged along the south side of the road, with a large manor farm on the northern side.

7

Discussion: the Archaeological Landscape of the SPTA

The story of human use of the Salisbury Plain Training Area is one of episodic habitation and abandonment, providing us with a largely deserted landscape littered with the detritus of earlier centuries; a legacy of settlements, villages, and fields, together with non-secular monuments such as causewayed enclosures, henges, barrows, shrines and churches. It is clear that from at least the early 4th millennium BC, when the earliest monuments were constructed, a process has taken place that has led to the extensive remodelling of the Plain, and indeed, the wider area.

We cannot be sure of the appearance of the natural landscape in which the first sites were constructed, but environmental samples from recent excavations on the Eastern Ranges (Bradley *et al* 1994), and those recently published for the Stonehenge area (Richards 1990; Cleal *et al* 1995), as well as the results from other isolated, as yet unpublished, excavations, enable us to make some broad observations. There are, of course, uncertainties in that it is unclear how far the information gained from molluscan and pollen analysis can be extrapolated beyond the immediate environment of the sampled areas. It has been suggested that chalkland in prehistory was cloaked in a close canopy woodland that was steadily cleared for agriculture at the beginning of the Neolithic (Evans 1975), was allowed to revert to secondary woodland during the Middle Neolithic, and was steadily converted to grassland during the Early Bronze Age (Watson 1982, 75). However, microclimate, slope, aspect, and soil type, are all likely to influence the pattern, and, as Allen observes, most evidence has come from valley sites rather than the chalk uplands (Allen *in* Cleal 1995, 43). The picture is by no means clear and it is probably unsafe to infer that vegetation and land-use was similar right across the Plain at any point in time.

Pine was present at Stonehenge in the Mesolithic period (op cit, 43), for here three definite, but up to five possible, post-pits were dug between 8500 and 7650 BC

(Cleal *et al* 1995, 55) in either an area of relatively open woodland dominated by pine and hazel or perhaps a substantial clearing close to open woodland cover. Closer to the river, woodland indicators thought to be of Mesolithic date, found under the banks at Durrington Walls and Woodhenge, include species that point to human influence; hazel at Woodhenge, for example, is thought to represent early regeneration (Allen *in* Cleal *et al* 1995, 256–7). This evidence for Mesolithic activity within the Avon valley is supported by finds of flints attributable to the same period from Upavon, and during this period (8500–4500 BC) much of the tree cover might have been removed, particularly along the river valleys, in order to facilitate the management and hunting of wild game. There is continuing discussion concerning the burning of forest to encourage game; Moore (1997), however, has recently provided fresh insight into the natural processes of regular forest fires, particularly of the underwood, indicating that much woodland might not have been as closed as formerly believed. Hunting in dense woodland can be difficult and Coy (1982, 288) has pointed out that it relies heavily on the use of clearings. Work in other parts of southern England, most notably on the Somerset Levels (Orme and Coles 1985), suggests that by the Neolithic, the landscape, and woodland in particular, might have been utilised or managed with some order. It seems likely, therefore, that the chalk supported a patchwork of open and closed woodland, extensive areas of open or grazed land and other formerly open but self-regenerating areas.

The earliest securely dated environmental evidence for the Neolithic in the area comes from the Coneybury 'anomaly' to the south of Stonehenge where there is evidence for grassland in the early 4th millennium BC (Bell and Jones 1990). Cereal grains (emmer wheat) found here might have been locally derived, although it is just as plausible that they were brought to the site from a distance (Carruthers 1990). Elsewhere, there is little evidence of cereal cultivation at this time. Six-rowed barley has been found in a Later Neolithic context at Winterbourne Stoke and emmer wheat at Upavon (Grose 1964, 59), but it is generally thought that the economy of the Earlier Neolithic was largely based on dairying (Grigson 1982). In areas where clusters of monuments occur, for example, around Tilshead, Warminster, and Robin Hood's Ball, more extensive areas might have been open. At Stonehenge the Earlier Neolithic landscape comprised areas of scrubby woodland, as well as open grassland (Allen in Cleal et al 1995, 56). The Amesbury 42 long barrow, built in the middle of the 4th millennium BC, was apparently constructed in well-established grassland (Entwistle 1990, 56), as were the Netheravon Bake long barrow and the Lesser Cursus (Richards 1990).

The construction of the first monuments must have made a profound impact on the landscape, with the banks, ditches and mounds clearly being designed and placed so as to maximise visibility. As we have seen, many of the long barrows were placed so as to be visible from a particular direction; in the majority of cases this is looking away from the chalk, from the valleys and lower-lying plains where it is assumed the majority of the population resided at this time. Certainly, the monuments speak of a landscape that was becoming heavily demarcated with, perhaps, notions of territory, community and, possibly, also ownership. It might be that the monuments were constructed by a number of groups of people who practised a mobile lifestyle, moving from area to area, but who were in the process of becoming more sedentary (Whittle 1997, 21). The importance of ancestral rights and claims to land would have been of great significance in this scenario and it is, therefore, no surprise that the earliest monuments are overtly concerned with burial and a regard for ancestors (Bradley 1998, 54).

As in the area to the south around Stonehenge, flint scatters of Neolithic date occur close to Robin Hood's Ball, in association with a number of contemporary pits of unknown purpose. Another flint accumulation, also of Neolithic date, along with a number of ditches and some undated postholes, has been identified at Copehill Down, to the south of Tilshead (Anon 1988a, 176–7). Late Neolithic activity in

the form of a ditch and four pits at Larkhill (Wainwright et al 1971, 78–82) might be indicative of settlement sites on the bluff overlooking the narrow floodplain of the River Avon, but, as it lies only a short distance to the north of Durrington Walls, it is possible that it represents extramural activity associated with the henge. However, it is difficult to interpret the nature of this evidence with so few diagnostic features or artefacts. If settlements were generally located on the valley floors alongside the major streams, they are now likely to be covered by alluvial/colluvial deposits of some depth. It has been noted elsewhere that many Neolithic sites occur on well-drained sands or pebble deposits close to, rather than on, Clay-with-flints. In this context the various Neolithic surface finds from Sidbury Hill are of particular interest, given the local proximity of the Reading Beds to Clay-with-flints.

Some woodland regeneration is evident during the Middle Neolithic, but the main monuments on the southern periphery of the Training Area, namely Durrington Walls, Woodhenge and Stonehenge, were probably constructed in grassland between 2550 and 1600 BC (Allen in Cleal et al 1995, 52). Thereafter, the landscape appears to have been much more open; molluscan data and soil profiles of early grassland from a number of sites immediately south of the military area, including Boscombe Down (Richardson 1951), Earls Down Farm (Christie 1964), Greenland Farm (Christie 1970), Amesbury (Kerney in Christie et al 1964) and the North Kite (Evans 1984, 26), emphatically make this clear. Some of the mounds that form the King Barrows Ridge cemetery to the east of Stonehenge comprise turf stacks (Cleal and Allen 1994) that must be the result of stripping considerable areas of ground, indicating the contemporary presence of wider grassland. A turf stack was also encountered in a bell barrow at Snail Down (Thomas and Thomas 1955, 137–8).

The concentration of so many funeral monuments between Bulford and Everleigh indicates that the landscape was intensively utilised, with large tracts possibly having been reserved for burial. Indeed, it is possible that the downs themselves were considered to be a sacred area, but, given that round barrows were perhaps being built and used over a period of 500 years, the concentration might represent the construction of little more than one barrow per year.

Figure 7.1
Sarsen boulders lying in the ditch of Figheldean 31 long barrow close to Robin Hood's Ball, 3km north of Stonehenge.

Fleming (1971, 159) considered that the barrow concentration was too great for that expected of local communities and suggested that they represented the activities of transhumant pastoralists. It can be observed, however, that barrow cemeteries were placed at regular distances from each other, approximately 2km apart along the Avon, for example, and such clusters are likely to indicate ancestral associations (or a stake in the landscape), if not outright territoriality. The lack of settlement evidence might suggest that secular activities were excluded from these areas or, alternatively, that settlement during this period is not being recognised due to its ephemeral nature.

Like that of the long barrows, the general position of round barrows implies that the focus of attention was not the chalk downland itself but rather the river valleys. Richards noted that in the area around Stonehenge there is some evidence for settlement among the barrows and suggests the presence of early fields there (Richards 1990, 274–5). Temporary or small-scale subsistence was certainly possible without being constrained by the barrows, but the very intensity of barrows in some places suggests that the major settlement activity was taking place elsewhere in the landscape.

The problem of sarsen stones

Sarsen has figured prominently in archaeological literature about Wessex, particularly in the context of monuments such as Stonehenge and Avebury, and, more than 20 years ago, the Society of Antiquaries considered it important enough to promote a survey of remaining sarsen stones (Bowen and Smith 1977). The genesis of sarsen remains uncertain but it is generally accepted that a crust of siliceous sandstone, regarded as an Eocene (55–38 million years) deposit (Clark, *et al* 1967, 14–16) found in association with the Reading Beds and allied material that formerly covered the chalk, broke up and drifted down into valleys during periods of solifluction, leaving trails of material along valley bottoms.

Studies farther down the dip-slope have suggested that little sarsen remained on Salisbury Plain after deposits were removed during the later part of the Tertiary period (Green 1997a; 1997b, 261). On the higher ground little sarsen remains on the surface today, but occasional boulders have been noted along the Avon, and there is a cluster around Warminster (Manley 1928), coinciding with the area where archaeological records indicate the presence of sarsens in long barrows, as at Arn Hill and Boles Barrow (Cunnington MSS: Devizes Museum). A second group lies in the Amesbury–Bulford area (Fig 7.1) (Barron 1976, 84); a sarsen was noted in the Avon at Bulford (SU161433) (OS 2-inch map), for example, and a number of massive boulders lie close to the Robin Hood's Ball causewayed enclosure. Cunnington, too, recorded sarsen on the Plain, noting that such stones are '...found upon the Downs, a foot or two under the ground (where) their supefices are rounded by attrition...' and added in a footnote that '...others ploughed up near Stonehenge appear to have been bored through by the Teredo...' (Cunnington MSS Book 9: Devizes Museum). Although the Society of Antiquaries survey of sarsens remained incomplete, particularly in the military zone of the Plain, the SPTA survey did not set out to contribute to it. However, broken sarsen boulders were frequently encountered during fieldwork across the area. Observations along the Berril Valley near Imber, during the construction of a tank track, revealed extensive deposits of small sarsen boulders. The Society of Antiquaries study made clear the obstacle that sarsen represented to early settlers in terms of ground clearance (Bowen and Smith 1977, 185), and referred to the examples of 'Celtic' fields at Overton Down that were bounded by sarsens that were subsequently obscured by lynchet formation (op cit, 189). Excavation of an Early Iron Age midden at East Chisenbury revealed sarsen boulders that were neatly broken up and stratified within the deposit; clearly the process of sarsen clearance was well-established at this time, and continued into the historic period. Examples of this include a boulder, presumably from Water Dean Bottom, that has been moved to the door of the farmhouse at Compton, and a farmstead at Fiddington with substantial sarsen foundations. It is considered that clearance to create the extensive 'Celtic'

field systems resulted in many sarsen boulders being obscured by massive lynchets, thus countering claims of their overall geological absence from the area; the sarsen used at Stonehenge need not have come from the Marlborough Downs (*contra* Green 1997b).

Agricultural revolution

The findings from the present survey, together with earlier environmental reports, suggest that large areas of the landscape must have been opened up by the middle of the 2nd millennium BC, if we may assume that the coaxial field systems were laid out in open country. The establishment of such extensive systems demanded an open landscape or widespread clearance. The evidence from the Wilsford Shaft, dug in the Middle Bronze Age (*c* 1500 BC) 4km to the south of the Training Area but part of the same topographical block of downland, is unequivocal. The landscape by this time was notable for its lack of woodland cover (Ashbee *et al* 1989), and cereal pollen, which does not disperse widely from its source, was found in relatively high quantities, indicating local cultivation.

Elsewhere, Gingell has noted that many of the 'Celtic' fields on the Marlborough Downs had been abandoned by the Late Bronze Age (Gingell 1984). At Ebbesbourne Wake, in south Wiltshire, fields had become lynchetted, and perhaps gone out of use, by the time that a Bronze Age hoard was deposited there sometime between 1500 and 1200 BC (Shortt 1949). There is also some evidence to indicate that fields were in use during the currency of Deverel-Rimbury pottery, as early as 1600 BC. The extent of the ancient field systems recorded during the survey is a revelation, since it now appears that relatively little of the downs remained unploughed during the prehistoric and Roman periods. The superficial simplicity of the fields masks not only a complex sequence of construction but also a lengthy history of use. Often the earliest fields are oriented northeast–south-west. They pre-date not only the linear earthworks, which criss-cross the Plain and date to the end of the Bronze Age, but also, it appears, the earliest enclosures of Middle to Late Bronze Age date.

Dividing up the landscape in this way must have been revolutionary. The uniformity of design and the extensiveness of the layout of coaxial systems suggests that there must have been powerful social forces at work. It is difficult to escape the conclusion that they represent some form of central control or widespread cooperative agreement, perhaps as an attempt to rigidly control development. It is likely that the landscape was already notionally divided up before the creation of settlements, and field and linear boundaries of later prehistory and the field systems themselves would also have formed very prominent indicators of land tenure and use. The identity of those exercising control is less easy to define, and arguments for communal ownership or imposed hierarchy are both plausible. Whatever the forces at work, the preferences of individual farmers were made to fit an overall strategy in order to gain some form of social cohesion and, possibly, political strength. This must have been communicated in a way that made it clear that it was to work for the benefit of a community or an individual owner. The conformity of the coaxial systems would have been a very efficient communicator of social cohesion, and it might be that the lack of heavily defended settlements associated with the fields suggests that disputes and tensions resulting from their organisation and operation would have been resolved in a way that did not lead to violence. The creation of these fields is possibly linked to the first real, large-scale colonisation on a permanent basis. Before this, use might have been temporary or sporadic and confined to specific areas. The fields could have been laid out very quickly, so that large areas previously used only on a very piecemeal basis were opened up for exploitation. The degree of survey skills required to do this should not be underestimated. Although straight lines can be maintained across the landscape by the use of a few poles, the scale of the undertakings implies that fairly complex laying-out procedures must have been established.

While the layout often seems to have respected burial sites, it automatically swept aside traditional rights, claims and beliefs about land-use, and would have debarred open access grazing regimes over large areas. The orientation appears to have no agricultural advantage, and the alignment was retained across all topographical variations. It is surprising how widespread this orientation is in 'Celtic' field layout. The fields on Overton and Fyfield Downs on the Marlborough Downs (Fowler and Blackwell 1998) are, very broadly, similarly

oriented, as are those on Preshute Down, and this alignment extends to many field systems across a wide chronological span, even as far afield as Ballooerveld in Holland (Brongers 1976, 136; Harsema 1992, frontispiece).

The dominant axis of north-east–south-west could be seen as an attempt to maximise the use of sunlight, but many of the fields tilt away from the main direction of light; others are built on heavily shaded slopes and the majority are on plateaux where orientation is irrelevant. There are approximately fifteen coaxial field blocks that can be identified from the distribution map of archaeological sites (Fig i.1) and that share this very regular axial layout (Fig 3.4). There are six or so others that show alignments varying between 25° and 3° west of north, as well as other stretches of aggregate fields where it is impossible to define a single axial trend. Coaxial fields are found in all areas of the Plain, suggesting that, at this time, there was a good population spread across the entire colonised area. It is also worth speculating that all of the coaxial systems, laid out as part of the large-scale colonisation of the downs, are contemporary, although it is not clear how the fields functioned. Even if used for cultivation, much of the area might have been fallow at any one time and stock kept on the remainder. But it is possible that some fields were not used at all, especially if they lay at a distance from settlement, the boundaries simply demarcating plots of land that might be utilised in a variety of ways. We could speculate further and suggest that many of the fields at this early date were constructed solely to enclose formerly open terrain, bringing it under control in a symbolic manner, but performing no productive function. However, if the fields were in productive use, as part of a rotational pattern of farming, for example, this has enormous implications in terms of the carrying capacity of the land. By borrowing methods of statistical analysis from historical geographers it is possible to arrive at crude estimates of population for the Higher Plain during the later second millennium BC. Despite uncertainty about their full extent the largest coaxial field systems cover an area of 15 sq km, some 1500ha. On this basis each system would support some twenty-five families, possibly in excess of 100 people. Across the Training Area as a whole, coaxials would support at least 2,000 individuals.

153

No settlement contemporary with the earliest coaxial field systems has been identified and it might be that habitation sites lay at the edges of the system and were subsequently included within later field intakes. It appears, for example, that many aggregate systems, often on a different alignment, represent later infilling of the landscape, the irregular nature of their boundaries reflecting the morphology of previous settlement. In areas where fieldwalking is feasible, there are indications of open settlement occurring among the fields, although this is unlikely to be contemporary with the initial layout. Scatters of flint and Deverel-Rimbury pottery were frequently recorded among the 'Celtic' fields on Brigmerston Down (Bradley *et al* 1994, 35), for example, but it is rarely possible to suggest whether such scatters pre- or post-date the fields.

There is also good evidence for extensive tracts of pasture, supporting the thesis that a well-developed mixed farming regime had been established by the end of the 2nd millennium BC. Bradley *et al* (1994) suggest that the area now given over to military training was, in the late 2nd and early 1st millennia BC, primarily used for pasture with sheep, pig, cattle and horse being exploited. The construction of a network of linear boundaries defining these pastoral zones truncated many of the fields and molluscan analysis indicates that they were established in a landscape of established grassland with long-standing 'short-grazed pasture' (Allen *in* Cleal *et al* 1995, 333), the fields evidently having fallen out of use. On the Eastern Range the only identifiably wooded areas at this time were the hilltops of Windmill Hill and Sidbury Hill, both of which were covered in oak, ash and elder (Bradley *et al* 1994, 120). At the latter site this must represent local woodland regeneration before the construction of the linear ditch system and the hillfort at the beginning of the 1st millennium BC, since the hilltop appears to have been used sporadically from at least the Neolithic period onwards.

While linear earthworks consistently cut through 'Celtic' fields, no well-defined date range has been produced for them. Some are dated by close associations with Plain Ware pottery to perhaps *c* 1200–1000 BC at the earliest, although there is likely to be considerable variation, with many being recut during landscape reorganisation during the 8th–5th centuries BC (op cit, 142).

The fact that the linear earthworks consistently slight 'Celtic' fields indicates that the regime typified by the enclosing of land within small fields was no longer adhered to in the same way. Again, the chronology of events is unclear and it is also uncertain just how extensive the disruption was. Certainly, by the beginning of the 1st millennium BC there had been a significant shift towards stock rearing, with arable still present but much reduced. The presence of high numbers of sheep at the East Chisenbury Early Iron Age midden site provides a clear indication of the dominant species in this area. The available evidence for this site suggests that most of the animals there were consumed in (sacrificial) feasting activities, and it might be that prestige and social ranking was assessed or won on the size of the flocks of sheep and conspicuous consumption of their meat.

The linears appear to have performed a number of functions, perhaps initially forming territorial boundaries but later being used as trackways. This latter use is certainly evident at a number of the Romano-British settlements such as Knook, Chapperton Down, and Church Pits, where linear ditches were adapted and utilised as main streets. Overall, however, the long-held view that linears represent 'ranch' boundaries must still be considered. Indeed, a lack of other contemporary archaeological features close by, or within, these areas reinforces the interpretation that the downs were used for pastoral purposes, and that the cooperative control implied by the coaxial fields had undergone a transformation. The construction of linear ditches must have also been a cooperative venture, but reflects different social needs and perhaps also a degree of competition. These boundaries clearly played an important role in symbolically dividing the landscape, although they might also have had important economic functions.

Enclosures

Angled and rectangular enclosures were the most commonly observed Bronze Age settlement form. The majority of sites remain undated but, by analogy with examples elsewhere in southern England, including those on Cranborne Chase (Barrett *et al* 1991) and the Marlborough Downs (Gingell 1984), they can be dated to the Later Bronze Age. Up to twenty enclosures of this type have been recognised, including those at Ablington Furze, Figheldean, Church Ditches, Milston and Lidbury and several on Brigmerston Down. These are generally small, rectilinear in outline, often overlie fields and frequently occur close to linear earthworks. None of these sites appears to be associated with contemporary cultivation or to display evidence of intensive farmyard activity. The bulk of the evidence would suggest that rather than permanently occupied farmsteads, these enclosures might have been used on a seasonal basis by shepherds and their families tending the sheep on the downs, and in a similar manner perhaps to the medieval sheep enclosures and post-medieval barns. Apart from Church Ditches, for which Piggott's excavation remains unpublished, only Lidbury has seen excavation, and here Cunnington revealed two phases of construction over a period spanning 800 to 450 BC.

In contrast, later enclosures display a wider variety of shapes and sizes, usually circular or oval, surviving for the most part as cropmarks around the periphery of the Training Area and along the margins of the river valleys. What little is known of them from survey and excavation suggests that they most probably date to the late 1st millennium BC, with a substantial number continuing to be occupied well into the Roman period. Sites such as Chisenbury Trendle and Widdington Farm are associated with scratch-cordoned bowls (6th–5th century BC) in their earliest phases. Mancombe Down, with a small sherd of furrowed bowl dating to at least the 8th century BC is earlier, but it is uncertain whether or not this pottery was residual from an earlier unenclosed phase of the site (Fowler *et al* 1965). Whether these represent typical isolated farms or the equivalent of field barns is unclear, but in at least one case, Coombe Down, the enclosure formed a precursor for the Romano-British settlement.

Perhaps the most spectacular discovery during the survey was that of a massive midden mound of the Early Iron Age at East Chisenbury. Only a few comparable sites are known elsewhere in England; East Chisenbury stands alone, however, because it survives above ground. Survey and excavation here clearly mark this as a site of international importance. Furthermore, it is apparent that, as indicated above, this is no mere collection of rubbish and might represent the curated remains of feasts and associated celebrations.

Ritual concerns are perhaps also reflected in many of the hillforts. Five have been previously classified within the Training Area, the largest of which, with an area of 27.5ha, is Casterley Camp. The term 'hillfort' covers a wide morphological diversity and this is apparent within the surveyed examples. Traditional interpretations of hillforts as primarily defensive structures, are brought into question by the varying defensive capabilities of these sites. There is a similar diversity in their topographical setting and only one, Sidbury Camp, that is located on a prominent hilltop, might be thought of as having a strategic advantage. The others are placed in a variety of locales, most often spurs or plateaux. At Casterley Camp, the enclosing boundary is so ephemeral in nature that it could never have been used in a defensive manner. Instead, the banks and ditches are used to demarcate an area that had been important to local people over a long period of time, as suggested by the finds of Neolithic and Bronze Age material here. This is not to say that there was continuous occupation; it is the sense of place, the recognition of the site's preceding significance, that is being given added definition by the creation of the surrounding earthworks. The location of the entrance so far downslope at the head of a coombe further negates the defence argument, and seems placed so as to facilitate access from the deep re-entrant into which it faces. Given the indications of a contemporary local economy heavily dependent on sheep, the site might have provided a market function, with the location of the entrance designed for access by flocks. To accompany this activity there might have been a range of other social events, some of which were, possibly, ceremonial in nature; it is no surprise, therefore, that in the Late Iron Age and possibly earlier, a *Viereckschanze* or ritual enclosure, was constructed in the middle of the site. At this time, one segment of the defences was refurbished but the remainder of the circuit was untouched. This rebuilding of only one segment can have had no defensive purpose and seems best interpreted as an attempt to create a visually impressive, and perhaps symbolic, façade for the enclosure. It is curious, too, that the hinterland appears to be genuinely devoid of 'Celtic' fields and might have been an area of managed woodland or, alternatively, deliberately reserved from cultivation.

The construction of the enclosure in a field-free enclave would have served to highlight and give a focus to its placement. It sits at the head of a coombe that gives direct access to the Avon Valley 1.5km to the west, thus facilitating its easy inclusion within any existing riverine trade or communication network.

Similar arguments of indefensibility can be used of Scratchbury, where the ramparts, although more substantial, are so far downslope that large portions of the interior are visible from the valley floor to the south and west. This hillfort incorporates a number of earlier burial mounds within the interior, and we can speculate that living among the remains of the dead created a symbolically charged environment for the inhabitants. With the earlier burial mounds, settlement and massive ramparts and ditches, Scratchbury would have been a focal and very strategic location for the interception of river-borne transport and trade, and, lying close to the watershed between the river systems of the Avon and Stour, it is feasible that the site functioned as a 'market' in much the same way as Casterley Camp. Its near neighbour, Battlesbury, might not be contemporary, but it too is a remarkably visible site, being prominently located at the mouth of the Wylye valley. Travellers using this route would have been confronted by stunning views of the site when approaching from the west.

Finds of Romano-British material at Sidbury, Casterley Camp and Battlesbury suggest that these sites continued to function after the Roman Conquest. Again, more work is needed to clarify their role at the time of the Claudian campaigns, but it is suspected that they might have featured among the twenty or so hillforts taken by Vespasian in AD 43–4 (Cunliffe 1991, 202). At Coombe Down we catch a glimpse of an extremely important but transient event. Here, an open village replaced the double concentric Iron Age enclosure so that on the surface no trace of the enclosure exists. This almost certainly involved levelling the enclosure, thus creating an emphatic break with the past, since its course along the western arc has been reused as a terraced track within the later settlement. Here we can see an example of the process by which the scattered, isolated, enclosed farms of the late 1st millennium BC are replaced by large, open nucleated villages, many with an integrated street pattern, and it is tempting to conclude that this change resulted directly from Roman control.

The level of activity during the Iron Age at Knook Castle is unknown because of the effects of later cultivation. Positioned so close to the Romano-British settlement at Knook West, the community there would have perceived it as the major feature in the surrounding landscape, and yet it does not appear to have been utilised as a settlement at this time. Its only entrance faces southeast, away from the village.

A new order...

The evidence from environmental assessment indicates that arable exploitation continued throughout the Iron Age, though of unknown extent and density, and was further developed throughout the first two centuries of the 1st millennium AD (Bradley *et al* 1994, 105; 108). The thin soils would have required a considerable amount of fertilizer and many fields must have held stock; it is presumed, therefore, that some form of rotational system was practised. It is unclear whether the field boundaries supported hedgerows, but the need for wood for construction and fuel implies that areas of managed woodland existed somewhere locally.

A decline in the rate of colluvial build-up, in association with molluscan analysis, noted on excavations at Chisenbury Warren and Coombe Down, points to a temporary abandonment of the fields sometime between the late 2nd and early 3rd centuries (Entwistle 1993). The reasons for this might be found in events happening elsewhere in the Roman world and their effects on the regional economy. In any case, this was a short-lived episode and thereafter the extent of field systems and settlement reached its zenith on the downland.

The true scale of Romano-British settlements on the Plain can only now be appreciated. One village, on Cheverell Down, was rediscovered, while a number of others were noted through aerial survey. Prominent among these is that found on the western flank of the Avon valley at Fifield Folly. Here, a number of pits, ditches and areas of darkened soil suggest the existence of a settlement contemporary with those elsewhere in the area, subsequently confirmed by finds of Roman pottery on the ploughed surface of the field. The surviving earthwork sites have been shown by a combination of aerial and ground survey to be remarkably complex and detailed, set within their attendant landscapes of fields and roads. Several of them, such as Charlton Down and Chapperton Down, are enormous, sprawling concentrations of settlement with interlinked roads and fields, and suburb development utilizing 'greenfield' sites. Any notions of Salisbury Plain as a deserted 'no-man's land' during the Roman era (Frere 1987, 266) can be dismissed.

The identification, principally by geophysical survey, of a number of villas in the surrounding valleys, further undermines the traditional view and provides a context for the presence of such large settlements on the Higher Plain. It seems likely that these villas and settlements formed the integrated basis for heavy arable exploitation of the area. Much of the grain produced on the downs would have been processed, then exported via the villa estate centres.

...and decline

There is good reason to believe that a number of the Romano-British settlements continued to be occupied, albeit in a much reduced form, in the early 5th century. Elsewhere, pollen diagrams indicate that after c AD 400 there was decreasing use of land for arable purposes at the expense of regenerating woodland (Turner 1981, 71–2), although it seems most unlikely that the Higher Plain reverted entirely to woodland. Grass-tempered pottery and a possible sunken-featured building from excavations at Coombe Down (Entwistle et al 1994), point to activity continuing, or being resumed, well beyond the 5th century. A small percentage of the fields might have continued in use and the decline in cultivation might have been a long drawn-out affair rather than a rapid abandonment. Initially, unencumbered by the constraints of cultivated fields, there was probably some mobility among inhabitants leading ultimately to the abandonment of the Higher Plain.

Between the end of the period of Roman rule and the Norman Conquest it is difficult to gauge the sequence of events. The forms of settlement and land-use are at present unknown, but there is strong evidence to suggest that the area, or perhaps more particularly its river valleys, played host to substantial settlement. The tripartite distinction within estates between valley meadow, arable and downland pasture, that lasted until the modern era, might have

been established at this time. The relationship of boundaries to Romano-British settlements is interesting. It has been repeatedly demonstrated that the relict Romano-British villages are either partially enclosed by, or lie close to, the valley settlement's territorial boundary in the medieval period. This might suggest that, on a local level at least, there was a residual link to these places; the Higher Plain settlement, even when it was finally abandoned, was a place where the ancestors had lived and tilled their fields. These links between the valley and Higher Plain might not necessarily have been formed by a continuous tract of land; valley settlements might have had detached holdings, like the later detached territories of some medieval parishes, with the remainder of the Plain remaining a largely unallocated zone. We see the relationship between Higher Plain holdings and the valley settlements later becoming more firmly established in the 9th and 10th centuries, as the charter boundaries show.

Finds of early Saxon artefacts, such as spearheads, jewellery, and pottery are relatively rare. However, the five spearheads from Marden Down, two of which are H1 type dating to the 5th century, are significant since they were recovered from an area close to the Romano-British village on Charlton Down. Other indications of settlement are also missing but there is a strong suspicion that, away from the Higher Plain, in the valleys and around the periphery of the chalk escarpment, many of the present-day settlements might have had a Saxon, and indeed possibly a Roman, origin. The finding of three early Saxon brooches at Upavon and on the lower slopes in the area where the Avon valley opens out to the Vale of Pewsey, is also noteworthy. Later Saxon finds are more evident along the Avon valley, and together with the place-name evidence, would strongly suggest that settlement was concentrated along the valleys at this time. The present valley settlements show a variety of forms, from the agglomerated hamlet to the compact regular row. Hindurrington is the only example of complete medieval desertion, although others such as Gore, Choulston, Alton and Syrencot, only survive as later farmsteads. There is, however, good evidence for settlement shrinkage and shift along the Avon, Till and Bourne valleys and on the flanks of the chalk escarpment. Shift from an earlier core can be seen at Imber, where the church is isolated on the higher ground some distance from the manor, with the remainder of the village lying principally on the valley floor. A number of other modern settlements, such as Tilshead, also mask earlier origins.

Although it is clear that some 'continuous' boundaries were established by the 10th century, the earthwork evidence of territorial boundaries crossing ridge-and-furrow (probably dating to the 13th or 14th centuries), suggests that there was some later realignment of boundaries, possibly before the 16th century (the Duchy of Lancaster's perambulations would suggest that the boundaries were demarcated by this time). The linearity of many of the boundaries also shows that the Higher Plain was in pasture.

The relationship of early Saxon secondary burials in barrows to the continuing occupation of the Higher Plain settlements needs to be explored. Interestingly, none of the interments in long barrows occur to the east of the Avon valley, although there are three from round barrows, adding emphasis to the differences in the archaeological record on either side of the river. It has also been suggested that settlement on the Higher Plain continued, albeit at a reduced level, beyond the 5th century and it therefore seems conceivable that the interments in barrows might have been of inhabitants of these Higher Plain settlements. The barrows were clearly significant features in the landscape, continuing in use as repositories of the dead or as boundary markers; they might therefore have also been regarded as sacred to the Anglo-Saxons as they were in earlier periods.

Anglo-Saxon minsters have been identified at a number of places on the fringes of Salisbury Plain, at Warminster, Upavon, Netheravon, Tilshead and possibly Heytesbury (Hase 1994, 53). Hints of later Saxon ecclesiastical administrative boundaries enclosing the parochia, have also been identified. At Netheravon, the parochia probably included much the same area as the Elstub Hundred boundary and included Netheravon, Enford, East and West Chisenbury, and Fittleton. West Chisenbury is securely linked to Netheravon since the medieval chapel-of-ease at West Chisenbury was dependent on Netheravon. The break-up of the parochia in Wessex, generally dating from the 9th to the later 12th century (op cit, 62), is instanced here by the grant of Enford to St Swithun's (Winchester) in the mid-10th century, which effectively left Chisenbury

detached from Netheravon. As Hase notes, grants of this kind invariably led to the foundation of a new local church, no longer dependent on the minster. In this case Enford church was no longer tied to the old minster at Netheravon. A church is implied at Enford at the time of the Domesday Survey when a priest held land here (Thorn and Thorn 1979, 2.10).

Much of the Training Area, apart from the Central Range and the area to the west of Tilshead as far as Imber, lay within the royal forests of Chute and Selwood (Grant 1959, 449; 453). These forests were probably created by at least the late 11th century and included much open downland that might have been interspersed with small pockets of scrub and woodland. Chute Forest also contained three royal parks; two at Ludgershall and another, smaller example at Everleigh. The effect that the creation of these forests had on the region is not entirely clear, although it appears to have had little impact on the settlement pattern. However, it is interesting to note that the temporary cultivation noted on the Higher Plain lies within areas not subject to Forest Law, that is, the area of the Central Range around Thornham Down, Church Pits, and farther west at Knook, suggesting perhaps that tithings within the forest might have been inhibited from extending cultivation onto the Higher Plain.

Cultivation of the Higher Plain appears not to have been carried out in any concerted manner until the post-medieval period. Although it is only evident where there is an absence of earlier 'Celtic' fields, later estate and enclosure maps show that cultivation extended deep into the Higher Plain, including the interiors of hillforts such as Casterley and Battlesbury. This is particularly noticeable in the parishes of Market Lavington and Erlestoke where practically the whole of the Higher Plain was being cultivated by the late 18th century. Much of this cultivation was carried out from the villages, the farm workers being obliged to journey each day from the valley settlement; it was not until the late 18th and early 19th centuries that the Higher Plain was again settled in a controlled manner. The field barns of the late 18th century were distributed on both sides of the River Avon; the later farmsteads were more conspicuous in the west, although they might well have been more prevalent during other periods of agricultural expansion such as the 13th and early 14th centuries.

The archaeology of warfare

The most recent episode of 'dislocation' of the Higher Plain occurred in the early 20th century when military acquisition resulted in the abandonment of the newly established post-Enclosure farmsteads and the area reverted to grassland. In this respect, the region is unlike many other areas in England where marginal land has been intensively cultivated and new settlements established in hitherto unsuitable places.

The military use of the Plain can broadly be characterised by a series of 'zones of activity'. The valleys, however, remained the focus of settlement with regular garrisons, built initially on a grid pattern, dominating the edge of the former medieval villages of Bulford, Tidworth, Ludgershall and Warminster. Larkhill is unique in this respect since it lies on the Higher Plain close to its principal 'zone of activity', the artillery range. Another zone was the area of the rifle ranges. These are situated close to the garrisons and temporary camps and within easy reach of the soldiers. Although the area of the rifle range might be quite small, the 'zone of activity' is much larger due to the inherent danger, and as such precludes other forms of training.

The largest zone is the artillery 'impact area'. Although small pieces of shrapnel are sometimes encountered elsewhere on the Higher Plain, suggesting other, unspecified impact areas, the two main impact zones lie to the north of Larkhill. Despite the considerable amount of munitions that have been detonated in these areas during the past one hundred years, much of the underlying archaeology can still be recognised. However, in areas of more intense activity, particularly where there have been mines or bombing, much of the archaeology is difficult to interpret.

Analysis of military fortifications from the 19th and 20th centuries has, until recently, been concerned with the more prominent sites such as the coastal defences and the 'stop line' trenches constructed during the Second World War. Little detailed work, however, has been undertaken on the trench systems since, by their very nature, they leave only slight evidence either in the form of earthworks or crop marks (cf Smith 1995). Trenches were designed as ephemeral earthworks, built specifically to provide protection for troops for a relatively short period of time when attacked or when defending an area. On Salisbury Plain the trenches have been mapped in detail and we now have an understanding of their siting and construction. These trenches are, apart from the notable exceptions of other military training areas such as at Otterburn or Dartmoor, among the few remaining areas in England where an appreciation of their overall scale and landscape setting can be gained.

8
Conclusion

We have recorded the physical remains as they survive and provided as detailed a commentary as possible on their conditions and morphologies. We have also sought to go beyond this by considering other aspects that have left no direct physical trace, but that have had a profound impact on where and why sites developed.

We have noted, for instance, that certain locations were used repeatedly and were perhaps seen as significant places in the landscape throughout a long period. There is a tendency for monuments to be built on or alongside earlier monumental landmarks. Not only do we see this at cause-wayed enclosures such as Robin Hood's Ball, but also in later millennia: Late Bronze Age enclosures, such as those on the Bulford Ranges, are constructed on the sites of earlier activity even though the builders might only have perceived this by the presence of different vegetation and old artefactual debris. Hillforts, in their association with earlier barrows, enclosures and linear earthworks, form part of this process and seem continually to re-emphasise locations of ancestral activity. The later Iron Age and Roman structures within Casterley Camp, identified as a possible *Viereckschanze*, show that this process continued. In the Roman period, however, there appear to be many changes in belief, and the altar and plaque of Minerva from Charlton indicate that new gods were respected. The reuse of earlier burial mounds in the Anglo-Saxon period re-emphasised the sacredness and symbolic importance of ancestral linkages and tenure of the landscape.

It is also clear that prominent natural landmarks such as hilltops and river valleys were imbued with special meaning. The tendency for round barrows to avoid the most prominent hilltops might, on the one hand, suggest that the latter were cloaked in woodland at the time. On the other hand, and more plausibly, they were ignored because the barrows were built to emphasise the importance of springs and springlines, as well as the river and stream networks. The fact that the builders of the burial mounds avoided the most distinctive landmark in the area is striking, and suggests perhaps that it was taboo, 'out-of-bounds' or reserved for some other purpose. The importance of Sidbury Hill is confirmed by the length of activity on its summit, with its focus of linear earthworks and with the construction of the hillfort.

This book records the archaeological remains across a substantial part of chalk downland. In doing so the project attempted to record the archaeology as objectively as possible. However, at an early stage it became apparent that perceptions of monuments and landscape were largely conditioned by the restrictions of modern paraphernalia. Throughout much of southern England, modern boundaries, paths and roads force the traveller to move through the landscape in a heavily prescribed manner. For the visitor who is free to roam, a subtly different landscape emerges and a return to earlier patterns of movement, as on parts of the SPTA, becomes possible. Routes to and from Roman settlements and fields are used again simply because it is now apparent that they were the most economical routes available. Likewise, movement within settlements is best done along the original streets and lanes. A number of the barrow cemeteries also make sense in this regard: they marked the position of bourne holes and springs, and were placed so as to be seen from the most frequented thoroughfares, the river valleys.

To travel across the Training Area is a stimulating journey that highlights the real differentiation apparent within what, superficially, appears to be a homogeneous landscape. The survey, both aerial- and ground-based, faced many more specific problems. The disentangling of older archaeological features from those that result directly from recent military damage was a major achievement; the difficulty of differentiating shell craters and other scars

from scarps associated with settlement and fields should not be underestimated. The experience of walking along streets leading to, and then through, deserted Romano-British settlements, taking smaller lanes that lead to individual house compounds or others that lead out into the surrounding fields, is awe-inspiring. The experience offers a connection with the past that is possible in only a few other places in England, such as on Dartmoor or in the Cheviots. On the SPTA, the visible intensity of past land use, the remarkable degree of preservation, and its current fossilised state, set it apart.

Eight million shells have landed on and around the Charlton settlement since military occupation began and it seems strange that the remains that so peacefully escaped

the worst of historic agriculture should be so violently shaken now. This use of the landscape is the most revolutionary of all, for by its very nature it is the final use (Fig 8.1). It is impossible to assess the number of unexploded shells but it is expected to run into tens of thousands and many were noted during the course of this survey. Thus it is unsafe for the land to be used for anything else. There is new growth; safe from human interference, the land has returned to a wild state and supports some of the finest flora and fauna of the British Isles. It is likely that the Charlton Down settlement and, indeed, much of the archaeology still visible on the SPTA, will remain long after most archaeological sites in the lowlands of southern England have succumbed to the excesses of the 21st century.

Figure 8.1
Land use on the Central Ranges. The view from an observation post on the Larkhill Impact Area showing targets in the foreground. Artillery shellfire pounds the Impact Area daily. The vehicle hulks provide scale.

Song of the Dark Ages

by Francis Brett Young

We digged our trenches on the down
Beside old barrows, and the wet
White chalk we shovelled from below;
It lay like drifts of thawing snow
On parados and parapet:

Until a pick neither struck flint
Nor split the yielding chalky soil,
But only calcined human bone:
Poor relic of that Age of Stone
Whose ossuary was our spoil.

Home we marched singing in the rain,
And all the while, beneath our song,
I mused how many springs should wane
And still our trenches scar the plain:
The monument of an old wrong.

But then, I thought, the fair green sod
Will wholly cover that white stain,
And soften, as it clothes the face
Of those old barrows, every trace
Of violence to the patient plain.

And careless people, passing by,
Will speak of both in casual tone:
Saying "You will see the toil they made:
The age of iron, pick and spade,
Here jostles with the Age of Stone."

Yet either from that happier race
Will merit but a passing glance;
And they will leave us both alone:
Poor savages who wrought in stone –
Poor savages who fought in France.

Francis Brett Young was stationed on Salisbury Plain between 1915 and 1918 with the Royal Army Medical Corps (Crawford 1999, 6) and his poems were published in 1919 by Collins.

Concordance

List of sites mentioned in the text

Space restriction does not permit a full inventory of sites to be included here. The full archive is available for consultation at the National Monuments Record Centre (NMRC) and the sites included here are those mentioned in the text. Each site mentioned has been given a suffix, where appropriate (NMR number), that comprises the Ordnance Survey 1:10 000 quarter sheet followed by a unique reference number (for example, SU 25 SW 9); this makes it possible to cross-reference to the more detailed archive held in Swindon. The subject matter is arranged chronologically, following discussion of themes, such as burial, ritual, settlement or agriculture in each chapter.

Concordance table

Type	site	grid reference	NMR number
Airfield	Larkhill	SU 140435	–
Airfield	Netheravon	SU 165495	–
Airfield	New Zealand Farm	ST 973508	–
Airfield	Rollestone	SU 094448	–
Airfield	Upavon	SU 155545	–
Anti-Tank Range	Shrewton Folly	SU 095475	SU 04 NE 38
Castle	Ludgershall	SU 26385118	SU 25 SE 3
Causewayed Enclosure	Robin Hood's Ball	SU 10204595	SU 14 NW 3
Causewayed Enclosure	Scratchbury Inner	ST 912442	ST 94 SW 17
Chapel	Compton	SU 134521	SU 15 SW 93
Chapel	Coombe	SU 148505	SU 15 SW 31
Chapel	Gore	SU 01315039	SU 05 SW 5
Chapel	Knighton	SU 155455	SU 14 NE 73
Chapel	West Chisenbury	SU 13645298	SU 15 SW 44
Church	Amesbury	SU 15184143	SU 14 SE 120
Church	Enford	SU 14065163	SU 15 SW 18
Church	Everleigh	SU 205540	SU 25 SW 200
Church	Figheldean	SU 15274749	SU 14 NE 74
Church	Fittleton	SU 14624954	SU 14 NW 37
Church	Heytesbury	ST 92504255	ST 94 SW 3
Church	Milston	SU 162452	SU 14 NE 250
Church	Netheravon	SU 14794839	SU 14 NW 18
Church	Tidworth	SU 235490	SU 24 NW 163
Church	Tilshead	SU 03474798	SU 04 NW 28
Church	Upavon	SU 13545504	SU 15 NW 11
Church	Warminster	ST 87394508	ST 84 NE 15
Enclosure	Ablington Furze	SU 18494816	SU 14 NE 26
Enclosure	Brigmerston East 1	SU 20834766	SU 24 NW 2
Enclosure	Brigmerston East 2	SU 20784762	SU 24 NW 2
Enclosure	Brigmerston U	SU 20374740	SU 24 NW 52
Enclosure	Casterley Interior	SU 11595346	SU 15 SW 5
Enclosure	Chisenbury Field Barn	SU 15855346	SU 15 NE 44
Enclosure	Chisenbury Trendle	SU 15205380	SU 15 SE 7
Enclosure	Church Ditches	SU 088519	SU 05 SE 12
Enclosure	Coombe Down	SU 193520	SU 15 SE 117
Enclosure	Dunch Hill	SU 20704801	SU 24 NW 7
Enclosure	Dunch Hill/Figheldean	SU 20654800	SU 24 NW 7
Enclosure	East Chisenbury	SU 146573	SU 15 SW 34
Enclosure	Edington Hill	ST 92705250	ST 95 SW 43
Enclosure	Everleigh	SU 20755264	SU 25 SW 69
Enclosure	Lidbury	SU 16655340	SU 15 SE 6
Enclosure	Maddington Down	SU 03814311	SU 04 NW 19
Enclosure	Mancombe Down	ST 89504710	ST 8 3NE 3
Enclosure	Marden Down	SU 07635355	SU 05 SE 4

Enclosure	Milston Down	SU 20734659	SU 24 NW 51
Enclosure	Netheravon	SU 14854698	SU 14 NW 107
Enclosure	Pewsey Hill	SU 16755765	SU 15 NE 42
Enclosure	Snoddington Hill	SU 24594544	SU 24 NW 27
Enclosure	Stoke Hill	SU 96345211	ST 95 SE 87
Enclosure	Warren Hill	SU 25714773	SU 24 NE 5
Enclosure	Widdington Farm	SU 12755411	SU 15 SW 33
Farmstead	Compton	SU 132521	–
Farmstead	Copehill Farm	SU 029462	–
Farmstead	Eastcott Down Farm	SU 038539	SU 05 SW 72
Farmstead	Enford Farm	SU 127507	SU 15 SW 114
Farmstead	Greenland Farm	SU 068470	–
Farmstead	Keeper's Farm	SU 058473	–
Farmstead	Newfoundland Farm	SU 107478	–
Farmstead	Pond Farm	SU 044525	–
Farmstead	Prospect Farm	SU 073491	–
Farmstead	Slay Down	SU 089503	–
Farmstead	Summer Down	SU 060509	SU 05 SE 81
Farmstead	Widdington Farm	SU 124535	–
Farmstead	Wilsford Down Farm North	SU 074523	–
Field Barn	Compton Bake	SU 099505	SU 05 SE 80
Field Barn	Compton Field Barn	SU 118514	SU 15 SW 118
Field Barn	Honeydown Barn	SU 082488	–
Field Barn	Old Barn	SU 028529	SU 05 SW 71
Field Gun Emplacements	Imber	ST 955455	ST 94 NE 67
Field Gun Emplacements	Orcheston Down	SU 075475	SU 04 NE 40
Garden	Middleton	ST 908446	ST 94 SW 44
Garden	Tilshead Lodge	SU 026473	SU 04 NW 65
Henge	Weather Hill	SU 20645260	SU 25 SW 65
Hillfort	Battlesbury Camp	ST 898456	ST 84 NE 4
Hillfort	Bratton Castle	ST 90035160	ST 95 SW 1
Hillfort	Casterley Camp	SU 115535	SU 15 SW 5
Hillfort	Knook Castle	ST 960444	ST 94 SE 2
Hillfort	Scratchbury Camp	ST 912443	S T 94 SW 1
Hillfort	Sidbury Hill	SU 216505	SU 25 SW 37
Impact Area	Chapperton Down	ST 995478	–
Impact Area	Knook Down	ST 960455	–
Linear Earthwork	Church Pits	SU 054490–SU075459	SU 04 NE 1
Linear Earthwork	Dunch Hill	SU 209485–SU 231436	SU 24 NW 11
Linear Earthwork	Figheldean Down	SU 180497–186493	SU 14 NE 23
Linear Earthwork	Old Ditch West	ST 877493–ST 948449	LIN 87
Linear Earthwork	Old Nursery Ditch	SU 07875148– SU11755015	SU 05 SE 11
Linear Earthwork	Sidbury Double	SU 210521– SU 215508 SU	25 SW 166
Linear Earthwork	Snail Down	SU 204519–SU211520	SU 25 SW 167
Linear Earthwork	Tidworth Down	SU 214486–SU 211483 SU	24 NW 145
Lodge Tilshead	Lodge	SU 024475	SU 04 NW 65
Long Barrow	Arn Hill (Warminster 1)	ST 87394706	ST 84 NE 5
Long Barrow	Boles Barrow (Heytesbury 1)	ST 94204676	ST 94 NW 20
Long Barrow	Bratton 1	ST 90035160	ST 95 SW 2
Long Barrow	Durrington 24	SU 12484439	SU 14 SW 23
Long Barrow	East Down (Tilshead 7)	SU 05984944	SU 04 NE 7
Long Barrow	Ell Barrow (Wilsford N 3)	SU 07305138	SU 05 SE 22
Long Barrow	Figheldean 31 (Alton Down)	SU 10894588	SU 14 NW 5
Long Barrow	Fittleton 5	ST 19895168	SU 15 SE 16
Long Barrow	Heytesbury Field (Heytesbury 4)	ST 92504150	ST 94 SW 1
Long Barrow	Imber Down (Imber 4a)	ST 96199418	ST 94 NE 7
Long Barrow	Kill Barrow (Tilshead 1)	SU 04 NW 11	SU 00014789
Long Barrow	Knighton Down (Figheldean 27)	SU 12794531	SU 14 NW 14
Long Barrow	Knook 2	ST 95614460	ST 94 SE 21

Long Barrow	Knook Down 5	ST 96754625	ST 94 NE 18
Long Barrow	Middleton Down	ST 91864595	ST 94 NW 16
	(Norton Bavant 14)		
Long Barrow	Milston (1) Milston Firs	SU 18954595	SU 14 NE 125
Long Barrow	Milston 39	SU 21704629	SU 24 NW 93
Long Barrow	Milston 40	SU 21704635	SU 24 NW 34
Long Barrow	Netheravon 6	SU 11434667	SU 14 NW 41
Long Barrow	Netheravon Bake (a)	SU 11424668	SU 14 NW 7
Long Barrow	Netheravon Bake (b)	SU 10814655	SU 14 NW 59
Long Barrow	Norton Bavant	ST 92564595	ST 94 NW 28
	(Norton Bavant 13)		
Long Barrow	Old Ditch Barrow (Tilshead 2)	SU 02324686	SU 04 NW 9
Long Barrow	Oxendean Down (Warminster 6)	ST 90244717	ST 94 NW 17
Long Barrow	Sheer Barrow (Figheldean)	SU 16864822	SU 14 NE 12
Long Barrow	Tilshead Lodge (Tilshead 5)	ST 02104750	ST 04 NW 12
Long Barrow	Tinhead (Edington 7)	ST 93795240	ST 95 SW 13
Long Barrow	White Barrow (Tilshead 4)	SU 03304686	SU 04 NW 3
Medieval Borough	Ludgershall	SU 265505	SU 25 SE 3
Medieval Settlement	Ablington	SU 15854675	SU 14 NE 209
Medieval Settlement	Alton Magna	SU 15034670	SU 14 NE 210
Medieval Settlement	Bulford	SU 166437	SU 14 SE 281
Medieval Settlement	Choulston	SU 151485	SU 14 NE 83
Medieval Settlement	Compton	SU 133520	SU 15 SW 76
Medieval Settlement	Coombe	SU 14965040	SU 15 SW 31
Medieval Settlement	Durrington	SU 157448	–
Medieval Settlement	East Chisenbury	SU 140525	SU 15 SW 43
Medieval Settlement	Enford	SU 141516	SU 15 SW 84
Medieval Settlement	Everleigh	SU 205540	SU 25 SW 132
Medieval Settlement	Figheldean	SU 152472	SU 14 NE 82
Medieval Settlement	Fittleton	SU 148498	SU 14 NW 109
Medieval Settlement	Gore	SU 013504	SU 05 SW 5
Medieval Settlement	Haxton	SU 147493	SU 14 NW 102
Medieval Settlement	Hindurrington	SU 166444	SU 14 SE 348
Medieval Settlement	Imber	ST 966486	ST 94 NE 22
Medieval Settlement	Imber Coney Site	ST 95504876	ST 94 NE 37
Medieval Settlement	Knighton	SU 155455	SU 14 NE 73
Medieval Settlement	Knighton Farm	SU 15504550	SU 14 NE 73
Medieval Settlement	Longstreet	SU 14205140	SU 15 SW 46
Medieval Settlement	Middleton	ST 90754456	ST 94 SW 44
Medieval Settlement	Milston	SU 16354525	SU 14 NE 211
Medieval Settlement	Netheravon	SU 14804844	SU 14 NW 104
Medieval Settlement	Orcheston St George	SU 059449	SU 04 SE 161
Medieval Settlement	Orcheston St Mary	SU 059456	SU 04 NE 39
Medieval Settlement	Syrencot	SU 160460	SU 14 NE 234
Medieval Settlement	Tidworth	SU 235490	–
Medieval Settlement	Tilshead	SU 037478	SU 04 NW 29
Medieval Settlement	Upavon	SU 135556	SU 15 NW 71
Medieval Settlement	West Chisenbury	SU 13645298	SU 15 SW 44
Medieval Settlement	Widdington	SU 124536	SU 15 SW 68
Midden	East Chisenbury	SU 146573	SU 15 SW 22
Military Camp	Bulford	SU 1843	–
Military Camp	Larkhill	SU 1344	–
Military Camp	Ludgershall	SU 2549	–
Military Camp	West Down South	SU 0647	–
Military Railway	Larkhill	SU 115446	–
Military Railway	Tidworth	SU 238485	–
Military Trenches	Knook Down	ST 965455	ST 94 NE 67
Military Trenches	Market Lavington	SU 043518	SU 05 SW 73
Military Trenches	Market Lavington	SU 048518	SU 05 SW 73

Military Trenches	Perham Down	SU 249460	SU 24 NW 164
Military Trenches	Shrewton Folly	SU 087468	SU 04 NE 40
Military Trenches	Slay Down	SU 084511	SU 05 SE 84
Neolithic Pits	Copehill Down	SU 017453	SU 04 NW 61
Park	East Chisenbury	SU 13955255	SU 15 SW 43
Park	Everleigh	SU 2055	SU 25 NW 66
Park	Imber	ST 965489	ST 94 NE 64
Pillow Mound	Conegar Hill	ST 948448	ST 94 SW 33
Pillow Mounds	Luccombe Bottom	ST 924522	ST 95 SW 18, 91, 92
Pillow Mounds	Piquet Hill	ST 926523	ST 95 SW 4
Prehistoric Fields	Dunch Hill	SU 214478	SU 24 NW 139
Prehistoric Fields	Figheldean Down	SU 185495	SU 14 NW 213
Prehistoric Fields	Lidbury	SU16655340	SU 15 SE 6
Prehistoric Fields	Orcheston Down	SU 0748	SU 04 NE 36
Prehistoric Fields	Snail Down	SU 219520	SU 25 SW 18
Prehistoric Fields	Tidworth Golf Course	SU 214478	SU 24 NW 14
Prehistoric Fields	Upavon Golf Course	SU 147552	SU 15 NW 47
Ridge-and-furrow	Thornham Down	SU 0951	SU 05 SE 7
Rifle Range	Bulford	SU 2045	–
Rifle Range	Mancombe Down	ST 8946	–
Rifle Range	Robin Hood's Ball	SU 102458	–
Rifle Range	Rushall Down	SU 0850	–
Rifle Range	Wilsford Down	SU 0752	–
Romano-British Settlement	Beach's Barn	SU 18605120	SU 15 SE 87
Romano-British Village	Chapperton Down	ST 99704760	ST 94 NE 11
Romano-British Village	Charlton Down	SU 088525	SU 05 SE 10
Romano-British Village	Cheverell Down	ST 969503	ST 95 SE 10
Romano-British Village	Chisenbury Warren	SU 177537	SU 15 SE 18
Romano-British Village	Church Pits	SU 07404830	SU 04 NE 6
Romano-British Village	Compton Down	SU 191520	SU 15 SW 2
Romano-British Village	Coombe Down	SU 192521	SU 15 SE 117
Romano-British Settlement	Fifield Folly	SU 140498	SU 14 NW 100
Romano-British Village	Knook Down East	ST 96704460	ST 94 SE 42
Romano-British Village	Knook Down West	ST 96004440	ST 94 SE 41
Romano-British Village	Maddington Down	SU 04904450	SU 04 SW 19
Romano-British Village	Upavon Down	SU 096522	SU 05 SE 3
Romano-British Village	Wadman's Coppice	ST 952494	ST 94 NE 6
Round Barrow	Collingbourne Ducis 3 (a)	SU 22195227	SU 25 SW 51
Round Barrow	Collingbourne Ducis 4	SU 22055202	SU 25 SW 116
Round Barrow	Collingbourne Kingston 6	SU 21555194	SU 25 SW 101
Round Barrow	Collingbourne Kingston 7	SU 21645202	SU 25 SW 103
Round Barrow	Collingbourne Kingston 8	SU 21685205	SU 25 SW 104
Round Barrow	Collingbourne Kingston 13	SU 21785211	SU 25 SW 105
Round Barrow	Collingbourne Kingston 14	SU 21815214	SU 25 SW 106
Round Barrow	Collingbourne Kingston 15	SU 21845216	SU 25 SW 107
Round Barrow	Figheldean 39	SU 18854912	SU 14 NE 39
Round Barrow	Milston Down 45 (a)	SU 20434597	SU 24 NW 78
Round Barrow	Nine Mile River Mound	SU 20104750	SU 24 NW
Round Barrow	Robin Hood's Ball	SU 10054606	SU 14 NW 3
Round Barrow	Rough Down	ST 966493	ST 94 NE 4
Round Barrow	Silk Hill	SU 19054689	SU 14 NE 172
Round Barrow	Silver Barrow	SU 04554723	SU 04 NW 5
Round Barrow	Slay Barrow	SU 08755117	SU 05 SE 9
Round Barrow	Westbury 7	ST 88544950	ST 84 NE 30
Round Barrow Cemetery	Barrow Clump Group	SU 165469	SU 14 NE 1
Round Barrow Cemetery	Brigmerston Firs	SU 194477	SU 14 NE 5
Round Barrow Cemetery	Brigmerston Plantation	SU 204477	SU 14 NE 50
Round Barrow Cemetery	Cow Down	SU 229515	SU 25 SW 30
Round Barrow Cemetery	Durrington Down Group	SU 118441	SU 14 SW 71

Round Barrow Cemetery	Everleigh	SU 184560	SU 15 NE 22
Round Barrow Cemetery	Goat Wood Group	SU 199479	SU 14 NE 48
Round Barrow Cemetery	Hare Warren Group	SU 216472 (centre)	SU 24 NW 45
Round Barrow Cemetery	Milston Down 1	SU 204460 (centre)	SU 24 NW 47
Round Barrow Cemetery	Milston Down 2	SU 213467 (centre)	SU 24 NW 1/42/44/56/94
Round Barrow Cemetery	Milston Firs Group	SU 18924595	SU 14 NE 9
Round Barrow Cemetery	Netheravon Down	SU 11034775	SU 14 NW 13
Round Barrow Cemetery	Seven Barrows Group	SU 218486	SU 24 NW 20
Round Barrow Cemetery	Silk Hill	SU 191467	SU 14 NE 29/49
Round Barrow Cemetery	Sling Camp Group	SU 197446 (centre)	SU 14 SE 51
Round Barrow Cemetery	Small Arms Range	SU 201452 (centre)	SU 24 NW 35
Round Barrow Cemetery	Snail Down	SU 218520	SU 25 SW 9, 10
Saxon Burial	Elston	SU 068453	SU 04 NE 27
Saxon Burial	Perham Down	SU 24404833	SU 24 NW 64
Saxon Burial	Shrewton	SU 066445	SU 04 SE 1
Saxon Burial	Tidworth	SU 232493	SU 24 NW 55
Saxon Burial	West Chisenbury	SU 13615317	SU 15 SW 11
Sheep Enclosure	Figheldean Dow	SU 18464905	SU 14 NE 25
Sheep Enclosure	Imber Brook	ST 989473	ST 94 NE 65
Sheep Enclosure	Orcheston Down	SU 07184747	SU 04 NE 24
Sheep Enclosure	Shepherd's Garden	SU 085514	SU 05 SE 83
Sheep Enclosure	Upavon	SU 14755525	SU 15 NW 62
Sheep Enclosure	Wadman's Coppice	ST 952494	ST 94 NE 6
Sheep Enclosure	Warden's Down	ST 90855090	ST 95 SW 8
Sheep Enclosure	Wilsford Down	SU 085529	SU 05 SE 82
Splinter Proof Shelter	Larkhill Impact Area	SU 089488	–
Strip Lynchets	Battlesbury	ST 902455	ST 94 NW 18
Strip Lynchets	Bishopstrow Down	ST 91954560	ST 94 NW 47
Strip Lynchets	Bratton	ST 91855125	ST 95 SW 79
Strip Lynchets	Charlton	SU 105557	SU 15 NW 27
Strip Lynchets	Compton	SU 119517	SU 15 SW 74
Strip Lynchets	East Chisenbury	SU 143531	SU 15 SW 37
Strip Lynchets	Middle Hill	ST 908448	ST 94 SW 20
Strip Lynchets	Strawberry Hill	ST 970520	ST 95 SE 30
Unenclosed Settlement	Hill Bottom Farm	ST 985521	ST 95 SE 86
Unenclosed Settlement	Marden Down	SU 075542	SU 05 SE 77
Villa	Compton	SU 133522	SU 15 SW 120
Villa	Netheravon 1	SU 148482	SU 14 NW 19
Villa	Netheravon 2	SU 147474	SU 14 NW 24
Warren	Everleigh	SU 176 538	–
Warren	Fittleton Warren	SU 144496	–
Warren	Imber	ST 95454880	ST 94 NE 37
Warren	Warren Down	SU 046517	–
Warren	Warren Farm	SU 253473	–
Warren	Warren Plantation	SU 098463	–
Water Feature	Charlton Down	SU 08455215	SU 05 SE 76
Water Feature	Wadman's Coppice	ST 95154925	ST 94 NE 6
Water Meadows	Compton	SU 135520	SU 15 SW 119
Water Meadows	Hindurrington	SU 165445	SU 14 SE 344
Water Meadows	West Chisenbury	SU 137530	SU 15 SW 44

Bibliography

Abbreviations used

WAM Wiltshire Archaeological and Natural History Magazine

Aldsworth, F G 1974 'Towards a pre-Domesday geography of Hampshire – a review of the evidence'. Unpublished BA dissertation, Univ Southampton

Allen, M J 1995 'Before Stonehenge', *in* Cleal, R, Walker, K E and Montague, R 1995 *Stonehenge in its Landscape: Twentieth-century Excavations* (English Heritage Archaeol Rep No 10, 41–62). London: English Heritage

Andrews, J and Dury, *A 1773 Map of Wiltshire* (reduced facsimile edn in atlas form with an introduction by Crittal, E Wilts Record Society 1952 rep 1968, 1974 Devizes)

Annable, F K 1958 'Excavation and fieldwork in Wiltshire, 1958'. *WAM* **57**, 17

— 1960 'Excavation and fieldwork in Wiltshire, 1957'. *WAM* **57**, 2–17

Anon 1860 'Duchy of Lancaster: survey of its manors in co. Wilts, taken 33 Eliz (AD 1591)'. *WAM* **6**, 186–200

— 1901a *Annual Report (July 10th) 13th Congress of Archaeological Societies* (Society of Antiquaries). London

— 1901b 'Annual Report of the School of Gunnery'. Unpublished MSS Badley Library, Royal School Artillery, Larkhill

— 1902a *Minutes of the Proceedings of the War Office Salisbury Plain Committee from first meeting on 11 May 1897 to last meeting on 25 April 1902*. London: HMSO

— 1902b 'Annual Report of the School of Gunnery'. Unpublished MSS Badley Library, Royal School Artillery, Larkhill

— 1915a *Report of the Committee on Ancient Earthworks and Fortified Enclosures* (Congress of Archaeological Societies). London: Society of Antiquaries

— 1915b 'Note from the front: part 3: Further notes on field defences'. Unpublished MSS Badley Library, Royal School Artillery, Larkhill

— 1918 *Field Works for Royal Artillery*. London: Charles and Son

— 1966 'Excavation and fieldwork in Wiltshire, 1965'. *WAM* **61**, 102–8

— 1967 'Excavation and fieldwork in Wiltshire, 1966'. *WAM* **62**, 124–31

— 1973 *Report of the Defence Lands Committee, 1971–3 Chaired by the Rt Hon Lord Nugent*. London: HMSO

— 1981 'Wiltshire Archaeological Register for 1978–9'. *WAM* **74/5**, 201–8

— 1983 *Archaeology in the Salisbury Plain Training Area*. Wiltshire Library & Museum Service, Trowbridge, Wilts

— 1985 'Wiltshire Archaeological Register for 1983'. *WAM* **79**, 254–9

— 1986 *Report 1984–1985*. Salisbury Plain Training Area Archaeological Working Party, Property Services Agency, W Region

— 1988a 'Excavation and fieldwork in Wiltshire 1987'. *WAM* **82**, 176–82

— 1988b 'Wiltshire Archaeological Register for 1986'. *WAM* **82**, 183–6

— 1990 'Wiltshire Archaeological Register for 1987 and 1988'. *WAM* **83**, 224–35

— 1991 'Wiltshire Archaeological Register for 1989'. *WAM* **84**, 146–51

— 1994 'Excavation and fieldwork in Wiltshire 1992' *WAM* **87**, 149–59

— 1997a 'Excavation and fieldwork in Wiltshire'. *WAM* **90**, 151–60

— 1997b *British Trench Warfare 1917–1918: a Reference Manual*. London: Imperial War Museum

Applebaum, S 1954 'The agriculture of the British Early Iron Age'. *Proc Prehist Soc* **20**, (1), 103–14

Arnold, J, Green, M, Lewis, B and Bradley, R 1989 (1988) 'The Mesolithic of Cranborne Chase'. *Proc Dorset Nat Hist & Archaeol Soc* **110**, 117–26

Ashbee, P 1960 *The Bronze Age Round Barrow in Britain*. London: Phoenix House

— 1984 *The Earthen Long Barrow in Britain*. 2 edn. Norwich

Ashbee, P, Bell, M and Proudfoot, E 1989 *Wilsford Shaft: Excavations 1960–62* (English Heritage Archaeol Rep No 11). London: English Heritage

Aston, M and Lewis, C (eds) 1994 *The Medieval Landscape of Wessex*. Oxford: Oxbow

Barrett, J Bradley, R and Green, M 1991 *Landscape Monuments and Society: the Prehistory of Cranborne Chase*. Cambridge: Cambridge Univ Press

Barrett, J and Corney, M C 1991 'The Iron Age', *in* Barrett, J, Bradley, R, and Green, M (eds) *Landscape Monuments and Society: the Prehistory of Cranborne Chase*. Cambridge: Cambridge Univ Press, 225–42

Barron, R S 1976 *The Geology of Wiltshire: a Field Guide*. Moonraker Press

Bedford, His Grace the Duke of, 1849 'On labourers' cottages'. *Journal of the Royal Agricultural Society of England* **10**, 185–7

Bell, M and Jones, J 1990 'Land mollusca' *in* Richards, J *The Stonehenge Environs Project* (English Heritage Archaeol Rep No 16). London: English Heritage, 154–8

Bennett, Rev Canon, 1887 'The Orders of Shrewton'. *WAM* **23**, 33–9

Bettey, J H 1986 *Wessex from AD 1000*. Harlow: Longman

Blackmore, H P 1804 'Discovery of flint implements in the higher level gravels at Milford Hill, Salisbury'. *Archaeol J* **21**, 243–5

Bond, J 1994 'Forests, chases, warrens and parks in medieval Wessex' *in* Aston, M and Lewis, C *The Medieval Landscape of Wessex* (Oxbow Monograph 46). Oxford: Oxbow, 115–58

Bonney, D 1966 'Pagan Saxon burials and boundaries in Wiltshire'. *WAM* **61**, 25–39

— 1976 'Early boundaries and estates in Southern England', *in* Sawyer, P (ed) *Medieval Settlement*. London: Edward Arnold, 72–82

Bowen, H C 1961 *Ancient Fields*. London: Brit Assoc for the Advancement of Science

— 1978 ' "Celtic" fields and "ranch" boundaries in Wessex', *in* Limbrey, S and Evans, J G (eds) *The Effect of Man on the Landscape: the Lowland Zone*, CBA Res Rep 21, 115–22

Bowen, H C and Fowler, P J 1962 'The archaeology of Fyfield and Overton Downs, Wilts (interim report)'. *WAM* **58**, 98–115

— 1966 'Romano-British rural settlements in Dorset and Wiltshire', *in* Thomas, C (ed) *Rural Settlement in Roman Britain*, CBA Res Rep 7, 43–67

Bowen, H C and Smith, I F 1977 'Sarsen stones in Wessex: the society's first investigations in the evolution of the landscape project'. *Antiq J* **57**, 186–96

Bradley, R 1984 *The Social Foundations of Prehistoric Britain*. London: Longmans

— 1992 'The excavation of an Oval barrow beside the Abingdon causewayed enclosure, Oxford'. *Proc Prehist Soc* **58**, 127–42

— 1998 *The Significance of Monuments*. London: Routledge

Bradley, R, Entwistle, R and Raymond, F 1994 *Prehistoric Land Divisions on Salisbury Plain: the Work of the Wessex Linear Ditches Project* (English Heritage Archaeol Rep No 2). London: English Heritage

Bradley, R and Richards, J 1978 'Prehistoric fields and boundaries on the Berkshire Downs' in Bowen, H C and Fowler P J (eds) *Early Land Allotment* (Brit Archaeol Rep 48, 53–60). Oxford

Branigan, K 1976 *The Roman Villa in South-west England*. Bradford-on-Avon: Moonraker Press

Bristow, R, Mortimore, M and Wood, C 1997 'Lithostratigraphy for mapping the chalk of southern England' *Proc Geol Assn* **108** (4), 296–315

Brongers, J A 1976 *Air Photography and Celtic Field Research in the Netherlands*. Nederlandse Oudheden 6. Amersfoort

Brown, G 1996 'West Chisenbury: settlement and land-use in a chalk downland landscape'. *WAM* **89**, 73–83

Brown, G, Field, D and McOmish, D 1994 'East Chisenbury midden complex, Wiltshire', in Fitzpatrick, A P and Morris, E L (eds) *The Iron Age in Wessex: Recent Research* (Association Française D'Etude de L'Age du Fer, 46–9)

— (in prep) *A Midden Site of the Late Bronze Age/Early Iron Age Transition at East Chisenbury, Wiltshire*

Burgess, C B, Topping, P, Mordant, C and Maddison, M 1988 *Enclosures and Defences in the Neolithic of Western Europe* (Brit Archaeol Rep Supp Series 403). Oxford

Cam, H M 1944 'Manerium cum Hundredo: the Hundred and Hundredal Manor', in Cam, H M (ed) *Liberties and Communities in Medieval England*. Cambridge: Cambridge Univ Press, 64–90

Care, V 1979 'The production and distribution of Mesolithic axes in southern Britain'. *Proc Prehist Soc* **45**, 93–102

Carruthers, W 1990 'Carbonised plant remains', in Richards, J *The Stonehenge Environs Project* (English Heritage Archaeol Rep No 16). London: English Heritage, 250–52

Catt, J 1978 'The contribution of loess to soils in lowland Britain', in Limbrey, S and Evans, J G (eds) *The Effect of Man on the Landscape: the Lowland Zone* (CBA Res Rep 21, 12–20)

Chadwick, S E and Thompson, M W 1956 'Note on an Iron Age habitation site near Battlesbury Camp, Warminster', *WAM* **56**, 262–4

Charlton, D B and Day, J C 1977 'An archaeological survey of the Ministry of Defence Training Area, Otterburn, Northumberland'. Unpublished MSS

Christie, P 1964 'A Bronze Age round barrow on Earls Farm Down, Amesbury'. *WAM* **59**, 30–45

— 1970 'A round barrow on Greenland Farm, Winterbourne Stoke'. *WAM* **65**, 64–73

Clark, M J, Lewin, J and Small, R J 1967 *The Sarsen Stones of the Marlborough Downs and their Geomorphological Implications* (Southampton Res Ser in Geography 4). Univ Southampton

Cleal, R and Allen, M J 1994 'Investigation of tree damaged barrows on King Barrow Ridge, Amesbury'. *WAM* **87**, 54–84

Cleal, R, Walker, K E and Montague, R 1995 *Stonehenge in its Landscape: Twentieth-Century Excavations* (English Heritage Archaeol Rep No 10). London: English Heritage

Cobbett, W 1830 *Rural Rides*. 1967 edn Middlesex: Penguin

Collingwood, R G and Myres, J N L 1937 *Roman Britain and the English Settlements*, 2 edn Oxford: Clarendon Press

Colt Hoare, R C 1810 *The Ancient History of Wiltshire, Vol. 1*. London: Miller

— 1821 *The Ancient History of Wiltshire Vol 2*. London: Miller

Cope, D 1976 'Soils in Wiltshire I, sheet SU 03 Wilton'. Soil Survey, Harpendon

Corney, M C 1989 'Multiple ditch systems and Iron Age settlement in central Wessex', in Bowden, M, Mackay, D and Topping, P (eds) *From Cornwall to Caithness* (Brit Archaeol Rep 209, 111–28). Oxford

— 1997a 'New evidence for the Romano-British settlement by Silbury Hill'. *WAM* **90**, 139–50

— 1997b 'The origins and development of the "small" town of Cunetio, Mildenhall, Wiltshire'. *Britannia* **28**, 337–50

Cossons, A 1959 'Roads', in Crittal, E (ed) *A History of Wiltshire* 4, Victoria County History. London: OUP, 254–71

Coy, J 1982 'Woodland mammals in Wessex', in Bell, M and Limbrey, S (eds) *Archaeological Aspects of Woodland Ecology* (Brit Archaeol Rep S 146, 287–96). Oxford

Crawford, D J 1976 'Imperial estates', in Finley, M I (ed) *Studies in Roman Property*, 35–70. London

Crawford, O G S 1924 *Air Survey and Archaeology*. 2 edn (1928). Ordnance Survey, Southampton

— 1929 'Air photography for archaeologists', *Ordnance Survey Professional Papers* **12**

— 1937 *Ordnance Survey 1:25 000 Salisbury Plain, Old Sarum Sheet*. Ordnance Survey, Southampton

— 1953 *Archaeology in the Field*. London: Dent

Crawford, O G S and Keiller A 1928 *Wessex from the Air*. Oxford: Clarendon Press

Crawford, T S 1999 *Wiltshire and the Great War*. Reading: DPF Publishing

Crittall, E 1980a 'Everleigh', in Crowley, D A (ed) *A History of Wiltshire* 11, Victoria County History. London: OUP, 135–42

— 1980b 'Collingbourne Ducis', in Crowley, D A (ed) *A History of Wiltshire* 11, Victoria County History. London: OUP, 108–15

Cross, D A E 1971 'Narrow-gauge railway on Salisbury Plain'. *WAM* **66**, 184–5

Cunliffe, B 1973 'Saxon and medieval settlement pattern in the region of Chalton, Hampshire'. *Med Archaeol* **14**, 1–12

— 1991 *Iron Age Communities in Britain*. 3 edn London: Routledge

Cunnington, B H and Cunnington, M E 1913 'Casterley Camp excavations'. *WAM* **38**, 53–105

Cunnington, M E 1910a 'A medieval earthwork near Morgans Hill'. *WAM* **36**, 590–98

— 1910b 'Notes on the Roman antiquities in the Westbury Collection at the Museum, Devizes'. *WAM* **36**, 464–77

— 1914 'List of long barrows in Wiltshire'. *WAM* **38**, 379–415

— 1917 'Lidbury Camp'. *WAM* **40**, 12–36

— 1924 'Pits in Battlesbury Camp'. *WAM* **42**, 368–73

— 1930a 'Romano-British Wiltshire'. *WAM* **45** 166–216

— 1930b 'Saxon burials at West Chisenbury'. *WAM* **45**, 84

— 1932 'The demolition of Chisenbury Trendle'. *WAM* **46**, 1–3

— 1939 *An Introduction to the Archaeology of Wiltshire, From the Earliest Times to the Pagan Saxons*. Devizes

Cunnington, W 1856 'On the mammalian drift of Wiltshire and its fossil contents'. *WAM* **4**, 129–42

— 1889 'Notes on the Bowl's Barrow'. *WAM* **24**, 104–17

Curtis, L F, Courtney, F M and Trudgill, S T 1976 *Soils in the British Isles*. London: Longmans

Curwen, E C 1930 'Neolithic camps'. *Antiquity* **4**, 22–54

Dark, K and Dark, P 1997 *The Landscape of Roman Britain*. Stroud: Sutton

Davis, T 1811 *General View of the Agriculture of Wiltshire: Drawn up and Published by Order of the Board of Agriculture and Internal Improvement*. London

Defoe, D 1724–6 *A Tour through the Whole Island of Great Britain*. rep 1979 Harmondsworth: Penguin

Delair, J D and Shackley, M L 1978 'The Fisherton brickpits: their stratigraphy and fossil contents'. *WAM* **73**, 3–18

Drewett, P 1975 'The excavation of an oval burial mound of the third millennium BC at Alfriston, East Sussex, 1974'. *Proc Prehist Soc* **41**, 119–52

— 1986 'The excavation of a neolithic oval barrow at North Marden, West Sussex, 1982'. *Proc Prehist Soc* **52**, 1986, 31–51

Duke, R E H 1914 'Notes on the Hydes of Wilts and Cheshire'. *Wiltshire Notes and Queries* 7, 1911–1913, 160–61

Eagles, B N E 1994 'The archaeological evidence for settlement in the fifth to seventh centuries AD', *in* Aston, M and Lewis, C (eds) *The Medieval Landscape of Wessex* (Oxbow Monograph 46). Oxford: Oxbow, 13–22

— 2001 'Anglo-Saxon presence and culture in Wiltshire', *in* Ellis, P (ed) *Roman Wiltshire and after*. Bath: Wilts Archaeol Nat Hist Soc, 199–233

Ekwall, E 1960 *The Concise Oxford Dictionary of English Place-names*. 4 edn. Oxford: Clarendon Press

Ellis, P (ed) 2000 *Ludgershall Castle, Wiltshire: a Report on the Excavations by Peter Addyman, 1964–1972*. Wiltshire Archaeol Natur Hist Soc Monogr Ser **2**

Engleheart, G H 1915–17 'Romano-British? Cemetery at Imber, Wilts'. *WAM* **39**, 500–1

English Heritage (forthcoming) *The Field Archaeology of South Wiltshire*.

Entwistle, R 1990 'Land mollusca', *in* Richards, J *The Stonehenge Environs Project* (English Heritage Archaeol Rep No 16). London: English Heritage, 105–9

Entwistle, R, Fulford, M and Raymond, F 1993 *Salisbury Plain Project 1992–3: Interim Report*. Univ Reading

— 1994 *Salisbury Plain Project 1993–4: Interim Report*. Univ Reading

— (in prep) *Romano-British Settlements on Salisbury Plain*. Univ Reading

Esmonde Cleary, A S 1989 *The Ending of Roman Britain*. London: Batsford

Evans, J 1864 'On some recent discoveries of the flint implements in drift deposits in Hants and Wilts'. *Quart J Geol Soc London* **20**, 188–99

— 1872 *The Stone Implements, Weapons and Ornaments of Great Britain*. London: Longmans

Evans, J G 1968 'Periglacial deposits on the Chalk of Wiltshire'. *WAM* **63**, 12–26

— 1975 *The Environment of Early Man in the British Isles*. London: Elek

— 1984 'The environment of the Late Neolithic and Early Bronze age and a Beaker Age burial'. *WAM* **78**, 7–30

Evans, J G and Simpson, D D A 1991 'Giant's Hills 2 Long Barrow, Skendleby, Lincolnshire'. *Archaeologia* **109**, 1–48

Everson, P, Brown, G and Stocker, D 2000 'A landscape context', *in* Ellis, P (ed) 2000, 97–119

Fagg, C G 1923 'On the recession of the chalk escarpment'. *Trans Croydon Nat Hist Soc* **9**

Feachem, R W 1971 'Unfinished hillforts', *in* Hill, D and Jesson, M (eds) *The Iron Age and its Hillforts*. Southampton: Millbrook Press, 19–40

Field, D 1999 'Ancient water management on Salisbury Plain', *in* Pattison, P, *et al* (eds), *Patterns of the Past: Essays in Landscape Archaeology for Christopher Taylor*. Oxford: Oxbow

Findlay, D C, Colborne, G J N, Cope, D W, Harrod, T R, Hogan, D V and Staines, S J 1984 *Soils and their Use in South-west England*. Soil Survey of England and Wales Bull 14, Harpenden

Fleming, A 1971 'Territorial patterns in Bronze Age Wessex'. *Proc Prehist Soc* **37**, pt 1, 138–66

— 1987 'Co-axial field systems: some questions of time and space'. *Antiquity* **61**, 188–203

— 1988 *The Dartmoor Reaves*. London: Batsford

Fowler, P J 1966 'Two finds of Saxon domestic pottery in Wiltshire'. *WAM* **61**, 31–7

— 1975 'Continuity in the landscape? Some local archaeology in Wiltshire, Somerset and Gloucestershire', *in* Fowler, P J (ed) *Recent Work in Rural Archaeology*. Bradford on Avon: Moonraker Press, 121–36

Fowler, P J and Blackwell, I 1998 *The Land of Lettice Sweetapple: an English Countryside Explored*. Stroud: Tempus

Fowler, P J, Musty, J W G and Taylor, C C 1965 'Some earthwork enclosures in Wiltshire'. *WAM* **60**, 52–74

Freeman, J 1995 'Tilshead', *in* Crowley, D A (ed) *A History of Wiltshire* 15, Victoria County History. London: OUP, 263–75

Frere, S 1987 *Britannia: a History of Roman Britain*. 3 rev edn London: Routledge & Kegan Paul

Gaffney, V and Tingle, M 1989 *The Maddle Farm Project* (Brit Archaeol Rep 200). Oxford

Gardiner, J 1984 'Lithic distributions and Neolithic settlement patterns in central southern England', *in* Bradley, R and Gardiner, J (eds) *Neolithic Studies*. Oxford: Brit Archaeol Rep **133**, 15–40

Gelling, M 1978 *Signposts to the Past. Place-names and the History of England*. London: J M Dent

Gifford, J 1957 'The physique of Wiltshire' *in* Pugh, R B (ed) *A History of Wiltshire* 1, pt1, Victoria County History. London: OUP, 1–20

Gingell, C 1978 'The excavation of an early Anglo-Saxon cemetery at Collingbourne Ducis'. *WAM* **70/71** (for 1975–6), 61–98

— 1984 *The Marlborough Downs: a Later Bronze Age Landscape and its Origins* (Wilts Archaeol & Nat Hist Soc Monograph 1). Devizes

Goddard, Rev E H 1913 'A list of Prehistoric, Roman, and Pagan Saxon antiquities in the county of Wiltshire arranged under parishes'. *WAM* **38**, 153–378

Gover, J G B, Mawer, A and Stenton, F M 1939 *The Place-names of Wiltshire* (English Place Name Soc 16). Cambridge

Graham, A and Newman, C 1993 'Recent excavations of Iron Age and Romano-British enclosures in the Avon Valley, Wiltshire'. *WAM* **86**, 8–57

Grant, R 1959 'Royal forests', *in* Crittall, E *A History of Wiltshire* Vol IV. London: Oxford Univ Press, 391–460

Green, C 1997a 'Stonehenge: geology and prehistory'. *Proc Geol Assn* **108**, 1–10

— 1997b 'The provenance of rocks used in the construction of Stonehenge', *in* Cunliffe, B and Renfrew, C (eds) *Science and Stonehenge* (Proc of Brit Academy 92, 257–70). Oxford

Griffiths, N 1982 'Early Roman metalwork from Wiltshire'. *WAM* **7** (1983), 49–59

Grigson, C 1982 'Porridge and Pannage: Pig Husbandry in Neolithic England', *in* Bell, M and Limbrey, S (eds) *Archaeological Aspects of Woodland Ecology*. BAR International Series **146**, 297–314

Grinsell, L V 1941 'The Bronze Age round barrows of Wessex'. *Proc Prehist Soc* **7**, 73–113

— 1952 'A Palaeolithic handaxe from Heytesbury'. *WAM* **54**, 436–7

— 1953 *The Ancient Burial Mounds of England*. 2 edn. London: Methuen

— 1957 'Archaeological gazetteer', *A History of Wiltshire* 1, pt 1, Victoria County History. London: OUP, 21–272

— 1974 'Disc barrows'. *Proc Prehist Soc* **40**, 79–93

Grose, J D and Sandell, R E 1964 'A catalogue of prehistoric plant remains in Wiltshire'. *WAM* **59**, 58–67

Grundy, G. B 1919 'The Saxon land charters of Wiltshire'. *Archaeol J* **76**, 143–301

Guido, M 1980 (for 1977/8) 'An Iron Age burial from Battlesbury'. *WAM* **72/3**, 177–8

Guy, R 1981 'A history of Gunnery Wing, Royal School of Artillery 1929–1980'. Unpublished MSS Badley Library, Royal School Artillery, Larkhill

Harding, P A and Bridgeland, D R 1998 'Pleistocene deposits and Palaeolithic implements at Godolphin School, Milford Hill, Salisbury'. *WAM* **91**, 1–10

Hare, J N 1994 'Agriculture and settlement in Wiltshire and Hampshire', in Aston, M and Lewis, C (eds) *The Medieval Settlement of Wessex*. Oxford: Oxbow, 159–69

Harrison, B 1995 'Field systems and demesne farming on the Wiltshire estates of Saint Swithun's Priory, Wiltshire, 1248–1340'. *Agricultural Hist Rev* 43, pt 1, 1–18

Harsema, O H 1992 *Geschiedenis in het Landschap*. Netherlands: Drenthe Museum

Hase, P 1994 'The church in the Wessex heartlands' in Aston, M and Lewis, C (eds) *The Medieval Settlement of Wessex*. Oxford: Oxbow, 47–81

Haslam, J 1984 'The towns of Wiltshire', in Haslam, J (ed) *Anglo-Saxon Towns*. Chichester: Phillimore, 87–147

Hawkes, C F C 1939 'The excavations at Quarley Hill, 1938'. *Proc Hants Field Club* 14, 136–94

Hawley, Lt Col W 1910 'Notes on barrows in south Wilts'. *WAM* 36, 615–28

— 1923 'Romano-British villages on Upavon and Rushall Downs, excavated by Lt Col Hawley'. *WAM* 42, 227–30

Headlam, J 1937 *The History of the Royal Artillery from the Indian Mutiny to the Great War*. Woolwich: Royal Artillery Institution

Hingley, R 1989 *Rural Settlement in Roman Britain*. London

Hodder, I 1976 'The distribution of Savernake Ware'. *WAM* 69 (1974), 67–84

Hooke, D 1988 'Regional variation in southern and central England, the Anglo-Saxon period and its relationship to land units and settlement', in Hooke, D (ed) *Anglo-Saxon Settlements*. Oxford: Blackwell, 123–51

James, N D G 1987 *Plain Soldiering: a History of the Armed Forces on Salisbury Plain*. Salisbury: Hobnob Press

Johnson, P and Walters, B 1988 'Exploratory excavations of Roman buildings at Cherhill and Manningford Bruce'. *WAM* 82, 77–91

Jukes-Brown, A J 1901 *The Cretaceous Rocks of Britain 1* (Memoir of the Geological Survey of the UK). London: HMSO

— 1905 *The Geology of the Country South and East of Devizes* (Memoir of the Geological Survey of the UK). London: HMSO

Kerridge, E 1951 *Agrarian Development of Wiltshire, 1540–1640*. Univ London, PhD Thesis

— 1953 'The floating of the Wiltshire watermeadows'. *WAM* 60, 105–18

Kinnes, I 1979 *Round Barrows and Ring-ditches in the British Neolithic* (Brit Mus Occ Paper 7). London

— 1992 *Non-megalithic Long Barrows and Allied Structures in the British Neolithic* (Brit Mus Occ Paper 52). London

Kinnes, I, Gibson, A, Ambers, J, Bowman, S, Leese, M, and Boast, R 1991 Radiocarbon dating and British Beakers: the British Museum programme *Scottish Archaeol Rev* 8, 35–68

Land Classification Survey 1947 *Land Classification of Gloucestershire, Somerset and Wiltshire*. Univ Bristol, Arrowsmith

Lawson, A J 1994 'Potterne', in Fitzpatrick, A P and Morris, E L (eds) *The Iron Age in Wessex: Recent Work*. Dorchester: Association Française de l'Age du Fer

Lewis, C 1994 'Patterns and Processes', in Aston, M and Lewis, C (eds) *The Medieval Settlement of Wessex*. Oxford: Oxbow, 171–94

Lewis, C, Mitchell-Fox, P and Dyer, C 1997 *Village, Hamlet and Field: Changing Medieval Settlements in Central England*. Manchester: Manchester Univ Press

London, V C M 1979 *The Bradenstoke Cartulary*. Devizes: Wilts Record Soc

Lukis, Rev 1867 'Notes on barrow diggings in the Parish of Collingbourne Ducis'. *WAM* 10, 85–103

Manley, V Strode 1928 'A regional survey of the Warminster District 2'. Unpublished MSS, Salisbury Local History Library

Margary, I 1955 *Roman Roads in Britain*. London: Phoenix House

McKinley, J I 1999 'Further excavations of an Iron Age and Romano-British enclosed settlement at Figheldean, near Netheravon'. *WAM* 92, 7–32

McKinley, J I, & Heaton, M, 1996 'A Romano-British farmstead and associated burials at Maddington Farm, Shrewton'. *WAM* 89, 44–72

McOmish, D 1996 'East Chisenbury: ritual and rubbish at the British Bronze Age – Early Iron Age transition'. *Antiquity* 70 (267), 68–76

Meaney, A 1964 *A Gazetteer of Early Anglo-Saxon Burial Sites*. London

Megaw, J V S 1967 'Notes on Iron Age and Neolithic material from Sidbury Camp'. *WAM* 62, 115–17

Mercer, R 1988 'Hambledon Hill, Dorset, England', in Burgess, C B, Topping, P Mordant, C and Maddison, M *Enclosures and Defences in the Neolithic of Western Europe* (Brit Archaeol Report S Ser 403). Oxford: Brit Archaeol, 89–106

Moore, J 1997 'The infernal cycle of fire ecology', in Topping, P (ed) *Neolithic Landscapes* (Neolithic Studies Group Seminars Papers 2, 33–40). Oxford

Mortimore, R and Wood, C 1986 'The distribution of flint in the English chalk, with particular reference to the "Brandon Flint Series" and the high Turonian maximum', in Sieveking, G de G and Hart, M B (eds) *The Scientific Study of Flint and Chert: Proceedings of the Fourth International Flint Symposium 10–15 April 1983*. London: Cambridge Univ Press, 7–42

Nan Kivell, R de C 1925 'Objects found during excavations on the Romano-British site at Cold Kitchen Hill, Brixton Deverill 1924'. *WAM* 43, 180–91

— 1926 'Objects found during excavations on the Romano-British site at Cold Kitchen Hill'. *WAM* 43, 327–32

Nenk, B S, Margeson, S and Hurley, M 1993 'Medieval Britain and Ireland'. *Med Archaeol* 37, (1992), 240–313

Orme, B J and Coles, J M 1985 'Prehistoric woodworking from the Somerset Levels: 2 Species selection and prehistoric woodlands', in Coles, J M Orme, B J and Pouillard, S E (eds) *Somerset Levels Papers* 11, 7–24

Pevsner, N 1975 *The Buildings of England: Wiltshire*. rev Cherry, B 2 edn 1991 rep (first pub 1963). Harmondsworth: Penguin

Phillips, C W 1936 'The Excavation the Giant's Hill Long Barrow, Skendleby, Lincolnshire'. *Archaeologia* 85, 37–106

Piggott, S 1938 'The Early Bronze Age in Wessex'. *Proc Prehist Soc* 4, 52–106

— 1973 'The Wessex Culture of the Early Bronze Age', in Crittall, E (ed) *A History of Wiltshire* 1, pt 2, Victoria County History. London: OUP, 352–75

Pine, J 1998 *Cadley Road Collingbourne Ducis Wiltshire – an Assessment of the Excavation for Berkeley Homes (Hampshire) Limited* (Thames Valley Archaeological Services Report 98/9)

Rawlings, M and Fitzpatrick, A P 1996 'Prehistoric sites with a Romano-British settlement at Butterfield Down, Amesbury'. *WAM* 89, 1–43

RCHME 1970 *An Inventory of the Historical Monuments in the County of Dorset 2: South-east*. London: HMSO

— 1979 *Stonehenge and its Environs*. Edinburgh: Edinburgh Univ Press

— 1987 *Churches of South-East Wiltshire*. London: HMSO

Read, C J 1885 'The flint implements of Bemerton and Milford Hill, near Salisbury'. *WAM* 22, 117–23

Reid, C 1903 *The Geology of the Country around Salisbury* (Memoir of the Geological Survey of the UK). London: HMSO

Richards, J 1990 *The Stonehenge Environs Project* (English Heritage Archaeol Rep No 16). London: English Heritage

Richardson, K 1951 'The excavation of an Iron Age village on Boscombe Down West'. *WAM* **54**, 123–68

Robinson, P H 1977 'A local Iron Age coinage in silver and perhaps gold in Wiltshire'. *Brit Numis Journ* **47**, 5–21

— 1987 'Saxon burials at Elston, Orcheston'. *WAM* **45**, 132

— 1995 'Miniature socketed bronze axes from Wiltshire'. *WAM* **88**, 60–68

— 1997 'A Roman inscription from Charlton Down'. *WAM* **90**, 141–43

Roe, D 1969 'Part I: Palaeolithic (an archaeological survey and policy for Wiltshire pt 1)'. *WAM* **64**, 1–18

Scott-Jackson, J 1992 'Lower Palaeolithic finds at Wood Hill, East Kent: a geological and geomorphological approach to an archaeological problem'. *Lithics* **13**, 11–16

Sellwood, L 1984 'Tribal boundaries viewed from the perspective of numismatic evidence', *in* Cunliffe, B and Miles, D (eds) *Aspects of the Iron Age in Central Southern Britain* (OUCA Monograph 2, 191–204)

Sherratt, A 1996 'Why Wessex? The Avon route and river transport in later British prehistory'. *Oxford Journ of Archaeol* **15** (2), 211–34

Shortt, H de S 1949 'A hoard of bangles from Ebbesbourne Wake, Wilts'. *WAM* **53**, 104–12

Smith, N 1995 'Military Training earthworks in Crowthorne Wood, Berkshire: a survey by the Royal Commission on the Historical Monuments of England'. *Archaeol J* **152**, 422–40

Smith, R 1981 *The Future of Archaeology in the Salisbury Plain Training Area*. Wiltshire Library and Museum Service, Trowbridge, Wiltshire

Solano, E J (ed) 1915 *Field Entrenchments – Spadework for Riflemen*. London: John Murray

Sparks, W W and Lewis, W V 1958 'Escarpment dry valleys near Pegsdon, Hertfordshire'. *Proc Geol Assn* **69**, 26–38

St John Hope, W H 1914 Proceedings. *Proc Society Antiqs Lond* 2nd series **26**, 100–119

Stevenson, J 1980 'Netheravon' *in* Crowley, D A (ed) *A History of Wiltshire* 11, Victoria County History. London: OUP, 165–81

— 1995a 'Ludgershall', *in* Crowley, D A (ed) *A History of Wiltshire* 15, Victoria County History. London: OUP, 119–33

— 1995b 'Bulford' *in* Crowley, D A (ed) *A History of Wiltshire* 15, Victoria County History. London: OUP, 61–70

— 1995c 'North Tidworth', *in* Crowley, D A (ed) *A History of Wiltshire* 15, Victoria County History. London: OUP, 153–63

Stokes, E 1914 *Abstracts of Wiltshire Inquisitions Post Mortem* (Edward III. AD 1327–1377). London: British Record Society

Stone, J F S 1937 'A Late Bronze Age habitation site on Thorney Down, Winterbourne Gunner, S. Wilts'. *WAM* **57**, 640–60

Struth, P and Eagles, B N E 1999 'An Anglo-Saxon barrow cemetery in Greenwich Park', *in* Ainsworth, S, Field, D and Pattison, P (eds) *Patterns of the Past: Essays in Landscape Archaeology for Christopher Taylor*. Oxford: Oxbow, 37–52

Stukeley, W 1776 *Itinerarium Curiosum*. London

Taylor, C C 1971 'Settlement patterns in pre-Saxon Britain', *in* Ucko, P, Tringham, R, and Dimbleby, G W (eds) *Man, Settlement and Urbanism*. London: Duckworth, 109–13

— 1994 'The regular village plan: Dorset revisited and revised', *in* Aston, M and Lewis, C (eds) *The Medieval landscape of Wessex*. Oxford: Oxbow, 213–18

— 1997 'Dorset and beyond', *in* Baker, K and Darvill, T (eds) *Making English Landscapes* (Bournemouth Univ School of Conservation Sciences Occ Paper 3 and Oxbow Monograph 93). Oxford, 9–25

Taylor, C, Everson, P and Wilson-North, R 1990 'Bodiam Castle, Sussex'. *Med Arch* **34**, 155–7

Thomas, C 1978 'Types and distribution of pre-Norman fields in Cornwall and Scilly', *in* Bowen, H C and Fowler, P J (eds) *Early Land Allotment* (Brit Archaeol Rep 48). Oxford: Brit Archaeol, 7–16

Thomas, N 1960 *A Guide to Prehistoric England*. London: Batsford

— (forthcoming) *Excavations at Snail Down*. London: English Heritage

Thomas, N and Thomas, C 1955 'Excavations at Snail Down, Everleigh 1953, 1955: an interim report'. *WAM* **56**, 127–48

Thomas, R J C 1997 'Penally Camp'. *Sanctuary* **26**, 5–6

Thorn, C and Thorn, F 1979 *Domesday Book 6, Wiltshire*. Chichester: Phillimore

Thurnam, J 1869 'On ancient British barrows, especially those of Wiltshire and adjoining counties. Part 1 Long barrows'. *Archaeologia* **42**, 161–244

— 1871 'On ancient British barrows, especially those of Wiltshire and the adjoining counties. Part 2 Round barrows'. *Archaeologia* **43** (2), 285–544

Tilley, C 1994 *A Phenomenolgy of Landscape*. Oxford: Berg

Timby, J (forthcoming) *The Origins of the Savernake Industry*

Tinsley, H M 1981 'The Bronze Age', *in* Simmons, I and Tooley, M (eds) *The Environment in British Prehistory*. London: Duckworth, 218–49

Turner, J 1981 'The Iron Age', *in* Simmons, I and Tooley, M (eds) *The Environment in British Prehistory*. London: Duckworth, 250–81

Van Arsdell, R D 1994 *The Coinage of the Dobunni*. Oxford Univ Comm for Archaeology

Wainwright, G J, Donaldson, P, Longworth, I H and Swan, V 1971 'The excavation of prehistoric and Romano-British settlements near Durrington Walls, Wiltshire'. *WAM* **66**, 76-128

Walls, T and Cotton, J 1980 'Palaeoliths from the North Downs at Lower Kingswood'. *Surrey Archaeol Colls* **72**, 15–36

Watson, P V 1982 'Man's impact on the chalklands: some new pollen evidence', *in* Bell, M and Limbrey, S (eds) *Archaeological Aspects of Woodland Ecology* (Brit Archaeol Rep S 146). Oxford: Brit Archaeol, 75–92

Welch, C 1997 *An Investigation of a Possible Trench 'Model' on the Site of the First World War Camp at Rugeley* (Staffordshire County Council Research Report No. 2)

Whimster, R 1981 'Burial Practices in Iron Age Britain. A Discussion and Gazetteer of the Evidence *c* 700 BC–*c* AD 43'. BAR British Series **90** (i): Oxford

Whitaker, W and Edmonds, F H 1925 *The water supply of Wiltshire*. (Memoir of the Geological Survey of the UK). London: HMSO

Whittle, A 1997 'Moving on and around: Neolithic settlement mobility', *in* Topping, P (ed) *Neolithic landscapes* (Neolithic Studies Group Seminar Papers 2, 15–22). Oxford

Williams, H 1997 'Ancient landscapes of the dead: the reuse of prehistoric and Roman monuments as Early Anglo-Saxon burial sites'. *Med Archaeol* XLI, 1–32

Williams, P and Newman, R 1998 *Excavations at Grove Farm, Market Lavington, Wiltshire, 1986: the Development of a Romano-British, Anglo-Saxon, and Medieval Settlement of Wessex* (Archaeology Report 15)

Williamson, T 1997 'Fish, fur and feather: man and nature in the Post-Medieval landscape', *in* Barker, K and Darvill, T (eds) *Making English Landscapes*. Oxford: Oxbow, 92–117

Williamson, T and Loveday, R 1988 'Rabbits or Ritual? Artificial Warrens and the Neolithic Long Mound Tradition'. *Archaeol J* **145**, 290–313

Willis, G W 1947 'Hampshire Palaeoliths and Clay-with-flints'. *Proc Hants Field Club* **16**(3), 253–56

Wilson, D M and Hurst, D G 1969 'Medieval Britain in 1968'. *Med Archaeol* **13**, 230–87

Wymer, J J 1987 *The Archaeology of Surrey to 1540 AD* (Surrey Archaeological Society).

Yorke, B 1995 *Wessex in the Early Middle Ages*. London: Leicester Univ Press

Index

Page numbers in **bold** refer to illustrations or tables. Page numbers in **bold** between [ ] refer to fold-outs. This is not an index to the Concordance.

A

aerial photography
 barrows, 21, **22**, **23**, 41, 43, **47**, 50
 'Celtic' fields, 15, 63, **112**, **118**
 Central Impact Area, 57, **90**
 earthworks, xi, 11, 56, 71, **80**
 field systems, 63
 hangars, 147
 hillforts, **37**, 75, **76**, 79, **80**, **81**
 Iron Age settlement, 82, 83, 84
 military trench earthworks, 139
 prehistoric enclosures, **34**, **35**, **36**, **72**, **83**
 Roman villas, 105
 Romano-British field systems, 100
 Romano-British settlements, 14, **16**, **94**, 97, 98, **101**, 156
 Romano-British track networks, 108
 SPTA earthwork survey (RCHME), xi
 water meadows, **136**
 see also Cambridge University Collection of Aerial Photographs; RAF; ring ditches; surveys; USAAF; Wiltshire County Council
aerial transcription; *see* aerial photography; surveys
afforestation, 5; *see also* timber; trees; woodland
Agricultural Depression (19thC), 4, 117
agricultural tenancies, 4
agriculture
 and ancient monuments, xv, 2, 21, 33, 52
 cereal production, 104, 149
 landscape damaged by, 13
 loess and, 8
 Lower Chalk and, 8
 marginal land, 119–121, 159
 medieval, 114
 Parliamentary Enclosure and, 12
 post-medieval, 3, 115, 158
 post-World War II, 1
 prehistoric 3, 51, 81, 152–4
 Romano-British, xv, 88, 93, **93**, 100–4
 see also arable agriculture; barns; cattle; chalk; coaxial field systems; farming; geology; land use; livestock; military (policy); ploughing; sheep; soils; water meadows

air photography; *see* aerial photography
air warfare, 147
airfields, 4, **139**, 147; *see also* aerial photography; communications; geophysical surveys; RAF bases; Royal Flying Corps
altars, 93, 160
Alton Down (gun pit), 144
Amesbury, 106, 145, 150
ancient fields, xiii, 51, 152; *see also* 'Celtic' fields; field systems; fields; linear earthworks; lynchets
ancient landscape, xii
ancient monuments, viii; *see also* barrows; monuments; Stonehenge
Andrews and Dury, map of Wiltshire (1773), 10
Anglo-Saxon
 burials, xv, 110, 160
 charters, 10
 land use, 12
 minsters, 158
 occupation, 109–11
 see also pottery; Saxon secondary burials; settlement(s)
animal hospital (at Fargo), 145
animals; *see* bones; cattle; game; horses; hunting; rabbits; red deer; sheep
anti-tank warfare, 142, **143**, 144, **146**
antiquarian record, 13, 21, 27, 48, 110
Antiquarian Society; *see* Society of Antiquaries
antlers, 27, 50; *see also* artefacts; red deer
arable agriculture
 and archaeology, xv, 2
 Iron Age, 156
 landscape and, 12
 military policy, effect on, 4, 133, 138, 159
 parish tithings and, 113
 post-Roman period, 157
 Romano-British period, 100, 157
 sheep and, 115, 133, 154
archaeological
 evidence, viii, 119, 144, 147
 landscape, 18, **42**, [**64–5**], [**97–98**], **107**, 149–51
 record, ix, xi, 13, 152
 remains, xi, 2, 11, 51, 87, 88, 160
 see also archaeological sites
Archaeological Site Group (ASG) Management Plans, x

archaeological sites
 conservation of, viii, 18
 damage to, on SPTA, 11
 distribution maps, [**xviii–1**], **52**
 Higher Plain, 3
 Salisbury Plain, viii, x, 13
 see also maps; monuments
Archaeological Working Party, ix
archaeology
 arable agriculture and, 2
 of chalk downland, xii, 160
 of impact areas, 147
 prehistoric period, 51
 Romano-British period, 87
 of Salisbury Plain, 6
 shelling and, xii
 of warfare, **140**, 159
 Wessex downland and, 13
 Wiltshire Archaeology Service, ix
armoured training (SPTA), viii
Army Field Training Centre, viii
Arn Hill, 22, 29, 152
arrowheads, 32; *see also* artefacts; causewayed enclosures; flints; weapons
artefacts
 axe-hammers, 50
 axes, 33, 50, 73
 Bronze Age, 68
 burial monument excavations and, 13
 flint scrapers, 32
 Iron Age, 78, 86
 Romano-British, xv, 13, 93, **93**, 104, 107
 Saxon, 157
 seal boxes, **108**
 spindle whorls, 73
 see also agriculture; coins; pottery; weapons
artillery, 137, 142, 159
ashes, 34, 50
Augustinian priory (Honeydown Ridge), 113
Avebury, 151
Avon (river), 1
 agriculture and, 3
 Anglo-Saxon settlement, 109
 barrows, 24, 33, 35, 40, 46, 50
 bifaces from terraces, 7
 drainage for SPTA, 9
 Iron Age settlement, 82, 84
 linear earthworks, 61
 medieval settlement, 124, **125**
 Mesolithic activity, 149
 Romano-British settlements, 88, 95, 100, 104
 Saxon finds, 157
 valley as thoroughfare, 2
 see also communications; East Chisenbury (midden); rivers; valleys; water meadows
axe-hammers, 50
axes, 33, 50, 73

B

'bakeland' (Orcheston Down), 20; *see also* pasture
balloons, 14, 147
banks
 barrows, 35
 and ditches, 12, 70, 79, 88, 128, 131
 field boundaries, 51, 53
 hillforts, 77, 155
 and linear earthworks, 56
 modern military, 140, 143
 see also dams
barns, 97, 118, **121**, 155; *see also* field barns
barracks, 137, 139, 142
barrow cemeteries, 17, 40, **41**, **42**, **43**, 44–**46**, 46, 48, 53, 110, 151, 160
barrows, **42**, 76
 associations of, 40
 as boundary markers, 113, 158
 Bronze Age, 12, 73
 chronology, 39
 distribution pattern near Stonehenge, 50
 groupings, 23
 land use and, 33, 110
 and linear earthwork chronology, 61
 maps and plans, 14, **62**
 siting of, 43–8
 see also antiquarian record; barrow cemeteries; bell barrows; bowl barrows; cone barrows; disc barrows; henges; long barrows; pond barrows; round barrows; saucer barrows; 'short' long barrows
Battlesbury, 48, 68
Battlesbury Camp, 13, 74, 78, 156
Beach's Barn, 88, 104
Beacon Hill, 22, 48
Beaker period, 40
Beaker pottery, 43
bell barrows, 39, 40, 150
berms, 21, 39, 143
BGS; *see* British Geological Survey
bifaces, 7, **8**
Boles Barrow, 7, 23, **25**, **27**, 28, 30, 111, 152
bones, 68
 animal, 31, 73
 human, 27, 29, 30, 31, 74, 78, 100, 111
 see also burial mounds; causewayed enclosures; cemeteries; long barrows; pavements; settlements

boroughs, 129
boundaries, xv
  banks, 51, 52, 88
  barrows and, 158
  estates and, 112–113
  fencing and, 119
  hillforts, 74
  linear earthworks, 64, 113, 114, 154
  lynchets, 12
  medieval, 157, 158
  medieval settlements, 124, 126, 128
  modern, and landscape perception, 160
  prehistoric enclosures, **11**, 73
  tithings, 61, **110**, 113, 116, 121
  see also banks; ditches; Hundreds; linear boundaries; parish boundaries
Bourne (river), 1
  barrow cemeteries, 46, 48
  bifaces, 7
  linear earthworks, 61, 64
  saucer barrows, 35
  settlement (5th/7thC), 109
  Weather Hill henge, 33
bourne holes, 9, 10, 160; *see also* barrow cemeteries
bowl barrows, 33, **38**, 40, 43, 121
Bowl's Barrow; *see* Boles Barrow
bowls, 70, 73, 155; *see also* pottery
bracelets, 13; *see also* jewellery
Brett Young, Francis, 162
brick, xii, 14, 93, 118; *see also* building materials
Brigmerston, 9, 46, **72**
  'Celtic' fields, 154
  prehistoric enclosures, 68, 70, 72, 155
British Geological Survey (BGS) map, 6, 10; *see also* surveys
Broadbury Banks, 79
Bronze Age
  burial monuments, 12, 14, 19, 40, 75; *see also* round barrows
  burial mounds, 20
  chalk downland, 149
  enclosures, 154, 160
  fields, 20, 52, 53
  hoard (Ebbesbourne Wake), 152
  metalwork, 79
  monuments on SPTA, 21, 149
  pottery, 68, 71
  well, 10
brooches, 104, 109; *see also* jewellery
building materials
  brick, xii, 118
  chalk, 58
  concrete, 138, 145
  corrugated iron, 144, 145
  geology and, 5
  from Romano-British settlements, 93, 105

sandstone, 90, 105
stone, xii, 14, 98, 104, 115
timber, 50
see also barrows; earthworks; linear earthworks; sarsen stones
building platforms, xvi, 94, 100, **116**, **120**, 124, 126, 128
buildings
  aeronautical, 147
  hunting lodges, 120
  medieval (at Ludgershall Castle), 131
  Romano-British period, 87, 90, 98, 105
  sheep enclosures, 115
  sunken-featured, 100, 109, 157
  see also barns; building materials; garrisons; houses; hut platforms; huts; platforms; villas
Bulford
  Anglo-Saxon finds, 109
  barracks, 137
  barrow, **38**
  field systems, 53
  garrison, 5, 159
  medieval settlement, 124, **125**
  rifle ranges, 4, **17**, 40, 48, 142, 143, **145**, 160
  sarsen stone, 152
bunkers, 144, 147
burgage plots, 129
burial monuments
  chronology, 39
  excavations, 13, 15
  landscape and, 17, 20, 23, 43, 50, 150, 151
  later prehistoric period, 51
  linear earthworks and, 64
  rivers and, 24
burial mounds, xv
  Beaker period, 40
  funeral activity, 31
  incorporated in hillfort, 156
  reuse in Anglo-Saxon period, 160
  on SPTA, 21, 48, 74
  see also barrows; bones; burials; cemeteries; pavements; pillow mounds
burials (Saxon), xv, 109, 110, 112, 158; *see also* barrows; bones; burial mounds; cemeteries; infants; skeletons
butt-beaker sherds, 84
Butterfield Down, 104

C

cairns, 27, 29, 48; *see also* long barrows
Cambridge University Collection of Aerial Photographs (CUCAP), xii

camps (20thC), 5, 20, 120, 137, 138, 139; *see also* Battlesbury Camp; Casterley Camp; Knook Castle; Scratchbury Camp; Sidbury Camp
'carriers', 132; *see also* water meadows
cartographic evidence; *see* maps
Casterley Camp
  annexe, **81**
  antiquarian survey, 13, 15, **15**
  hillfort, **59**, 74, **76**, 79, 155, 160
  linear earthworks, 58
  prehistoric enclosure, 84
castles; *see* Ludgershall Castle
cattle, 21, 32, 71, 79, 95, 118, 154; *see also* agriculture; bones; farming; horses; pasture; sheep
causewayed enclosures, xv, 18, 21, 24, 31–3, **34**, **35**, **36**, 160
causeways, 10, 31, **33**, **38**, 95; *see also* roads; tracks
cavalry training (19thC), xv, 137, 138
'Celtic' field lynchets, 18
'Celtic' fields, xiii, 2, 3, 13, 51–6, **58**, 73, 82, **112**
  boundaries and, **67**, 113, 114, 126
  coaxial systems, 53, 63
  dating, 52, 154
  landscape and, 12, 17
  and long barrows, 24, **26**, **30**
  maps and plans, 14, 15, **16**, **52**, **62**
  modern military activity and, 138, **138**, 142, **143**, 144
  reused, 19, **42**, 115, **118**
  Romano-British settlement and, 98, 103, **106**
  sarsen stones and, 152
  see also Battlesbury (hillfort); field systems; lynchets; ridge-and-furrow
cemeteries, 40–3
  Anglo-Saxon, 109, 111
  Bronze Age, 75
  Iron Age, 78
  prehistoric, xv, 33, 35
  Romano-British, 100
  see also barrow cemeteries; barrows; henges
Central Impact Zone, xii, 56, **57**, **90**
Central Range, xiii, 4, 12, 61, 100, **107**, 118
ceramic fine wares, 100; *see also* pottery; roofs
cereals, 16, 32, 104, 150, 152, 157
chalk, 5, 58; *see also* chalk downland; chalk pavements; downs; Lower Chalk; Middle Chalk; Upper Chalk

chalk downland, xv, 1
  agriculture, 8
  archaeology and, xii, 160
  'Celtic' fields, 51, 152
  farms, 117
  landscape, 114
  parish boundary pattern, 112
  recolonisation of (20thC), 147
  routes through, 75
  sarsen stones, 151
  strip lynchets, 115
  water supply, 10, 90, 132
  woodland (in prehistory), 149
  see also burial monuments; burial mounds; settlement(s)
chalk pavements, 27, 28; *see also* long barrows
Chalk Summit, 8
chapels, 126
Chapperton Down
  linear earthwork, **66**
  monument (19thC), **3**
  Romano-British settlement, 88, 98, 154, 157
  trench system (20thC), 142, **144**
Charlton (parish), 13
Charlton Down
  ancient fields, 52
  dam and reservoir, 10, **91**
  Romano-British settlement, xv, 16, **16**, 88, 90, **92**, 102, 107, 157, 161
Cheverell Down (Romano-British settlement), 88, 100, **102**, 156
children (inhumation), 50
Chisenbury Field Barn (settlement sequence), 81
Chisenbury Priory, **124**
Chisenbury Trendle, 68, 70, 155
Chisenbury Warren
  excavation and molluscan analysis, 156
  Iron Age settlement, 98
  linear settlement, 17
  rabbit warren enclosure, 120
  Romano-British settlement, 88, 98, **99**, 100, **101**
Chitterne, 2, 111
chronology
  antiquarian record and, 48
  burial monuments, 39
  disc barrows, 39
  landscape development (Church Pits), 20
  landscape survey and, 18
  linear earthworks, 61
  long barrows, 27
  Romano-British sites, 13, 16
  see also dating
Church Ditches (prehistoric enclosure), 12, **91**, 155
Church Pits, 10, 20, 88, 154

churches, 4, 139
  Amesbury, 106
  Domesday Survey and, 124, 158
  Figheldean, 126
  Imber, **148**, 157
  Ludgershall, 129
  Manningford Bruce, 104
  see also minsters; Wessex (parochia)
Chute Forest, 111, 131
cists, 27, 48; *see also* long barrows; pits
clay, xv, 74
Clay-with-flint, 2, 6, 8, 150; *see also* flints; soils
climate, 8, 9
cloth trade (14th/15thC), 3; *see also* sheep
coaxial field systems, 19, 53, 54, **55**, 56
  aerial survey, 63
  extent and layout, 152, 153
  and linear earthworks, 61, 62, 152
  see also 'Celtic' fields
Cobbett, William, 12
coffins (Romano-British period), 100
coins
  Iron Age, 3, 84, 86
  Roman, 13, 93, 104, 105
Collingbourne Ducis, 40, 48, 109
Colt Hoare, Sir Richard, 13, 33, 34, 48, 51, 81
Combesdeane Well, 100; *see also* ponds; water management
communications
  military, 144
  modern, Salisbury Plain, 5, 121
  Romano-British period, 17, 87, 98, 107–8
  routes through chalk downland, 75
  routeways to Higher Plain, 18
  trench systems, 140
  valleys, 18, 123
  see also airfields; railways; roads
compact villages, 89–98; *see also* Romano-British (settlements)
Compton
  burial mound, 39
  hollow way, 123
  pottery finds, 109
  round barrow, **40, 113**
  sheep washing, 117
  strip lynchets, 115
  water meadows, 132, **135**
Compton Down, 12, 88, 95, **95**, 105, 123
cone barrows, 50; *see also* barrows
Conegar Hill (pillow mound), 121
Coneybury 'anomaly', 149
Conservation Groups, viii, x, 18
'contour reaves', 64; *see also* Old Ditch West

contours, xi; *see also* relief map of SPTA
Coombe Down, xv
  excavation, and molluscan analysis, 156
  grass-tempered pottery, 157
  hollow way, **122**
  Iron Age enclosure replaced by open village, 156
  lynchet trackway, 87
  prehistoric enclosures, 70, 155
  Romano-British settlement, 10, 81, **82**, 88, 98
  sunken-featured building, 109, 157
corrugated iron, 144, 145; *see also* building materials
counterscarps, 78; *see also* banks; ditches; hillforts; ramparts; scarps
county inventories, 14
Cow Down, 43, 46, 48
Cranborne Chase, 22, 24, 52, 154
cremations, 31, 73; *see also* long barrows
cropmarks, xi, 12, 68, 84, 144, 155
crops, 115, 133; *see also* agriculture; cereals; water meadows
cryoturbation, 7
cultivation,
  19thC, Higher Plain, **13**
  post-Roman, **111**, 114–115
  Romano-British, 100–4
  spade-dug in Iron Age, 98
  see also agriculture; arable agriculture; cereals; farming
Cunetio; *see* Mildenhall
Cunnington, William, 13, 48, 121

D

dairying, 71, 150
dams, 90, **91**, 94, 100; *see also* water management
Dartmoor, 64, 137, 159, 161
databases, ix, xii
dating
  Bronze Age settlement enclosures, 154
  'Celtic' field lynchets, 18
  'Celtic' fields, 53
  field systems, 52, 56, 152
  hominid activity on SPTA, 8
  linear earthworks, 18, 61, 154
  long barrows, 27
  Neolithic burial monuments, 39
  ponds, earliest construction of, 10
  prehistoric enclosures on SPTA, 70
  sequence at Stonehenge, 18
  strip lynchets, 115
  see also chronology; Coneybury 'anomaly'; documentary evidence; molluscan

evidence; pollen analysis; radiocarbon dates
Defence Land Service (DLS), 5
defences, 131, 155
Defoe, Daniel, 3, 12
Department of the Environment, x
depopulation, 138, 157; *see also* population
depressions (Romano-British settlements), 90; *see also* hollows; pond barrows
deserted settlements, 112, **128**, **132**
development sequence (barrow cemeteries), 43
Deverel-Rimbury
  enclosure, and 'Celtic' fields, 52
  pottery, 40, 53, 72, 152, 154
  see also 'Celtic' fields; dating (enclosures, field systems)
dew ponds, 11, 20, 118; *see also* ponds; reservoirs
disc barrows, 36, **38**, 40, 43, 50
distribution patterns; *see also* maps
  ancient fields, 52
  barrows near Stonehenge, 50
  Bronze Age round barrows, 12
  Iron Age coins, 84
  Neolithic monuments on SPTA, **24**
  prehistoric settlement, 12, **52**
ditches
  with banks, 12, 77, 155
  bell barrows and, 39
  causewayed, 40
  henges and, 33
  hillforts, 74, 155
  Iron Age enclosure, 83
  linear earthworks and, 56
  long barrows, 21, 24, 27, 31
  modern military, 142, 143, 147
  pond barrows, 35
  Romano-British period, 156
  sheep enclosures and, 115
  Wessex Linear Ditch System, 57
  see also banks; linear ditches; ring ditches
Dobunni, 3, 84, 86
documentary sources; *see also* maps
  10th-century charters, 111
  agricultural leases, 4
  Anglo-Saxon charters, 10
  county inventories, 14
  Domesday Book, 3, 109, 123, 126
  Salisbury & Winchester Journal (1897), 137
  Saxon Charter (AD 934), 10
  tax assessment (1334), 129
Domesday Survey, 3, 109, 123, 126
door furniture, 13, **93**
double-linears, 62
downland; *see* chalk downland; downs
downs, xv

Bronze Age, 50
  medieval period, xvi
  morphology, 6
  ploughed in prehistoric period, 152
  settlement (20thC), 9, 117–118, 147
  see also chalk downland
drainage (Salisbury Plain), 9–11, **9**; *see also* Avon (river); rivers; water management
droveways, 20, 115, 116, 121; *see also* communications; roads; tracks
Duchy of Lancaster, 113, 158
dugouts, 140
Dunch Hill, 57, 68, 71
dung; *see* livestock; sheep
Durotriges, 3, 83, 86
Durrington, 27, 46, 104, 109
Durrington Walls, 1, 33, 149, 150

E

Early Iron Age; *see* Iron Age
earthworks, 2
  ancient, preservation of, viii
  archaeological remains, 11, 87, 88
  'Celtic' fields and, 51, 52
  farmstead remains (19thC), 117, **120**, **121**
  field kitchen remains, 138
  Ludgershall Castle, 131, 132, **134**
  medieval settlement remains, **123**, 124, 126, 128
  military (19th/20thC), 138, **139**, 144, 159; *see also* trenches
  reused, 120, 142
  survey on SPTA (RCHME), ix, xi
  water meadows (remains), 132
  see also banks; barrows; dams; linear earthworks; monuments
East Chisenbury
  Anglo-Saxon settlement, 109
  excavations at, 9
  linear ditches, 58
  location, 74
  medieval settlement, 124, 127
  midden, xv, 51, **60**, **70**, 73–4, 152, 154, 155
  prehistoric settlement, 68, 73
  strip lynchets, 115
Eastcott, **120**
Eastern Range, xiii, 4, 36, 61, 154
economy; *see* market economy; markets; medieval (economy); trade
Ell Barrow, 21, 43
emmer wheat, 32, 149; *see also* agriculture; cereals
emparking, 131
emporia, 84; *see also* trade
enclosure (Parliamentary), 12, 20, 117

enclosures
  'banjo' type, 84
  Bronze Age, 154–6
  and 'Celtic' fields, 52
  enclosed settlements, xiii, 87
  farmstead remains (19thC),
    118
  formed by linear earthworks,
    57, 61
  hillforts and, 74, 84
  Iron Age, 10, **11**, 14, 56, 82, 84,
    91, 155
  for livestock, 95, 100
  plans of, **69, 71**
  prehistoric, xiii, 12, 51, 67–73,
    83
  for rabbit warrens, 120
  ritual, 79, 84
  town defences (Ludgershall),
    131
  see also causewayed enclosures;
    'Celtic' fields; field systems;
    Parliamentary Enclosures;
    settlement(s); sheep
    (enclosures for)
Enford, 109
English Heritage, ix, x
entrances
  causewayed, 95
  henges, **37**
  hillforts, **59**, 77, 155
  Iron Age enclosure
    (Netheravon), 83
  military trench systems
    (20thC), 142
  prehistoric fields, 56
  Romano-British fields, 100
  round barrows and henges,
    compared, 33
environmental evidence (Neolithic
  period), 149
Environmentally Sensitive Areas
  (ESA), 2
erosion, 21
estate maps, **122**, 126
estates, 20, 106–7, 112, 113, 121,
  129, 133, 137
Everleigh, 14, 50, **110**
excavation trenches, 10, **14**, 24,
  31, 98
excavations
  Beach's Barn, 104
  Butterfield Down, 104
  Casterley Camp, 6, 79
  Charlton Down, 16, 90, 93
  Chisenbury Trendle, 70
  Chisenbury Warren, 98
  Church Ditches, 155
  Conegar Hill, 121
  Coombe Down, xv, 10, 81, 98,
    157
  Cow Down, 48
  Dunch Hill, 68
  Durrington, 104
  East Chisenbury, 6, 9, 73, 152,
    155
  Eastern Ranges, 149

Lidbury, 10, 68, 155
long barrows (internal features),
  28
Mancombe Down, 73
Marlborough Downs (sheep
  enclosures), 115
Netheravon, 83, 104
Netheravon Bake, 27
Robin Hood's Ball, 18, 32
Romano-British settlements,
  88, 90
Scratchbury, 32
Sidbury Camp, 74
Sidbury Hill, 62
Silk Hill, 40
Sling Camp, 34
Snail Down, 17, 35, 40, 43,
  53
Strawberry Hill, 68
Widdington Farm, 70, 82, 155
see also antiquarian record;
  barrows; Colt Hoare, Sir
  Richard; Cunnington,
  William; linear earthworks;
  sunken-featured buildings

F

false-crests, 22, **42**, 46, 57, 62
farming
  arable, in Roman period,
    100
  Bronze Age settlement
    enclosures and, 155
  coaxial field systems, 153
  geology and, 5
  intensive, ancient monuments
    destroyed by, xv, 52
  military training on SPTA and,
    137, 138
  mixed, 3, 154
  prehistoric period, 51
  rabbit-, 120
  Romano-British, 87
  see also agriculture; arable
    agriculture; cattle; farms;
    farmsteads; field systems;
    ploughing; sheep
farms, 3, 4, 20, 117, 119, 144
farmsteads, 117, **117**, **119**, **120**,
  121, 138; *see also* downs;
  farms
Farrer, Percy, x, 14
fences, xi, 51, 119, 138
FIBUA (Fighting In Built-Up
  Areas), 4
fibulae, 83, 84, 105
field barns, 117, **117**, **119**, 158
field boundaries, 95; *see also*
  boundaries; field systems;
  linear boundaries
field evidence, 12, 21, 40
field gun emplacements, 144–5
field lynchets; *see* lynchets
field systems, 17, 19
  'Celtic', xiii
  dating, 52, 152

prehistoric, 51–6, 90
Romano-British settlements,
  94, 97, 100, 105
statistics, xiii
see also coaxial field systems
fields, xv, 3
  'aggregate', 56
  boundaries for, 95
  Bronze Age, 20, 152
  and linear earthworks, 62
  prehistoric on Marlborough
    Downs, 73
  prehistoric on SPTA, 51, 52
  ridge-and-furrow, 12
  Romano-British period, xv, 87,
    100, 157
  see also 'Celtic' fields; coaxial
    field systems; field systems
fieldwalking, xi, xii, 70, 106, 126,
  154
Fifield Folly, 84, 156
Figheldean
  Anglo-Saxon finds, 109
  Bronze Age settlement
    enclosure, 155
  excavations, 16
  fields, 63, **65**
  medieval settlement, **125**,
    126
  military camps and bases
    (20thC), 5
  sheep enclosure, 14, **117**,
    118
Fighting In Built-Up Areas
  (FIBUA), 4
firing practice, 4
First World War, viii, 5, 100, 139,
  140, 144; *see also* Brett
  Young, Francis
fishponds, 126
Fittleton, 21, **26**, 120
flint, xii, 6, 27, 28, 32, 48, 90,
  150, 154
flints
  agriculture and, 8
  chipped, 14
  drainage of SPTA, effect on, 9
  Mesolithic period, 149
  Neolithic period, 150
  prehistoric extraction of, 6
  as settlement evidence, 68
  shaft-sinking techniques for, 10
flora and fauna (SPTA), 2, 7,
  161
footings, 90; *see also* building
  materials
forestry, 5; *see also* afforestation;
  timber; trees; woodland
forests, 111, 131, 158
fortifications (19th/20thC), 159
forts, 84, 87; *see also* hillforts
funeral activity, 31; *see also* barrow
  cemeteries; barrows; burial
  monuments; burials; long
  barrows
funerary landscape, 43, 50
furlongs, 114; *see also* ploughing

G

game, 119, 149
gardens, 120, 128, 132
garrisons, xvi, 5, 139, 159
geology, 1, 5, 6, 7; *see also* sarsen
  stones
geophysical surveys, xii, 81, 82,
  83, **85**, 104, 105, 157; *see
  also* aerial photography
'ghost' villages, 147
glass, 106
gods, 160; *see also* altars; Minerva;
  ritual; shrines
Gore (medieval hamlet), 126, 157
government (Roman), 106
'grain driers', 104; *see also* cereals
grass-tempered pottery, 157
grassland, 1, 149, 154
  military policy and, 4, 138, 159
  monuments and, xi, 28, 150
  and prehistoric enclosures, 12
  see also grazing; pasture; sheep
grave goods, 48
grazing, 18, 32, 113; *see also*
  grassland; pasture
Great Hall (Ludgershall Castle),
  131
Greenland Farm, 7, 20, 150
Grooved Ware pottery, 43
Grovely Ridge, xiii
gun pits, **19**, 20, 139, 144, 145

H

Hambledon Hill, Dorset, 32, 79
hamlets, 124, 126
hangars, 147
Hawley, Colonel, 16, 48, 104, 107
Haxton (medieval settlement),
  124, **125**
henges, 21, 33, **37**; *see also*
  Durrington Down;
  Stonehenge; Weather Hill;
  Woodhenge
Heytesbury North Field, **14**, 27,
  27, 28, **29**, 31, 39
Higher Plain
  cultivation (19thC), **13**
  cultivation, post-medieval
    period, 158
  farming, Romano-British
    period, 157
  military acquisition and, 159
  pasture, medieval period, 158
  population, 153
  rabbit-farming, 120
  re-colonisation (19thC), 117
  routeways to, 18
  settlements, 2, 109, 157
  tented camps on, 138
hillforts, xv, **52**, **59**, 74–81, 155
  and barrows, 75, 160
  paired, 79
  postulated (Ludgershall), 131
  Scratchbury, **37**
  see also enclosures

hilltops, 65, 74, 154, 155, 160; *see also* hillforts; linear earthworks; topography
Hindurrington, 126, 132, 133, **136**, 157
hollow ways
  incorporated in water meadow, 133
  medieval, 81, **122**, 123, 126, 128
  Romano-British settlements and, 97, 98
  Upavon Down, 88, 94
  see also communications; roads; tracks
hollows, 62, 73, 94, 97, 98; *see also* depressions; pond barrows; ponds; rabbits; scarps
horses, 120, 121, 138, 154
hospitals, 139; *see also* animal hospital
house platforms, 94, **130**
houses, 68, 118, 127; *see also* building materials; buildings; huts
Hundreds, 111, 113, 158
hunting, 119, 149; *see also* agriculture; land use
hut platforms, 76, 95
huts, 51, 139
hypocausts, 14, 104; *see also* agriculture; cereals; Romano-British settlement

I

Imber, **148**
  church, and settlement shrinkage, 157
  earthworks reused for warren, 120
  'ghost' village, 147
  gun pits, 144
  long barrow, **27**
  manor house, 4, 127
  ridge-and-furrow cultivation, 52
  settlement, 2, **116**
  soil stripes, 7
  stone-axe, 50
  water supply, and place name, 11
Imber-Chitterne Brook, 9, 117; *see also* rivers; water management
Impact Area (Central Range), xii, 12
impact areas, xvi, 12, 147, 159
imperial estate (theory), 106–7
infantry, 4, 137, 142; *see also* rifle ranges
infants (inhumation), 50
inhumations, **52**, 109; *see also* burials
interments; *see* barrow cemeteries; barrows; bones; burial monuments; burial mounds; burials; cemeteries; cremations

Iron Age
  agriculture, 81, 98, 156
  cemeteries, 78
  enclosed settlements, 81–6
  enclosures, 14, 56, 84
  finds, 32
  midden, xv, 152, 155
  pits, 79
  ponds, 10
  pottery, 68, 70, 74, 79, 83, 90, 106
  ritual enclosure, 155
  shrine, 90
  sites, 3
iron
  smelting, 98
  weapons, 111

J

jewellery, 13, 83, 105, 109, 157

K

Kill Barrow, **30**, 31, **66**
Knighton Down (long barrow), 21, 24, 43
Knook, 13, 14, **25**, 56, 74, 79
Knook Down
  archaeological landscape, [64–5], **96**
  earthworks, **80**, **146**
  hillfort, 14
  long barrow, 21, **25**, 28, 111
  military trenches, **140**, 142, **143**
  pond, 10
  Romano-British village, 88, 95, 104, 154

L

La Tene I (*fibula*), 83
Land Classification Survey (1947), 8; *see also* surveys
land use
  Agricultural Depression and, 117
  Archaeological Site Group (ASG) Management Plans and, x
  army training land, and conservation, viii
  barrows and, 33, 110
  continuity of, xv, 20, 98
  current, management of, xii
  downs in Early Bronze Age, 50
  garrison infrastructure, effects on, 139
  linear earthworks and, 64
  marginal agricultural land, 119
  military policy and, xv, 4, 117
  modern, 4
  Neolithic Age, 24
  prehistoric period, 51
  Salisbury Plain, post-Roman period, 109
  sarsen stone clearance and, 152

unexploded shells and, 4, 161
  see also agriculture; barrows; farming; landscape; ploughing; sheep; warfare
landscape
  ancient, survival of, ix
  burial monuments, 17, 20, 43, 50, 110, 150, 151
  'Celtic' fields, 56
  chalk, Anglo-Saxon use of, 12
  Church Pits, development sequence for, 20
  climate and, 9
  coaxial field systems and, 152
  historic, xi
  hunting, effect on, 119
  impact areas, effect on, 147
  linear earthworks and, 61, 154
  Ludgershall Castle, 131
  modern boundaries, and perception of, 160
  Neolithic, 150
  parks and, 131
  prehistoric monuments and, 21, 33, 51, 160
  Romano-British fields and, 100
  see also agriculture; barrows; burial mounds; farming; funerary landscape; geology; geophysical surveys; land use; monuments; ploughing
lanes (Ludgershall market), 131
Larkhill, 5, 137, 145, 147, 150, 159
Late Neolithic burial mounds, 20
lead weights, 104; *see also* Romano-British settlement
leases (agricultural), 4
Lidbury
  enclosure, **53**, 155
  excavations, 10, 15
  prehistoric enclosure, **11**, 73, 116
  prehistoric fields, 53, 56
linear boundaries, xiii, 2, 19, **54**, 56, **57**, **58**, **62**, 64, **67**, 71
  hillfort location, 79
  landscape and, 17, 20, 51, 154
  prehistoric pasture and, 154
  Romano-British settlements and, 97, 98, 103, 108
  Tilshead hunting lodge and, 120
linear configurations (barrow cemeteries), 43
linear ditches, 52, 53, 79, 97, 114, 155
linear earthworks, 13, **32**, **52**, 56–66, **67**
  and burial monuments, 64, 65
  and 'Celtic' fields, **42**, 56, 152, 154
  construction, 58, 64
  dating, 61, 154

enclosures formed by, 57, 61, 72
  parish boundaries and, 113
  prehistoric land use and, 51
  reused as thoroughfares, 19, 65, 95, 98, 154
  siting of, 57, 58, 61, 64
  spinal linears, 64
  statistics, xiii
  target butts, 143
  see also double-linears; linear boundaries; Old Ditch West; Old Nursery Ditch; SPTA
linear villages, 98–100; *see also* Romano-British (settlements)
Littlecott (Romano-British building), 105
livestock, 10, 17, 52, 154; *see also* cattle; horses; sheep
loess, and early agriculture, 8
long barrows, xiii, 21
  air photography, **22**, **23**, 47
  antiquarian record, 27
  county inventories for, 14
  dimensions, **23**
  ditches and, 21, 24
  groupings, 23
  internal excavation features, **28**
  pavements, 27
  pits, 28
  plans of, **25**, **26**, **29**, **30**, 47
  profiles of, **27**
  radiocarbon dating, 27
  Saxon burials and, 110
  siting, 22, 150, 151
  slighted by 'Celtic' fields, 24
  statistics, xiii
  see also antiquarian record; barrows; 'short' long barrows
Longstreet (medieval village), **123**
Lower Chalk, 6, 8; *see also* chalk downland; chalk pavements; downs; Middle Chalk; Upper Chalk
Lower Plain, 8
Ludgershall, 5, 129, 137, 159
Ludgershall Castle, 131–2, **134**
lynchets, 19, 56, 70, 72, 73, 82
  as boundaries, 12, 113
  distinct from 'Celtic' fields, 51
  negative, 51, 109
  reused in modern military trenches, 142
  Romano-British period, 87, 98, 100
  sarsen stones and, 152
  see also 'Celtic' fields; linear earthworks; strip lynchets

M

machine gun posts, 142
malting kilns, 104; *see also* agriculture; cereals

management strategies (SPTA land use), x, xii, xvi
Mancombe Down, 73
  furrowed bowl sherd from, 155; *see also* pottery
  Iron Age enclosure, 14
  rifle range, 142
Manningford Bruce, 104
manor houses, 4, 124, 127
maps; *see also* plans
  Anglo-Saxon activity, **110**
  barrows, location of, 14
  British Geological Survey (BGS) map, 6, 10
  'Celtic Fields of Salisbury Plain', 15
  estates and enclosures, **122**, 159
  farmstead distribution (19thC), 117, **119**
  field barns (19thC), 118, **119**
  geology of SPTA, 7
  manorial complexes, 126
  military earthworks, 139, **139**, 159
  relief map of SPTA, **9**
  Romano-British sites, **87**
  round barrow distribution, **49**
  Salisbury Plain, military use of, **4**
  and sheep washing, 117
  SPTA, location of, **1**
  SPTA, monument distribution, **24**, **49**, **52**
  Tilshead village (19thC), 128
  Wiltshire (Andrews and Dury, 1773), 10
  see also National Mapping Programme (NMP)
Marden Down, 67, **68**, 157
market centres (Romano-British), 107–8; *see also* Ludgershall
market cross (Ludgershall), 131
market economy, xv, 87; *see also* Romano-British period
Market Lavington, 12, 126, **141**, 142, 147, 158
markets (Ludgershall), 131; *see also* market centres; trade
Marlborough Downs, xiii, 5, 13, 52, 73, 116, 152, 154
meat, 115, 154; *see also* East Chisenbury (midden); sheep
medieval
  parish boundaries (on SPTA), 112, 157
  ploughing, 12
  ridge-and-furrow cultivation, 20, 114
  settlements, 123–8, **123**, 129, 157
  sheep farming, xvi, 115; *see also* sheep
  towns, 128–131

metalwork, 79, 84, 93; *see also* artefacts; coins; jewellery; weapons
methodology (SPTA earthworks survey by RCHME), xi
middens; *see* East Chisenbury
Middle Chalk, 6, 8; *see also* chalk downland; chalk pavements; downs; Lower Chalk; Upper Chalk
Mildenhall (Cunetio), 87, 108
milestones, 123; *see also* communications; roads
military
  camps and bases, 5, 120
  damage to landscape, **48**, 94, 95, 161; *see also* shelling
  earthworks, 139
  equipment (1stC), 87
  estate, 2, 121, 137, 145
  fortifications (19th/20thC), 159
  government (Roman), 106
  infrastructure on SPTA, 139
  land purchase, xv
  policy, effect on land use, 4, 117, 133, 159
  settlement (20thC), **5**, 147, 159
  targets, xi, 143, 147
  training, xvi, 2, 137
  see also railways; roads; Salisbury Plain; trenches
Milston, 23, 34, 35, 133
Milston Down, 22, 41, 72, 155
Milston Firs (long barrow), **27**, **47**
Minerva (bronze plaque), 93, 160
Ministry of Defence (MoD), x, 2, 5, 13, 18, 20
minsters, 158; *see also* chapels; churches; monastic houses; parishes
MoD; *see* Ministry of Defence
molluscan evidence, 100, 149, 150, 154, 156
monastic houses, 113, 114
monuments
  construction materials for, 5
  damaged by military activity, viii, 24, **48**
  damaged by ploughing, 12
  destruction of, 11
  effect of agriculture on, 2
  and landscape, 149, 150
  maps for location of, 14, **24**
  military trench earthworks as, 139
  and SPTA, viii, 149
  survival of, 11, 88, 160
  Wiltshire Library and Museum Service, x
  see also barrows; burial monuments; linear earthworks; Scheduled Monuments; Stonehenge
mortar, 14; *see also* building materials
mortuary structure, 50
musketry, 142; *see also* rifle ranges

N
Nadder (river), 1
nails, 13
National Mapping Programme (NMP), xi
negative lynchets, 51
Neolithic Age, 20, 21, 24, **24**, 31, 39, 149, 150; *see also* Coneybury 'anomaly'
Netheravon
  airfield, 4, 139, 147
  Anglo-Saxon minster, 158
  barrows, **25**, 40, **85**, 111
  hunting box (18thC), 120
  Iron Age settlement, 82, 83
  manor house, 126
  Roman villa settlement, 104
  'valley fort', 84
Netheravon Bake (long barrow), **23**, 24, 27, 150
New Zealand Farm, 67, 147
Nine Mile River, 9, 11
  barrow cemeteries sited near, 40, 46, 48, 50
  long barrows, 22
  medieval settlement, 124
  round barrows, 33
  saucer barrows, 35
  Saxon burials, 111
  prehistoric enclosures, 70
Norman Conquest, 157
Nugent Report (1973), viii, x

O
observation posts, 147
occupation patterns; *see* depopulation; population; settlement(s)
Old Bake Barn, 118
Old Ditch Barrow, 21, 23, **26**, 28, 31, 39
Old Ditch West, **52**, 56, 61, 64
Old Nursery Ditch, 46, **52**, 57, 61, 62, 64, 103, 114
Old Sarum, 15, 109
oppida, 84
Orcheston (medieval village), 124
Orcheston Down
  archaeological landscape sequence, 18–20
  'Celtic' fields and linear ditch, **16**
  field systems, 54
  gun pits, 144
  linear earthwork, 64
  plans, 14, **19**
  sheep enclosure, **117**
Orcheston estate, 20
organic-tempered pottery, 109
outfields, 115
Overton Down (sarsen field boundaries), 152

P
parchmarks, 24, 68, 105
parish boundaries, **34**, **110**, 111, 112, 121
parishes, 158
parks (Ludgershall Castle), 131
Parliamentary Enclosures (18th/19thC), 12, 20, 117
pasture, xv, 8, 12, 113, 114, 138, 154
pavements (long barrows), 27, 31
Pepys, Samuel, 2
perambulations, 113, 158; *see also* estates; parish boundaries
Perham Down (rifle ranges), **138**, **141**, 142
Petrie, Flinders, 14, **15**, 16
Pewsey Vale; *see* Vale of Pewsey
pewter vessels, 104
photography; *see* aerial photography
pillow mounds, 121; *see also* rabbits
Pit Mead (Roman villa), 104
pits, 27, 28, 32, 67, 79, 150, 156; *see also* cists; long barrows
place-names, 111, 112, 115, 121, 124, 157
the Plain; *see* Salisbury Plain
Plain Ware pottery, 61, 154
plans, xi,
  barns and farmstead earthworks, **121**
  barrows, **62**
  Charlton Down (dam), **91**
  Colt Hoare inventory of, 13
  East Chisenbury (midden), **60**
  enclosures, **69**, **71**, **83**, **91**
  Figheldean Down, **65**
  Heytesbury North Field, **14**
  hillforts, 77, **78**
  Knook Down, [**64–5**], **96**
  Lidbury, **53**
  long barrows, **25**
  medieval settlements, **123**, **125**, **126**, **127**, **128**, **129**
  military trench systems, **141**
  Orcheston Down, **16**, **19**, [**20–21**]
  Robin Hood's Ball, **15**
  Romano-British villages, **88**, **89**, **92**, **95**, **102**, **103**
  round barrows, **38**, **44–46**
  water meadows, **135**, **136**
platforms
  farm building remains (19thC), 118
  hillforts, 78
  on lynchets, 115
  military camp remains, 120
  pond barrows, 35
  Romano-British settlements, 90, 94, 95, 97, 98, 100
  unenclosed settlements, 67
  see also building platforms; hut platforms; pavements; pottery

Pleistocene drift, 6
ploughing
  field systems and, 54
  furlongs, 114
  linear earthworks damaged or
    destroyed by, 20, 56, 71,
    79, 84
  monuments damaged or
    destroyed by, xv, 12, 21, 46,
    73, 94, 98, 100
  negative/positive lynchets
    formed by, 51
  prehistoric period, 152
  see also agriculture; arable
    agriculture; Defoe, Daniel;
    farming; ridge-and-furrow
pollen analysis, 149, 152, 157
pond barrows, 34
ponds
  dating earliest construction of, 10
  fishponds, 126
  Romano-British settlements
    and, 10, 97, 98, 100
  sheep washing, 117
  tented camps, 138
  see also dew ponds; hollows;
    reservoirs; water
    management
population, xv, 3, 5, 51, 84, 153;
    see also depopulation;
    settlement(s)
post-medieval agriculture, 3, 114,
    158
post-pits, 8, 149
post-Roman period, 109, **111**
postholes, 43, 67, 150
pottery, xii
  Anglo-Saxon, 109, 157
  Bronze Age, 68, 71
  Deverel-Rimbury, 40, 53, 72,
    152, 154
  from East Chisenbury midden,
    73, 74
  grass-tempered, 157
  Iron Age, 68, 70, 74, 79, 83, 84,
    90, 106
  Plain Ware, 61, 154
  Romano-British period, 13, 81, 93,
    94, 98, 100, 106, 109, 156
  Savernake ware, 84, 108
  from Silver Barrow long barrow,
    31
  from Snail Down barrow
    cemetery, 43
  see also bowls
prehistoric period, 21, 51
  agriculture, 6, 81, 152–4
  'Celtic' fields, 53, 56
  enclosures, xiii, 12, 67–73, 116
  flint extraction, 6
  funerary landscape, 33
  hillforts, 74
  linear earthworks, 56
  settlement, 50, 67, 81
  see also barrows; East
    Chisenbury midden; field
    systems

Q
Quaternary geology, 6
quernstone, **93**, 107

R
rabbits, 72, 120, 121
radiocarbon dating, 27, 32; see also
    chronology; dating
RAF, xii, 5, 15; see also aerial
    photography; airfields;
    surveys
railways, 3
  military, 24, 139, 145; see also
    communications
ramparts, 48, 76, 79, 131, 156
ramps, 115, 131; see also
    agriculture; lynchets
ranges, 4; see also Central Range;
    Eastern Range; rifle ranges;
    Western Range
RCHME (Royal Commission on
    the Historical Monuments
    of England), earthworks
    survey, ix, x, xii, 18, 34, 93
Reading Beds, 6, 74, 150, 151
Reading University projects, xiii,
    18
re-cutting
  linear earthworks, 65, 154
  long barrows and, 21
red deer, 32; see also antlers; game
re-entrants, 24, **30**, 46, 100, **114**,
    142
*Register of Grave Groups of the
    Wessex Culture*, 48
relief map of SPTA, **9**; see also
    maps
'rents', 131
reports; see English Heritage;
    Nugent Report; Wiltshire
    County Archaeologist
reservoirs, 10, 20, 90, 138; see also
    water management
ridge-and-furrow
  and 'Celtic' fields, 51, **112**, 114
  cultivation, xv, 52, 61, 73
  fields, 12
  medieval, 114, 20
  parish boundaries and, 114
  water meadows, 132
rifle ranges, xvi, 4, 137, 139,
    142–4, **145**, 159
rilling, 7
ring ditches, **22**, 33, 46, **49**, **85**
ringwork (Ludgershall Castle),
    131
ritual, xv
  altar, 93
  enclosures, 79
  and hillforts, 155
  miniature socketed axes, **108**
  see also Viereckschanzen
rivers, 1
  burial monuments and, 24, 27,
    46, 50, 160

drainage of SPTA, 9
henges and, 33
winterbournes, 9
see also Avon; Bourne; Imber-
    Chitterne Brook; Nadder;
    Nine Mile River; Till;
    valleys; Water Dean Bottom;
    water management; Wylye
roads, 2, 17, 127
  linear earthworks reused for, 65
  military (20thC), 121, 139
  Romano-British period, 87,
    107, 157
  see also communications;
    droveways; routeways;
    tracks
Robin Hood's Ball
  causewayed enclosure, 18, 31,
    34, **35**, 160
  flints at, 14, 150
  long barrows and, 24
  plan of site (Petrie), 14, **15**
  rifle ranges (abandoned), 144
  round barrows and, 43
  sarsens, 152
Rollestone, 5, 147
Roman
  coins, 13, 93, 104, 105
  pottery, 100, 106, 156
  villas, xv, 87, 104–6, 157
Roman Empire, 13, 84, 87, 93,
    104, 156
Romano-British
  agriculture, xv, 100–4; see also
    field systems
  building material, 105
  buildings, 87; see also Roman
    villas
  finds (in hillforts), 156
  forts (suggested), 87
  government, 106
  period, 87
  sites, map of, **87**
Romano-British settlement(s), xv,
    2, 13, 81, **82**, 84, 87, **90**,
    94, **99**
  boundaries (7thC) and, 112
  pattern, 88–9
  sites, 3, 12
  on SPTA, xv
  streets, 19, 20, 65, 98, 100,
    154, 161
  villages, xv, 17, 88, **92**, **95**, 98,
    102
  water management, 10, 20, 90,
    98, 100
  see also artefacts; communi-
    cations
roofs, 90, 105, 118
round barrows, xiii, xv, 21, 33–50,
    58, 70, **113**
  Bronze Age, distribution pattern
    for, 12
  burials (Saxon period), 110
  distribution map, **49**
  excavations, 16, 48
  and land use in Bronze Age, 50

plans of, **38**, **44**, **45**
prehistoric enclosures and, 73
profiles of, **39**
Robin Hood's Ball and, 14, 43
siting of, 43, 48, 151
statistics, xiii
types, 33, **43**
routeways, 18, 56, 108, 124; see
    also communications; roads;
    trackways
Royal Air Force; see airfields; RAF
Royal Commission on the
    Historical Monuments of
    England (RCHME),
    earthworks survey, ix, x, xii,
    18, 34, 93
Royal Flying Corps, 14
rubbish, 52, 74, 109, 155
Rushall Down, 14, **16**, 118, 143,
    147

S
Salisbury (Sorviodunum), 3, 98,
    108
Salisbury Plain, 2
  Avon (river), 9
  'Celtic fields' mapped, 15
  communications (modern),
    121, 123
  geology, 1, 5
  land use, 109, 139
  local economy, 5
  mapping of trenches on, 159
  military estate, creation of
    (1897), 137
  military use, map of, **4**
  modern agriculture and, 13
  rabbits, 120
  Romano-British period, 156,
    157
  sarsen stones, 152
  sheep, 3
  see also chalk downland; downs;
    Marlborough Downs;
    sheep; trade
Salisbury Plain Training Area
    (SPTA); see SPTA
sarsen stones, 2, 151–2
  long barrows and, 24, 27, 29, 31
  and settlements, 152
saucepan pot, 81; see also
    artefacts
saucer barrows, 35–6
Savernake ware, 84, 108; see also
    pottery
Saxon
  burials, 112, 158
  jewellery, 157
  settlement pattern, 111
Saxon Charter (AD 934), 10; see
    also documentary sources
scarps
  hillforts, 78
  lynchets and, 51, 115
  prehistoric settlements and, 67,
    72, 75

and shell craters, 161
see also counterscarps; hollows
Scheduled Monuments
   (database), ix
scratch-cordoned bowls, 155; *see also* pottery
Scratchbury Camp, 13, 32, **36**, **37**, 74, 156
Second World War, 139, 159
settlement(s), xv
   Anglo-Saxon, 109
   'Atrebatic', 82
   barrow cemeteries and, 151
   Battlesbury hillfort, 78
   and development of landscape, 17
   Domesday Survey, 109, 123
   on downland, 9, 17
   Early Bronze Age, 50, 154–6
   Higher Plain and, 2
   Iron Age, 81–6
   medieval, patterns of, 123–8, 129
   modern, patterns of, xvi, 5, 147, 159
   paired, 124
   prehistoric period, 51, 67, 81, 98
   removal of, East Chisenbury (17thC), 127
   river valleys and, 3, 113
   roads and, 17
   Romano-British, xv, 2, 10, 12, 81, 84, 87, 88, 98, 104
   sarsen stone clearance and, 152
   unenclosed (open), 67–70, **68**, 73, 84, 87, 88
   water supply and, 9, 10, 70
   see also barrows; boundaries; enclosures; garrisons; platforms; pottery; springs; villages
sheep, xvi, 3, 12
   and arable agriculture, 133
   dung, 73, 115
   enclosures for, xv, 14, 71, 100, **105**, **114**, 115–117, **118**, 155
   Iron Age, 154
   washing, 117
   winter feed for, 133
   see also East Chisenbury (midden); livestock; water meadows
Sheer Barrow, **33**
shelling
   and archaeology, xii, **140**, 159
   damage to monuments from, 33, 94, 95, 147
   and scarps, 161
shelters; *see* splinter-proof shelters
Shepherd's Garden, 115
sherds, 84, 109, 155; *see also* pottery
'short' long barrows, 18, 27, **31**; *see also* barrows; long barrows

Shrewton Folly, 144, **146**
shrines, 86, 90; *see also* altars
Sidbury Camp (hillfort), 13, 74, **77**, 155
Sidbury Hill, 6, 48, 57, **58**, 62, 100, 154, 160
Silk Hill, 33, 35, **38**, 40, **41**, 46
Silver Barrow, 31
Sites of Special Scientific Interest (SSSI), 2
siting of
   dew ponds, 11
   long barrows, 22
   round barrows, 46
skeletons, 29, 30, 31, 100, 111; *see also* bones; burial mounds; cemeteries; long barrows; pavements
slate (roofs), 118; *see also* building materials
Slay Barrow, 33, 46
Slay Down, 62, **141**, 142
Sling Camp, 34, 40, 48
Small Arms Range, 39, 40
Snail Down
   barrow cemetery, 17, 40, **42**, 43, **48**, 65, 150
   barrows and cemeteries, siting of, 46
   Bronze Age field systems, 53
   hollow way, 123
   landscape, **47**
   linear earthworks, 62
   Romano-British settlement, 89
Society of Antiquaries, 151, 152
socketed axes, 73, **108**
socketed iron spearhead, 111
soil, 52, 58
   exhaustion, 106, 156
   marks, xi, 7, 12, 68, 144
   profiles, 150
   stripes, 7
   see also geology; molluscan evidence
soils, 8–9
solar tower (Ludgershall Castle), 131
Somerset Levels, 149
Song of the Dark Ages, 162
Sorviodunum; *see* Salisbury
spearheads (Saxon), 157
spindle whorls, 73, **74**
splinter-proof shelters, 144–5, 147
springs, 9, 24, 50, 70, 160
SPTA (Salisbury Plain Training Area), xv, 1, **1**, 2
   aerial reconnaissance and, 14
   ancient fields, 51; *see also* 'Celtic' fields
   ancient monuments, viii, ix, 11, 21, **24**, 31
   archaeological landscape, 149–51, 161
   Archaeological Working Party, ix
   barrow cemeteries, 43, 46

barrows, xv, 21, 27, 36, 48
   coaxial field systems, 53, 153
   current land use, management of, x, xii
   flora and fauna, viii, 2, 7, 161
   geology, map of, **7**
   grazing rights, 18
   henges, 33
   hillforts, xv, 74, 160
   Iron Age settlement on, 84
   landscape, 1, 12
   linear earthworks, 56, 57
   lynchets, 52
   medieval parishes, 112
   MoD, and archaeology of, 18
   modern military activity and, viii, 5, 139, 161
   prehistoric enclosures, 73; *see also* enclosures
   relief map of, **9**
   Romano-British settlement, 87, 95, 104–6, 156
   woodland, 5
   World Wars I and II, 139
   see also communications; Cranborne Chase; Dartmoor; Marlborough Downs; railways (military); Salisbury Plain; sheep; statistics; surveys; Wessex Linear Ditch System
SSSI (Sites of Special Scientific Interest), 2
standing stones, 29; *see also* sarsen stones
statistics, xiii, **43**, 153; *see also* long barrows (dimensions)
stock; *see* cattle; horses; livestock; sheep
stone, xii, 93
   axes, 50; *see also* artefacts
   buildings, 98, 115, 118, 131
   footings, 90
stone-sockets, 29
Stonehenge, xv, 1, 7, 24, 33, 61
   and ancient fields, 52
   and barrow distribution, 50
   Neolithic landscape, 150
   post-pits, 149
   and secular activity, 18, 151
Stonehenge and its Environs, 18
strap union (Iron Age), 83
Strawberry Hill, 68, 115
streets
   hutted camps and, 139
   linear earthworks used as, 19, 20, 65, 154
   medieval settlements, 124
   Romano-British settlements, 90, 95, 98, 100, 156
strip lynchets, 51, **113**, 115, **129**; *see also* lynchets
Stukeley, W, 51
sunken-featured buildings, 100, 109, 157
survey techniques (coaxial field system lay out), 153

surveys
   aerial, xi, 14, 156
   of ancient field systems, 152
   of archaeological sites on Salisbury Plain, 13
   Casterley Camp (by Crocker), **15**
   Domesday, 112, 123
   English Heritage, ix, x, 160
   Farrer, Percy, 14
   geophysical, xii, 81, 82, 157
   Land Classification Survey (1947), 8
   methodology (RCHME survey), x
   of sarsen stones (Antiquarian Society), 151, 152
   of SPTA earthworks (RCHME), ix, xi
   Wiltshire County Council aerial survey (1991), ix

T

tanks (warfare), 4, **48**, 144
target butts, 143
targets, ix, 147
tegula, 100; *see also* buildings; pottery; roof tiles
tenancies (agricultural), 4
tented camps, **137**, 138
terraces
   earthwork, 82
   gravel and brickearth, 7
   Ludgershall Castle, 131
   and lynchets, 115
   medieval settlements, 124
   Romano-British settlements, 87, 90, 95, 98, 102
   see also geology; rivers
Thames Valley, 84
Thornham Down, 56, 64, **111**, **112**
Tidworth, 4, 5, 53, 61, 138, 159
tiles, 90, 104, 105
Till (river), 1, 4
   bifaces, 7
   long barrows, 24
   medieval settlements, 124, 128
   Roman villa site (possible), 106
   routeways to, 18
   siting of barrows near, 50
Tilshead
   Anglo-Saxon minster, 158
   biface from, **8**
   Lodge, 27, **27**, 120, **122**
   long barrows, 43
   medieval town, 128, **133**
   settlements, 2, 89, 158
timber (burial monument), 50; *see also* wood
Tinhead, 21, 22
Tithe Commutation Act (1836), 117
Tithe maps, 126
tithings, 61, **110**, 112, 116, 126, 158

tofts, 124, 128
topography
    geology of Salisbury Plain, 5
    hillforts and, 74, 155
    linear earthworks, 61, 62, 64
    modern military trenches and,
        142
    tithing boundaries, 112
    and types of water meadows,
        132
Total Stations EDM equipment,
    xi
towns, 5, 128–31; see also
    garrisons; oppida
tracks, xi, 17, **30**, 90, 94, **94**, 109
    on coombe terraces, 10
    on earthworks, 65, 97, 156
    on lynchets, 87
    see also communications; roads
trackways; see tracks
trade, 3, 84, 87, 107, 121
Training Area; see SPTA
trees, 5, 20, 32, 118, 119, 128; see
    also timber; woodland
trench systems, xvi, 139–42
trenches, 78
    evaluation at East Chisenbury, 44
    excavation, 10, **14**, 24, 31, 98
    military, 95, 100, 109, **138**, 139,
        140, **142**, **143**, 159; see also
        trench systems
tribes, 3
troops, 137
turf, 27, 29, 58, 150; see also
    grassland; long barrows

U

unenclosed (open) settlements,
    67, **68**, 73; see also
    enclosures; settlements
unexploded shells, 4
Upavon, 9, 13, **106**
    airfield, 4, 147
    Anglo-Saxon minster, 158
    emmer wheat, 150
    hollow way, 88, 94
    Mesolithic period, flints, 149

modern military camps, 5
    Romano-British village, **89**, 94,
        107, 108
    Saxon brooches, 157
    sheep enclosure, 14, **114**, 116
    strip lynchets, 115
Upper Chalk, 6, 8; see also chalk
    downland; chalk
    pavements; downs; Lower
    Chalk; Middle Chalk
Urchfont, 111; see also place-
    names
urns, 73
USAAF, xii; see also aerial
    photography

V

Vale of Pewsey, 5, 9, 27, 81,
    104
'valley fort' (Netheravon), 84
valleys, 1
    burial monuments and, xv, 27,
        46, 160
    Hundreds and, 113
    and landscape (medieval
        settlement), 123
    Pleistocene drift, 6
    settlements in, 3, 109, 129,
        159
    and water meadows, 132
    see also barrow cemeteries;
        barrows; communications;
        rivers
Vespasian (Roman Emperor AD
    69), 13, 156
Viereckschanzen, 79, 84, 155, 160;
    see also altars; enclosures;
    hillforts; ritual
villages
    aerial transcription and, 17
    'artificial', 4
    compact, 89–98
    'ghost', 147
    Iron Age enclosure replaced by,
        156
    linear, 98–100
    medieval, **123**, 124, 128

modern military, **5**
    Romano-British, xv, **16**, **88**, 89,
        94, **95**, 98
villas, xv, 87, 104–6, 157; see also
    Romano-British settlement

W

Wadman's Coppice, 10, 88, 100,
    103, **104**, 116
War, Under Secretary of State for,
    137
War Office, 4; see also Ministry of
    Defence
Warden's Down (sheep
    enclosures), 100, **105**, 116
warfare, 2, 142, 147, 159
Warminster, 4, 137, 142, 152,
    158, 159
warrens, 120, 121
Water Dean Bottom (river), 6,
    105, **113**, 117, 152
water garden, 127
water management, 9–11
    downland farmsteads (19thC),
        118
    East Chisenbury village, **124**
    modern military activity, 137
    Romano-British settlements,
        19, 90, 100, 103, **104**
    for sheep washing, 117
    see also dams; dew ponds;
        ponds; reservoirs; rivers;
        settlement; water meadows;
        water table; water tanks;
        wells
water meadows, 52, 124, 132–3,
    135, **136**
water table, 10, 24
water tanks, 20
watercourses (and barrows), 46,
    50
weapons, 111; see also arrowheads;
    artefacts; artillery;
    spearheads
Weather Hill, 33, **37**, 100
wells, 9, 10
Wessex, xv, 112, 114, 124, 151, 158

'Wessex' burials, 40
Wessex Culture, 1, 48
Wessex Linear Ditch System, 57
West Chisenbury (socketed iron
    spearhead), 111
West Lavington, 12, 142
Westbury Ironworks, 108
Western Range, xiii, 4, 13, 61
White Barrow, **32**
Wickham Green, 111, 112
Widdington Farm, 70, 82, 117, 155
Wilsford Shaft, 10, 152
Wiltshire, 10, 39, 129, 133
Wiltshire Archaeology Service, ix
Wiltshire County Archaeologist
    (monument damage report,
    1983), x
Wiltshire County Council (aerial
    survey, 1991), ix; see also
    aerial photography; surveys
Wiltshire Library and Museum
    Service, x
Windmill Hill, 154
Winterbourne Stoke, 150
winterbournes, 8, 10, 24; see also
    rivers
wood, 27, 31, 33, 50, 100
Woodhenge, 1, 24, 33, 149, 150
woodland, 8, 111, 149, 150, 152,
    154, 157; see also
    afforestation; forests;
    hunting; trees
wool, 12, 115
World War I, viii, 5, 139, **140**, 144
World War II, 139, 147
Wylye valley, 2, 156
Wylye river, 1, 9
    barrows and, 23, 48, 50
    bifaces found near, 7
    hillforts and, 74
    Hundreds, 113
    linear earthworks and, 61, 64
    settlement, 3, 86, 95, 114
    shrine, 86
    strip lynchets, 115
    valley as boundary, 3
    villa, 104 (Pit Mead)
    water meadows (17thC), 133